A BEGINNER'S GUIDE *to the* MMPI-A

A BEGINNER'S GUIDE *to the* MMPI-A

Carolyn L. Williams and James N. Butcher

American Psychological Association • Washington, DC

Published by
American Psychological Association
750 First Street, NE
Washington, DC 20002
www.apa.org

To order
APA Order Department
P.O. Box 92984
Washington, DC 20090-2984
Tel: (800) 374-2721; Direct: (202) 336-5510
Fax: (202) 336-5502; TDD/TTY: (202) 336-6123
Online: www.apa.org/pubs/books
E-mail: order@apa.org

In the U.K., Europe, Africa, and the Middle East, copies may be ordered from
American Psychological Association
3 Henrietta Street
Covent Garden, London
WC2E 8LU England

Typeset in Meridien by Circle Graphics, Inc., Columbia, MD

Printer: Maple-Vail Book Manufacturing Group, York, PA
Cover Designer: Mercury Publishing Services, Rockville, MD

The opinions and statements published are the responsibility of the authors, and such opinions and statements do not necessarily represent the policies of the American Psychological Association.

Library of Congress Cataloging-in-Publication Data

Williams, Carolyn L., 1951-
  A beginner's guide to the MMPI-A / Carolyn L. Williams and James N. Butcher. — 1st ed.
    p. cm.
  Includes bibliographical references and index.
  ISBN-13: 978-1-4338-0938-5
  ISBN-10: 1-4338-0938-9
  1. Minnesota Multiphasic Personality Inventory. I. Butcher, James Neal, 1933- II. Title.

  BF698.8.M5W55 2010
  155.2'83—dc22
                                        2010035700

British Library Cataloguing-in-Publication Data
A CIP record is available from the British Library.

Printed in the United States of America
First Edition

For the Zajicek family: Karrie, Jason, Brandon, and Brittany.
Wishing you joy and success on your adventures through adolescence.

Contents

8

Putting It All Together: An Interpretive Strategy and Report Writing 195

9

The Feedback Loop: Sharing MMPI–A Information With Adolescents and Parents 221

Preface

The genesis of this book can be traced back to more than a decade ago when the American Psychological Association (APA) asked one of us to write *A Beginner's Guide to the MMPI–2*. That book, now in its third edition, is designed to provide a brief introduction to the Minnesota Multiphasic Personality Inventory—2 (MMPI–2) for professionals—physicians, attorneys, counselors, social workers—who encounter the MMPI–2 in their work with clients but who do not have in-depth training in psychological testing or research. It became clear over time that many psychologists also found the MMPI–2 *Beginner's Guide* a useful tool as part of their graduate training and as a professional resource for interpreting the MMPI–2.

We knew for several years that we wanted to do a similar book for the Minnesota Multiphasic Personality Inventory—Adolescent (MMPI–A), which became the most widely used clinical personality inventory for adolescents after its release in 1992. Given our early work on the MMPI–A, we are pleased that it became such a valuable instrument for understanding adolescent problems and behaviors. We are grateful to Susan Reynolds of APA Books for prodding us in 2008 to develop *A Beginner's Guide to the MMPI–A*. Too many other books, journal articles, research projects, and something called "life" kept interfering with our goal of writing this companion guide to the MMPI–A for practitioners working with adolescents.

Even though at this point in our careers we are both retired from the University of Minnesota, we are pleased with this task—although, as with all projects of this scope, it did replace for a time other plans we had. We thought our career work would be incomplete without publishing this book. It's been a decade since the publication of the second edition of our *Essentials of MMPI–2 and MMPI–A Interpretation*, which provided comprehensive guidelines for both versions of the instrument. Today, however, there is new research to incorporate into recommendations for use of the MMPI–A.

We began this book while we completed several other projects: the revision of our computerized interpretive system for the MMPI–A, the *Minnesota Report: Adolescent Interpretive System;* joint projects on new developments with the MMPI–2; Carolyn's work on alcohol and drug use prevention projects for adolescents; and Jim's updating of the MMPI–2 *Beginner's Guide* and completion of five other books related to the MMPI–2 and MMPI–A. Fortunately, these projects are all interrelated, with one informing the other. We will admit, however, that we are hoping for a time with fewer deadlines as we continue to learn that emeritus professors are just as prone to being overcommitted as those on the full-time payroll.

As with *A Beginner's Guide to the MMPI–2*, we have multiple goals for this volume:

- Provide a brief and readable overview of what the MMPI–A is and does.
- Introduce the MMPI–A within a developmental framework and provide an historical perspective on what is known about adolescence and the various influences on adolescent behavior and personality (Chapter 1).
- Explain how the test was developed to describe and predict behavior in a broad range of clinical settings (Chapter 2).
- Using as little jargon as possible, explain the various scores, scales, profiles, and the like that are used to interpret the MMPI–A (Chapters 2–5 and 8).
- Walk the reader through test administration and how the MMPI–A fits into a psychological evaluation (Chapter 3).
- Describe the use of the MMPI–A across cultures and around the world (Chapter 6).
- Demystify computerized interpretive systems for the MMPI–A and demonstrate how they can be used (Chapter 7).
- Illustrate how to combine all the information from the MMPI–A into an interpretive report (Chapter 8).
- Recommend "best practices" MMPI–A feedback sessions (Chapter 9).
- Use case material from adolescents to highlight all the above.

Although we provide information from the scientific literature to highlight the research base that supports our recommendations on how to use the MMPI–A, we did not write this book as a comprehensive research resource. Rather, we hope that it provides a practical guide to the test's use with adolescents from a developmental perspective. We hope that we have struck the right chords in selecting research material and practical examples that can give the beginner a sound introduction to the use of the MMPI–A and can serve as a guide for seeking further information. Appendix A lists MMPI–A studies by topic—a starting point for those wanting to learn more about the research underlying the MMPI–A.

Like the MMPI–2 *Beginner's Guide,* we assume this book will have readers with diverse backgrounds, interests, and knowledge of psychology. That presents a challenge for selecting how much information to include, on the one hand, and how to avoid being superficial, on the other hand. Fortunately, we had the previous book and its readers as a guide. That showed us that we could write an easy-to-understand book that would be useful to a variety of readers.

We encourage our readers to use this book to suit their needs. For example, instructors and graduate students in a beginning course on the MMPI–A may find relevant reading in each chapter. Practicing psychologists (those new to the MMPI–A or those wanting an up-to-date resource) also are likely to find relevant practical information in each chapter. We would like psychologists to pay particular attention to the last chapter on feedback because this is an innovative way to use the MMPI–A that doesn't get the attention it deserves. Newcomers to the MMPI–A may find the Glossary a useful resource for looking up MMPI–A terms; it both defines the terms and refers readers to specific chapters for more detailed information.

Psychiatrists, social workers, or counselors wanting an introduction to the test might pay closest attention to Chapters 4 and 5 on the various MMPI–A scales and Chapter 8 on what makes up an MMPI–A report. Attorneys can use this book as a resource to look up information about the MMPI–A scales (again, Chapters 4 and 5) and how the test should be administered (Chapter 3) to see if their client's MMPI–A results conform to how the test should be used. Users of the Minnesota Report will find important information about that computerized system in Chapter 7. However, even if a reader does not use the Minnesota Report, the computerized interpretations in Chapter 7 demonstrate how a narrative report based on MMPI–A scores is written (i.e., numerous case examples illustrate what can be included in an interpretive narrative based solely on MMPI–A measures, the sex of the individual, and the setting in which the MMPI–A was administered).

We would like to acknowledge the considerable assistance we received from colleagues over the course of developing this book. We thank Mera Atlis, Myron Atlis, Stephen Finn, Reneau Kennedy, Pamela Schaber, and Natalia Zhukova for providing case material used in this book. We are particularly grateful to Pamela Schaber and Stephen Finn for recommending articles and chapters about collaborative assessment and their helpful reviews of the last chapter on feedback.

Over the years we've worked with many psychologists, graduate students, adolescents, and their parents—all have informed this book, and we have fond recollections of experiences with many. Some of our case material also came from our research and clinical files of these previous collaborations. APA Books sought the advice of two anonymous reviewers who provided detailed comments that greatly strengthened our book. Likewise, both our development and production editors, Susan Herman and Harriet Kaplan, respectively, ably guided the book through its last stages. We relied on Verla Johansson's graphic skills to design many of the figures and exhibits and Betty Kiminki to double-check (and find) references for us.

There has been increasing attention paid to how conflicts of interest may influence professional judgment or recommendations. Although we receive royalties for our books on the MMPI instruments and for the Minnesota Reports, first developed for the MMPI and then revised for the MMPI–2 and MMPI–A, we do not receive any royalties from sales of the MMPI–2, MMPI–A, any of the scales we developed (or recommend) for these instruments, or any MMPI–2 or MMPI–A translations into foreign languages. We were part of the group of researchers who decided during the MMPI Restandardization Project to forgo royalties on the versions of these instruments resulting from their work. This decision allowed us to make changes to and recommendations about the instrument without any financial consequences. Similarly, other psychologists for more than 60 years developed scales and translations for the MMPI instruments without financial gains, but that tradition changed for some starting in 2003. We believe that psychologists, like physicians, should be forthcoming in disclosing all sources of their income (e.g., royalties, practice income, professional consulting fees, workshop fees, and the like), as well as their research funding sources, when making recommendations to practitioners. Complete disclosure statements for each of us can be found at the MMPI–2/MMPI–A Research Project Website (http://www1.umn.edu/mmpi/disclosure.php).

Finally, we would like to recognize the continued support of our daughter Holly Butcher, Jim's daughter Sherry Butcher Wickstrom, Sherry's husband Mark Wickstrom, and Jim's son Jay Butcher and wife Cindi Butcher. Not only did we make the journey through adolescence with our children, we also experienced it through wonderful grandchildren, Bryce Thompson, Nic and Neal Younghans, and Sarah and Ben Butcher.

A
BEGINNER'S
GUIDE *to the*
MMPI-A

Understanding Adolescence
A Conceptual Framework for Personality and Behavior

1

Do I really see what's in her mind?
Each time I think I'm close to knowing
She keeps on growing
Slipping through my fingers all the time.[1]

I n a melancholy moment during the musical *Mamma Mia*, the mother of a young woman captures nicely one of the many challenges facing psychologists attempting a clinical assessment of an adolescent. Adolescents are growing, changing, and evolving. They can be elusive individuals to understand, given all the psychological, biological, and social changes beginning around the 2nd decade of life. Although they may reach out for help from professionals such as psychologists, frequently it is others (e.g., parents or teachers) who prompt the referral for a psychological evaluation, compounding the difficulties in trying to understand their issues.

The Minnesota Multiphasic Personality Inventory—Adolescent (MMPI–A; Butcher, Williams, et al., 1992) is the most widely used and researched self-report inventory for young people. It is based on decades of empirical research. Its rich foundation of reliability and validity studies includes

---

[1]From "Slipping Through My Fingers," words and music by Benny Andersson and Bjorn Ulvaeus. Copyright © 1981 Universal/Union Songs Musikforlag AB (Sweden). All rights in the United States and Canada controlled and administered by Universal–Polygram International Publishing, Inc. and EMI Waterford Music, Inc. Exclusive print rights for EMI Grove Park Music, Inc. Administered by Alfred Publishing Co., Inc. All rights reserved. Used by permission of Hal Leonard Corporation and Alfred Music Publishing Co., Inc.

those based on the original MMPI (Hathaway & McKinley, 1940) as well as those that have accumulated since the publication of a separate instrument designed for adolescents in 1992 (Appendix A in this volume contains a list of studies by research topic published since the release of this instrument almost 20 years ago). The MMPI–A provides the assessment psychologist with a comprehensive approach to understanding an adolescent's personality and psychopathology, two key components for addressing referral questions about a young person's mental health status.

This book is a beginner's guide for interpretation of the MMPI–A. It addresses the multiple factors that are important to a personality assessment of adolescents using the MMPI–A, details the development and psychometric features of the MMPI–A, and provides a roadmap for interpreting the widely used MMPI–A scales and indicators in clinical evaluations. Although the MMPI–A is often but one part of a comprehensive psychological evaluation, it is beyond the scope of this volume to detail these broader types of psychological assessments. Although we mention other parts of a psychological evaluation in this book, our focus remains primarily on how to use the MMPI–A. An understanding of the developmental issues during adolescence is essential to our topic. We begin this book with an historical perspective of our knowledge of adolescence from antiquity to today.

Observations About Adolescence Across the Ages

There are deep historical origins for the recognition of the importance of developmental changes from childhood to adolescence and from adolescence to adulthood for understanding behavior and personality. Long before Piaget's theory of cognitive development, Erikson's theory of identity formation, and Kohlberg's stages of moral development, ancient and medieval authorities had already identified various stages of human development. These authorities did not always agree on the number of stages or when the transitions are made, but they all described certain characteristics that would unfold through a natural process. Ancient Greek, Roman, and early Christian and Islamic scholars, including Pythagoras (circa 580–500 BCE), Hippocrates (circa 460–375 BCE), Plato (428–347 BCE), Aristotle (384–322 BCE), Ptolemy (circa 90–168 CE), St. Augustine (354–430 CE), and Avicenna (circa 980–1037 CE) are among those commenting on adolescent development (Bakke, 2005; Burrow, 1986; Rawson, 2003).

The 4th-century BCE scholars Aristotle and Plato, not surprisingly, had influential ideas about adolescent development. Aristotle identified the period from puberty to age 21 as the last of three preadult periods (Berzonsky, 2000). His other childhood periods were infancy (birth to 7 years) and young childhood (from age 7 to puberty). Santrock (2007) pointed out that Aristotle's emphasis on the development of self-determination during adolescence is consistent with current views of some of the key themes of adolescence, including autonomy, identity, and career choice. Aristotle described other characteristics of adolescents (e.g., egocentrism, impulsivity, moodiness).

Plato recognized the importance of cognitive development during adolescence, indicating that reasoning first appears during this time period; hence children should spend time in sports and music, whereas adolescents can study science and mathematics (Berzonsky, 2000; Santrock, 2007). Plato described children as both intellectually and physically soft and malleable, "wax tablets" (referring to a reusable and portable writing device used during antiquity and the Middle Ages). He emphasized that age-appropriate texts must be selected to avoid a negative influence on the moral development of youth (Bakke, 2005).

"EMERGING ADULTHOOD'S" ANCIENT ROOTS

It is interesting that the concept of "emerging adulthood," which has been called a new theory of development from the late teens through the 20s (Arnett, 2000), has quite ancient roots as well. Although Arnett (2000) indicated that sweeping demographic shifts in the past 50 years led him to conclude that the period between the ages of 18 to 25 should be considered distinct in the human life cycle and not just a brief transition into adulthood, observers in other times had similar ideas. For example, Burrow (1986) quoted the Persian physician and scholar Avicenna (circa 980–1037 CE): "The ages are four in all. There is the age of growing up, which is called the age of adolescence and commonly lasts until the age of 30" (p. 15). Similarly, Shahar (1992) indicated that there were confraternities of children from age 10 years in 15th-century Florence and that separate confraternities for late adolescents began at 19 years for those "too old to be among boys and too young to be among mature men" (p. 23).

SEPARATE, BUT NOT EQUAL:
BOYS AND GIRLS IN HISTORY

Early observers recognized the gender differences in maturation and described normative expectations for behaviors at the various stages. There was wide agreement that an adolescent stage began around age 12 for girls and age 14 for boys, but there was not a uniform marker for the beginning of adulthood, at least for boys. The age of maturity for boys varied from 18 to 35 years. A postadolescent phase of development, *juventus,* included young men in military training who had yet to take a wife. Dante in *Convivio* (written between 1304 and 1307 CE) indicated that *adolescentia* only ended at age 25 with the completion of rational development and economic independence—although, like today's "emerging adults," some did not become independent by age 25 (Shahar, 1992).

The transition to adulthood for girls was much more abrupt than the long intermediate transition to full adulthood afforded boys. Girls exited adolescence through marriage, which often occurred close to puberty; they experienced sexual initiation and pregnancy quite early (Hanawalt, 1993). Both Plato and Aristotle categorized children with other marginal groups in classical civilizations, asserting that they are like women, slaves, or animals, and their lack of reason inhibits the expression of ethical behavior (Bakke, 2005). Although there was sensitivity to child development and great importance attached to education, it was primarily for boys and not girls (Rawson, 2003). This lack of gender equality with regard to both interest in and opportunities for girls is a distinguishing feature separating modern theories of adolescent development from the past.

SHAKESPEARE DESCRIBES STAGE THEORY

By the beginning of the modern period, there was widespread acceptance of the stage theory of the human life cycle, with Shakespeare, writing around 1599, describing seven developmental stages in Jacques's monologue from *As You Like It* (Act 2, Scene 7):

> All the world's a stage,
> And all the men and women merely players;
> They have their exits and their entrances,
> And one man in his time plays many parts,
> His acts being seven ages.

Shakespeare, like others before and after, highlighted the prominence of sexuality and heightened emotionality during adolescence. Interested readers can explore Shakespeare's descriptions of human development to old age by doing an online search with the phrase "all the world's a stage."

SEXUALITY, MORALITY, AND THOSE PEER GROUP INFLUENCES

Controlling adolescent sexuality is a theme across many time periods. For example, Bakke (2005) described St. Augustine's criticisms that his father did not provide sufficient guidance to help him resist sexual desires and thereby avoid sinful behaviors. Augustine's *Confessions* (2.3.6), written around 397 CE, includes the following concerns:

> The thorn-bushes of my lust shot up higher than my head, and no hand was there to root them out. Least of all my father's: for when at the baths one day he saw me with unquiet adolescence my only covering, and noted my ripening sexuality, he began at once to look forward eagerly to grandchildren, and gleefully announced his discovery to my mother. . . . She . . . started up in devout fear and trembling.

Early Christian writers indicated that adolescents had greater responsibility than younger children for their behaviors because of the onset of reasoning during this stage (Bakke, 2005). However, as early as the 3rd century CE, parents were cautioned about being overly permissive given negative peer group influences that could encourage children to "go with those of their own age and meet together and carouse; for in this way they learn mischief" (Bakke, 2005, p. 180).

BEGINNING OF THE SCIENTIFIC STUDY OF ADOLESCENCE

The scientific observation of child and adolescent development expanded in the 18th to early 20th centuries. One of Rousseau's (1762/1979) five books in *Emile, or On Education* deals with Emile's education during adolescence. The education of Sophie, Emile's wife to be, is detailed in the last book. Rousseau argued that puberty should be considered a second birth given its profound emotional effects (Savage, 2008). Goethe's novel, *The Sorrows of Young Werther,* published in 1774, expanded on Rousseau's description of adolescence as a time of storm and stress, a description also included in *Adolescence,* the seminal work by G. Stanley Hall (1904) in the early 20th century (Arnett, 1999; Savage, 2008).

The formal study of adolescent development was given great impetus by Hall (1904) when he brought together, as a formal discipline, information from a variety of fields to address the development of youth. One of Hall's great breakthroughs was the recognition that the adolescent period was not just biologically determined by puberty but socially constructed as well (Savage, 2008). In addition, Hall, like others before him, recognized that adolescence extended beyond the teen years, until age 21 in girls and 25 in boys. Arnett (2006) assessed Hall's contributions as follows:

> A century later, his views continue to be part of the core knowledge of the field of adolescent psychology, in areas including the prevalence and sources of depressed mood in adolescence; the rise in crime rates during the teens and specific patterns of delinquency; heightened sensation seeking in adolescence and its relation to risk behavior; susceptibility to

media influences; increased orientation toward peers and relational aggression in girls; and biological development during puberty—among others. (p. 190)

Influences on Adolescent Personality and Behavior

As we have seen, there is a rich historical context for understanding adolescents that must be considered when using the MMPI–A as part of a psychological evaluation. Figure 1.1 provides a conceptual framework for considering the various influences on a young person's personality and behavior. In addition to considerations at the individual level (e.g., biological, cognitive, identity formation, increased social demands and expectations), adolescents must be understood within their families, various peer groups, school community, local community, and the more general society in which they live (Perry, Williams, & Veblen-Mortenson, 2009).

INDIVIDUAL OR INFLUENCES FROM WITHIN

Research at the commencement of the 21st century benefits from sophisticated techniques such as magnetic resonance imaging (MRI),

FIGURE 1.1

Influences on adolescent personality and behavior. From *Project Northland Program Guide for Effective Alcohol-Use Prevention in School and Communities* (p. 3), by Cheryl L. Perry, Carolyn L. Williams, and Sara Veblen-Mortenson, 2009. Copyright 2009 by Hazelden Foundation, Center City, MN. Reprinted with permission of Hazelden Foundation.

functional MRI, and event-related potential for describing the adolescent brain's responses to thinking and memory tasks (e.g., Rutter, 2007; Sowell, Thompson, & Toga, 2007; Tapert, Caldwell, & Burke, 2004–2005) that may underlie previous observations of adolescent development described earlier. Researchers are demonstrating that significant neuro-maturation occurs during adolescence, which likely results in greater cognitive efficiency and more cognitive control over behavior (e.g., Dahl, 2004; Lopez, Schwartz, Prado, Campo, & Pantin, 2008; Luna & Sweeney, 2004; Sowell et al., 2007; Spear, 2000; Zeigler et al., 2005).

Although it is true that overall brain size, weight, amount of cortical folding, and specialization of the brain's regions are in adult form by early childhood, more subtle changes, which have a significant impact on brain function and behavior, occur during adolescence and beyond (Luna & Sweeney, 2004). These include synaptic pruning, elaboration of dendritic arborization, increased myelination, and increased integration of the prefrontal cortex with other regions of the brain (Luna & Sweeney, 2004). Although the prefrontal cortex decreases in volume during adolescence, perhaps because of synaptic pruning, the subcortical gray matter and limbic system structures (septal area, hippocampus, and amygdala) increase in volume (Zeigler et al., 2005). These important structures are pictured in Figure 1.2. The prefrontal cortex has long been identified as involved with reasoning, planning, integrating information, abstract thinking, problem solving, judgment, and self-control; the amygdala is involved with emotions; and the hippocampus is involved with learning and memory (Lopez et al., 2008; Santrock, 2007; Zeigler et al., 2005).

The changes in brain structure and functioning are not all or nothing but gradual. Adolescents are gaining the ability for cognitive control over behavior; however, brain functioning is unlikely to be fully mature until adolescents are in their 20s (Lopez et al., 2008). Therefore, under "hot" high-demand situations (e.g., distracting stimuli, competing tasks, high affect, competing motivations like peer pressure), adult-level control of behavior by internal processes rather than external stimuli may fail, which offers an explanation of adolescents' greater propensity for risk taking (Dahl, 2004; Luna & Sweeney, 2004; Spear, 2000). Similarly, the continued development of the prefrontal cortex has direct implications for mood regulation as well as decision making (Lopez et al., 2008).

There are other important individual-level changes during adolescence, including changes in feelings of self-worth and self-esteem. Harter (2006) provided a valuable perspective on the development of self-esteem in several domains, including physical appearance, likeability by peers, athletic competence, academic competence, and behavioral conduct. Beginning in middle childhood, marked individual differences in self-esteem begin to emerge and will continue through adolescence and across the life span. Adolescents may become more negative in their

FIGURE 1.2

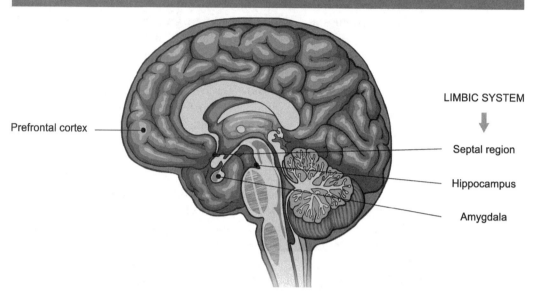

Prefrontal cortex

LIMBIC SYSTEM

Septal region

Hippocampus

Amygdala

Important areas of brain development and change during adolescence. From *Project Northland Program Guide for Effective Alcohol-Use Prevention in School and Communities* (CD-ROM), by Cheryl L. Perry, Carolyn L. Williams, and Sara Veblen-Mortenson, 2009. Copyright 2009 by Hazelden Foundation, Center City, MN. Reprinted with permission of Hazelden Foundation.

self-appraisal, resulting in part because they come to rely more on their use of social comparisons and the feedback they receive from peers. According to a meta-analysis, the greatest effect sizes emerged during late adolescence, with young men showing a slightly higher self-esteem than young women (Kling, Hyde, Showers, & Buswell, 1999).

Resilience, that is, the process of positive adaptation during or following significant adversity or risk, is another individual-level characteristic relevant to an appraisal of a young person's psychological adjustment. Resilient children and adolescents are described as having (a) cognitive, attention, and problem-solving skills; (b) effective emotion and behavioral regulation; (c) positive sense of self-worth; (d) hopefulness or a belief that life can have meaning; and (e) some aptitudes or characteristics that are valued by society, such as attractiveness or talent (see Masten, 2007; Masten, Cutuli, Herbers, & Gabrielle-Reed, 2009).

In addition to these individual factors that predict an adolescent's resilience, Masten (2007; Masten et al., 2009) described other important positive influences evident in Figure 1.1. These include (a) having at least one effective parent; (b) connections with one or more caring and competent adults; (c) having prosocial friends; (d) attending an effective school; (e) socioeconomic advantage; (f) affiliation with a religious group; and (g) living in an effective community (a safe environment with good resources including health care availability).

Dahl (2004) described a startling paradox: Even though adolescence is a developmental period of increasing strength and resilience (e.g., adolescents are stronger than those who are younger and show improvements in reaction time, immune function, and reasoning abilities), overall morbidity and mortality rates for adolescents increase 200%. The major sources of morbidity and mortality in adolescents (e.g., accidents, suicide, homicide, alcohol and drug abuse, and violence) are associated with problems of behavioral and emotional control. And, as Dahl pointed out, a second paradox is that adolescents have better reasoning and decision-making skills than those who are younger yet are more prone to erratic risk-taking behaviors.

Dahl (2004) suggested that the previously described neurobehavioral changes appear to be linked to pubertal development. These changes have significant effects on motivation and behavior of adolescents that require an interdisciplinary approach to achieve greater understanding of effective intervention and prevention strategies for youths. Others have proposed that the emergence of some of the major psychiatric illnesses during adolescence may be due to the individual's inability to develop a more mature brain that is capable of working in an integrated manner rather than to any loss of cognitive abilities (Luna & Sweeney, 2004). Steinberg et al. (2006) suggested that "adolescents who enjoy a supportive home, peer, school, and neighborhood context are buffered from the ill effects of the emotional-cognitive dysfunction" (p. 716).

EVEN AS AUTONOMY INCREASES, THE FAMILY REMAINS IMPORTANT

Figure 1.1 puts the adolescent's family as the next closest influence on his or her behavior. Family members remain important influences from early adolescence through emerging adulthood, even though adolescence is recognized as a time of increasing autonomy and movement from the family into a broader peer group culture (Arnett, 1999, 2000, 2006; Santrock, 2007). Today's families are no longer limited to two-parent households. Rather, other adults—stepparents, grandparents, the live-in partner of a parent, foster parents, or guardians—can be just as important to a young person as his or her biological parent and must be considered in a psychological evaluation (Josephson & the AACAP Work Group on Quality Issues, 2007). Siblings, cousins, or others with long-standing and binding ties may be part of a young person's family environment (Perry et al., 2009; Santrock, 2007). Older siblings may have important functions such as supervising younger siblings, an important influence on both the younger and the older sibling.

Views of parents' influence on their children have expanded in recent years beyond a consideration of the various parenting styles (e.g., authoritarian, authoritative, neglectful, and indulgent parenting) that can influence a young person's development to seeing parents in a managerial role of their child's social environment (Josephson & the AACAP Work Group on Quality Issues, 2007; Park & Buriel, 2006; Santrock, 2007). Parents can remain influential through their roles as managers or gatekeepers of social activities even as their children spend more time in the peer group. Parents are able to monitor their children's activities and maintain family routines encouraging completion of homework and participation in chores (Santrock, 2007).

In addition, many parents are able to select neighborhoods, schools, and extracurricular activities that directly affect the social opportunities available to the adolescent. At the same time, adolescents' wishes may affect parents' decisions as well. As evidence of the more active participation of adolescents in decisions about the choice of neighborhoods, Park and Buriel (2006) pointed out that residential mobility of the family increases after adolescents graduate from high school, perhaps because parents may be reluctant to disrupt an older teen's school and/or social environments.

NOT NECESSARILY NEGATIVE: THE UBIQUITOUS PEER GROUP

The peer group is the next significant influence on adolescent behavior in Figure 1.1. As noted earlier, descriptions about the harmful effects of negative peer group influences can be found as early as the 3rd century (Bakke, 2005). Although influences from the peer group are inevitable, they are not necessarily negative. Peer group influences are important as the young person's autonomy and separation from parents evolve during adolescence. Peer groups exist in the school or can be neighborhood based or centered on sports or other extracurricular activities, at religious institutions, or at after school or summer jobs (Perry et al., 2009; Santrock, 2007).

Competence within the peer group is important to psychological functioning. Eisenberg, Vaughan, and Hofer (2009) presented a model reflecting how children's temperament (e.g., individual differences in reactivity and self-regulation) influences their personality and how both these factors influence young people's status with peers, the quality of their behaviors with peers, and their friendships—all of which are associated with self-esteem, loneliness, adjustment, and other aspects of psychological functioning. The reader is referred to Rubin, Bukowski, and Laursen (2009) for a comprehensive discussion of peer group issues.

SCHOOL DAYS, SCHOOL DAYS

The school setting has multiple areas of influence on a young person's behavior. Its influences reach beyond "reading and 'riting and 'rithmetic." Teachers and administrators, as well as other personnel such as the school nurse or coaches, are role models. Schools that provide safe and fun after hours activities can have a positive impact on youth behavior. In addition, school policies on important problems such as alcohol and drug use—when enforced consistently—can also have significant impact on youth problem behaviors (Perry et al., 2007, 2009). The young person's behavior may differ substantially in these various contexts. This requires the assessor to examine functioning in all relevant domains before deciding if a young person's problems require treatment or simply reflect normative difficulties of adolescence (Steiner & Feldman, 1996).

LAST, BUT NOT INEVITABLY LEAST, COMMUNITY AND SOCIETAL INFLUENCES

The more distal influences in Figure 1.1—the local community and the broader society—can affect an adolescent's behaviors in a positive or negative fashion (Fulkerson, Pasch, Perry, & Komro, 2008; Leventhal & Brooks-Gunn, 2000; Perry et al., 2009; Rutter, 2007, Sampson, Morenoff, & Gannon-Rowley, 2002). Poverty, residential instability, single parenthood, and ethnic heterogeneity are examples of possible influences on both adolescent and parenting behaviors. Jencks and Mayer (1990), in what is now considered a classic framework for understanding how community differences can affect individual behavior, identified five models:

- Neighborhood institutional resources: Access to resources such as parks, libraries, recreational facilities, and services contributes to safe (i.e., police protection) and healthy environments.
- Collective socialization: This includes the presence of adult role models, supervision, monitoring, structure, and routine.
- Contagion effects: The presence of negative behaviors in neighbors or peers spreads to others.
- Competition: Scarce resources lead to competition among neighbors and peers.
- Relative deprivation: Individuals evaluate themselves in comparison with their neighbors.

Leventhal and Brooks-Gunn (2000) suggested that according to the first three of these models, high socioeconomic status neighborhoods confer benefits to adolescents, whereas the adverse is true for the competition and relative deprivation models. Furthermore, parents are thought to modify their parenting behaviors on the basis of the conditions in their communities. For example, in high-crime neighborhoods, parents may try to protect younger adolescents from being victimized by keeping them inside or prohibiting interactions with peers in the neighborhood, which could lead to the negative consequence of increasing discord with their child. On the other hand, neighborhoods with safe community resources and the presence of actively engaged adults providing supervision and positive role models can mediate the negative effects of poverty. Parents in more problematic neighborhoods may mediate the negative effects by sending their children to play under the supervision of adults in safer neighborhoods (Sampson et al., 2002). The reader is referred to Sampson et al. (2002) for a comprehensive review of neighborhood effects on adolescent behavior.

Other aspects of the broader social environment that influence adolescent behavior include the mass media, which has grown considerably in the past few years with technologies such as the Internet, social networking sites (e.g., Facebook, MySpace, Open Diary, Twitter, Vampirefreaks), and cell phones. These technological advances provide access to information and opportunities across the socioeconomic spectrum. However, messages about sexuality, alcohol and drug use, violence, body image, and the like are accessible to even the youngest adolescents. This requires more diligent monitoring from parents and other adults to mitigate the unhealthy messages reaching adolescents from these multiple sources, many of which were unknown just a few years ago.

Psychopathology in Adolescence

Adolescence is a period of vulnerability in which some young people experience the disruption caused by mental health problems (e.g., Spear, 2000; Steinberg et al., 2006). Although research over the past 40 years has shown that adolescence is not inevitably a time of storm and stress (Rutter, 2007; Steinberg et al., 2006), some disorders increase during adolescence, including social anxiety, panic disorders, depression, and substance abuse (Costello, Mustillo, Erkanli, Keeler, & Angold, 2003). The rates of mental disorders among adolescents have been reported to be comparable with those of adults (Costello et al., 2003; Roberts, Roberts, & Xing, 2007; Spear, 2000). For example, Roberts et al. (2007) found that, consistent with earlier studies, 17.1% of a sample of 4,175 adolescents (ages 11–17 years) in a metropolitan area met *Diagnostic and Statistical Manual of Mental Disorders* (4th ed., text revision; American Psychiatric Association, 2000) criteria for one or more disorders. The most prominent diagnoses were the anxiety disorders (6.9%), disruptive disorders

(6.5%), and substance abuse disorders (5.3%). Prevalence of mood disorders was 2.1%, with major depression being the most frequent and with both mania and hypomania at less than 1%.

An intriguing study by Cicero, Epler, and Sher (2009) suggests that there may be developmentally limited forms of bipolar disorder. Findings from recent epidemiological studies revealed that a "strikingly high prevalence of bipolar disorders in emerging adulthood (5.5%–6.2% among 18 to 24 year olds)" appeared to have resolved favorably by the latter half of the 3rd decade of life (3.1% to 3.4% in 25- to 29-year-olds; Cicero et al., 2009, p. 431). These authors hypothesized that the maturation of the prefrontal cortex by the 3rd decade of life might represent a key factor in resolving developmentally limited forms of bipolar disorder as well as other disorders marked by disinhibition (e.g., alcohol use disorders and some personality disorders).

Adverse life events tend to result in a higher likelihood of psychopathology (Flouri & Kallis, 2007). The likelihood of deviant behaviors is increased if the young person chooses to associate with antisocial peers (Masten, 2007). Some adolescents, especially those who have learning or developmental difficulties, may be especially challenged during this period with consequences for later development. For example, in a study of boys treated in childhood (i.e., ages 6–12 years) for hyperactivity (78% of this sample had parents who identified conduct problems as part of the boys' clinical picture), a significant number of them had higher rates of arrests, convictions, and incarcerations than a control group 30 years later (Satterfield et al., 2007). The authors concluded that hyperactive boys with conduct problems were at increased risk for adult criminality. However, it is also important to note that the majority of the sample did not become adult criminals.

Use of alcohol and other drug is a major risk factor during adolescence. By eighth grade, 32% of American youths have used alcohol in the past year, and 10% of them report heavy episodic use, defined as having five or more drinks in a row in the previous 2 weeks (Johnston, O'Malley, Bachman, & Schulenberg, 2008). Research has demonstrated a number of social and health problems associated with alcohol use during adolescence, including the progression to alcohol and other drug abuse and dependence, alcohol-related violence and injuries, automobile crashes, risky sexual behaviors, and school truancy and problems (e.g., Tobler, Komro, & Maldonado-Molina, 2009; Zeigler et al., 2005). There is increasing concern that alcohol use during adolescence may have profound effects on brain structure and neurocognitive deficits (e.g., Tapert et al., 2004–2005; Zeigler et al., 2005). Underage drinkers are susceptible to the immediate consequences of their drinking (e.g., hangovers, blackouts, alcohol poisoning) as well as brain damage and neurocognitive deficits that have implications for learning and intellectual development (Zeigler et al., 2005).

Adolescents under the age of 15 years who drink alcohol are estimated to be 4 times more likely to develop alcohol dependence in adulthood compared with those who delay drinking until age 18 or older (Grant & Dawson, 1997). Early alcohol use by 12-year-olds was related to more arrests and greater likelihood of substance abuse disorders at ages 20 to 22 years (Flory, Lynam, Milich, Leukefeld, & Clayton, 2004). It is clear that alcohol use at early ages is a signal of the greater likelihood of problems later in the life cycle.

Utility of the MMPI–A for Measuring Psychopathology

It is not coincidental that self-report inventories such as the MMPI–A first become useful measures for psychological evaluations at the commencement of adolescence, given all the developmental changes that come about with the emergence from childhood to adolescence. It would be impossible for participants to respond meaningfully to the MMPI–A item pool without having the ability to reason and reflect on how the individual items relate to their sense of self. In addition, some of the item content is simply not relevant to younger children's experiences or psychological understanding.

One of the first questions for a psychologist to address, particularly for the youngest adolescents, is whether the individual is mature enough to complete an MMPI–A (included in this assessment is whether he or she has the reading level for items at the fifth- to seventh-grade level). Not all young adolescents will be sufficiently mature or have the necessary reading level for the instrument. However, for those who are, the MMPI–A can be an important part of a psychological evaluation.

The MMPI–A is also useful for addressing compelling issues about the mental health status of adolescents over time. For example, one of the unique aspects of the MMPI instruments–their longevity—allowed a group of researchers to investigate changes over significant periods of time in psychopathology as measured by responses to the MMPI items (Twenge et al., 2010). A meta-analysis of studies published between 1938 and 2007 on MMPI, MMPI–2, and MMPI–A scores from high school ($N = 13,870$) and college ($N = 63,706$) students revealed that today's adolescents and young adults tend to score about 1 standard deviation higher on several MMPI Clinical Scales (i.e., Scale 2, Depression [D]; Scale 4, Psychotic Deviate [Pd]; Scale 6, Paranoia [Pa]; Scale 9, Hypomania [Ma]; see Chapter 4 for a complete list of the Clinical Scales) than earlier cohorts. These higher scores suggest more rejection of societal rules and norms, impulsivity, tendency to blame others for problems, and greater unhappiness in young people living today.

Do these MMPI differences reflect actual decreases in psychological health? Has the American culture's increased focus on money, appearance, and status, rather than earlier values promoting community and close relationships, led to poorer mental health outcomes for today's adolescents compared with earlier cohorts? Although Twenge et al. (2010) were able to control for response bias using two of the MMPI–A Validity Scales (Lie [L] and Correction [K]; see Chapter 4), they did not take into account changes in test administration procedures from the early days to current practices, covered in the next two chapters. Adolescents taking the test after the late 1960s were encouraged to answer all the items, which could theoretically contribute to higher scores in later cohorts. However, this study does raise intriguing questions about how some of the broader societal-level influences discussed in this chapter may be affecting the well-being of today's youths as measured by their scores on the MMPI–A Clinical Scales.

"Slipping Through My Fingers All the Time"

Any psychological assessment of an adolescent provides a snapshot of developing personality problems and mental health symptoms. Although many of the personality problems and symptoms revealed during an evaluation might reflect enduring problems, they may also be surpassed by other behaviors—positive or negative—as time passes. The very nature of adolescence is marked by change, growth, and development. Indeed, some of these behaviors and transitions have been described since antiquity. In the next chapter, we turn to a more in-depth discussion of the history of personality measures like the MMPI–A and the MMPI Restandardization Project that resulted in its development. We also introduce important components of the MMPI–A, including its substantial research base, scores, norms, and scales.

History and Development
of the MMPI–A 2

Do you find school a hard place to get along in?
Do you find home a hard place to get along in?
Do other children let you play with them?
          —(*Woodworth & Mathews, 1924*)

The MMPI–A's lineage can be traced directly back to the work of Robert Woodworth and his colleagues that occurred within 2 decades of the publication of G. Stanley Hall's *Adolescence* in 1904. Like Hall, Woodworth was a prominent psychologist of his time. After the United States entered World War I, the American Psychological Association commissioned Woodworth to develop a measure to identify soldiers most likely to develop "shell shock" on the battlefields in Europe. The Woodworth Personal Data Sheet contained 116 face-valid yes–no items, some of which will seem familiar to users of the MMPI instruments:

"Do you feel well rested in the morning?"
"Do you make friends easily?"
"Have you ever fainted away?"
"Did you ever run away from home?"

Woodworth (1919, 1920) conducted research primarily with older adolescents and young adults, comparing the responses of college students with a sample of draftees and returning soldiers with shell shock. The Personal Data Sheet was not, however, completed in time to be used during the war to select out draftees who were maladjusted (Woodworth, 1920).

Shortly afterward, to study the special problems of children and adolescents, Woodworth and Mathews (1924) published a 75-item version of the Personal Data Sheet for young people that included many of the same items as the adult version (e.g., see the items listed before the previous paragraph). They changed the context for some of the adult items (e.g., "Are you troubled with dreams about your work?" became "Are you troubled by dreams about your play?"). They dropped some content from the adult version of the Personal Data Sheet, particularly items dealing with sexuality and alcohol and other drug use.

Most of the items in the two versions of the Personal Data Sheet (i.e., Woodworth, 1920; Woodworth & Mathews, 1924), with perhaps a little tweaking to correct changes in word usage (e.g., *fainted* sounds better to the modern ear than *fainted away*), are related to personality constructs recognizable to psychologists today. The item content of the Personal Data Sheet included social adjustment, family issues, school problems, anxiety, fears, somatic complaints, and dreams, among others. There are a few interesting items that for the modern reader reflect a change in language usage and the understanding of human behavior, as in the case of the item, "Did you ever have St. Vitus' Dance?"[1]

A particularly startling item for contemporary psychologists, found on the adult version, is "Have you hurt yourself by masturbation (self-abuse)?" Woodworth (1920) and other psychologists such as G. Stanley Hall were, after all, products of the Victorian era. With the important exception of his description of masturbation, Hall's view of adolescent sexuality as normal and healthy was enlightened (Arnett, 2006): "It is, therefore, one of the cardinal sins against youth to repress healthy thoughts of sex at the proper age" (Hall, 1904, Vol. 2, p. 109).

The personality measures developed by Woodworth (1920; Woodworth & Mathews, 1924) were influential in the development of later personality scales, most notably, the MMPI, originally called a "multiphasic personality schedule (Minnesota)." Psychologist Starke Hathaway and psychiatrist J. C. McKinley developed the MMPI at the University of Minnesota Hospitals during the late 1930s and 1940s (e.g., Hathaway & McKinley, 1943). Their goal was to develop an efficient and effective means to assess mental health problems in psychiatric and medical settings. Eventually, the MMPI became the standard personality instrument in clinical evaluations and research of both adults and adolescents.

The popularity of the true–false MMPI was due in large part to its easy-to-use format and because its scales were based on well-established empirical validity for assessing clinical symptoms and syndromes (Butcher, 2011; Butcher & Williams, 2000). Another major contributor to the long-term success of the MMPI was its innovative validity scales, or the ability to assess the individual's test-taking atti-

---

[1] *Saint Vitus' Dance* is an alternate name for *Sydenham chorea*, a movement disorder that is one of the major signs of acute rheumatic fever (Medline Plus, 2010).

tudes. The Woodworth (1920; Woodworth & Mathews, 1924) measures lacked this crucial feature.

In this chapter we review the early application of the original version of the MMPI with adolescents and the MMPI revision program that included the development of the instrument to be more effective with adolescent populations. We provide a description of the normative population and clinical research samples that established the research basis for the application of the MMPI–A with adolescents in clinical and correctional applications. We describe the norms used to interpret MMPI–A scale elevations and other relevant terms necessary for understanding the instrument. Some of the fundamental terms are included in Exhibit 2.1.

The Pioneers in MMPI Assessments

Although the MMPI originally was developed, normed, and validated for adult populations, it rapidly came to be used with adolescents. However, unlike the Woodworth and Mathews Personal Data Sheet, no attempts were made to change the item content of the instrument for adolescents

EXHIBIT 2.1

MMPI–A FAQs: Scales, Correlates, and Code Types

What is an MMPI–A scale?
Personality scales like those on the MMPI–A are groups of items used to measure a particular construct, for example, depression, alcohol and other drug problems, or family conflicts.

What are the various sets of scales used for interpreting the MMPI–A?
There are five primary sets of MMPI–A scales used for interpreting the test: the Validity Scales, the Clinical Scales, the Supplementary Scales, the Content Scales, and the PSY-5 Scales. Chapters 4 and 5 provide detailed information about the MMPI–A Scales.

What is a scale correlate or descriptor?
Scale correlates, also known as scale descriptors, are symptoms, behaviors, attitudes, or motivations, experienced by adolescents that have been established by empirical validation research and found to be associated and with elevations on various MMPI–A scales.

What is a code type?
An MMPI code type is a subset of the highest elevated Clinical Scales in the clinical profile. The code type is obtained by rank ordering the highest scales in the clinical pro?le (usually excluding Scale 5, Masculinity/Femininity [*Mf*] and Scale 0, Social Introversion [*Si*]). A specific code type is made up of the highest 2 or 3 scale elevations (e.g., 2-7/7-2). Research has established empirical correlates or descriptors for MMPI–2 code types with adults, but the research is more equivocal for the utility of code types with adolescents.

during the first half century of its use. Nevertheless, the MMPI became the most frequently used personality measure across mental health, personnel, health, and correctional settings and was adapted widely in many countries (Butcher, 2010, 2011; Butcher & Williams, 2009).

IN THE BEGINNING . . . DORA CAPWELL ON MAIN STREET

The first MMPI-based personality study to evaluate the use of the test with adolescents was conducted by Dora Capwell, actually during the same time period that the original MMPI was being developed. Sauk Centre, Minnesota, the small town that inspired Sinclair Lewis's popular novel, *Main Street*, was the setting for Capwell's (1945a, 1945b, 1953) research project. The Minnesota Home School for Girls opened in Sauk Centre in 1911 to house and rehabilitate delinquent girls from ages 9 to 16 years. Incorrigibility and immorality were the leading causes for the girls' commitment in the early days. By 1948, the Home School for Girls served as the reception and diagnostic center for delinquent girls in Minnesota (Minnesota Department of Corrections, 2009).

Capwell, studying adolescent girls (a notable shift of attention from history's emphasis on adolescent boys), found that girls in a correctional facility produced similar MMPI patterns as adults with a history of acting-out problems. This provided the first confirmation of the validity of the MMPI with adolescents. Capwell administered the MMPI to 101 delinquent girls living at the Minnesota Home School. Notably, she hypothesized that the best comparison group for evaluating these troubled adolescents would be a sample of other adolescents who were not experiencing problems, not the adult sample developed by Hathaway and McKinley (1940, 1942) that came to be known as the "Minnesota Normals" (Exhibit 2.2). Therefore, her comparison sample consisted of

---

EXHIBIT 2.2

MMPI–A Trivia Questions: "Minnesota Normals"

Where did Starke Hathaway and J. C. McKinley find the "Minnesota Normals?"
In the waiting rooms, corridors, and cafeteria at the University of Minnesota Hospital. The "Minnesota Normals" became an abbreviation for the normative sample for the original MMPI—in use for almost 50 years. The MMPI normative sample was made up primarily of friends and family members of patients being seen at the hospital—if you were a patient at the hospital or said you were "under a doctor's care," then you were ineligible to be tested as part of the normative sample.

How did they decide the "Minnesota Normals" were normal?
The "Minnesota Normals" were a comparison or normative sample whose mental health status was never determined, despite the familiar, but misleading, nickname.

85 girls who attended Sauk Centre public school. In her research, Capwell concluded that of all the personality measures she studied, the MMPI most clearly differentiated her correctional sample from the normative comparison sample.

In the years that followed Capwell's original study, a number of others also focused on the personality of adolescents using the MMPI. Monachesi (1948, 1950a, 1950b, 1953) extended Capwell's findings for girls to boys. Hathaway, Hastings, Capwell, and Bell (1953) conducted a follow-up of the original Sauk Centre adolescent samples that provided additional support for the effectiveness of the MMPI items in understanding adolescents. The research by Capwell showing how the MMPI items were effective at describing troubled adolescents influenced a large number of additional studies over the following 20 years.

STARKE HATHAWAY AND ELIO
MONACHESI'S MAMMOTH PROJECT

Perhaps the largest longitudinal personality study of adolescents ever conducted was that of MMPI developer Starke Hathaway and his colleague Elio Monachesi, who headed the sociology department at the University of Minnesota (Hathaway & Monachesi, 1953, 1957, 1961, 1963). They initially tested 15,300 adolescents in the ninth grade throughout the state of Minnesota (i.e., about 89% of the ninth-grade students registered in public schools). They followed up this sample several years later examining variables such as school performance, school dropout rates, and delinquent behaviors. Their research provided substantial support for the sensitivity of the MMPI to adolescent problems in health, mental health, and correctional or juvenile delinquency settings. This study demonstrated personality factors associated with delinquency and high school dropout. For example, Scale 4, Psychotic Deviate (*Pd*); Scale 8, Schizophrenia (*Sc*); and Scale 9, Hypomania (*Ma*) were "excitatory" scales or were found to be associated with high rates of delinquency, whereas Scale 2, Depression (*D*) and Scale 0, Social Introversion (*Si*) were found to be "inhibitory" scales or were associated with lower rates of delinquency. As we will see in the next section, data from this study of Hathaway and Monachesi were instrumental in others' research on the use of the MMPI with adolescents for many years. Exhibit 2.3 provides a list of questions about MMPI–A norms and scores to assist in understanding the next section.

PHILIP MARKS AND OTHERS DEVELOP
ADOLESCENT NORMS FOR THE MMPI

In addition to not changing the item wording or content for adolescents, Hathaway and Monachesi's (1963) studies on the MMPI with adolescents did not include the development of adolescent-specific norms. At

---

EXHIBIT 2.3

MMPI–A FAQs: Norms and Scores

What is an MMPI–A raw score?
On a personality test like the MMPI–A, a raw score is the number of items the adolescent endorsed in the scored direction on any given measure (e.g., scale, subscale, component scale).

What are MMPI–A norms?
Norms for psychological tests like the MMPI–A provide data that are used to compare an individual's raw scores relative to scores from others his or her sex and age by means of a standard score. MMPI standard scores are called *T* scores, and these are used for interpreting both the MMPI–A and MMPI–2.

What is a T *score?*
A *T* score is a standard score developed for the original MMPI that enables an individual's raw scale score to be compared with a normative group—the "Minnesota Normals" in the case of the original test and adults. An individual's raw score is converted to a *T* score—a distribution of positions on a continuum that has been generated from responses of a normative sample. *T* scores fall on a distribution in which the mean score is 50 and the standard deviation is 10. MMPI–A *T* scores come in two types: linear and uniform *T* scores, to be described later in the chapter.

---

this time, psychologists used raw-score to *T*-score conversion tables generated from adult responses to the MMPI (i.e., the Minnesota Normals) when assessing an adolescent client or conducting comparative research with adolescents. However, by the 1970s and 1980s, four sets of norms for adolescents were developed for the original MMPI. Peter Briggs and Philip Marks (cited in Dahlstrom, Welsh, & Dahlstrom, 1972) developed the first specific adolescent norms using a small subset of the adolescent data collected by Hathaway and Monachesi (*n* = 437 males and 419 females). Dahlstrom et al. (1972) included this adolescent norm set in an appendix as *T*-score conversion tables.

Shortly after the publication of his first adolescent norm set, Philip Marks, working with other colleagues, developed the second set of adolescent norms. Marks, Seeman, and Haller (1974) augmented the normative sample developed by Briggs and Marks with additional samples of adolescents from Alabama, Kansas, North Carolina, and Missouri. This second norm set included 949 boys and 854 girls. Even with the addition of subjects from other states, the norms were not representative of the U.S. population and did not include diverse groups of adolescents.

Gottesman, Hanson, Kroeker, and Briggs (1987) developed the third adolescent norms using a more complete set of the data that Hathaway and Monachesi (1963) accumulated. According to Archer (1987), who reprinted these norms in an appendix, these norms were based on responses from approximately 14,000 ninth graders (age 15 years) tested between 1948 and 1954 by Hathaway and Monachesi (1963) and 3,500 12th graders (age 18 years) retested between 1956 and 1957.

All three of these sets of adolescent norms were hampered by the instructions used by Hathaway and Monachesi (1963) during their data collection, limiting their use as part of a normative comparison group in later years when test administration instructions changed. Hathaway and Monachesi allowed adolescents in their studies to omit items they did not want to answer, which resulted in a higher level of Cannot Say scores compared with later use of the MMPI when the instructions were to answer all the items. Higher Cannot Say scores led to an overall lowering of the mean scale scores in Hathaway and Monachesi's subjects. This resulted in higher scores for adolescents who later were encouraged to answer all the items when compared with normative samples based in large part on Hathaway and Monachesi's data.

The fourth set of adolescent norms was developed by Colligan and Offord during the 1980s and published by Archer (1987) and Colligan and Offord (1989). Colligan and Offord collected their normative data using the original version of the MMPI. They obtained responses from 691 girls and 624 boys between the ages of 13 and 17. They randomly sampled 11,930 households in Minnesota, Iowa, and Wisconsin that were within a 50-mile radius of the Mayo Clinic in Rochester, Minnesota. In telephone interviews of a subset of these households, Colligan and Offord found that more than 10% of these households included adolescents within the appropriate age groups. They located 1,412 adolescents for the study. The original version of the MMPI was administered in an uncontrolled situation; that is, the materials were mailed to these households for the adolescent to complete. They obtained a completion rate of 83% for girls and 72% for boys.

Despite these varied efforts to develop effective norms for adolescents with the original MMPI, many practitioners continued to use the adult norms for the MMPI with adolescents. The continued use of the adult norms for interpreting adolescent profiles required that the interpreter use "clinical judgment." Because use of the adult norms tended to characterize adolescents as more pathological than use of the adolescent norms, clinicians were advised to somehow take this into account to avoid overinterpreting psychopathology.

PHILIP MARKS, ROBERT ARCHER, AND OTHERS DEVELOP SCALE CORRELATES AND CODE TYPES

Despite the problems with norms, the use of the MMPI in studying adolescent populations and for assessing clients was extensive in the 1970s and 1980s. A great deal of research was aimed at exploring the clinical correlates of MMPI scale elevations and two-point code types in adolescent patient populations (refer back to Exhibit 2.1 on p. 21 for descriptions of scale correlates and code types). In addition to their normative work, Marks et al. (1974) also conducted a clinical study of 834 adolescent outpatients from clinics in several states during 1965–1970. They obtained clinical and behavioral rating information for use in developing empirical correlates for MMPI code types. Marks and colleagues reported that many of their MMPI adolescent code type descriptors were similar to the correlates that had been found in adult studies. The Marks et al. MMPI codebook became a widely used resource guide to interpreting adolescent MMPI profiles during the 1970s and 1980s.

Several studies by Archer and his colleagues reported that adolescent clinical patients tended to produce behavioral relationships to the Clinical Scales similar to adult patients. Archer, Gordon, Giannetti, and Singles (1988) found that correlates of single-scale high point elevations for Scale 1, Hypochondriasis (Hs); Scale 3, Hysteria (Hy); Scale 4, Psychopathic Deviate (Pd); Scale 8, Schizophrenia (Sc); and Scale 9, Hypomania (Ma) in an inpatient sample of 112 adolescent inpatients showed behaviors that were very similar to descriptors reported for the Clinical Scales in studies of adult patients. In another study, Archer, Gordon, Anderson, and Giannetti (1989) found that the behavioral correlates of the Welsh's Anxiety (A) and Repression (R) scales, the MacAndrew Alcoholism Scale (MAC), and Barron's Ego Strength scale (Es) were similar to the results of adult inpatients as with adolescents. Archer and Gordon (1988) found that Scale 8 elevation was an effective and sensitive indicator of the presence of schizophrenic diagnoses in a sample of adolescent inpatients as with adults.

USEFUL, BUT CUMBERSOME TO INTERPRET

During the 1980s the MMPI continued to be widely used in both research studies and clinical applications with adolescents. However, as described earlier, there were five different norm sets (four from adolescent samples and the adult Minnesota Normals) from which to choose, each with significant limitations. There were other issues, too, hampering interpretations of MMPI profiles from adolescents. C. L. Williams (1986) identified three main differences in MMPI profiles from adults and adolescents that contributed to more difficulties in interpreting adolescents' profiles: (a) item endorsements, (b) code types, and (c) elevation. C. L. Williams (1986) and Butcher and Williams (2000) described how the item-level endorsement differences between adults and adolescents likely contributed to the elevated T scores for adolescents when using the adult normative sample. Adolescents more frequently endorsed items indicating urges to do harmful or shocking things, ideas of reference, and feelings of unreality, to name a few examples. Although these differences are understandable from a developmental perspective, they also indicate that the items are not psychometrically equivalent with adults and adolescents.

One of Hathaway and Monachesi's (1963) findings, that a "no high point" code type (e.g., none of the Clinical Scales above a *T* score of 54) was more prevalent in adults compared with adolescents, led to their hypothesis that "normal personality" may be more prevalent in adults than in adolescents (note the influence of the storm-and-stress model of adolescence on these MMPI pioneers). However, this definition of normal personality was soon discarded (Butcher & Williams, 2000). Although the 4-9/9-4 code type was the most frequent code type for adolescents in both clinical and general population settings (Marks et al., 1974; C. L. Williams & Butcher, 1989b), attempts to validate the adolescent code type approach subsequent to Marks et al. (1974) have not been successful (Ehrenworth & Archer, 1985; Peña, Megargee, & Brody, 1996; C. L. Williams & Butcher, 1989b). Fortunately, though, many studies did validate the behavioral correlates for scale elevations (see Archer and colleagues' work described earlier and C. L. Williams & Butcher, 1989b).

By the 1980s, it was also clear that adolescents from normative samples score at least one standard deviation higher than the adult Minnesota Normals on the Infrequency (*F*) Validity Scale and several Clinical Scales, including Scale 4, Psychopathic Deviate (*Pd*); Scale 6, Paranoia (*Pa*); Scale 7, Psychasthenia (*Pt*); and Scale 9, Hypomania (*Ma*) (Butcher & Williams, 2000). Another compounding problem was that the widely used Marks et al. (1974) adolescent norms did not yield mean *T* scores of 50 for normal adolescents, as did the adult norms. And, surprisingly, Ehrenworth and Archer (1985) found that interpretative statements for adolescents' MMPI profiles that were based on Marks et al.'s (1974) adolescent norms and adolescent code type descriptors were rated less accurate than interpretations based on adult norms and adult descriptors or adolescent norms and adult descriptors. All these issues emerging from the research and clinical use of the MMPI with adolescents led to widely varying interpretive strategies (Butcher & Williams, 2000; C. L. Williams, Butcher, Ben-Porath, & Graham, 1992), each of which is described below.

Adult Interpretive Strategy

In the adult interpretive strategy, there is no need for any special procedures. Norms, scale correlates, and code type descriptors derived from adult populations are used. Starke Hathaway, the developer of the MMPI, favored the use of adult norms with adolescents to avoid masking adult and adolescent differences (C. L. Williams, 1986). Unlike Woodworth and Mathews's (1924) development of the Personal Data Sheet for adolescents, Hathaway made no changes to the MMPI item content when he used the instrument with adolescents.

Marks et al. (1974) Interpretive Strategy

Marks et al.'s (1974) interpretive strategy uses the adolescent norms and adolescent code type descriptors.

Mixed Interpretive Strategy

The mixed interpretive strategy uses Marks et al.'s (1974) adolescent norms with the scale correlates and code type descriptors derived from adult populations.

Archer Combined Interpretive Strategy

This strategy was originally developed for the MMPI by Archer in 1987 by combining Marks et al.'s (1974) code type descriptors with those identified from a review of the descriptors found in adult texts (Graham, 1977; Greene, 1980; Lachar, 1974). Those found in both the adolescent and adult texts were assumed to be more robust. Archer (1987) recommended using the Marks et al. (1974) adolescent norms, not the adult norms. Archer (1992a, 2005) adapted this strategy for the MMPI–A and his computerized system for interpreting the MMPI–A (Archer, 1992b, 2003).

Williams and Butcher Scale Descriptor Interpretive Strategy

Because of the problems in defining and classifying code types in adolescent samples, as well as findings of limited validity for many of the traditional MMPI code type descriptors in adolescent samples, C. L. Williams and Butcher (1989b) recommended an approach focusing on the empirically based scale descriptors found in C. L. Williams and Butcher (1989a) for the original MMPI. This strategy was adapted for the MMPI–A (Butcher & Williams, 1992a, 2000; Butcher, Williams, et al., 1992; C. L. Williams et al., 1992) and the Minnesota Reports, a computerized interpretive system for the MMPI–A (Butcher & Williams, 1992b, 2007), and is the approach recommended in this beginner's guide as well.

And Even More Problems

In addition to these multiple and sometimes contradictory interpretive strategies, other problems were also noticeable when using the original MMPI with adolescents. The MMPI item pool did not sufficiently address adolescent problems and behaviors to the degree necessary to provide comprehensive evaluation of adolescent problems. The items were written for adults and some were confusing to adolescents. When the MMPI Restandardization Project began in the early 1980s, one of its goals was to determine the feasibility of developing a specific form of the test for adolescents.

The MMPI Restandardization Project and Development of MMPI–A

The original MMPI underwent a major revision in the 1980s guided by a committee appointed by the test publisher, the University of Minnesota Press. The initial members of the MMPI Restandardization Committee were W. Grant Dahlstrom and James N. Butcher. Within the first few months, they invited John R. Graham to join the committee. These three individuals designed the research plan, selected the instruments to include, developed two separate experimental forms of the MMPI for study, decided on strategies for the normative data collection, and then solicited help from psychologists around the United States to participate in local efforts to collect the required data for the normative sample. In addition, Butcher and Graham developed and carried out multiple clinical studies in conjunction with the Restandardization Project, and they recruited Carolyn L. Williams to work with them on the adolescent research projects.

After the restandardization study was designed and data collection completed for the development of the MMPI–2, Auke Tellegen joined the Restandardization Committee for the purpose of developing the *T*-score conversion tables. Exhibit 2.4 lists frequently asked questions regarding the two types of *T* scores. Tellegen's other major contribution to the MMPI–2 was the development of two new Validity Scales, Variable Response Inconsistency (*VRIN*) and True Response Inconsistency (*TRIN*), which were incorporated into both the MMPI–2 and MMPI–A. The MMPI–2 was released in 1989 (Butcher, Dahlstrom, Graham, Tellegen, & Kaemmer, 1989), and its manual was updated in 2001 (Butcher, Graham, Tellegen, Ben-Porath, & Kaemmer, 2001). Another change in the Restandardization Committee occurred once the MMPI–2 was published. Dahlstrom decided not to participate further in the development of the MMPI–A, and the University of Minnesota Press replaced him on the committee with Robert Archer in 1989.

The first phase of the Restandardization Project involved revising, updating, and expanding the original MMPI item pool to modernize the language. The Restandardization Committee identified several problems with the original items, including colloquial or obsolete language, sexist or masculine-oriented language, awkward wording, grammatical problems, ambiguities, and religious items referring only to Christianity (C. L. Williams, Ben-Porath, & Hevern, 1994). These items were either rewritten or eliminated (e.g., items related to religion and bowel and bladder functioning were dropped). The 16 items that were repeated in the original MMPI appeared only once in the new item pool. Newer items were

---

EXHIBIT 2.4

MMPI–A FAQs: Types of *T* Scores

---

*What is the difference between linear and uniform **T** scores?*
Linear *T* scores were developed for the original MMPI. The uniform *T* distribution was developed for the MMPI–2 during the Restandardization Project from a composite of all of the Clinical Scale scores (and other scale sets like the Content Scales and PSY-5 Scales). The uniform *T* score distribution approximates the linear *T* distribution. However, it allows for a more effective comparison across scales in that the percentile values for the scales are more comparable for uniform *T* scores. Like the linear *T* score distribution, uniform *T* scores have a mean of 50 and a standard deviation of 10. Uniform *T* scores were developed for the MMPI–A following the procedures used for the MMPI–2. Both types of *T* scores are used on the MMPI–A.

*How do I use linear **T** or uniform **T** scores to interpret an MMPI–A?*
Cut-off scores are points on the linear *T* or uniform *T* score distributions that are used to signify an elevated or moderately elevated scale score. An MMPI–A score of $T = 65$, which is one and a half standard deviations above the mean (and is at the 92nd percentile if it is a uniform *T* score), indicates that the score is elevated in the interpretable range suggesting that the construct being measured by that scale is likely to be prominent in the adolescent's clinical presentation. A *T* score of 60 to 64 indicates a moderate elevation; therefore less certainty that the scale correlates or descriptors apply to the individual. *T* scores below 59 are in the normal range. Chapters 4 through 8 in this volume describe in detail how to interpret MMPI–A scales.

---

added that addressed clinical or personality problems not covered sufficiently in the original item pool.

At the same time these improvements were being made to the MMPI item pool, the Restandardization Committee decided to develop two separate experimental booklets, Form AX for adults and Form TX for adolescents, each containing 704 items (Exhibit 2.5). The development of a separate booklet for adolescents was a departure from Hathaway's original work, and the test publisher, the University of Minnesota Press, was cautious about developing a new form of the test for adolescents. Empirical research was required before any decision was made about whether there would be a separate version of the instrument for adolescents.

EXHIBIT 2.5

MMPI Trivia Question: Forms AX and TX

Ever wondered why Form AX and Form TX of the MMPI used during the Restandardization Project each contained exactly 704 items?

SIMPLE—That was the maximum amount of items that could be included on one page, front and back, computer answer sheet.

FORM TX OF THE MMPI

The MMPI restandardization data collection for adolescents was conducted using Form TX, a 704-item inventory that contained all 550 original MMPI items plus 58 new items also included in the adult experimental booklet, Form AX, that resulted in the MMPI–2. These items were added to the test to address problems not covered sufficiently in the original MMPI (e.g., substance abuse, eating problems, suicide potential, amenability to treatment). In addition, 96 adolescent-specific items were added to Form TX that had not been included in the adult experimental version.

Butcher and Graham asked Carolyn Williams to review the literature on adolescent personality and development, and the three of them wrote these new items based on this literature review. The new adolescent-specific content included problem areas such as negative peer influences, identity formation, problems with family or school, and attitudes toward or experiences with sexuality.

NORMATIVE SAMPLE DATA COLLECTION

A primary goal of the adolescent normative data collection research was to develop reference norms that represented adolescents living in the United States with particular attention to minority group inclusion. The data collection sites for the MMPI–A normative study were obtained from both public and private schools. Several regions of the United States, encompassing California, Minnesota, Ohio, North Carolina, Virginia, New York, Pennsylvania, and Washington, provided a more diverse and heterogeneous normative group than was available in earlier adolescent norm development.

The normative sample includes 805 boys and 815 girls between the ages of 14 and 18 years. During the Restandardization Project, data were collected from adolescents as young as 12 and 13 years. However, it was difficult to recruit sufficient numbers of younger subjects. School principals and other administrators in elementary, middle, and junior high schools were reluctant to grant permission for the 3-hour testing session, indicating it would be too taxing for 12- and 13-year-olds. They also expressed concerns about some of the objectionable item content (e.g., items that assume sexual behaviors) in Form TX for younger adolescents (Butcher, Williams, et al., 1992).

By the time of the publication of the MMPI–A, only 173 subjects ages 12 and 13 were available for inclusion in the normative sample, with an additional 170 subjects age 13 years, collected by Archer in Norfolk, Virginia. The Infrequency (*F*) scale scores of these younger subjects were compared with the older subjects and were found to be considerably higher, suggesting problems in understanding the items (Butcher, Williams, et al., 1992). Rather than delaying the release of the

MMPI–A while attempting to recruit additional younger subjects with the shorter and less objectionable MMPI–A booklet (Butcher, Graham, Williams, & Kaemmer, 1992), we decided to limit the MMPI–A normative sample to subjects between 14 and 18 years (Butcher, Williams, et al., 1992). Archer (1992a) included linear *T*-score conversion tables in an appendix from the 13-year-old subjects he collected.

In addition to collecting data using Form TX, the restandardization study also included a Biographical Information Form and a Life Events Form, developed in collaboration with Williams, to study and identify demographic and life stressors of the samples included in the norms (C. L. Williams & Uchiyama, 1989). Procedures varied slightly depending on schools' differing requirements for psychological testing. However, data were typically collected in groups ranging in size from 5 to 100 students with approximately one proctor for every 25 students. A complete description of the normative sample for the MMPI–A can be found in Butcher, Williams, et al. (1992).

CLINICAL VALIDITY STUDY

C. L. Williams and Butcher (1989a, 1989b; C. L. Williams et al., 1992) conducted a large clinical validity study to verify the utility of the MMPI–A in practical applications. This clinical sample was also used to develop several new adolescent-specific scales to more clearly focus on adolescent behavior and problems (McNulty, Harkness, Ben-Porath, & Williams, 1997; Sherwood, Ben-Porath, & Williams, 1997; Weed, Butcher, & Williams, 1994). C. L. Williams and Butcher (1989a, 1989b) tested 420 boys and 293 girls from inpatient alcohol/drug treatment units, psychiatric units, day treatment centers, and special school programs. Subjects completed Form TX of the MMPI and the Restandardization Project's Life Events and Biographical Information Forms. In addition, information about the subjects was obtained from the Devereux Adolescent Behavior Rating Scale (a therapist rating scale; Spivack, Haimes, & Spotts, 1967), the Child Behavior Checklist (a parent rating scale; Achenbach & Edelbrock, 1983), and a Record Review Form developed by the investigators for this study. These external data sources provided descriptors for the MMPI–A Clinical and Content Scales (Butcher, Williams, et al., 1992; C. L. Williams & Butcher, 1989a; C. L. Williams et al., 1992). On the basis of the results of their clinical evaluation research using Form TX, the MMPI–A was approved for publication, given that the Clinical Scales showed strong external validation for adolescent problems.

DEVELOPMENT OF THE MMPI–A BOOKLET

Once the MMPI–2 was completed in 1989, the newly reconstituted Restandardization Committee turned to the development of the MMPI–A booklet (Butcher, Graham, et al., 1992) and manual (Butcher, Williams, et al., 1992). The first task was to reduce the 704-item Form TX to a more manageable booklet of 478 items for adolescents (Butcher, Graham, et al., 1992). As was the case with the MMPI–2, a primary goal was to ensure continuity with the original MMPI by retaining the key Validity and Clinical Scales, as well as important Supplementary Scales (MacAndrew Alcoholism Scale [*MAC*], Anxiety [*A*], and Repression [*R*]). Changes made to improve the item content for these scales on Forms AX and TX were incorporated into the MMPI–A. In addition, items for the newly developed alcohol and drug problem scales, the MMPI–A Content Scales, and the new *VRIN* and *TRIN* Validity Scales were included in the MMPI–A booklet. Items that did not function as intended with adolescents as they did with adults were removed from some of the scales, most notably Scale *F*, the Infrequency Validity Scale. Two long Standard Scales (Scale 5, Masculinity [*Mf*], and Scale 0, Social Introversion [*Si*]) were shortened to reduce the number of items in the MMPI–A booklet. The items in the MMPI–A booklet are arranged so that the traditional Validity and Clinical Scales can be scored if a young person only responds to the first 350 items. Butcher, Williams, et al. (1992) provided detailed information about the changes in the MMPI items that are in the MMPI–A booklet (Butcher, Graham, et al., 1992).

Despite the best efforts at revising the item pool for Form TX to make the items more appropriate for adolescents, 26 items were discovered during the final stages of the project that were still written from an adult perspective (e.g., the past tense was used to described present adolescent behaviors). Therefore, two studies examined the psychometric performance of rewritten versions of Form TX items that more clearly indicated that the items were referring to current, not past, behaviors or problems (Archer & Gordon, 1994; C. L. Williams et al., 1994). These rewritten items were included on the MMPI–A.

DEVELOPMENT OF THE MMPI–A NORMS

The norms for the MMPI–A, as in the MMPI–2, were developed using statistical procedures that produced *T* scores similar to those linear transformations used for the original MMPI. In addition, both the MMPI–A and the MMPI–2 use primarily uniform *T* scores with equivalent percentile ranks for each level of *T* score. For example, a *T* score of 65 falls at approximately the same percentile rank, the 92nd, for each scale.

Most MMPI–A scales (e.g., the original Clinical Scales 1–4 and 6–9; the Content Scales; the Personality Psychopathology Five [PSY-5] Scales) are interpreted using uniform *T* scores. There are a few exceptions in which linear *T* scores are used, most notably the Validity Scales and the Supplementary Scales, which include the MacAndrew Alcoholism Scale— Revised (*MAC–R*), Alcohol/Drug Problem Proneness (*PRO*), Alcohol/Drug Problem Acknowledgment (*ACK*), Anxiety (*A*), and Repression (*R*). The mean of each scale distribution, regardless of whether the transformation used is uniform or linear, is a *T* score of 50 and a standard deviation of 10. This assures that the interpretive levels for the MMPI–A were generally comparable with those for the MMPI. The MMPI–A manual provides more details about linear and uniform *T* scores and the statistical formulas used to derive them.

Some adolescents in clinical settings actually produce MMPI–A profiles without substantial clinical elevation on the adolescent norms. Normal range clinical profiles in psychiatric settings require close evaluation to determine the potential causes of low scale elevation. For example, some adolescents in mental health or juvenile delinquency settings may be motivated to underreport psychopathology (see Fontaine, Archer, Elkins, & Johansen, 2001; Hilts & Moore, 2003, for additional information). Close attention to the MMPI–A Validity Scales and indicators described in Chapter 4 is useful in those circumstances.

The MMPI–A: A Dynamic Instrument

The publication of the MMPI–A booklet, manual, and other test materials in 1992 did not mark the end of active research on this instrument but the beginning. Like the MMPI–2, the MMPI–A is a dynamic instrument given the efforts of psychologists in the United States and around the world. As research accumulates, changes are incorporated into the MMPI–A. Appendix A lists research studies since its publication highlighting its dynamic nature. One example of significant additions to the MMPI–A is the development of the PSY-5 Scales by McNulty, Harkness, et al. (1997). Another is the updating of the Adolescent Interpretive System of the MMPI–A to take into account research on the instrument during the 13 years after its release in 1992 (Butcher & Williams, 2007).

Following the historical and conceptual framework for understanding adolescent behavior and personality in Chapter 1, this chapter detailed how the MMPI–A came to be and introduced important terminology that must be understood when using the instrument. The remaining chapters in this beginner's guide focus on the use of the MMPI–A based on research and our clinical experiences with the instrument. Of course, the first steps in using the MMPI–A are to administer and score it, among the topics in our next chapter.

The Nuts and Bolts: Administering, Scoring, and Augmenting MMPI–A Assessments

3

"Read each statement and decide whether it is *true as applied to you* or *false as applied to you*."

—(Butcher, Graham, et al., 1992)

If you want to know what troubles someone, there is no better starting point than asking directly what he or she is feeling or thinking. The simple instructions in the MMPI–A booklet—read a list of true–false statements and decide if the statement applies to you—contributes to its utility in psychological assessments. Many young people find it easier to be open about their problems by responding to true–false questions on an answer sheet than in initial clinical interviews with an adult. Adolescents, who are often not self-referred but brought into the assessment by others, may be unwilling, distrustful, or otherwise have difficulty responding to interview questions. Administration of the MMPI–A early in the intake process can facilitate disclosure. The clinician can then address the young person's MMPI–A responses in a follow-up interview, which often reveals further clinically relevant information, as we discuss in Chapter 9.

Details, Details

Several factors need to be considered in administering and scoring the MMPI–A. These include sex, age, and reading level of the young person; test administration procedures;

and test versions and scoring procedures (Archer, 2005; Butcher & Williams, 2000; Butcher, Williams, et al., 1992). Some of these factors are necessary for determining what scoring templates to use; others are important for determining whether the young person has the skills or maturity to complete the MMPI–A, as we'll discover below.

BOY OR GIRL?

The responses of adolescent girls and boys, like those of women and men, differ somewhat across the pool of items on the test. Because of the differential pattern of responding by men and women, the original MMPI authors developed separate norms for the two sexes. Therefore, on the MMPI–A, as on the MMPI and MMPI–2, individuals' responses to the test are compared with individuals of the same sex from the general population. This tradition was maintained in the development of the MMPI–A. Accurate MMPI–A interpretation is dependent on choosing the appropriate norms (i.e., boys or girls) against which the adolescent's profile is to be compared. In addition, some scale descriptors apply only to one sex (Butcher & Williams, 2000; Butcher, Williams, et al., 1992; C. L. Williams & Butcher, 1989a).

AGE?

As described in Chapter 2, the normative and clinical samples used to develop the MMPI–A were limited to adolescents between the ages of 14 and 18 years. Persons who are 19 or older should be administered the MMPI–2 because its norms are the appropriate comparison since there are no 19 and older individuals in the MMPI–A normative sample. Exhibit 3.1 has a FAQ about using the MMPI–A with young adults.

There is overlap in the upper age limit for the MMPI–A and MMPI–2 because 18-year-olds were included in each instrument's normative sample. Therefore, the clinician has the option of administering either instrument with an 18-year-old, depending on the circumstances. Figure 3.1

EXHIBIT 3.1

MMPI–FAQ: The Not Quite "Emerged" Adult

I am evaluating a 20-year-old patient who acts more like a 16-year-old. Wouldn't the MMPI–A be more appropriate for this individual?

No, the MMPI–2 should always be selected for evaluating individuals aged 19 and above—only with 18-year-old individuals can either the MMPI–A or MMPI–2 be administered. This is because 18-year-old subjects were included in each instruments' normative samples.

FIGURE 3.1

MMPI–A

If the 18-year-old is still living in his or her parents' home and attending high school, then the MMPI–A is likely to be more relevant to his or her life circumstances.

ON THE OTHER HAND

MMPI–2

If the 18-year-old is living independently, including in a college, university, or military setting, then the MMPI–2 is perhaps more appropriate.

General rule of thumb for 18-year-olds.

provides a general rule of thumb for deciding which instrument to administer to an 18-year-old.

Recall that it was difficult to get permission from school administrators to collect data from students ages 12 to 14 years, in part due to the length of the testing session and in part due to the objectionable content in Form TX of the MMPI used to develop the MMPI–A (see Chapter 2, p. 31). Those younger subjects tested with Form TX during the Restandardization Project produced higher Infrequency (*F*) scores, hence the decision to eliminate subjects younger than 14 years from the normative sample. However, beginning with the original MMPI and now the MMPI–A, experts have indicated that useful information can be obtained from adolescents as young as 12 or 13 years if they read well enough to understand the items (e.g., Archer, 2005; Butcher & Williams, 2000; Janus, de Groot, & Toepfer, 1998; Lucio, Hernandez-Cervantes, Duran, & Butcher, 2010; Peña, Megargee, & Brody, 1996; Rouse et al., 2009; Toyer & Weed, 1998; C. L. Williams, 1986; C. L. Williams &

Butcher, 1989a). Special attention is needed when the test is administered to those ages 12 and 13 years, especially to ensure these youngsters have the appropriate reading level. Both the MMPI–A manual (Butcher, Williams, et al., 1992) and Butcher and Williams (2000) provide guidelines for using the test with younger subjects.

READING LEVEL?

The practitioner should determine whether the client's English language proficiency is sufficient to understand the items before administering the MMPI–A. The MMPI–A manual provides reading difficulty estimates of the items; most are at the fifth- to seventh-grade levels (Butcher, Williams, et al., 1992). If the administrator has questions as to whether the adolescent can comprehend the questions, then it may be helpful to administer a standardized reading test or see if the school records indicate reading level. A quick appraisal of the adolescent's reading level can be made by asking him or her to read out loud the first few items in the booklet.

During the course of the normative and clinical data collection, Williams and her research assistants began compiling a list of words that received the highest number of questions from subjects completing Form TX. Table 3.1 contains that list of words and the MMPI–A booklet number in which the word appears. It may be useful to have these words and their definitions handy when administering the test. Butcher and Williams (2000) provided a list of standardized definitions and explanations used during the Restandardization Project for the words in Table 3.1.

MMPI–A Administration Procedures

There are several different test versions available for administering the MMPI–A depending on the client's needs. They include reusable test booklets, an audio CD version for those with limited reading skills, a computer-administered version, and translated versions. Each version of the MMPI–A has the same number of items and an identical item order. Most adolescents in the United States can complete the booklet version in English, and many have a preference for taking the test on the computer. Computer administration typically takes less time and has the additional advantage of immediate and accurate scoring and interpretation if a computerized interpretive report is purchased (see Chapter 7 for more information).

In cases where the adolescent is not a native English speaker, a translated version of the test in the adolescent's language might be available

TABLE 3.1

Words on the MMPI–A That May Be Unfamiliar to Adolescents

Word	Item No.
Anxiety	281
Fitful	36
Shrink	27
Apt	280, 377
Judgment	40
Sociable	46
Benefit	324
Lacking	70
Soul	250
Brood	203
Law enforcement	120
Spirits	417
Condemned	219
Laxatives	30
Stranger	235
Crowd	316, 335
Lecture	411
Stress	424
Disturbed	36
Object	191
Success	326
Editorial	48
Quarrels	70
Tender	143
Excessively	247
Self-confident	223
Unpardonable	230
Fault	269

Note. Numbers in the second column refer to the item numbers in the MMPI–A booklet (Butcher, Graham, et al., 1992).

(see Butcher, 1996; Butcher, Cabiya, Lucio, & Garrido, 2007; Butcher, Cheung, & Lim, 2003; Butcher, Derksen, Sloore, & Sirigatti, 2003). A number of translated versions of the MMPI–A have been published and are available for testing adolescents who are originally from different countries and have not acculturated to the English language. Chapter 6 presents information about the translated versions of the MMPI–A available for adolescents from culturally different backgrounds.

The MMPI–A should be administered in a private, controlled, and comfortable setting to ensure that the adolescent takes the task seriously and is not disturbed by external circumstances. It should never be given to the young person to complete at home or in his or her room in an inpatient or residential facility. Nor should parents, siblings, other family members, or peers be present during the testing session. If the MMPI–A is administered to several adolescents at the same time, then a test proctor should be present at all times.

The instructions that are printed on the first page of the MMPI–A booklet (Butcher, Graham, Williams, & Kaemmer, 1992) should be read aloud to assure that the test is taken in a standard manner. If the adolescent is left in a private room to complete the MMPI–A, then the test administrator should check back at regular intervals of 10 to 15 minutes to "see how you're doing and if you have any questions." As noted before, it is important that the adolescent be able to read at the fifth- to seventh-grade levels. Psychologists should avoid setting up a failure experience for the young person by administering the MMPI–A to someone without the requisite reading skills or attention span to complete the test. The audio CD version is an option for those with more limited reading skills. However, it can become quite tedious for the young person, so frequent breaks and reinforcement, described in the next paragraph, are essential for this administration procedure.

Most young people can complete the 478-item MMPI–A in one session of 45 minutes to 1 hour. Others could benefit from shorter sessions of 20 to 30 minutes. Frequent breaks and positive reinforcement from the test administrator for their attention or hard work can be valuable. In some inpatient settings, tangible reinforcement may prove useful for those adolescents who are easily distracted or have difficulty with paper-and-pencil tasks.

MMPI–A Scoring Options

There are two basic scores on the MMPI–A: raw scores and T scores (see Exhibit 2.3, p. 24). A raw score is simply the actual number of items on a particular scale that an adolescent has answered in the scored direction. T scores are standard scores that enable the comparison of the individual's raw score with average scores from the normative sample. Raw scores and T scores can be obtained either by hand scoring or computer scoring. By far, computer scoring offers the quickest and most accurate scores and profiles. If at all possible, that is the recommended procedure, which we describe in detail in Chapter 7.

However, cost considerations and low volume lead some psychologists to use hand-scoring procedures. Answer sheets and their corresponding plastic templates are available commercially to aid in the process by showing only the items contained on a specific scale, one template per scale. That is, the scoring templates are plastic overlays placed on an individual's MMPI–A answer sheet. These templates contain holes that allow the scorer to "see and count" the items for the scale being scored. Once counted, the raw scores for each scale are entered into the appropriate lines that are printed on the bottom of the MMPI–A profile sheet.

There are separate profile sheets for plotting the raw scores for the Validity, Standard, Content, Supplementary, and Personality Psychopathology Five (PSY-5) Scales to use when hand scoring the MMPI–A. Figure 3.2 provides a profile sheet of the Basic Scales (i.e., Validity and Standard) for Rachel, a 14-year-old girl in the eighth grade. As can be seen in this figure, the scale names and raw scores are plotted on the x-axis, and the T score equivalents for the raw scores appear along the y-axis (Ts range from 30 to 120).

Once the psychologist or assistant obtains the raw scores from the templates for the Validity and Standard Scales, they are entered along the

FIGURE 3.2

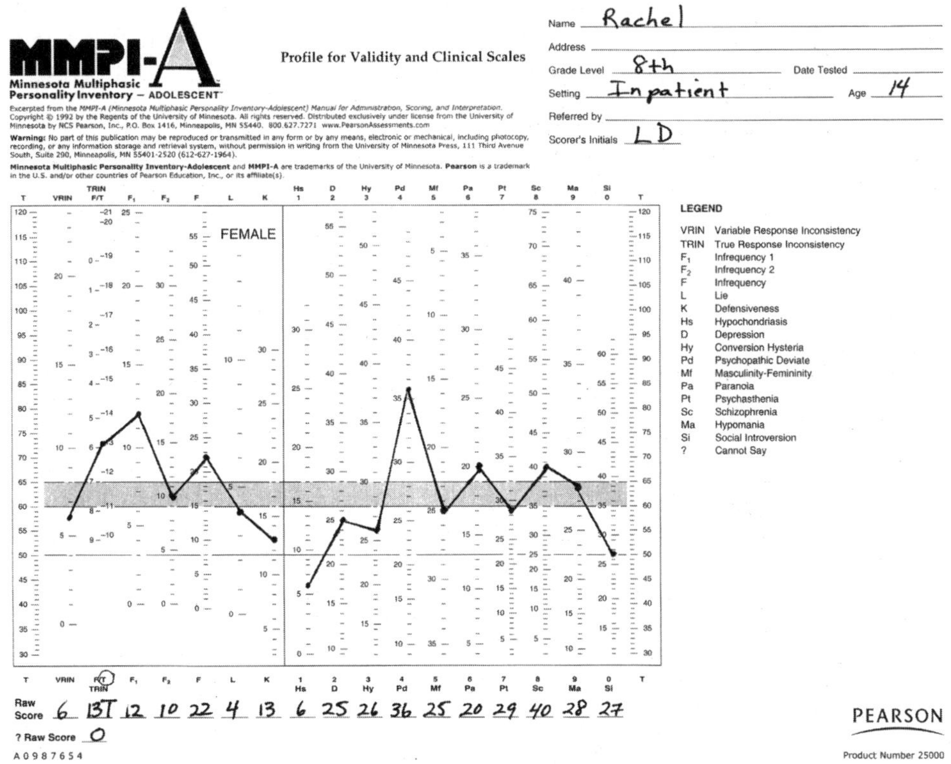

Rachel's hand-scored profile of the Basic Scales. Profile sheet reproduced by permission of the University of Minnesota Press. All rights reserved. "Minnesota Multiphasic Personality Inventory®—Adolescent" and "MMPI®-A" are trademarks owned by the University of Minnesota.

bottom of the profile as shown in Figure 3.2 (note the word *Female* on Rachel's profile). On the back of Rachel's Basic Scales profile is a similar profile for boys. It is important to make sure that the correct side of the profile sheet is used for plotting the scores, otherwise a fairly common error results. That is, scores for a boy sometimes are inadvertently plotted on the side of the profile for girls or vice versa. As described earlier, the norms and resulting *T* scores are different for boys and girls, hence the need for separate profile sheets for each.

The profile sheet for the Validity and Standard Scales in Figure 3.2 prominently shows important interpretive features:

- The line indicating a *T* score of 50 is in bold and indicates the average score of the normative sample on any given scale along the *y*-axis.
- The line indicating a *T* score of 65 is in bold and indicates a high scale elevation with interpretable scores.
- There is a shaded area from a *T* score of 60 to 64 and indicates a moderate scale elevation that can be interpreted cautiously.

When the person scoring the MMPI–A completes entering the raw score information for the Basic Scales, the process has to be repeated for the Content, Supplementary, and PSY-5 Scales, a time-consuming process that is subject to clerical errors, hence our preference for computer scoring. Chapter 7 provides case examples of the scales, subscales, content component scales, and item-level indicators that are provided in our computerized interpretive system, the Minnesota Reports (Exhibit 3.2).

EXHIBIT 3.2

MMPI–A FAQs: Computer Scoring and Interpretation

What is a computerized interpretive system?

Given its objective scoring and empirically derived scale descriptors, the MMPI and its successors, the MMPI–2 and MMPI–A, lend themselves to computerized interpretative systems. In these systems, a computer scores the MMPI–A and then using objective criteria, the computer generates an interpretation of the individual's scores based on decision rules developed by the author(s) of the system. More information about computerized systems is in Chapter 7.

What are the Minnesota Reports?

The Minnesota Reports are a widely used computerized interpretive system developed originally by James Butcher for the MMPI. There are now four Minnesota Reports written for the MMPI–2, and one written by James Butcher and Carolyn Williams for the MMPI–A. Examples of the Minnesota Report are provided in Chapters 6 through 9 of this volume.

Sources to Augment a Personality Assessment With the MMPI–A

A personality assessment of a young person is not complete without consideration of all the primary influences on a young person's behavior described in Chapter 1, not just the individual or influences from within. It is essential to consider information about the peer group, school, community, and society influences (Figure 1.1, p. 8). Both the young person and his or her family can provide an indication of the adolescent's behaviors in these contexts. In some cases teachers or coaches may have a relevant perspective. The following are some important questions to address in assessing the young person:

- Does he or she have friends?
- Does he or she become involved in school-related social activities?
- Does he or she engage in social activities or events outside the family?
- Does he or she spend an inordinate amount of time alone?
- What is his or her experience with alcohol and other drug use?
- Have there been any problem behaviors with peer groups, such as staying out all night without permission, running away, vandalism, and so on?
- Has there been a history of reported bullying in the adolescent's relationships with peers (including online—see below)?
- What is the young person's perception of the safety of his or her environment?
- Which of the mass media does he or she use?
  - Do the parents monitor their teen's media use?
  - Is there a computer or television in his or her bedroom?
  - What musicians/songs does he or she like? What types of messages are in the songs (e.g., prodrug or prosuicide)?
  - Does he or she use social networking sites? How prevalent is the use of these sites in his or her peer group? Have there been problems with inappropriate postings on these sites in his or her peer group?
  - What websites does he or she visit? (This is especially important for assessing problems related to eating disorders, suicide, sexual behaviors.)
  - Does he or she use a cell phone? Is the content of text messages an issue (e.g., harassing messages to or from peers, "sexting")?

The MMPI–A is but one component of a personality assessment of an adolescent. Although it is a comprehensive self-report inventory of personality and psychopathology, other techniques are necessary to complete a personality assessment. If the referral questions are broader than an evaluation of personality and psychopathology, then other assessment procedures will be necessary for a comprehensive psychological evaluation. (See Reynolds & Kamphuis, 2003, for a comprehensive discussion of intellectual, achievement, and aptitude assessment in children and adolescents.) Other assessment techniques to use concurrently with an MMPI–A include interviews with the adolescent, parent interviews, parent and teacher rating scales, school records and performance, projective techniques, information from intelligence tests, and MMPI–2 and MMPI–A assessments of other family members.

THE CLINICAL INTERVIEW

Conducting an effective and successful interview in the clinical assessment context is an extremely important area for consideration. There are several resources that can be consulted for reviewing the interview process with adolescents (e.g., Craig, 2009; Orvaschel, 2006). Within the first few minutes of a clinical interview, the adolescent's level of cooperation with the assessment, his or her understanding of its purpose, and his or her willingness to discuss the situation that led to the referral may become evident. In addition to covering the presenting complaint and the adolescent's perspective on any problems, the psychologist also needs to consider the assets the client possesses and personal resources he or she brings to the situation. For example, several developmental psychologists have underscored the importance of understanding the adolescent's capacities for dealing with stress that can occur at various points during normal development described earlier (Masten, 2007; Masten, Cutuli, Herbers, & Gabrielle-Reed, 2009).

Mental health professionals need to obtain a relevant and comprehensive picture of the adolescent's family situation and relationships to place other personality information into appropriate context (Josephson & the AACAP Work Group on Quality Issues, 2007). Interviewing the adolescent with family members, as well as separately, can be informative. Is the young person more or less comfortable talking in the presence or absence of his or her parents? A joint interview can allow for behavioral observations of the family's communication style. An understanding of the adolescent in a family assessment usually requires the following:

- Gathering information on relevant family relationships to determine the important influences in the adolescent's life;
- Determining if there is a history of trauma or abuse;
- Considering family communication patterns;
- Obtaining family history of health problems;

- Obtaining history of psychiatric problems, substance abuse, or criminal involvement of close family members; and
- Gaining an understanding of family decision-making processes.

BEHAVIOR RATING SCALES

One useful approach to getting information from parents (or other important adults including teachers) is the use of behavior ratings. Parent and therapist rating scales were used as criterion measures for new scales in the development of the MMPI–A, such as the MMPI–A Content Scales, as well as for assessing the validity of the original scales and code type correlates (Butcher, Williams, et al., 1992; C. L. Williams & Butcher, 1989a, 1989b; C. L. Williams, Butcher, Ben-Porath, & Graham, 1992). Behavior rating scales of adolescent problems can also be informative about an individual adolescent. Mash and Barkley (2007) described their use.

Information from parent rating scales not only provides additional information about the adolescent's behavior but also serves as a valuable means of incorporating or enlisting parents into the evaluation process. Parents need to feel that their concerns are being addressed and their role is acknowledged. Sometimes the parents' perception of the adolescent's behavior may not match what is apparent from the MMPI–A, which will require additional assessment on the part of the psychologist.

SCHOOL RECORDS AND PERFORMANCE

School records and consultations with teachers and other school personnel about the adolescent's behavior in the classroom and elsewhere can be useful for understanding an adolescent's psychological adjustment. In addition to academic performance, questions about the history of any behavior problems observed at school, changes in behavior or affect, disciplinary actions taken, referrals to school counselors, peer relationships, interactions with parents, participation in extracurricular activities, and relationships with teachers and other adults are likely to reveal relevant information. If school problems are significant, behavioral observations in that environment may be helpful.

PROJECTIVE TECHNIQUES

Projective tests such as the Rorschach Inkblot Test (Weiner, 2003; Weiner & Meyer, 2009) and the Thematic Apperception Test or TAT (Aronow, Altman Weiss, & Reznikoff, 2001; Cramer, 2004; Murray, 1943) can augment an MMPI–A assessment. The Rorschach and TAT are among the most widely used psychological tests with adolescents (Archer & Newsom, 2000). The ways in which the adolescent responds to inkblots or ambiguous pictures provide samples of how the young person problem-solves or makes decisions. Hypotheses about underlying motivations, needs, attitudes, and worries can be generated. For example, an individual might report seeing human figures as friendly and cooperative or as being conflictual, serving as clues to how others are viewed. How the adolescent relates to the examiner provides a sample of behavior in interpersonal situations with a helping professional.

Caution is suggested regarding the use of projective techniques, however. Despite widespread use, both the Rorschach and TAT have been criticized. Concerns have been raised that the Rorschach is vulnerable to overpathologizing by incorrectly identifying a large number of nonpatients as being psychologically disturbed (Wood, Nezworski, Garb, & Lilienfeld, 2001). Proponents of the Rorschach provide another perspective (see Ganellen, 2001; Weiner & Meyer, 2009). Similarly, Lilienfeld, Wood, and Garb (2001) criticized the TAT on several grounds, including that it provides unreliable and invalid personality descriptions and lacks an effective scoring system.

INTELLIGENCE TESTS

Although not developed or intended for use in personality assessment, intelligence tests provide supplementary information about the adolescent's behavior and cognitive functioning that can aid in the overall evaluation. The Wechsler Intelligence Scale for Children—Fourth Edition (ages 6–16), the Wechsler Adult Intelligence Scale—Fourth Edition (ages 16–90), and the Stanford–Binet Intelligence Scale (ages 2–85+) tend to require 2 to 3 hours to administer. This time period provides for observations about how the individual approaches intellectual or cognitive tasks that can be used to generate personality-based hypotheses (e.g., did he or she appear anxious, frustrated, or careless during the assessment?). The estimate of the individual's intellectual functioning provided can help determine if the expectations (either internal or external) for the young person are consistent with his or her abilities or if too much or too little is being demanded.

MMPI–2 AND MMPI–A ASSESSMENTS OF SIGNIFICANT OTHERS

Butcher and Pope (2006) pointed out that a clear advantage for using the MMPI–A is its parallel instrument, the MMPI–2, which can be used with other family members, such as parents, thereby reducing the frequently occurring tendency to single out the referred adolescent as the only family member with problems. They noted that adolescents are more willing to complete the test if they know that their parents and/or siblings may be tested with a similar instrument.

C. L. Williams (1986) presented a case study of a 15-year-old patient and how original MMPI profiles from her 17-year-old brother and her mother and father were useful in revealing problems beyond the presenting complaint of a noncompliant adolescent who had poor school performance and increasing time away from home. In addition, giving the MMPI to significant others of the referred adolescent may lessen the young person's perceptions of being the family's scapegoat (C. L. Williams, 1986). Tharinger and colleagues (Tharinger et al., 2008; Tharinger, Finn, Wilkinson, & Schaber, 2007) presented case examples and techniques for using the MMPI–2 with parents of referred children and adolescents as part of a therapeutic assessment strategy, a topic described in the last chapter of this book.

Next Up

Now that we've covered the details of MMPI–A test administration and scoring, as well as how other assessment procedures provide additional information for a psychological evaluation, we are ready to consider how to evaluate the young person's responses to the test items. The next two chapters introduce the various scales used for MMPI–A interpretations, followed by chapters covering how to make culturally inclusive interpretations and use of computerized testing.

Getting Down to the Basics
Validity and Standard Scales

4

What's the next step after I administer and score the
   MMPI–A?
How do I begin the interpretive process?
Which scales do I look at first?
                    —*Beginners' FAQs about MMPI–A interpretations*

The Validity and Standard Scales are the starting point for
understanding a young person's performance on the MMPI–A.
These scales are basic to the MMPI–A, as well as to the
MMPI–2, because they are direct descendants from the original MMPI scales developed by Hathaway, McKinley, and their
colleagues. They establish the equivalency of the MMPI to its
successors. Without the Validity and Standard Scales' presence
on the MMPI–2 and MMPI–A, the 50 years of accumulated
research and clinical practice with the original MMPI would
not have been relevant to the MMPI–2, introduced in 1989, or
the MMPI–A, introduced in 1992.

The following original MMPI Validity Scales are also on
the MMPI–A:

- *L* or Lie (15 items on MMPI; 14 on MMPI–A)
- *K* or Defensiveness (30 items on both MMPI and
  MMPI–A)
- *F* or Infrequency (64 items on MMPI; 66 on MMPI–A).

Three other MMPI–A validity measures also come directly
from the original MMPI:

- Cannot Say score, abbreviated by *CS* or sometimes with
  a question mark (?). *CS* is simply a count of the number
  of items an adolescent does not answer. As such, it is

not a scale but better considered a validity indicator or measure. Because it is not a scale and the item content of *CS* varies by test taker, there are no *T* scores. It is the only MMPI–A measure that is interpreted with a raw score.

- Percent True is the percentage of items answered true. Some individuals will not comply with the assessment by filling in all or most items as true. When more than 95% of the items are endorsed as true, the MMPI–A is invalid.
- Percent False is the percentage of items answered false and is interpreted the same way as Percent True.

Many MMPI–2 and MMPI–A experts use the terms Basic, Clinical, and Standard Scales interchangeably. However, there are some subtle distinctions that can be confusing to beginners. The Clinical Scales are the Scales 1–4 and 6–9 developed by Hathaway and McKinley to measure common diagnostic groupings of their patients seen at University of Minnesota Hospitals in the 1940s. The Standard Scales are made up of the Clinical Scales plus Scales 5 and 0, which measure personality characteristics, not clinical syndromes, hence the origin of the term Standard Scales. Like the Clinical Scales, Scales 5 and 0 have been a part of the MMPI since its earliest days. The term Basic Scales is sometimes used to refer to both the Validity and Standard Scales.

The term Clinical Scales is used most precisely to describe the original set of eight scales developed by Hathaway and McKinley. These eight scales appear on the MMPI, MMPI–2, and MMPI–A. They are equivalent measures across these three versions of the instrument:

- Scale 1 or *Hs* or Hypochondriasis (33 items on MMPI; 32 on MMPI–A)
- Scale 2 or *D* or Depression (60 items on MMPI; 57 on MMPI–A)
- Scale 3 or *Hy* or Hysteria (60 items on both MMPI and MMPI–A)
- Scale 4 or *Pd* or Psychopathic Deviate (50 items on MMPI; 49 on MMPI–A)
- Scale 6 or *Pa* or Paranoia (40 items on both MMPI and MMPI–A)
- Scale 7 or *Pt* or Psychasthenia (48 items on both MMPI and MMPI–A)
- Scale 8 or *Sc* or Schizophrenia (78 items on MMPI; 77 on MMPI–A)
- Scale 9 or *Ma* or Hypomania (46 items on both MMPI and MMPI–A)

Shortly after the introduction of the eight Clinical Scales, two personality measures were added to the original MMPI's set of Clinical Scales:

- Scale 5 or *Mf* or Masculinity–Femininity (60 items on MMPI; 44 on MMPI–A)
- Scale 0 or *Si* or Social Introversion (70 items on MMPI; 62 on MMPI–A)

These 10 scales came to be known as the Standard Scales and are equivalent measures on the MMPI, MMPI–2, and MMPI–A. The Standard Scales are essentially the same measures on the MMPI–A as on the original version of the instrument. The changes in the number of items on these scales and the language improvements to the items did not result in significant changes in the psychometric properties of the Validity and Standard Scales (Archer & Gordon, 1994; Butcher, Williams, et al., 1992; C. L. Williams, Ben-Porath, & Hevern, 1994).

As we indicated in Chapter 3, the MMPI–A scales are interpreted using standardized *T* scores, not raw scores. Throughout the rest of this book, we will give recommendations for various interpretations based on *T* scores. These recommendations should not be considered absolutes. Suggested cutoff scores can change over time given new research. Furthermore, some of these recommendations can be modified for particular clinical decisions or settings. For example, one might use a slightly higher cutoff score for invalidity on the *F* scale than the ones suggested below when the base rate of extreme responding is higher in settings with adolescents with more extreme symptoms of psychopathology, as in inpatient settings.

The MMPI–A Validity Scales and Indicators

The Basic Scales profile begins with the Validity Scales, which were just one of the many signature achievements of Hathaway and McKinley (1940, 1942) in the development of the MMPI (Butcher & Williams, 2009). Earlier instruments like Woodworth's (1920) Personal Data Sheet did not have a method of determining the test-taking attitudes of the individual being assessed. Because not all people are motivated—or able—to reveal accurately on self-report inventories psychological difficulties they may be experiencing, the innovative validity measures are important contributions to personality assessment.

The MMPI–A Validity Scales provide methods of identifying random or inconsistent responding, underreporting, and overreporting. Since the publication of the MMPI–A, a number of studies provide further guidance for how to use the validity indices in detecting potentially problematic profiles. These studies include research on underreporting symptoms (e.g., Baer, Ballenger, & Kroll, 1998; Stein & Graham, 1999); overreporting or symptom exaggeration (e.g., Lucio, Duran, Graham, & Ben-Porath, 2002; Stein, Graham, & Williams, 1995); random responding (e.g., Archer, Handel, Lynch, & Elkins, 2002; Baer, Kroll, Rinaldo, & Ballenger, 1999; Pinsoneault, 2005); and response inconsistency (e.g., Handel,

Arnau, Archer, & Dandy, 2006). These studies, combined with what we know from research on the original instrument, are used to inform the recommendations in the next section.

More than any other psychological test in use today, the MMPI instruments pay careful attention to the response styles that the test taker uses to respond to items in order to determine whether their responses will result in a valid and interpretable protocol. In addition to *CS, L, K,* and *F* (introduced earlier), several other validity measures were included on the MMPI–A:

- *TRIN* or True Response Inconsistency scale (24 item-response pairs),
- *VRIN* or Variable Response Inconsistency scale (50 item-response pairs),
- F_1 or Infrequency Subscale 1 (33 items), and
- F_2 or Infrequency Subscale 2 (33 items).

The validity indicators address problems such as whether the adolescent has been careless or negligent in responding or whether he or she attempted to foil the assessment by omitting items or responding in an uncooperative fashion, such as answering all items true or false or responding inconsistently in other ways. The *TRIN* and *VRIN* scales provide further assessment of inconsistent responding. Other MMPI–A Validity Scales measure both overreporting and underreporting of symptoms. The *F* scale and its subscales assess whether the young person is trying to appear more disturbed than he or she actually is by responding to an extreme number of unusual or rarely endorsed items. Two scales, *L* and *K,* evaluate whether the adolescent is attempting to present an overly "glowing" personality picture by denying even minor problems.

CANNOT SAY (*CS*) SCORE

Some adolescents who are reluctant to participate in the evaluation or who are easily distracted may omit responses to MMPI–A items. After the test has been administered, it is important to examine the answer sheet to determine if any items were not completed (Exhibit 4.1). If there are more than 10 *CS* responses, the adolescent should be asked to complete the omitted items before his or her MMPI–A is scored. The *CS* score is the total number of unanswered items on the test answer sheet. A high number of item omissions can reflect a defensive protocol or reading comprehension problems. In any event, large numbers of omitted items may result in artificially lower scale scores. *CS* raw scores above 30 that are distributed throughout the booklet indicate an invalid profile (Butcher & Williams, 2007; Butcher, Williams, et al., 1992).

If the young person has omitted 29 or fewer items but is unavailable to complete the missing items, then it is crucial to the evaluation to determine if the pattern of item omissions has affected some scales

---

EXHIBIT 4.1

MMPI–A Helpful Hint: Test Administration

Examine those answer sheets and booklets after each test administration!

Sometimes, believe it or not, adolescents don't follow the test administration instructions completely. They have been known to write comments on the answer sheets or in the booklet. A quick look at the answer sheets can reveal invalidating response patterns like all true, all false, or random responding. Item numbers can be circled, qualifiers added to their responses, extraneous marks made, and so on. You also want to make sure that the MMPI–A booklet is pristine for the next test-taker without any comments from previous test-takers.

---

more than others. For example, *CS* raw scores of 10 to 29 occurring after item number 350 will not affect the scores on most of the Basic Scales (with the exception of *TRIN, VRIN,* and F_2). All the items for these scales are included in the first 350 items of the booklet; therefore they can be interpreted with confidence in this circumstance. The Content, Personality Psychopathology Five (PSY-5), and Supplementary Scales all have items that appear after item number 350 and could be affected if the missing items are concentrated at the back of the booklet. Therefore, scores on those scales may be affected by underreporting when *CS* raw scores of 10 to 29 appear solely in the second half of the booklet.

Computer-scoring programs indicate for each MMPI–A scale the percentage of items endorsed for any given scale. The Minnesota Report lists each omitted item. Unfortunately, this information is unlikely to be available in the case of hand-scored profiles. Such information is useful in determining whether a lower score is due to a significant number of omitted items on that scale or if the low score resulted even with most, if not all, the items being answered by the young person.

PERCENT TRUE AND PERCENT FALSE INDICATORS

Another strategy some adolescents adopt to avoid responding to the MMPI–A is to simply fill in the answer sheet without reading the items. Responses can be made in a random fashion or using a pattern such as answering all true or all false. The Percent True Index is the percentage of items in which the adolescent has endorsed items as "true." Very high percentages, 95% or higher, reflect an uncooperative response set and an invalid approach to the test.

Computer-scoring programs provide this and the Percent False indicator. In the absence of computer scoring, however, simply examining the answer sheet will quickly reveal this pattern and the next, the Percent False Index. In addition, the MMPI–A profile for all true responding is quite distinctive, as revealed in Jeff's MMPI–A hand-scored profile in Figure 4.1.

A high percentage of false responses indicates an individual who responded to the items with an extreme denial of problems. A Percent False Index of 95% or higher indicates an invalid MMPI–A protocol that should not be interpreted. Examination of the adolescent's answer sheet will reveal this pattern. The MMPI–A profile for "all false" responding is also quite distinctive, as revealed in Katherine's MMPI–A hand-scored profile in Figure 4.2.

It is not a coincidence that both Jeff and Katherine (Figures 4.1 and 4.2) produced invalid MMPI–A profiles when being evaluated in forensic settings. All true, all false, and random responding, as well as other types of invalid responding, are common in these settings. The Validity Scales and indicators increase the utility of the MMPI–A in court evaluations and juvenile detention facilities to assist in identifying types of invalid responding to the MMPI–A.

FIGURE 4.1

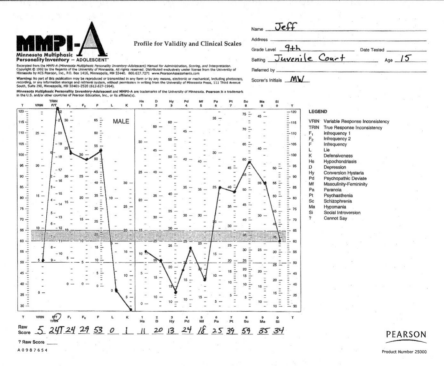

Jeff's hand-scored Basic Scales: All True Profile. Profile sheet reproduced by permission of the University of Minnesota Press. All rights reserved. "Minnesota Multiphasic Personality Inventory®-Adolescent" and "MMPI®-A" are trademarks owned by the University of Minnesota.

FIGURE 4.2

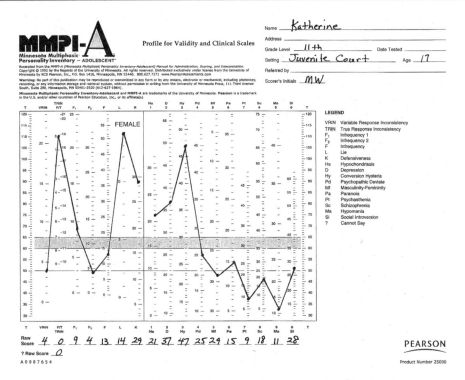

Katherine's hand-scored Basic Scales: All False Profile. Profile sheet reproduced by permission of the University of Minnesota Press. All rights reserved. "Minnesota Multiphasic Personality Inventory®-Adolescent" and "MMPI®-A" are trademarks owned by the University of Minnesota.

TRUE RESPONSE INCONSISTENCY (*TRIN*)

TRIN is a response inconsistency scale that evaluates the tendency for some adolescents to respond to the items in an inconsistently true or false manner. The scale comprises item pairs whose content is directly opposite in meaning, for example:

1. I like rap music.
2. I hate rap music.

If those two items were on the MMPI–A (they are not), they would be good candidates for the *TRIN* scale because it is inconsistent to respond "true" to both items, just as it is inconsistent to respond "false" to both items. When adolescents respond inconsistently to the *TRIN* item pairs by answering "true" to both items in the pair, one point is added to the *TRIN* raw score; if the adolescent responds inconsistently by answering "false" to both items in the pair, one point is subtracted from the *TRIN* raw score (a constant is added to the *TRIN* raw score to avoid negative values).

A high *TRIN T* score followed by the letter "T" indicates a tendency to indiscriminately answer "true" to the items. This is referred to as an acquiescent response style (i.e., a "yea-saying" response set). A very high *TRIN T* score followed by the letter "F" indicates a tendency to answer "false" indiscriminately, producing a nonacquiescent response style (i.e., a "nay-saying" response set). Such response styles suggest that the resulting profiles may be invalid and uninterpretable. The following are recommended guidelines for interpreting *TRIN*:

- *T* scores ≤ 69T or 69F: These scores suggest the adolescent was consistent in his or her responding to the MMPI–A items and appeared to take their meaning into account when responding to the MMPI–A.
- *T* scores of 70T to 74T: These are moderately elevated scores suggesting a somewhat careless and inconsistent response style with a tendency of answering "true" without carefully considering the item meaning.
- *T* scores of 70F to 74F: These are moderately elevated scores suggesting a somewhat careless and inconsistent response style with a tendency of answering "false" without carefully considering the item meaning.
- *T* scores ≥ 75T: These are high elevation scores suggesting the adolescent was markedly inconsistent in responding to the MMPI–A items by endorsing "true" without carefully considering the item meaning. The MMPI–A profile is likely invalid and should not be interpreted.
- *T* scores ≥ 75F: These are a high elevation scores suggesting the adolescent was markedly inconsistent in responding to the MMPI–A items by endorsing "false" without carefully considering the item meaning. The MMPI–A profile is likely invalid and should not be interpreted.

VARIABLE RESPONSE INCONSISTENCY (*VRIN*)

To understand the *VRIN* scale, consider possible responses to these two items:

1. Kanye West's music is good.
2. I like Kanye West's music.

It is consistent to respond "true" to both or "false" to both. However, it is inconsistent to respond "true" to Item 1 and "false" to Item 2 in this pair. The reverse applies as well: It is inconsistent to respond "false" to Item 1 and "true" to Item 2. If these items were on the MMPI–A (they are not), they would be good candidates for the *VRIN* scale.

The *VRIN* scale also includes the *TRIN* item pairs (i.e., *TRIN* is a subset of the *VRIN* scale measuring the specific response styles of yea-saying and nay-saying). The *VRIN* scale score is the total number of item pairs answered inconsistently. Higher *VRIN* scores suggest that the adolescent may have been responding to the MMPI–A items in an indiscriminate manner, such as a random response set. The following are guidelines for interpreting *VRIN:*

- *T* scores ≤ 69: These scores suggest the adolescent was consistent in his or her responding to the MMPI–A items and appeared to take their meaning into account when responding to the MMPI–A.
- *T* scores of 70 to 74: These are moderately elevated scores suggesting a somewhat careless and inconsistent response style.
- *T* scores ≥ 75: These are high elevation scores suggesting the adolescent was markedly inconsistent in responding to the MMPI–A items. His or her profile is likely invalid and should not be interpreted.

THE *F* OR INFREQUENCY SCALE

The *F* or Infrequency scale was developed for the original MMPI as a means of detecting whether a test taker was responding in an exaggerated manner that would raise questions about whether the person's responding was credible. Most people answer *F* items in the nonscored direction. People who endorse a large number of seemingly unrelated and rarely endorsed items are suspected of exaggerating their responses to the test. It turns out that adolescents and adults respond differently to some of the items that made up the original *F* scale developed for the MMPI (Exhibit 4.2).

High scores on the MMPI–A *F* scale suggest that extreme responding to the test has likely resulted in an invalid profile. This type of extreme responding might result from a number of factors, including reading difficulties, confusion, inconsistent or random responding,

---

EXHIBIT 4.2

MMPI–A Trivia Question: The Basic Scales

Which one of the Basic Scales changed the most from its MMPI version to its MMPI–A counterpart?

The *F* or Infrequency Scale on MMPI–A differs most substantially from its original version on the MMPI than any of the other Basic Scales. The changes made to *F* were required because of the different endorsement patterns for some F items by adolescents compared to adults (i.e., some of the original *F* items were not infrequently endorsed by adolescents in the normative sample). Only 37 of the original 64 MMPI F items (58%) are on the MMPI–A (Butcher & Williams, 2000).

symptom exaggeration (including malingering), or possibly serious psychopathology.

VRIN and *TRIN* scores are useful to rule in or rule out inconsistent responding as a contributor to a high *F* score. Extra test data are necessary to determine other reasons for highly elevated *F* scores. The following are general guidelines for interpreting *T* scores for the *F* scale:

- *T* scores < 59: These scores suggest the adolescent was cooperative and likely produced a valid profile that was unaffected by overreporting.
- Use *VRIN* to rule out inconsistent responding for the *F* elevations listed below. Further assessment is necessary to rule in or rule out the other reasons listed above for *F* elevations.
- *T* scores of 60 to 74: Scores in this range are considered valid although some extreme symptoms were reported. Adolescents in clinical settings can produce elevations in this range.
- *T* scores of 75 to 89: Scores in this range indicate that the adolescent endorsed an unusual number of rare and varied items. Although the profiles may be valid and can be interpreted with caution, the practitioner should note the elevation and explore the reasons for it. Some inpatients endorse a large number of extreme symptoms.
- *T* scores 90 to 99: Scores in this range indicate that the adolescent responded to the MMPI–A items by endorsing a wide variety of extreme and rare symptoms. Again, the practitioner should assess the underlying reasons for this endorsement pattern. The adolescent's protocol is likely to be invalid, and any inferences from it should note the problematic response pattern.
- *T* scores $\geq$ 100: Scores in this range are extremely unusual and invalid. The resulting MMPI–A should not be interpreted.

F_1 AND F_2 SUBSCALES

The *F* scale was divided into two subscales called F_1 and F_2. The F_1 items appear in the front half of the booklet, and the F_2 items appear in the back half. These scales also can be referred to as front *F* and back *F* for obvious reasons. These subscales give a picture of infrequent responding to items at the beginning of the booklet (i.e., the first 350 items) versus at the end of the booklet. For example, an adolescent might respond appropriately to the items in the first part of the booklet, then, part of the way through, get bored and begin to answer randomly. Another common mistake resulting in an elevated F_2 but not F_1 is misaligning the booklet item numbers with the numbers on the answer sheet. In both examples, a nonelevated F_1 score would indicate a valid performance on the front half of the booklet, whereas an elevated F_2 score would suggest an invalid or random response set to the second half of the booklet. This distinction made by F_1 and F_2 is important because the Basic Scales (excepting *TRIN, VRIN,* and F_2) appear in the first 350 items on the MMPI–A and can still be interpreted even in the presence of an invalidating response style in the second half of the booklet. The interpretive levels for the *F* scale in the above section apply to its subscales.

L OR LIE SCALE

The *L* scale is a measure of a rather unsophisticated or self-consciously "virtuous" test-taking attitude. Adolescents who score high on *L* endorse items that are unlikely because of their extremely virtuous claims. Elevated scores suggest that the individual is presenting him- or herself in an overly positive light, attempting to create an unrealistically favorable view of his or her adjustment. Because most of the *L* items are scored in the "false" direction, an elevated *TRIN* score indicating a nay-saying response style can help in its interpretation. The following are general guidelines for interpreting the *L* scale:

- *T* scores < 60: These scores suggest the adolescent was cooperative and likely produced a valid profile.
- Use *TRIN* to rule out inconsistent responding due to an acquiescent response style for the *L* elevations listed below.
- *T* scores of 61 to 69: Scores in this range are considered to be a valid MMPI–A performance, although the adolescent approached the test in a defensive and naïve manner that needs to be taken into consideration in developing an interpretation.
- *T* scores of 70 to 74: This relatively high elevation on *L* suggests a marginally valid MMPI–A. The adolescent attempted to present a favorable impression marked by claims of high virtue. The adolescent's test protocol may be invalid due to symptom underreporting. Elevated MMPI–A scale scores in the presence of elevated *L* scores can be interpreted. However, normal limits scale scores cannot be interpreted as a lack of psychological problems. Adolescents raised in highly religious backgrounds sometimes produce *L* scores in this range.
- *T* scores ≥ 75: This high elevation on *L* suggests an unusually defensive response and invalid pattern associated with highly virtuous responding to the MMPI–A items. The symptom scales are not likely to be interpretable due to underreporting.

K OR DEFENSIVENESS SCALE

The *K* scale was developed to assess a person's willingness to disclose personal information and discuss his or her problems. Persons who attain low scores are likely responding in an unusually open and frank manner. Moderately high scores reflect marginally valid protocols as a result of an uncooperative attitude toward the testing and a reluctance to disclose personal information. The following are interpretive guidelines:

- *T* scores < 45: Although scores in this range are considered valid, they can be associated with a person responding in an overly frank and open manner.
- *T* scores of 46 to 59: Scores in this range are considered a valid MMPI–A performance that is acceptably open and cooperative.
- Use *TRIN* to rule out inconsistent responding due to a non-acquiescent response style for the *K* elevations listed below.
- *T* scores of 60 to 69: Scores in this range are considered a valid MMPI–A performance; however, the adolescent approached the test in a somewhat defensive manner that should be taken into consideration in developing an interpretation. The adolescent may have been unwilling to share information about his or her problems.
- *T* scores of 70 to 74: This high elevation on *K* probably reflects an invalid response pattern as a result of the adolescent's defensiveness. Any interpretation of the adolescent's test protocol should be cautious, given the defensive approach shown. Given the defensive responding, the absence of symptoms on the MMPI–A scales is not an indication of well-being.
- *T* scores ≥ 75: This high elevation on *K* suggests an unusually defensive response to the MMPI–A items. The symptom scales are likely invalid due to underreporting.

INTERPRETING RACHEL'S VALIDITY SCALES

Now that we have covered the various Validity Scales and indictors, let us return to Rachel's MMPI–A Validity and Clinical Scales profile provided in Chapter 3 (Figure 3.2, p. 41) to illustrate how to use this information. The following is an interpretation of the validity of Rachel's MMPI–A profile:

Rachel completed all the items on the MMPI–A and produced a valid profile. However, there is evidence of possible symptom overreporting given her scores on *F* and its subscales. In addition, she had a tendency toward inconsistent responding in the "true" direction. This pattern of responding is not unusual with hospitalized adolescents, and her scores on the MMPI–A scales can be interpreted with these caveats in mind.

MMPI–A Standard Scales

Hathaway and McKinley (1940, 1942), building on the empirical scale development approach recommended by Paterson, Schneidler, and Williamson (1938), developed the MMPI Clinical Scales. In order for an item to be included on one of the Clinical Scales, it had to discriminate statistically among well-defined criterion groups of patients hospitalized at the neuropsychiatric division of the University of Minnesota Hospitals and a comparison group of individuals not under a doctor's care—remember those "Minnesota Normals" from Chapter 2?

The names of the Clinical Scales derive from diagnostic labels for the various patient groups used at the time the MMPI was created. Some of these scale names are familiar sounding to the modern ear (e.g., Depression, Schizophrenia), whereas others are quaint or downright odd (e.g., Psychopathic Deviate, Psychasthenia). Furthermore, Hathaway and McKinley (1942) classified patients into criterion groups based on psychiatric staff diagnosis even before the publication in 1952 of the widely used classification system, the *Diagnostic and Statistical Manual—Mental Disorders* (*DSM*; American Psychiatric Association, 1952). Despite the changes in diagnostic labels and rules over 70 years—a fifth edition is being developed—the MMPI Clinical Scales remain an important part of the MMPI–2 and MMPI–A interpretations (Exhibit 4.3).

WHAT IS THE REASON FOR THE LONGEVITY OF THE MMPI–A STANDARD SCALES?

Had Hathaway, McKinley, their colleagues, and successors limited the use of the Standard Scales to the prediction of the diagnostic concepts of the 1940s and 1950s, the MMPI would have been long forgotten, like

---

EXHIBIT 4.3

MMPI–A FAQ: Standard Scale Names

What names should I use for the Standard Scales?

You have three choices: full name, abbreviation, or number (e.g., Hypochondriasis or *H*s or Scale 1). In this book we use the three options interchangeably. Some MMPI experts prefer the scale number as the "name" because it avoids the use of the older terminology. We tend to use the scale numbers when giving feedback or other circumstances when talking about the MMPI–A with a layperson.

the Personal Data Sheet (Woodworth, 1920; Woodworth & Mathews, 1924). However, after these scales were developed empirically, and to this day, researchers use empirical methods to establish correlates or descriptors for those who score high on the MMPI–A Standard Scales contrasted with those who score lower. Many of the descriptors for these scales have been reestablished over and over as psychologists conducted research on these scales over time, as we discovered in Chapter 2. When a psychologist indicates an adolescent has an elevation on MMPI–A Scale 8, or any other of the Standard Scales, experts around the world know what descriptors likely apply to the individual with those elevations (Butcher & Williams, 2009).

As mentioned in Chapter 2, the MMPI–A is a dynamic instrument, adapted and changed when new research becomes available. This close relationship of new research guiding changes to the MMPI is evident in its first manual. About half of the Basic Scales were added to the original instrument after its first manual was published in 1942 (i.e., Scales 6, 7, 8, 9, 0, and the Validity Scale K were not in the first manual). Although Scales 3, 4, and 5 were included in the original MMPI manual, they were described as "preliminary." Hathaway and McKinley established this important strength of the MMPI: the ability to adjust its use when indicated by new research findings.

AVOIDING A COMMON INTERPRETIVE ERROR

Understanding how the MMPI–A Standard Scales were developed and researched is important for understanding how to interpret them. Because their descriptors are empirically derived and not content based, it is incorrect to interpret elevations on the Standard Scales as indicating the adolescent has "more" of the construct or symptoms or traits that the scale is designed to measure. Rather, T-score elevations on the various Standard Scales indicate a higher probability that the scale descriptors or correlates apply to a given adolescent. So, a T score of 90, contrasted with a T score of 61, on Scale 2, Depression, does not mean that the young person with the higher score is more depressed than the one with the lower score. Rather, the higher score indicates a greater probability that the scale descriptors apply to the adolescent. Other scales, such as the MMPI–A Content Scales, are interpreted differently given how they were developed, as we will see in Chapter 5.

Because the Standard Scales were developed using an empirical strategy of contrasting groups, some of these scales have quite heterogeneous content and resulting diverse correlates or descriptors. For that reason, Harris and Lingoes (1955, 1968) developed subscales for Scales 2, 3, 4, 6, 8, and 9 to facilitate the interpretation of these scales based on the content of the items the adolescent endorsed in the scored direction. Later, another group of researchers developed subscales for Scale 0 in the

MMPI–2 (Ben-Porath, Hostetler, Butcher, & Graham, 1989). When one of the Standard Scales is elevated, its corresponding Harris–Lingoes subscales can be examined to determine if the adolescent responded in the clinical range for all the content in the Standard Scale or if his or her item endorsements show a differential pattern of responding to the content of the given Standard Scale.

The Harris–Lingoes subscales should only be used if its parent Clinical Scale is elevated at a *T* score of 60 or higher and the subscale is elevated at 60 or higher. Because the Harris–Lingoes subscales are shorter than the Clinical Scales, their raw score standard deviations are substantially lower than those of the Clinical Scales: 1.33 to 4.25, median of 2.07, compared with 3.98 to 10.23, median of 5.4 (Peña, Megargee, & Brody, 1996). As Peña et al. (1996) pointed out, this means that a difference of only one or two raw scores contributes to substantial *T*-score differences that appear more clinically meaningful than is the case.

In the next sections of this chapter we describe the empirically based descriptors that can be used to interpret the MMPI–A Standard Scales. (Recall from Chapter 2, pp. 27–28, that code type correlates have not been sufficiently validated for use with adolescents, hence our recommendations to use a scale descriptor interpretive strategy for the Standard Scales.) We first provide background information for each of the Standard Scales from the original MMPI. Next we summarize the adolescent-specific and empirically derived descriptors for each of the Standard Scales based on conclusions from research conducted in conjunction with the Restandardization Project (C. L. Williams & Butcher, 1989a, 1989b), as well as information included in the MMPI–A manual (Butcher, Williams, et al., 1992) and information published since the manual (e.g., Archer & Krishnamurthy, 1997a; Cashel, Rogers, Sewell, & Holliman, 1998; Cumella, Wall, & Kerr-Almeida, 1999; Glaser, Calhoun, & Petrocelli, 2002; Holifield, Nelson, & Hart, 2002; Moore, Thompson-Pope, & Whited, 1996; Peña et al., 1996; Stage, 2000). The Harris–Lingoes subscales are described for those Standard Scales that have them (i.e., Scales 2, 3, 4, 6, 8, 9), as will the *Si* subscales. Exhibit 4.4 presents a general rule of thumb for interpreting the Standard Scales.

SCALE 1: HYPOCHONDRIASIS (*HS*)

Background

The *Hs* scale was developed originally to detect symptoms of pathological preoccupation with bodily function and physical illness, called hypochondiasis in the 1940s (that term survives in the *Diagnostic and Statistical Manual of Mental Disorders*, 4th ed., text revision [*DSM–IV–TR*]; American Psychiatric Association, 2000). The items selected by Hathaway and McKinley (1940, 1942) address complaints of physical symptoms that

---

EXHIBIT 4.4

MMPI–A Helpful Hints: Defining Elevated Scores for the Standard Scales

---

T scores > 65
High elevation that indicates high probability that the scale descriptors apply to the adolescent. The Harris–Lingoes and *Si* subscales can be used to augment interpretive statements for Standard Scale scores in this range.

T scores between 60 and 64
Moderate elevations indicating that the scale descriptors might apply to the adolescent. The Harris–Lingoes and *Si* subscales can be used to augment interpretive statements for Standard Scale scores in this range. Interpretive statements should be worded more tentatively.

T scores < 59
These scores are in the normal range. There is no empirical evidence that the scale descriptors apply to adolescents who score in this range. The Harris–Lingoes and *Si* subscales should not be used for scale scores in this range.

---

may be either vague or specific, as well as denial of good health. Today's diagnostic system recognizes five somatoform disorders in addition to hypochondrias (American Psychiatric Association, 2000). However, caution should be exercised when interpreting this scale, because some patients with chronic diseases or those seen in medical settings, particularly those having suffered a mild traumatic brain injury, may also obtain elevated scores. Typically, though, as elevations on Scale 1 exceed *T* scores of 65, the physical symptom picture becomes vague and psychological causation or influences become more likely. As indicated in the *DSM–IV–TR,* medical conditions or substance-induced etiologies must be ruled out before suggesting the young person's somatic compliants have a psychological rather than physiological origin.

Prior to the development of the MMPI–A, high scores on the *Hs* scale were associated with a number of personality traits in addition to reports of somatic symptoms, including pessimism, fatigue, being whiny, dysphoria, and being interested only in their own problems. High-scoring *Hs* clients can be critical and unwilling to take advice, even though they demand sympathy. They tend to seek medically oriented treatment and tend to terminate psychological therapy prematurely, particularly if it is suggested that their physical symptoms might have a psychological basis.

MMPI–A Scale 1 Descriptors

Many of the descriptors found in work with the original MMPI described earlier have been validated in studies on the MMPI–A (e.g., Cashel et al., 1998; Glaser et al., 2002; C. L. Williams & Butcher, 1989a). The following are descriptive statements that can be made for adolescents with elevations on Scale 1:

- High scorers tend to have an unusual number of somatic complaints and concerns compared with others their age, including pain, nausea, stomach problems, headaches, and dizziness.
- High scorers may feel depressed or cry frequently.
- High scorers may have concentration difficulties.
- High scorers can be clingy, whiny, and perfectionistic.
- High scorers tend to demand attention.
- Girls may have eating problems in addition to the somatic complaints.
- Girls are less likely than boys to engage in acting-out behaviors, including anger outbursts or fighting.
- Parents of boys report fearful, anxious, and worrying behaviors; they also indicate their sons have poor peer relations, can be teased, and feel unliked.
- This is an unusual elevation for adolescents, even more so for boys than girls. The treatment program may need to be modified to accommodate their clinical presentation.

There are no Harris–Lingoes subscales for the *Hs* given its relatively homogeneous item content.

SCALE 2: DEPRESSION (*D*)

Background

The Depression scale was developed to assess mood disturbances that occur solely or in combination with other personality problems (Hathaway & McKinley, 1942). Scale 2 items include sadness, anhedonia, difficulty concentrating, fatigue, psychomotor retardation, physical discomfort, and suicidal thinking. Studies on the original MMPI with both adults and adolescents provide descriptors including feelings of distress, hopelessness, anxiety, guilt, and tension. Individuals with high Scale 2 scores tend to be open to psychological treatment because of the high degree of discomfort they are experiencing.

MMPI–A Scale 2 Descriptors

Scale 2 is a well-validated measure of depression (e.g., Archer & Krishnamurthy, 1997a; Cashel et al., 1998; Cumella et al. 1999; C. L. Williams & Butcher, 1989a). The following descriptors apply:

- Symptoms of depression are likely prominent in the clinical presentation.

- Suicidal ideation or gestures may be present and should be evaluated.
- Low self-esteem may be present.
- High scorers may experience social withdrawal and possible poor peer relations.
- Tension and nervous behaviors may be present.
- High scorers may experience obsessions or compulsions.
- High scorers may be less likely to engage in acting-out behaviors.
- High scorers tend to be low in aggressive behavior
- Given the level of psychological distress, the adolescent may be willing to cooperate in psychological treatment.

Harris–Lingoes Subscales for D

There are five Harris–Lingoes subscales for Scale 2 that can be used to refine elevations on this scale:

- D_1, Subjective Depression (32 items). Depressed; unhappy; nervous; lack energy; few interests; not coping well; difficulties concentrating; feelings of inferiority; lack self-confidence; shy and uneasy in social situations.
- D_2, Psychomotor Retardation (14 items). Immobilized; listless; withdrawn; lack energy; avoid people.
- D_3, Physical Malfunctioning (11 items). Preoccupied with physical functioning; poor health; somatic complaints.
- D_4, Mental Dullness (15 items). Lack energy; tense; concentration problems; attention problems; lack self-confidence; life is empty; apathetic.
- D_5, Brooding (10 items). Ruminate; not happy; feel useless and inferior; feel life is not worth living; easily hurt by criticism; fear losing control of their thought processes.

SCALE 3: HYSTERIA (HY)

Background

Scale 3 was developed to determine if the individual is like patients who have developed "conversion-type hysterical symptoms" (Hathaway & McKinley, 1942, p. 7). Many Scale 3 items deal with vague physical complaints, whereas others represent naïveté and denial of psychological problems. Individuals who score high on Scale 3 have been shown to react to stress with somatic problems. In addition, they appear to have a strong need for attention and typically are quite sociable. Their relationships can be immature, and they may use their symptoms to manipulate others but seem to have little awareness of doing so. High *Hy* persons are often considered to seek secondary gain, such that they are reinforced by the avoidance of responsibility and attention seeking. Persons with high scores on *Hy* may not be responsive to traditional psychotherapy. Similar to the caveat for interpreting Scale 1 elevations, medical conditions or substance-induced etiologies must be ruled out before suggesting a conversion process is likely.

MMPI–A Scale 3 Descriptors

The adult correlates for *Hy* have been supported with adolescents (e.g., Cashel et al., 1998; C. L. Williams & Butcher 1989a). Research has also suggested that the *Hy* scale can be elevated among clients with eating disorders (Cashel et al., 1998; Cumella et al., 1999). Adolescents with elevations on Scale 3 are likely to have the following characteristics:

- Multiple somatic complaints, particularly in times of stress, may be reported.
- High scorers are unlikely to be socially withdrawn; indeed, they may be outgoing, talkative, and engaging.
- Boys may have suicidal ideations or gestures.

Harris–Lingoes Subscales for Hy

There are five Harris–Lingoes subscales for refining interpretations of Scale 3 elevations:

- Hy_1, Denial of Social Anxiety (6 items). Socially extroverted; comfortable in social settings; deny feeling shy or having difficulty talking to others.
- Hy_2, Need for Affection (12 items). Strong need for attention and affection; sensitive; trusting of others; optimistic; avoid confrontations with others; deny having negative feelings about other people.
- Hy_3, Lassitude–Malaise (15 items). Physically uncomfortable; poor health; unhappy; tired; weak; fatigued; concentration difficulties; poor appetite; sleep disturbance.
- Hy_4, Somatic Complaints (17 items). Physical complaints, such as headaches, dizziness, or problems with balance; use repression as a defense mechanism; may develop physical symptoms under stress.
- Hy_5, Inhibition of Aggression (7 items). Deny hostile or aggressive impulses; sensitive toward others; deny irritability; not aggressive toward others.

SCALE 4: PSYCHOPATHIC DEVIATE (*PD*)

Background

The *Pd* scale was developed to assess persons with an "absence of deep emotional response, inability to profit from experience, and disregard of social mores" (Hathaway & McKinley, 1942, p. 7). Although quite likable and able to give a good first impression, the members of the criterion group were also characterized by lying, stealing, truancy, alcohol or other drug addiction, and sexual promiscuity. Hathaway and McKinley (1942) indicated, "Many active professional persons have high scores, but their breaks are socially inocuous and are either disregarded by others or effectively concealed" (p. 8). From the earliest research forward, individuals with high Scale 4 scores are described as poor candidates for change through psychotherapy. Motivation for change is low.

McKinley and Hathaway (1944) created this scale by contrasting the responses of late adolescents and "emerging adults" (i.e., those ages 17 to 22 years; see Chapter 1 discussion of emerging adulthood) diagnosed as "psychopathic personality, asocial and amoral type" with those of the MMPI normative sample. The items emerging in this contrast reflect a variety of problems, including dissatisfaction with life, a difficult home environment, youth conduct offenses, resentment of authority, and lack of social anxiety. People with high *Pd* scores tend to exhibit chronic social maladjustment and negative attitudes toward authority. They characteristically have problems in relationships and seem unable to establish close bonds with others. High scorers are viewed as trying to manipulate other people for their own gain. Studies have shown that they tend not to experience guilt for this behavior; instead, they tend to externalize blame. High scorers on Scale 4 tend not to profit from negative or punishing experiences, thus they tend to repeat irresponsible behavior. Substance abuse is common among high scorers. In addition, high *Pd* scores are associated with aggression and criminal behavior.

Hathaway and Monachesi (1953, 1957, 1961, 1963) found Scale 4 to be one of the most prominent scales in terms of both elevation and frequency in the adolescent general population. The *Pd* scale was also found to be one of the markers for delinquent and aggressive behavior among adolescents and also prominent among those adolescents who dropped out of school.

One of the difficulties of interpreting high Scale 4 elevations is determining which of the many possible descriptors apply to a given young person. As we will see later in this chapter, the Harris–Lingoes subscales help focus on the descriptors. In the next chapter we will also discover other scales to use to refine the interpretation of a Scale 4 elevation.

MMPI–A Scale 4 Descriptors

Scale 4 is a well-validated measure of delinquent and acting-out behaviors in both adult and adolescent populations (e.g., Archer & Krishnamurthy, 1997a; Cashel et al., 1998; Glaser et al., 2002; Moore et al., 1996; Peña et al., 1996; Stage, 2000; C. L. Williams & Butcher, 1989a). The following descriptors apply:

- Multiple behavior problems are likely.
- Lying, cheating, stealing in the home and possibly elsewhere may be likely.
- High scorers may be runaways.
- High scorers tend to be high-risk taking.
- High scorers may be impulsive and resentful.
- High scorers may lack guilt or remorse for actions.
- Possible vandalism and other destructive behaviors may be likely.
- High scorers tend to have school problems like truancy, disobedience, and poor schoolwork.
- High scorers tend to have a negative peer group.
- High scorers tend to blame others for problems.
- Irritability, swearing, and anger outbursts are likely.
- Boys may engage in property damage and other juvenile offenses.
- Girls may be described as "boy crazy," tend to wear sexually provocative clothing, and may be sexually active and at risk for unprotected sex.
- Parents of boys report numerous problems, including cruelty toward others, temper tantrums, fighting, and other aggressive behaviors.
- Conduct problems are common among high elevation *Pd* adolescents.
- Boys may be at risk for suicidal ideations or gestures especially when in trouble for their behavior problems.

Harris–Lingoes Subscales for Pd

Harris–Lingoes subscales for Scale 4 elevations are as follows:

- Pd_1, Familial Discord (11 items). Home is unpleasant and lacking in love, support, and understanding; family is critical and controlling; desire to leave home.
- Pd_2, Authority Problems (10 items). Resent authority; trouble with the law; opinionated; tend to stand up for their beliefs; history of behavior problems in school; admit stealing; sexual acting out.
- Pd_3, Social Imperturbability (12 items). Feel comfortable and confident in social situations; exhibitionistic; opinionated.

- Pd_4, Social Alienation (18 items). Misunderstood, alienated, iso-lated, and estranged from others; lonely; unhappy; blame others; self-centered; insensitive; inconsiderate; some regret and remorse over past actions.
- Pd_5, Self-Alienation (15 items). Feel uncomfortable and unhappy with self; concentration problems; life is uninteresting or unre-warding; excessive use of alcohol.

SCALE 5: MASCULINITY–FEMININITY (*MF*)

Scale 5 was developed as an "interest scale" to measure "the tendency toward masculinity or femininity of interest pattern" or more explicitly:

> Every item finally chosen indicated a trend on the part of male sexual inverts[1] in the direction of femininity. Males with very high *Mf* scores have frequently been found to be either overt or repressed sexual inverts. However, abnormality *must not be assumed* on the basis of a high score without confirmatory evidence.
>
> Among females high scores cannot yet be safely assumed to have similar clinical significance, and the interpretation must be limited to measurement of the general trait. (Hathaway & McKinley, 1942, p. 8)

The initial criterion groups for Scale 5 were 13 gay men con-trasted with 54 heterosexual men, all soldiers (Lippa, 2005). Eventu-ally, Scale 5 was cross-validated against another widely used measure of masculine–feminine interests, the Attitude Analysis Interest Sur-vey developed by Terman and Miles in 1936 (see Lippa, 2005). Lippa (2005, p. 36) pointed out that even Terman and Miles in 1936 recog-nized that their scale could prove to be culturally limited because of their reliance on the differential item responding of men and women "in the present historical period of the Occidental culture of our own country."

Scale 5 items mostly deal with activities and preferences stereo-typically associated with one sex or the other. Men scoring high on the *Mf* scale tend to show more aesthetic interests considered more charac-teristic of women, whereas low-scoring men tend to be more interested in traditionally masculine activities. Women who score high on the *Mf* scale, on the other hand, tend to reject the stereotypically feminine role and behaviors prevalent before World War II and may prefer sports and other hobbies previously associated with men. The scale is highly asso-

---

[1]*Sexual inverts* or *sexual inversion* comes from a theory of homosexuality in vogue during the late 19th and early 20th centuries. It hypothesized a type of homosexuality in which men act like women and women act like men.

ciated with and influenced by educational attainment. C. L. Williams and Butcher (1989a) did not find, in their clinical samples, useful correlate information for the *Mf* score with adolescents.

MMPI–A Scale 5 Descriptors

Research and changing cultural norms regarding masculine and feminine interests suggest very cautious interpretive statements, if any, for Scale 5 elevations:

- He endorsed a number of interests beyond ones stereotypically identified as masculine.
- She endorsed a number of interests beyond ones stereotypically identified as feminine.

SCALE 6: PARANOIA (*PA*)

Background

Hathaway (1956) used as the initial criterion sample for this scale patients who were experiencing paranoid symptoms that were so severe that they required hospitalization. Thus many of the items on the scale are blatantly psychotic in nature. They reflect delusions of persecution and grandeur, as well as ideas of reference. Among some populations, it is possible to obtain an elevated score without endorsing any of these extreme items because there are also items dealing with emotional sensitivity, suspicion of the motives of others, dissatisfaction with life, and an idealistic denial of cynical attitudes. Thus, someone who feels oversensitive or under scrutiny may have moderate elevations. Scale 6 is a highly specific indicator of paranoia when it is quite elevated, but more modest elevations on *Pa* do not suggest severe delusional behavior. At extreme elevations, diagnoses of schizophrenia and paranoid disorders are common.

Moderate scores suggest suspicion and mistrust, but not always to a psychotic degree. Persons scoring in the moderate range tend to interpret innocuous interpersonal stimuli as threatening or insulting. They tend to react with anger to perceived slights and also to harbor grudges against others. Chronic social maladjustment is common even with moderate scores. Persons with elevated *Pa* scores are often viewed by others as guarded and suspicious. High scorers are often highly moralistic and may look down on those around them with contempt. People with high elevations on *Pa* are usually highly defensive, and they tend toward intellectualizing and blaming others for their problems. They have difficulty establishing an effective working alliance with the therapist and tend to terminate treatment early.

MMPI–A Scale 6 Descriptors

Research with the MMPI–A found more descriptors for clinical boys compared with clinical girls (e.g., Cashel et al.,1998; C. L. Williams & Butcher, 1989a).

- Difficulties in school, both academic and behavioral, are common with elevated scores from youths in school settings.
- Aggressive behavior and anger control problems are possible.
- High scorers are likely to have difficulties with interpersonal relationships.
- High scorers blame others for problems.
- Boys in clinical settings may display unusual behaviors, including ideas of reference, confusion, auditory hallucinations, gradiosity, odd grimaces, and vocalizations.
- Boys in clinical settings can be unpredictable, sneaky, easily upset, prone to acting out, and attention seeking.
- Parents of boys in clinical settings may observe numerous problems, including strange ideas and behaviors, obsessions and compulsions, concentration problems, impulsivity, feelings of persecution, and poor peer relationships.
- Girls in clinical settings may have increasing disagreements with parents.
- Incarcerated delinquent boys may have suicidal ideation or gestures.

Harris–Lingoes Subscales for Paranoia

There are three Harris–Lingoes subscales for interpreting Scale 6 elevations:

- Pa_1, Persecutory Ideas (17 items). Feel threatened, misunderstood, unfairly blamed, punished, and suspicious; distrust others; tend to blame others for problems.
- Pa_2, Poignancy (9 items). High-strung; sensitive; risk-takers; seek excitement.
- Pa_3, Naiveté (9 items). Very naive and optimistic attitudes about others; overly trusting; vulnerable to being hurt; high moral standards; deny feelings of hostility.

SCALE 7: PSYCHASTHENIA (*PT*)

Background

McKinley and Hathaway (1942) indicated that their criterion group of patients diagnosed with psychasthenia had excessive doubts, compulsions, obsessions, and unreasonable fears or phobias. They recognized that Scale 7 was made up of many items that are more general than specific compulsions or phobias, thus likely characterizing a more general personality makeup. They also noted the problems with finding sufficient patients hospitalized with this condition given that these problems were more prevalent in outpatient settings. (Their criterion group comprised 20 patients, including 2 adolescents; they ended up concluding that the 16-year-old criterion case may have been misdiagnosed!)

Persons with high scores on Scale 7 tend to express anxious preocccupation over their fears and insecurities. They often engage in ritualized acts as a means of alleviating this anxiety. Their anxiety is pronouned, and they tend to show agitation, worry, fear, difficulty concentrating, fatigue, insomnia, and tearfulness. Persons who obtain elevated *Pt* scale scores typically profit from psychological treatment as a result of their strong motivation for anxiety relief. However, it should be noted that their gains in therapy tend to be slow because they fear change and have difficulty coping with ambiguous circumstances.

MMPI–A Scale 7 Descriptors

Unexpectedly, Scale 7 was not associated with the anxiety measures on either the parent (Child Behavior Checklist) or therapist (Devereux Adolescent Behavior Rating Scale) rating scales (Butcher, Williams, et al., 1992; C. L. Williams & Butcher, 1989a). Other studies with adolescents provide support for Scale 7, however (e.g., Cashel et al., 1998; Lachar & Wrobel, 1990). The following are possible descriptors:

- High scorers may have generalized anxiety and concentration difficulties.
- High scorers may experience fear of dying or losing control.
- High scorers tend to be self-critical, tense, and nervous.
- High scorers on Scale 7 are somewhat unusual in mental health and alcohol and drug treatment centers for adolescents.
- The presence of depressed mood or anxiety symptoms (e.g., excessive fears, obsessions, compulsions) should be assessed further.
- Suicidal ideation or gestures should be assessed further.

There are no Harris–Lingoes subscales for the relatively homogeneous Scale 7.

SCALE 8: SCHIZOPHRENIA (*SC*)

Background

Hathaway and McKinley originally planned to develop separate scales for four types of schizophrenia (e.g., paranoid, catatonic, simple, and hebephrenic) that were recognized in the 1940s. At one point, according to Hathaway (1956), they attempted to develop more than 12 different scales! However, they were unable to make separate discriminations and decided to publish one scale for schizophrenia. Scale 8 measures a variety of symptoms associated with schizophrenia, including hallucinations, delusions, alienation from self and others, disturbed thinking, fearfulness, and dissatisfaction with life. Very high scores on Scale 8 are associated with the presence of a psychotic disorder and its underlying symptoms, including disorganization, confusion, and difficulty thinking clearly. Adolescents and young adults often score higher on this scale than adults. In addition, because some of the items on the scale are associated with unusual sensory experiences and cognitive deficits, some patients with neurological impairment or those who use psychoactive drugs may produce more elevated *Sc* scores. People who are experiencing severe emotional turmoil at the time of the evaluation may also obtain elevated *Sc* scores.

Some individuals with moderate elevations may not be actively psychotic, although they may have odd beliefs that are not necessarily delusional in nature but are "countercultural." These people tend to report feeling alienated and different from others, and they may have poor social skills. They may also show judgment difficulties. Individuals with high *Sc* scores show a relatively poor prognosis for traditional psychotherapy, in part because of the severity and long-standing nature of their problems. Moreover, they tend to have difficulties in interpersonal relationships resulting in communication problems in therapy. Individuals with elevated *Sc* scores tend to be prescribed psychotropic medication to assist in controlling their symptoms.

Hathaway and Monachesi (1961, 1963), in their work on the MMPI with adolescents, found the *Sc* scale to be one of the most prominent high-point scales among delinquents. Hathaway and Monachesi (1963) also reported that the *Sc* scale was associated with higher rates of school dropout. Hathaway (1956) reported that high Scale 8 boys, compared with high Scale 7 boys, have a higher delinquency rate and their crimes tend to be more severe. Later research using the MMPI–A with delinquents confirms the elevation of *Sc* in this population (e.g., Moore et al., 1996; Peña et al., 1996).

MMPI–A Scale 8 Descriptors

There are a number of descriptors for Scale 8 elevations from both the original MMPI research and MMPI–A studies. The correlates for boys indicate more acting-out behaviors than what is evident in girls:

- Behavior problems at home and school are likely as Scale 8 is elevated.
- Academic problems are possible in students in school settings.

- High scorers in clinical settings may display unusual behaviors, including ideas of reference, confusion, auditory hallucinations, gradiosity, odd grimaces, and vocalizations.
- High scorers in clinical settings can be unpredictable, sneaky, easily upset, prone to acting out, and attention seeking.
- Parents of boys in clinical settings may observe numerous problems, including strange ideas and behaviors, obsessions and compulsions, concentration problems, impulsivity, feelings of persecution, and poor peer relationships.
- Girls may report multiple somatic complaints.

Harris–Lingoes Subscales for Sc

Interpretations for the six Scale 8 Harris–Lingoes subscales are as follows:

- Sc_1, Social Alienation (21 items). Misunderstood; mistreated; family lacks love and support; hostility and hatred toward family members; loneliness; feel empty, being plotted against.
- Sc_2, Emotional Alienation (11 items). Depression; despair; wish they were dead; frightened; apathetic.
- Sc_3, Lack of Ego Mastery, Cognitive (10 items). Afraid of losing their mind; strange and unusual thoughts; feelings of unreality; concentration and attention difficulties.
- Sc_4, Lack of Ego Mastery, Conative (14 items). Life is a strain; depression; despair; worry; difficulty coping with everyday life; not much in life is interesting or rewarding; hopeless; wish they were dead.
- Sc_5, Lack of Ego Mastery, Defective Inhibition (11 items). Lost control of their emotions; impulsive; restless; hyperactive; irritable; laughing or crying spells; memory problems.
- Sc_6, Bizarre Sensory Experiences (20 items). Peculiar and strange experiences; blank spells; hallucinations; unusual thoughts; feel body is changing in unusual ways; oversensitivity; weakness; ringing in the ears.

SCALE 9: HYPOMANIA (*MA*)

Background

According to McKinley and Hathaway (1944), hypomania is the milder form of excitement that typically occurs as part of a manic-depressive psychosis. (This definition is consistent with the description of a hypomanic episode in the *DSM–IV–TR*.) The criterion group consisted of 24 inpatients with moderate or light symptoms (i.e., hypomania or mild acute mania) because the more severe cases could not complete the MMPI items. Scale 9 was developed to differentiate this patient group from the "Minnesota Normals" using similar procedures as for the other Standard Scales.

As scores on the Scale 9 increase, it is more likely that symptoms characterizing a hypomanic episode (e.g, grandiosity, rapidity of thought and speech, distractibility) are present. Extremely high scores on the scale can suggest psychotic symptoms, including hallucinations and delusions. However, a number of items on the *Ma* scale reflect acceptance of antisocial values, symptoms of dissociation, and attitudes related to family problems. Therefore, it is not unusual to find some individuals without psychiatric problems scoring in the clinical range on the *Ma* scale. Some individuals with moderate elevations may not meet full criteria for a mood disturbance, although several potentially problematic personality traits are suggested. High *Ma* scorers are reportedly impulsive, erratic, and have difficulty completing goals. In addition, persons with high *Ma* scores often have difficult interpersonal relations although, like high *Pd* scorers, the high-scoring *Ma* individual tends to make good first impressions with their sponteneity and creativity. Their involvement in these relationships, however, tends to be superficial and transient. These individuals are viewed as manipulative of other people. In addition, the high mood state of high *Ma* scorers can be very reactive, shifting unpredictably from joy to nervous agitation to explosive anger. Difficulties with family members, substance abuse, and the legal system are common. High *Ma* scorers typically do not seek therapy or make good candidates for psychotherapy, as their impulsivity prevents them from focusing consistently on productive therapeutic activities.

As they found for the *Pd* and *Sc* scales, Hathaway and Monachesi (1961, 1963) also found the *Ma* scale to be prominent in terms of both elevation and frequency in the general population of adolescents, as well as a marker for delinquent and aggressive behavior among adolescents.

MMPI–A Scale 9 Descriptors

In general, this is a well-validated MMPI–A scale (e.g., Archer, Gordon, Giannetti, & Singles, 1988; Cashel et al. 1998; Glaser et al., 2002; Peña et al., 1996; Stage, 2000; C. L. Williams & Butcher, 1989a) with the following empirical descriptors:

- High scorers tend to be enthusiastic and energetic, which may be taken to the extreme.
- Multiple behavior problems are likely, including lying, cheating, stealing, vandalism.
- High scorers are likely to have temper tantrums and act aggressively toward others.
- High scorers tend to be impulsive.
- High scorers are likely to associate with a negative peer group.
- High scorers tend to be hyperactive.

- High scorers may have oppositional behaviors.
- High scorers tend to be irritabile and argumentative.
- High scorers may be involved with alcohol and other drug use.
- Girls may be described as "boy crazy," tend to wear sexually provocative clothing, and may be sexually active and at risk for unprotected sex.

Harris–Lingoes Subscales for Ma

Harris–Lingoes subscales for refining interpretations of elevations on Scale 9 are as follows:

- Ma_1, Amorality (6 items). Selfish; dishonest; amoral; manipulative.
- Ma_2, Psychomotor Acceleration (11 items). Accelerated speech; overactive thought processes; excessive motor activity; restless; excited; elated without cause; easily bored; seek out excitement; impulsive; willing to do harmful or shocking things.
- Ma_3, Imperturbability (8 items). Deny social anxiety or caring about what others think of them; impatient; irritable.
- Ma_4, Ego Inflation (9 items). Unrealistic in their self-appraisals; resent others placing demands on them.

SCALE 0: SOCIAL INTROVERSION (*SI*)

Background

This is the only Standard Scale that was not developed by Hathaway and McKinley at the University of Minnesota. Drake (1946) developed it to measure the personality dimensions of introversion–extraversion using women students at the University of Wisconsin (there were too few men at the university during World War II). MMPI items that differentiated women who scored high on a measure of introversion/extroverson (i.e., the Minnesota Thinking–Social–Emotional Inventory) from those who scored low on it became the Scale 0 of the MMPI. Drake (1946) indicated that the scale was later validated with a sample of men.

People who score high on Scale 0 tend to be shy and reserved in social situations, whereas those who score low are extraverted and tend to be outgoing in social situations. High *Si* scorers tend to be excessively self-conscious and feel nervous in the presence of others. They are generally responsible, but their cautiousness and indecisiveness lead them to limit the number of novel experiences to which they are willing to expose themselves. Periodic episodes of anxiety or depression may cause them to seek treatment. Their reticence, however, makes it difficult to establish a working alliance with them, and they have may have trouble opening up to the therapist. Low scorers, on the other hand, display an opposite cluster of traits. They feel at ease in social situations and may be well-liked by others. These people are generally articulate, energetic, and competitive.

The *Si* scale is one of the most valuable measures on the MMPI instruments in that it assesses an important personality dimension, introversion–extraversion, that describes the manner in which the individual relates to others. Moreover, the *Si* scale addresses one of the more stable personality characteristics. This scale was shown to have a 5-year test–retest correlation of .85 (Spiro, Butcher, Levenson, Aldwin, & Bosse, 2000) and a 30-year retest of .73 (Leon, Gillum, Gillum, & Gouze, 1979). Therefore, the *Si* scale addresses one of the most enduring personality characteristics and can add a valuable perspective in making personality descriptions and predictions of change.

Hathaway and Monachesi (1961, 1963), reported that the *Si* scale was associated with lower rates of delinquency and acting-out behavior generally. C. L. Williams and Butcher (1989a), in their validity study of a large sample of adolescents in various clinical settings, found that the *Si* scale was associated with personality factors reported with the *Si* scale with adults.

MMPI–A Scale 0 Descriptors

The *Si* scale is a well-validated MMPI–A measure. Elevations are associated with some problems in social relationships:

- Social withdrawal and difficulties in interpersonal relationships are likely.
- High scorers are on the fringe socially; they may be bossed by peers.
- High scorers tend to daydream, stare blankly.
- High scorers can be suspicious of others, afraid of being hurt, unemotional.
- High scorers are likely to avoid competition.
- High scorers tend to be low in aggressive behavior.
- High scorers tend to be uninterested in or may be uncomfortable around the opposite sex.
- High scorers are unlikely to be part of a negative peer group or involved in alcohol or other drug use.
- High scorers are possibly anxious, depressed, or have suicidal ideations or gestures.

On the other hand, lower scores on Scale 0 (*T* score ≤ 45) indicate the following:

- Those with low scores are likely to be outgoing and friendly.
- Those with low scores are likely to be interested in the opposite sex.

Si *Subscales*

The interpretive hypotheses for the *Si* subscales are:

- *Si*$_1$, Shyness/Self Consciousness (14 items). Difficulty talking with people; shy; socially anxious; uncomfortable at parties; not sociable.
- *Si*$_2$, Social Avoidance (8 items). Dislike parties, dances, social gatherings, and crowds.
- *Si*$_3$, Alienation of Self and Others (17 items). Low self-confidence; distrustful; easily overwhelmed or disappointed; memory or concentration problems; impatient; ruminate; want to be happy like others.

MMPI–A STANDARD SCALE DESCRIPTORS OF SEXUAL ABUSE

Although both Butcher, Williams, et al. (1992)[2] and C. L. Williams and Butcher (1989a) reported significant relationships of several of the MMPI–A Standard Scales with indications in their treatment records of sexual or physical abuse, these possible correlates were not included in the above sections on descriptors for the Standard Scales. We do not recommend making these correlates part of an individual's MMPI–A interpretation because of the potential for harm of false positives (Butcher & Williams, 2000). However, these associations should remind the clinician to include an assessment of abuse in the psychological evaluation. In Chapter 9 we describe how questions about possible sexual abuse can be included in a MMPI–A feedback evaluation session. The MMPI–A Standard Scales that showed a relationship with sexual abuse in a clinical setting were Scales 1 and 7 (C. L. Williams & Butcher, 1989a) and 8 (Butcher, Williams, et al., 1992) for boys and Scales 4 and 8 for girls (Butcher, Williams, et al., 1992). A Scale 4 elevation was associated with physical abuse for boys (Butcher, Williams, et al., 1992). Holifield et al. (2002) found high Scale 1 and Scale 8 scores among adolescents who had been sexually abused. We will also see in the next chapter other MMPI–A scales that were associated with abuse.

---

[2]The clinical sample presented in the MMPI–A manual is a subset of the data collected by C. L. Williams and Butcher (1989a). Subjects between the ages of 12 and 13 years were excluded from the sample used in the MMPI–A manual when the decision was made to limit the normative sample to 14 to 18 years.

Interpreting Rachel's Standard Scales

Rachel's MMPI–A Basic Scale profile (Figure 3.2, p. 41) shows three prominent scale elevations ($T > 65$) that require consideration. We focus primarily on the *Pd* scale given its extreme elevation and prominence over the next two elevated scales, *Sc* and *Pa*. However, the interpreter should also pay attention to the *Sc* and *Pa* elevations because these measures can reveal severe cognitive and personality problems.

Rachel's MMPI–A *Pd* elevation suggests many behavior problems, including school maladjustment, family discord, and conflicts with authority. She is likely to be moody, resentful, and attention seeking. She tends to be rebellious, impulsive, and argumentative at times. She shows poor judgment and may get into trouble at school or with the law. She is likely to be self-centered and may show little remorse for difficult circumstances that she tends to create. Some adolescents with this test pattern may run away or lie to avoid punishment. She probably engages in risky behaviors and tends to seeks immediate gratification of her wishes. Sensation-seeking behavior is likely, and she may use alcohol or drugs. She may be sexually active, wear provocative clothing, be seen as "boy crazy," and be at risk for unprotected sex.

Because the Harris–Lingoes subscales for Rachel's profile were not scored by the clinician, it is not possible to use subscale information for clarifying her very high elevation on *Pd*. If this information had been available for the interpretation, the practitioner could have obtained a better idea about Rachel's problems by examining which content areas were most prominent in the three elevated scales. For example, her high elevation on *Pd* might be accounted for through her responding largely to items on Pd_1 (Family Problems) and Pd_3 (Social Imperturbability). In this case, Pd_2 (Authority Problems) would not be as pertinent in describing her clinical picture.

Similarly, the Harris–Lingoes subscales for *Pa* and *Sc* would have been useful in determining if her less extreme elevations on those Clinical Scales reflect endorsement of the blatantly psychotic items found in Sc_6 (Bizarre Sensory Experiences) and Sc_3 (Lack of Ego Mastery) or other emotional problems such as alienation, despair, and impulsivity apparent in the other *Sc* subscales. The *Pa* subscales would also have revealed if her elevation on that scale was due to endorsement of items in Pa_1 (Persecutory Ideas) or if they came about due to endorsement of items reflecting risk taking and sensation seeking (Pa_2), or naïveté and denial of feelings of hostility (Pa_3). For now, we can conclude that Rachel's elevations on *Pa* and *Sc* support the descriptors of multiple behavior problems at home and school, described above, as well as suggest she may be suspicious, overly sensitive, manipulative, and frequently misunderstands the motives of others.

The Next Step in MMPI–A Interpretations

Until the MMPI–A was introduced, most MMPI interpretations of adolescents such as Rachel ended with consideration of elevations on the Basic Scales covered in this chapter. Fortunately, as we will see in the next chapter, Rachel's clinician scored her MMPI–A for the Content and Supplementary Scales. Scores on those scales will be used to further develop Rachel's MMPI–A interpretation in the next chapter. In addition, the PSY-5 Scales will be described in this next chapter. Some of the scales covered in the next chapter were developed using the same empirical scale development techniques used for the Standard Scales described in this chapter. Others, however, used a different scale development strategy and thus require a different method of interpretation.

Beyond the Basics
MMPI–A Content Measures, PSY-5, and Supplementary Scales

5

But I already answered all these questions!
How come you keep asking me the same questions
again and again?
Didn't you even look at my answers?

This teenager, frustrated during a clinical interview when asked questions like the ones she answered on the MMPI–A, illustrates how sole reliance on the empirically derived Standard Scales does not facilitate direct communication between the client and the clinician. When this teen and others complete an MMPI–A, they do not approach the task with the idea of matching the responses of a particular criterion group versus another. Instead, they assume they are sharing (or declining to do so) their symptoms, beliefs, attitudes, and so forth with their psychologists. In other words, they respond to the content of the MMPI–A items and likely have the expectation that their psychologists will consider their responses to the MMPI–A items as part of the evaluation. In contrast, as we saw in the previous chapter, the empirically derived Standard Scales provide information to the psychologist about how likely a set of descriptors apply to a given individual. Item content becomes less important when examining and interpreting empirically derived scales.

Although the empirical scale construction strategy results in measures with high sensitivity for detecting mental health problems, the resulting Standard Scales contain items that overlap with other scales because the underlying constructs are complex and multidimensional (e.g., schizophrenia, somatization disorders). In addition, most of the Standard Scales contain heterogeneous item content, making the interpretations of these scales less straightforward. Because of these issues, even the early MMPI experts developed measures that provide more direct information about the content of the items endorsed by the patient than do the Standard Scales—remember the Harris–Lingoes subscales from the last chapter?

Two types of scales—empirically derived and content based—coexist in the MMPI-A. In addition, as we see in this chapter, there is also a set of item-level indicators in use today. Most of the scales considered in this chapter are content based (i.e., developed with procedures to assure more homogeneous grouping of items into scales than is the case with the Standard Scales). These include the set of MMPI–A Content Scales:

- Adolescent-Anxiety or *A-anx* (23 items on MMPI–2; 21 items on MMPI–A)
- Adolescent-Obsessiveness or *A-obs* (16 items on MMPI–2; 15 items on MMPI–A)
- Adolescent-Depression or *A-dep* (33 items on MMPI–2; 26 items on MMPI–A)
- Adolescent-Health Concerns or *A-hea* (36 items on MMPI–2; 37 items on MMPI–A)
- Adolescent-Alienation or *A-aln* (20 items on MMPI–A; not on MMPI–2)
- Adolescent-Bizarre Mentation or *A-biz* (23 items on MMPI–2; 37 items on MMPI–A)
- Adolescent-Anger or *A-ang* (16 items on MMPI–2; 17 items on MMPI–A)
- Adolescent-Cynicism or *A-cyn* (23 items on MMPI–2; 22 items on MMPI–A)
- Adolescent-Conduct Problems or *A-con* (23 items on MMPI–A; not on MMPI–2)
- Adolescent-Low Self-Esteem or *A-lse* (24 items on MMPI–2; 18 items on MMPI–A)
- Adolescent-Low Aspirations or *A-las* (16 items on MMPI–A; not on MMPI–2)
- Adolescent-Social Discomfort or *A-sod* (24 items on MMPI–2; 24 items on MMPI–A)
- Adolescent-Family Problems or *A-fam* (25 items on MMPI–2; 35 items on MMPI–A)
- Adolescent-School Problems or *A-sch* (20 items on MMPI–A; not on MMPI–2)
- Adolescent-Negative Treatment Indicators or *A-trt* (26 items on MMPI–2; 26 items on MMPI–A)

The Personality Psychopathology Five (PSY-5) Scales are another set designed to measure more homogeneous constructs than do the Standard Scales:

- Aggressiveness or *AGGR* (18 items on MMPI–2; 20 items on MMPI–A)
- Psychoticism or *PSYC* (25 items on MMPI–2; 21 items on MMPI–A)
- Disconstraint or *DISC* (29 items on MMPI–2; 23 items on MMPI–A)
- Negative Emotionality/Neuroticism or *NEGE* (33 items on MMPI–2; 22 items on MMPI–A)
- Introversion/Low Positive Emotionality or *INTR* (34 items on MMPI–2; 28 items on MMPI–A)

A final set described in this chapter, referred to as the Supplementary Scales, includes three scales designed to measure alcohol and other drug use problems:

- MacAndrew Alcoholism Scale—Revised or *MAC–R* (49 items on MMPI–2 and MMPI–A)
- Alcohol and Drug Problem Proneness Scale or *PRO* (36 items on MMPI–A)
- Alcohol and Drug Problem Acknowledgment Scale or *ACK* (13 items on MMPI–A)

Of the three Supplementary Scales, only *ACK* is a content-based measure. Both *MAC–R* and *PRO* were developed using empirical procedures involving contrasting groups similar to the Standard Scales described in the previous chapter. *MAC–R*, developed originally for the MMPI, is also included in the MMPI–2. *ACK*'s and *PRO*'s counterparts on the MMPI–2 are the 13-item Addiction Acknowledgment Scale and the 39-item Addiction Potential Scale.

With the exception of *MAC–R* and *PRO*, scales in this chapter contain groups of items that are face valid and relatively obvious in terms of their content. As an example, the Adolescent Depression scale contains items dealing with sadness and suicidal ideation. Similarly, the Alcohol and Drug Problems Acknowledgment scale, as its name aptly describes, consists of items about alcohol and drug use and related symptoms. Therefore, scores on these scales are influenced by a respondent's motivation to overreport or underreport symptoms. If a person chooses not to acknowledge certain problem areas, then he or she can simply not endorse those items on the scales in this chapter. Thus, careful evaluation of the level of cooperation of an adolescent's responding is important with regard to the interpretation of these scales.

These measures play an important role in interpretation by refining the focus of the interpretation of the Standard Scales by suggesting

MMPI–A Helpful Hints: Interpreting Content-Based Scales

Pay close attention to the Validity Scales and Indicators.

Examine Cannot Say score to insure item omissions will not affect elevations.

Scales in Chapter 5 can be more susceptible to underreporting and overreporting given their face valid item content.

Use the same *T*-score cut-offs for interpretations as for the Standard Scales.
> 65: High elevation
60 to 64: Moderate elevation
< 59: Normal range scores

Scores in the elevated ranges have a different meaning than the Standard Scales described in the last chapter.

As scale elevations increase on content-based measures, the adolescent has endorsed more symptoms or behaviors related to the constructs being assessed (e.g., he or she has more symptoms of anxiety or reports more problems with aggression).

which of the various descriptors for each Standard Scale should be emphasized, as we see later in the chapter. In addition, some of the scales in this chapter provide more detailed information about problem areas or issues that were not directly addressed by the Standard Scales, including, as examples, alcohol and other drug problems, low self-esteem, anger, and family problems. Exhibit 5.1 includes helpful hints about interpreting content-based scales described in the rest of this chapter.

MMPI–A Content Scales

BACKGROUND

Content interpretation and the development of content-based personality scales have been important additions to appraising responses on the original MMPI. Wiggins (1966) developed the most effective and widely used content scales for the original MMPI. These scales, summarizing the main item content themes in the test, produced scores that provided a perspective on the amount of personality and symptom information the client was willing to share in the test administration. When the MMPI was revised in the 1980s, a new set of content-based scales was developed for the MMPI–2 (Butcher, Graham, Williams, & Ben-Porath, 1989) and MMPI–A (C. L. Williams, Butcher, Ben-Porath, & Graham, 1992). This was necessary because of the large number of additional items that were added to the test and because some of the original items were eliminated for being outmoded or offensive. The MMPI–2 Content Scales were developed following the approach used by Wiggins in developing content scales. However, each of the new MMPI–2 Content Scales was also empirically validated against external criteria to assure that the scales had predictive validity.

The Content Scales developed for MMPI–A were initially based on the MMPI–2 Content Scales, with some changes to make them more appropriate for an adolescent population (C. L. Williams et al., 1992). These scales were derived following a multistep process that included rational, empirical, and construct-oriented test development strategies. The Content Scales assess homogeneous themes that have been externally validated in clinical samples (e.g., Archer & Krishnamurthy, 1997a; Arita & Baer, 1998; Cashel, Rogers, Sewell, & Holliman, 1998; Forbey, 2002; Forbey & Ben-Porath, 2003; Glaser, Calhoun, & Petrocelli, 2002; Kopper, Osman, Soman, & Hoffman, 1998; McGrath, Pogge, & Stokes, 2002; Peña, Megargee, & Brody, 1996; Rinaldo & Baer, 2003; C. L. Williams et al., 1992). Research has shown that the MMPI–A Content Scales provide incremental gains in clinically useful information beyond what is already provided by the MMPI–A Standard Scales (Forbey & Ben-Porath, 2003; Kopper et al., 1998; McGrath et al., 2002; Rinaldo & Baer, 2003).

In the development of the MMPI–A Content Scales, several important changes were made to the MMPI–2 Content Scales to make them more relevant and applicable to adolescents (C. L. Williams et al., 1992). Some MMPI–2 Content Scales were not included in the MMPI–A (e.g., the MMPI–2 Work Interference and Antisocial Personality scales) but, instead, other more adolescent-specific scales were developed (e.g., the School Problems and Low Aspirations scales were added to address behaviors, attitudes, and relational problems that may be interfering with an adolescent's ability to function in academic settings). The Conduct Problems and Alienation scales were added to assess acting-out problems and feelings of being misunderstood by others, respectively.

Content interpretation can be further refined by an examination of subgroupings of items within the MMPI–A Content Scales. That is, some Content Scales can be further subdivided to reflect more specific content. Sherwood, Ben-Porath, and Williams (1997) developed the Content Component Scales—subscales for each parent Content Scale representing a more focused problem area within the parent scale. Similar to the recommendations for the Harris–Lingoes subscales in the last chapter, an MMPI–A Content Component Scale should only be interpreted if its parent Content Scale is moderately elevated or higher and if it is elevated at 60 *T* score or higher. Surprisingly, as the reader will discover in Appendix A in the section on Content Scales, we were able to find only one doctoral dissertation exploring the utility and validity of the Content Component Scales in the almost decade and a half after their introduction.[1]

INTERPRETING THE *A-ANX* CONTENT SCALE

Adolescents who score high on the Adolescent Anxiety scale tend to be open and willing to talk about their concerns. They report

- multiple symptoms of anxiety;
- tension,
- somatic problems (e.g., heart palpitations, shortness of breath),
- sleep difficulties,
- worries,
- poor concentration,
- fear of losing their minds,
- not functioning well, and
- difficulty making decisions.

There are no component scales for *A-anx* given its straightforward and homogeneous content related to symptoms of anxiety.

INTERPRETING THE *A-OBS* CONTENT SCALE

Elevated scores on the Adolescent Obsessiveness scale reflect reports of

- decision-making difficulties;
- excessive ruminations, causing others to become impatient;
- worrying to excess;
- possible compulsive behaviors like counting or saving unimportant things; and
- being overwhelmed by their thoughts.

Like *A-anx,* this is a relatively homogeneous scale; hence component scales were not developed for it.

INTERPRETING THE *A-DEP* CONTENT SCALE

Adolescents scoring high on the Adolescent Depression scale tend to

- have significant depressive thoughts;
- report feeling uncertain about their future;
- acknowledge that they are uninterested in life;
- be moody and unhappy, cry easily, or feel hopeless and empty;

---

[1]The University of Minnesota Press issued an MMPI–A Manual Supplement in 2006 that includes sections on the PSY-5 Scales, critical items, and Content Component Scales. However, the Content Components section is essentially a reprinting of Sherwood et al. (1997) with no new research provided.

- possibly acknowledge thoughts of suicide or wish that they were dead;
- report uncertain futures;
- report beliefs they are condemned or feelings they have committed unpardonable sins; and
- see other people as unsupportive.

The following Content Component Scales were developed to augment interpretations of *A-dep* elevations over 60 *T*:

- *A-dep*$_1$ or Dysphoria (5 items): Multiple symptoms associated with depressed mood. Further evaluation to determine if the adolescent's symptoms meet the criteria for a major depressive episode.
- *A-dep*$_2$ or Self-Depreciation (5 items): Negative self-image, including feeling useless, helpless, worthlessness, having limited abilities, low self-confidence, and possible excessive or inappropriate guilt.
- *A-dep*$_3$ or Lack of Drive (7 items): Inability to get going or get things done, lack of drive and low motivation, apathy. Elevations over 65 *T* suggest markedly diminished interest or pleasure in all, or almost all, activities, a symptom of a major depressive episode.
- *A-dep*$_4$ or Suicidal Ideation (4 items): Careful assessment for potential suicide risk should be undertaken with the adolescent given that he or she has likely endorsed items reflecting suicidal ideation or death wishes.

INTERPRETING THE *A-HEA* CONTENT SCALE

Those scoring high on the Adolescent Health Concerns scale likely report

- multiple physical symptoms across several body systems;
- worries about their health,
- feeling sicker than most people,
- gastrointestinal symptoms (e.g., constipation, nausea and vomiting, stomach trouble),
- neurological problems (e.g., convulsions, dizzy and fainting spells, paralysis),
- sensory problems (e.g., poor hearing or eyesight),
- cardiovascular symptoms (e.g., heart or chest pains),
- skin problems,
- pain (e.g., headaches, neck pains), and
- respiratory troubles (e.g., coughs, hay fever, asthma).

There are three Content Component Scales for *A-hea* to help narrow down the areas in which symptoms are reported for scores at 60 *T* or higher:

- *A-hea*$_1$ or Gastrointestinal Complaints (4 items): Frequent complaints of stomachaches and related ailments.

- *A-hea₂* or Neurological Symptoms (18 items): Reports of symptoms commonly associated with neurological problems like headaches, tingling, convulsions, and loss of consciousness. Further assessment may be warranted to rule out the possibility of neuropsychological issues.
- *A-hea₃* or General Health Concerns (8 items): Numerous health concerns across different body systems, reports of generally poor health, worries about health, possible excessive absences from school.

INTERPRETING THE *A-ALN* CONTENT SCALE

Adolescents with elevations on the Adolescent Alienation scale endorse items indicating

- emotional distance from others;
- feelings of isolation;
- feeling that others give them a raw deal;
- thinking others dislike, misunderstand, and do not care about them;
- a preference for living alone;
- difficulty self-disclosing; and
- feeling that others prevent them from achieving success.

More specific interpretive information can be found for those scoring at 60 *T* score or above by examining the adolescents' differential responses to the three *A-aln* Content Component Scales:

- *A-aln₁* or Misunderstood (5 items): Others, including parents, do not understand them, leading them to withdraw from relationships or activities.
- *A-aln₂* or Social Isolation (5 items): Reports of isolation from and being uncomfortable in social situations, particularly with peers; may have social skill deficits.
- *A-aln₃* or Interpersonal Skepticism (5 items): Beliefs that others are not supportive, work against them, and are doing wrong to them.

INTERPRETING THE *A-BIZ* CONTENT SCALE

High-scoring adolescents on the Adolescent Bizarre Mentation scale are endorsing items reflecting unusual thought processes. They may

- have auditory, visual, or olfactory hallucinations;
- recognize that their thoughts are strange and peculiar;
- have paranoid ideations (e.g., they are being plotted against or that someone is trying to poison them); and
- believe that they have a special mission or powers.

Follow-up interviews should determine if these reports of psychotic symptoms occur during times of alcohol or drug use or if they fit the pattern of a psychotic disorder.

There are two Content Component Scales to assist in the interpretation of elevations on *A-Biz*:

- *A-biz*$_1$ or Psychotic Symptomatology (11 items): Endorsement of openly psychotic symptoms, suggesting the presence of delusions and hallucinations associated with some form of psychotic disorder or alcohol- or drug-related disorders.
- *A-biz*$_2$ or Paranoid Ideation (5 items): Acknowledgment of symptoms that are associated with the paranoid subtype of schizophrenia, delusional disorder, a personality disorder characterized by paranoid ideation, and/or an alcohol- or drug-related condition.

INTERPRETING THE *A-ANG* CONTENT SCALE

Individuals scoring high on the Anger Content scale, not surprisingly, experience anger control problems and tend to

- be irritable, impatient, hotheaded, annoyed, and stubborn;
- frequently feel like swearing or smashing things;
- have self-control problems; and
- be physically abusive to others.

These Content Component Scales can supplement interpretation of *A-ang* elevations:

- *A-ang*$_1$ or Explosive Behavior (8 items): Reports of explosive acts when angry, including breaking or destroying things and fistfights. May show symptoms related to a conduct disorder, oppositional defiant disorder, or intermittent explosive disorder.
- *A-ang*$_2$ or Irritability (8 items): Feelings of anger and irritability not necessarily expressed outwardly; may be impatient, argumentative, and easily annoyed.

INTERPRETING THE *A-CYN* CONTENT SCALE

Elevations on the Cynicism scale identifies adolescents with very negative attitudes about others. They tend to

- suspect others of having hidden or negative motives;
- believe others are only honest because they fear being caught;
- feel people are not trustworthy; and
- have negative attitudes about those close to them, not just people in general.

More specific interpretive information about elevated *A-cyn* scores can be obtained by examining the adolescent's differential responses to its two Content Component Scales:

- *A-cyn*$_1$ or Misanthropic Beliefs (13 items): Belief that people are interested only in their own welfare, not that of others; unlikely to turn to others for help or support because of their negative expectations about others.
- *A-cyn*$_2$ or Interpersonal Suspiciousness (9 items): Mistrustful and suspicious that others are out to get them and cause harm.

INTERPRETING THE *A-CON* CONTENT SCALE

Multiple behavior problems are endorsed by individuals with elevated scores on Conduct Problems scale, including

- bullying or intimidating or frightening others,
- being disrespectful,
- lying,
- shoplifting and stealing,
- breaking or destroying things,
- swearing, and
- viewing criminal behavior in a positive way.

The three Content Component Scales for *A-con* can be used for refining the interpretations of elevated scores:

- *A-con*$_1$ or Acting-Out Behaviors (10 items): Reports of problems with the law and antisocial behaviors such as stealing or shoplifting. These symptoms or behaviors are associated with conduct disorder or oppositional defiant disorder. The adolescent may also be experiencing difficulties with alcohol and/or other drug abuse.
- *A-con*$_2$ or Antisocial Attitudes (8 items): Endorsement of antisocial beliefs and attitudes indicating little respect for rules or the law and tolerance or even admiration for those who break the law.
- *A-con*$_3$ or Negative Peer Group (3 items): Association with a negative peer group that may be contributing to the adolescent's behavioral problems; susceptible to pressure to engage in antisocial behaviors and/or alcohol or other drug use.

INTERPRETING THE *A-LSE* CONTENT SCALE

Elevated scores on the Low Self-Esteem scale suggest that adolescents have a low opinion of themselves and

- do not believe others like them;
- feel unimportant;

- have many negative attitudes about themselves, including being unattractive, awkward, clumsy, useless, and a burden to others;
- lack self-confidence;
- find it difficult to accept compliments; and
- feel overwhelmed by all their faults.

More specific refinement in *A-lse* interpretations might be found by examining the adolescents' responses to two Content Component Scales:

- *A-lse*$_1$ or Self Doubt (13 items): Self-deprecatory thoughts including that others do not like them.
- *A-lse*$_2$ or Interpersonal Submissiveness (5 items): Acknowledgment of passive and dependent behaviors, including giving in to others easily, losing arguments, and following the advice or lead of others, showing little initiative.

INTERPRETING THE *A-LAS* CONTENT SCALE

Those who score high on the Low Aspirations scale endorse items indicating they

- are not interested in being successful in life,
- do not like to read or go to lectures,
- prefer work or activities that do not require them to be careful,
- have difficulty starting to do things, and
- believe others stand in their way of being successful.

There are two Content Component Scales to assist in interpretation of an adolescent's elevated *A-las* scores:

- *A-las*$_1$ or Low Achievement Orientation (8 items): Disinterest in learning about the world or reading.
- *A-las*$_2$ or Lack of Initiative (7 items): Endorsement of items suggesting passivity and apathy.

INTERPRETING THE *A-SOD* CONTENT SCALE

The Social Discomfort scale includes items indicating a dislike of being around other people. Adolescents who score high on this scale tend to

- dislike social events,
- prefer to be by themselves,
- prefer to sit alone rather than join a group, and
- have difficulty making friends.

The interpreter might find further interpretive statements in the two *A-sod* Content Component Scales:

- *A-sod*$_1$ or Introversion (14 items): Distant, withdrawn, dislike being with others or attending social events.

- *A-sod$_2$* or Shyness (10 items): Shy and uncomfortable in social situations, find it difficult to interact with new people they meet. An elevated score on this measure, along with a lower score on *A-sod$_1$*, suggests that the adolescent is unhappy with, and wishes to change, his or her life style.

INTERPRETING THE *A-FAM* CONTENT SCALE

There is considerable family discord among high scorers on the Adolescent Family Problems scale. They tend to

- describe their parents as angry, fault-finding, and not understanding them;
- feel they are punished unjustly;
- believe their families lack love;
- feel hatred toward family members;
- have lots of arguments; and
- be detached from their families.

The two Content Component Scales for *A-fam* may be of use in further clarifying the adolescents' attitudes toward their family:

- *A-fam$_1$* or Familial Discord (21 items): Family life characterized as full of arguments and anger; have considered leaving home.
- *A-fam$_2$* or Familial Alienation (11 items): Feelings of alienation and detachment to the family; no emotional support from family, disengaged.

INTERPRETING THE *A-SCH* CONTENT SCALE

School Problems is made of items reflecting both academic and behavior problems. Those who score high on this scale tend to

- have numerous problems in school,
- report failing or poor grades,
- possibly have been suspended from school,
- have negative attitudes toward teachers, and
- be unlikely to participate in school activities.

A-sch Content Component Scales include:

- *A-sch$_1$* or School Conduct (4 items): Acknowledges considerable acting-out behaviors at school; gets in trouble with school authorities; receives multiple disciplinary actions; and may also be at risk for the development of alcohol and/or other drug problems.

- *A-sch$_2$* or Negative Attitudes (8 items): Does not value school; resents teachers and school work; likely performs below ability level; and may get into trouble for not completing work or for truancy.

INTERPRETING THE *A-TRT* CONTENT SCALE

Those adolescents scoring high on the Negative Treatment Indicators scale report attitudes toward doctors and mental health treatment that may cause difficulties in establishing a therapeutic relationship. These adolescents

- do not believe that anyone can understand or help,
- report not being comfortable discussing some issues,
- do not want to change anything in their life,
- tend to think change is probably not possible,
- prefer giving up rather than facing a crisis or difficulty, and
- resent change agents like therapists.

More refined hypotheses for the interpretation of elevated *A-trt* scores might be found by examining adolescents' responses to its two Content Component Scales:

- *A-trt$_1$* or Low Motivation (11 items): Feeling apathetic, unmotivated, hopeless, or unable to change or help self.
- *A-trt$_2$* or Inability to Disclose (8 items): Uncomfortable discussing personal information, feelings of shame and/or guilt, belief that others will not understand them, and unable to open up to others, including members of the helping professions.

CONTENT SCALES CORRELATES OF SEXUAL ABUSE

As was the case with the Standard Scales, elevations on some of the Content Scales were associated with a history of sexual abuse (Butcher & Williams, 2000; C. L. Williams et al., 1992). For boys in a clinical sample with a base rate of 16% for sexual abuse, elevations on *A-dep, A-ang, A-lse, A-fam,* and *A-sch* were associated with having a history of sexual abuse noted in their treatment records. For girls in a clinical sample with a base rate of 48% for sexual abuse, only *A-fam* was associated with having a history of sexual abuse noted in their treatment records. However, these associations cannot be used for suggesting a given individual has been abused (Butcher & Williams, 2000). Rather, as we indicated in Chapter 4, these associations should be used as a reminder to the clinician to include an evaluation of abuse in the evaluation, which we illustrate in Chapter 9.

MMPI–A Personality Psychopathology Five Scales

BACKGROUND

The Personality Psychopathology Five (PSY-5) Scales include five measures designed to assess the major dimensions of personality, also known as the "Big Five," using the MMPI–2 item pool (Harkness, 2009). The PSY-5 Scales are hypothesized to measure the major personality traits or psychological structures underlying enduring behavioral dispositions that are characteristic of human beings: Aggressiveness (*AGGR*), Psychoticism (*PSYC*), Disconstraint (*DISC*), Negative Emotionality/Neuroticism (*NEGE*), and Introversion/Low Positive Emotionality (*INTR*).

McNulty, Harkness, Ben-Porath, and Williams (1997) adapted the MMPI–2 PSY-5 Scales for adolescents following a rational-statistical approach. They initially used the 104 PSY-5 items from the MMPI–2 that also appeared in the MMPI–A booklet and used a group of 150 undergraduates to classify the items into the five personality constructs defining the PSY-5 Scales. The participants were next asked to review the other items on MMPI–A to determine if they appropriately related to any of the PSY-5 constructs. Twenty-five additional items were included in the measures. This preliminary set of MMPI–A PSY-5 Scales were then studied further to determine if they possessed both internal statistical and external validity using item analyses, reliability analysis, and factor analysis to assess their psychometric characteristics. The authors used the external validity data that had been collected by Williams and Butcher reported in the MMPI–A test manual to validate the MMPI–A scales for confirming the predictive validity of the PSY-5 measures.

The interpretation of the PSY-5 Scales evolved from both the original construct definitions developed by Harkness (1992; Harkness & McNulty, 1994) and from a number of construct validity studies with both the MMPI–2 PSY-5 Scales (e.g., Harkness, McNulty, & Ben-Porath, 1995) and the MMPI–A PSY-5 Scales (McNulty, Harkness, et al., 1997). High and moderate elevations on the PSY-5 Scales are defined the same as with the other MMPI–A scales in this chapter.

INTERPRETING THE *AGGR* SCALE

The PSY-5 Aggressiveness scale includes content dealing with instrumental aggression (i.e., aggression that is used to achieve one's goals). Adolescents may display

- intimidating or acting-out behaviors,
- assaultive or physical aggression, and
- sexual acting-out behaviors.

INTERPRETING THE *PSYC* SCALE

The Psychoticism scale addresses the test taker's possible disengagement or withdrawal from reality. Adolescents may show

- symptoms of sensory and perceptual distortions,
- unusual beliefs or thinking,
- withdrawn behaviors,
- bizarre behaviors, and
- delusions or other psychotic symptoms.

INTERPRETING THE *DISC* SCALE

High Disconstraint scores are associated with characteristics such as risk taking, impulsivity, and rejection of traditional moral values. These adolescents may have

- impulsive, acting-out, and irresponsible behaviors;
- possible history of drug use;
- possible sexual acting-out behaviors; and
- possible juvenile offenses.

INTERPRETING THE *NEGE* SCALE

The Negative Emotionality/Neuroticism scale assesses the tendency for adolescents to experience negative affect and internalizing behaviors. High-scoring adolescents tend to be

- worried and anxious,
- guilt prone, and
- withdrawn.

In addition, girls may have somatic complaints.

INTERPRETING THE *INTR* SCALE

The Introversion/Low Positive Emotionality scale is associated with an inability to experience positive emotions and to engage positively with others. Adolescents may have

- feelings of depression, including anhedonia;
- low achievement motivation; and
- few or no friends.

MMPI–A Item-Level Indicators

BACKGROUND

The use of specific item responses, also known as *critical items,* has been a useful approach for understanding what a given individual communicates as he or she responds to a personality measure such as the MMPI–A. The first use of item responses in personality assessment was by Woodworth (1920), who thought specific item responses, or *starred items* as he called them, could have special meaning in understanding the client. Woodworth got it right calling them starred items instead of critical items (Exhibit 5.2). Single items or small clusters of items are unreliable psychometric measures, and too much importance is attached to these items with the label "critical items." However, these items can highlight areas for follow-up when a young person endorses an item indicating, for example, suicidal ideation, illegal activities, eating problems, and the like.

In the original MMPI, several investigators developed item sets to focus on specific problem areas. Grayson (1951) made the first effort to incorporate individual item data into MMPI interpretation. Grayson selected his items rationally, simply by reading through the MMPI and selecting items he thought reflected important problem areas. Other more comprehensive and empirically derived items sets were published for the MMPI and then modified as necessary for MMPI–2 (e.g., Koss & Butcher, 1973; Lachar & Wrobel, 1979).

Forbey and Ben-Porath (1998) developed a set of item-level indicators specifically for adolescents because the MMPI–A contains many new adolescent-specific items that could address adolescent problems more directly. They used the MMPI–A normative sample and item responses from a clinical sample of 419 adolescents (288 boys and 131 girls) between 13 and 18 years. Initially they examined the endorsement frequencies of the clinical participants compared with the normative sample to highlight items that were likely focusing on adolescent problems. Next, they sent the potential problem area items to 11 practitioners who were familiar with the MMPI–A. The clinicians were asked to indicate

---

EXHIBIT 5.2

MMPI–A FAQ: Item-Level Indicators (aka "Critical Items")

How "critical" are the MMPI–A Critical Items?

Not very, if you know the meaning of the word *critical* (i.e., crucial, essential, dangerous, life threatening). For that reason, what others have labeled *MMPI–A "Critical Items"* we refer to in this book as the *MMPI–A item-level indicators.*

those items that they felt to be critical or that required the practitioner's attention. They also examined the items from the Koss–Butcher and Lachar–Wrobel MMPI–2 item lists and the new items from the MMPI–A list. Items judged to be relevant to problem assessment were placed into categories based on their content.

These item-level indicators are printed out in computer-scoring programs as a way to alert the practitioner to specific items the adolescent endorsed. These items could be followed up in clinical interview or used to clarify elevations on the Standard Scales (e.g., multiple endorsements of the items in the Hallucinatory Experiences, Paranoid Ideation, and Unusual Thinking categories may prove useful for interpreting *Pa* and *Sc* elevations).

LIST OF ITEM-LEVEL INDICATORS

There are 15 categories of item-level indicators on the MMPI–A, each with too few items to use as a scale:

- Aggression (3 items)
- Anxiety (6 items)
- Cognitive problems (3 items)
- Conduct problems (7 items)
- Depression (Includes suicidal ideation, 6 items)
- Eating problems (2 items)
- Family problems (5 items)
- Hallucinatory experiences (5 items)
- Paranoid ideation (9 items)
- School problems (5 items)
- Self-denigration (5 items)
- Sexual concerns (4 items)
- Somatic complaints (9 items)
- Substance use/abuse (9 items)
- Unusual thinking (5 items)

Chapter 9 illustrates how the item-level indicators can be helpful in planning a feedback session.

MMPI–A Supplementary Scales

Several additional or supplementary scales are included as part of an adolescent's MMPI–A scores. Figure 5.1 has Rachel's hand-scored profile for the Content Scales described above and the Supplementary Scales

FIGURE 5.1

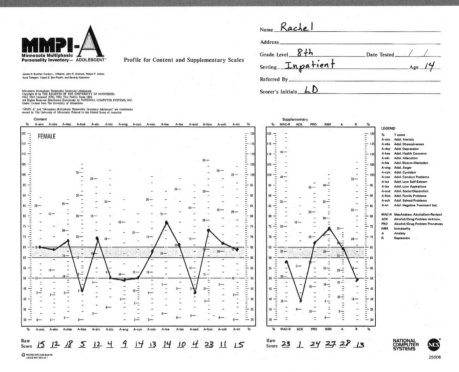

Rachel's hand-scored profile of Content and Supplementary Scales. Reproduced by permission of the University of Minnesota Press. All rights reserved. "Minnesota Multiphasic Personality Inventory®—Adolescent" and "MMPI®–A" are trademarks owned by the University of Minnesota.

described in this section. Remember Rachel's hand-scored profile of the Validity and Clinical Scales first presented in Chapter 3 (Figure 3.2, p. 41) and interpreted in Chapter 4 (pp. 60 and 80–81)? The first three scales on the supplementary profile in Figure 5.1 are the alcohol and drug problem scales. They are the most important to include as part of an adolescent's interpretation.

The next scale on the supplementary profile in Figure 5.1 is the Immaturity scale. It was developed during the MMPI Restandardization Project as a way of measuring Loevinger's (1976) concept of ego development using the MMPI–A item pool (Archer, 2005). The Welsh Anxiety (A) and Repression (R) scales come from the original MMPI and are essentially the first two factors to emerge from factor analyses of the MMPI Standard Scales (Butcher, Williams, et al., 1992; Welsh, 1956). These scales, largely used for research, will not be described further in this chapter.

MacANDREW ALCOHOLISM SCALE

Background

MacAndrew (1965) developed his scale (*MAC* on MMPI; *MAC–R* on MMPI–2 and MMPI–A) to discriminate between alcohol-abusing patients and general psychiatric patients who were not substance abusers. This scale has been substantially evaluated and found to discriminate well between alcoholic and nonalcoholic patients in adults (e.g., Craig, 2005). The *MAC* scale was also found to be successful in assessing adolescents (e.g., Andrucci, Archer, Pancoast, & Gordon, 1989; Wolfson & Erbaugh, 1984). When the MMPI was revised in the 1980s, the *MAC* scale was considered to be sufficiently valid and useful that it was revised to become a part of the MMPI–2. The revised version of the MacAndrew scale for MMPI–2 and MMPI–A includes four new items to replace four of the original items that were dropped in the test because they contained objectionable content (Butcher, Graham, Williams, & Ben-Porath, 1989). *MAC–R* has been shown to be a useful assessment measure for use with adolescents (e.g., Gallucci, 1997; Micucci, 2002).

Interpreting MAC–R

Moderate elevations on *MAC–R* (*T* scores between 60 and 64) should be considered as possibly indicating a pattern of stimulus-seeking behaviors that put the adolescent at risk for substance abuse problems. Those who attain *MAC–R* scores equal or greater than 65 *T* have a stronger probability of developing substance problems given their personality features of stimulus seeking. Because this is an empirically derived scale, interpretive statement should reflect a greater probability that the young person has personality characteristics of individuals who develop alcohol- and drug-related problems and

- may be at risk for developing problems of addiction,
- may have already developed problems with alcohol and other drug use, and
- are likely to engage in risk-taking and stimulus-seeking behaviors.

ALCOHOL/DRUG PROBLEM PRONENESS SCALE

Background

The *PRO* scale was developed empirically by contrasting groups of adolescents in drug and alcohol treatment with adolescents who were in general psychiatric treatment settings (Weed, Butcher, & Williams, 1994). The 34 items included on the *PRO* scale empirically differentiated adolescents in alcohol or drug treatment from those in mental health treatment. Therefore, the methods of deriving the *PRO* scale were similar to those used in the development of the original version of *MAC*. However, adolescent samples and an expanded item pool covering adolescent behaviors resulted in a scale with different item content than *MAC–R*. The *PRO* scale is a useful assessment measure for identifying adolescents who have personality features that put them at risk for alcohol and other drug use problems (e.g., Gallucci, 1997; Micucci, 2002; Stein & Graham, 2001, 2005).

Not surprisingly, given that *MAC–R* was developed with adults and *PRO* was developed with adolescents, the interpretive statements differ somewhat. Both scales identify individuals with personality characteristics associated with a greater probability of the development of alcohol or drug use problems (e.g., risk taking and stimulus seeking). However, as is apparent below, the *PRO* scale measures features more likely in adolescents with alcohol and drug problems (e.g., being in a negative peer group, family and school problems).

Interpreting PRO

As with all the other MMPI–A scales, there are two levels for interpretation: moderate and high scores. An adolescent who attains a moderate elevation on *PRO* should be considered as possibly having substance use problems or at risk for developing them; higher elevations suggest a stronger likelihood of problems or their development. The content of the items on *PRO* suggests other interpretive statements as well, including

- negative peer group influences,
- stimulus-seeking and risk-taking behaviors,
- friction with parents,
- behavior problems at school, and
- poor judgment.

ALCOHOL/DRUG PROBLEM ACKNOWLEDGMENT SCALE

Background

The *ACK* scale is a content-based measure designed to assess how willing an adolescent is to acknowledge alcohol or other drug use (Weed et al., 1994). It was developed using a combined rational/empirical test development strategy. Items were selected that recorded the adolescent's acknowledged involvement with alcohol or other drugs. Next, the items were correlated with the entire item pool to determine if there were other items that were empirically associated with these behaviors. Items were kept on the scale when they improved discrimination between non–substance abusers and substance abusers. The scale was cross-validated using additional samples. As in the *PRO* scale, the *ACK* scale has been found to be an effective measure since its initial development (e.g., Gallucci, 1997; Micucci, 2002; Stein & Graham, 2001, 2005).

Interpreting ACK

Like other content-based measures, the higher the elevation on the *ACK* scale, the more behaviors the adolescent has endorsed that are consistent with those who have alcohol and other drug problems. Descriptors include

- openly acknowledged alcohol, marijuana, or other drug use;
- problems such as fighting when using;
- relying on alcohol or other drugs in social situations;
- others have commented on their problem use; and
- reports of having bad habits.

What Rachel's Content and Supplementary Scales Add to Her MMPI–A Interpretation

When we left Rachel at the end of Chapter 4, we had some unanswered questions about how to refine the interpretation of her extreme elevation on the *Pd* Clinical Scale and more modest elevations on *Pa* and *Sc*. One thing that leaps off the page of her Content Scales profile (Figure 5.1) is her willingness to tell us how badly she feels given her high elevations on *A-lse* and *A-dep* and moderate elevations on *A-anx* and *A-obs*. Her acting-out problems must be considered in the context of her internalizing symptoms as well. Rachel reports feeling badly, is uncertain about her future, and likely worries. She may have thoughts about suicide or dying. Her problems occur in the two major settings of the adolescent's world: home and school. She has no one she can trust (see *A-aln* descriptors), and it will be a challenge for the clinician trying to establish a therapeutic relationship with her (moderate elevation on *A-trt*). Her elevations on *A-aln* and *A-dep* combined with her average score on *A-biz* suggest that her *Pa* and *Sc* scores may be more related to content reflecting alienation, despair, impulsivity, and risk taking rather than florid psychotic symptoms.

Although willing to admit to internalizing problems and significant behavior problems at home and school, Rachel endorsed only one item on *ACK*, despite achieving a high elevation on *PRO* (Figure 5.1). This indicates that she denies problematic alcohol and other drug use but has personality and behavioral characteristics associated with adolescents in substance abuse treatment units. Some of these characteristics are also correlates of her other MMPI–A scale elevations (e.g., risk taking, sensation seeking, family and school problems). An assessment of possible substance abuse problems is indicated. Rachel's elevation on *PRO* can be used in a feedback session to begin a discussion of her use of alcohol and other drugs in a nonthreatening way. Chapter 9 describes how MMPI–A feedback sessions can be used for further information gathering and illustrates these techniques with another adolescent, Kayla.

In the event that the practitioner plans to incorporate a clinical diagnosis in his or her clinical report, then information related to the possibility that Rachael shows poor impulse control, acting-out behavior, and anger control problems that are reflected in the Clinical Scale elevations, especially *Pd*, should be used. For example, the clinical diagnosis of one of the disruptive behavior or conduct disorders should be considered. Further assessment of her alcohol or other drug use could result in one of the substance-related disorders.

The impulsivity and poor judgment Rachel acknowledged on the MMPI–A scales should figure prominently in any treatment planning. She may be a poor candidate for traditional, insight-oriented psychotherapy given the personality characteristics associated with her prominent scale elevations. The practitioner might consider behavior therapy that includes clearly stated contingencies that need to be consistently followed if behavior change is to be expected. Such a behavioral approach might prove useful in the school setting as well. Her intense negative feelings may actually serve as a motivator for change despite her likely belief that change or improvement is not possible. Symptom relief of her depressive and anxious feelings, perhaps through a cognitive–behavioral approach, might be helpful. In addition, consideration of the high level of family discord should be considered in any treatment planning as well.

To Finish or Not to Finish Scoring

This concludes our discussion of Rachel's MMPI–A interpretation because her clinician did not score any of the other MMPI–A scales and indicators included in this chapter. Recall in the last chapter that her Harris–Lingoes and *Si* subscales were not scored either. As we mentioned earlier, hand-scoring the MMPI–A is a time-consuming process, so some clinicians choose not to score all the scales, subscales, component scales, or the item-level indicators that we recommend for interpretation. Although the reader probably wants to know how Rachel's MMPI–A interpretation would be informed if these other measures were available, this case illustration demonstrates a real-world application of the instrument, with only some of the MMPI–A measures available for interpretation.

We use our preferred method, computer-scored MMPI–A protocols, for seven cases in the rest of this book (Iliya in Chapter 6; Emily, Jeremy, Tyler, and Grace in Chapter 7; José in Chapter 8; and Kayla in Chapter 9). One additional case, Joseph in Chapter 6, is also hand-scored, but his clinician scored the PSY-5 Scales. Stay tuned to see these final eight cases demonstrating how all the measures covered so far are integrated into MMPI–A interpretations.

Globalization of the MMPI–A
Making Culturally Inclusive Interpretations

6

Our lives are all different and yet the same.

—*entry from Thursday, 6 July, 1944 in*
The Diary of a Young Girl *(Frank, 1947/1993, p. 255)*

When 15-year-old Anne Frank wrote that observation in her diary, she and seven others had been hiding from the Gestapo for 2 years. She was comparing herself with the two other adolescents who hid in the cramped Secret Annex, her sister Margot and her confidant Peter (with whom she had shared her first kiss in April). Anne's full statement began with "We all live with the object of being happy" (1947/1993, p. 255). Her diary entry went on to describe similar cultural backgrounds of the three adolescents living in the Secret Annex, including being brought up in "good circles" with opportunities for learning and reason to hope for much happiness. Within a month of this diary entry, the possibilities for future happiness ended with the capture of the eight people hiding in the Annex and the deaths of all in Nazi concentration camps except Anne's father Otto.

Anne's statement exemplifies the complexity of the task facing psychologists evaluating adolescents from different ethnic, language, religious, or cultural backgrounds. It is reminiscent of emic and etic approaches to understanding cultural influences on personality and behavior (see descriptions in Cheung, 2009; Triandis, 2007). An *emic* understanding assumes uniqueness within each cultural group (we are different), whereas an *etic* approach assumes attributes that can be found in most, if not all, cultures (we are the same).

The MMPI instruments are examples of etic personality measures that have been widely researched and used around the world. An emic approach to assessing personality uses indigenous personality theories and measures. Cheung (2009, p. 52) provided descriptions of Asian indigenous personality constructs that focus on "the relational nature of human experience in a social and interpersonal context." The concepts of "harmony" or "face" in China (Cheung, 2009) and of "*amae*" or "sweet indulgence" or "indulgent dependency" in Japan (Cheung, 2009; Triandis, 2007) are examples of emic personality constructs.

Both etic and emic principles are important for understanding personality and behavior across cultures. However, as Cheung (2009) pointed out, cross-cultural validation of the international versions of the MMPI–2 (and MMPI–A) provides clinicians in other countries access to the research database accumulated on the MMPI instruments. This, in turn, results in psychological assessments based in scientific studies that would be difficult to match if only indigenous tools were used in different cultures (Cheung, 2009). Before turning to a discussion of the international use of the MMPI–A, we begin this chapter by returning to the conceptual framework presented in Chapter 1 for understanding a young person's personality and behavior. We will see the importance of considering both emic and etic factors when conducting psychological assessments across cultures.

Different, Same, Emic, Etic Understandings of Adolescence

The conceptual framework emphasizing the importance of individual, family, peer, school, community, and societal influences on adolescents is described in Chapter 1 (see Figure 1.1, p. 8). Regardless of culture, these overarching influences are likely important across many, if not all, populations (i.e., they are etic constructs). However, in this section, we describe how they can vary across populations, thereby providing emic examples of differences in how these universal influences may vary across cultures. Because the MMPI–A is used to assess behavioral and psychological problems, our overview focuses primarily on the potential for negative outcomes. However, the reader is reminded to consider the positive aspects in the young person's cultural background in the evaluation. Good nutrition, prenatal and well-child medical care, supportive religious communities, and a global community connected by technology are but a few examples of positive cultural influences that may vary by community.

Recall that the individual-level influences are represented by the picture in Chapter 1 of the adolescent in the center of Figure 1.1 (p. 8). Brain growth and development during adolescence was one of the individual-level influences described in Chapter 1. These processes can be affected by factors such as inadequate nutrition, lead poisoning, viral encephalitis, or cerebral malaria—examples of problems with higher probabilities of occurrence in some geographic areas or populations than others. Refugees or migrants from the developing world may have greater exposure to these types of problems (for more details, see Westermeyer, Williams, & Nguyen, 1991; C. L. Williams & Westermeyer, 1983, 1986).

As we indicated in Chapter 1, family influences are not limited to mainstream notions of family as two-parent households. The amount of influence of various family members can differ across cultural or ethnic groups. For example, patterns of internal migrations can either enhance or disrupt family relations in some minority groups (e.g., the tendency for some American Indian adolescents to move between living in the city with one set of family members and on the reservation with another set; this also affects school or educational influences). In addition, some migrations produce large numbers of unaccompanied minors with their special needs and considerations (Westermeyer et al., 1991; C. L. Williams & Westermeyer, 1983, 1986). In contrast, the strong bonds in extended families in some cultures can enhance adolescent development by providing other adults to share in supervising and supporting the young person when parents cannot be available.

Acculturation, or the process groups and individuals go through when they come into contact with another culture, and the sometimes accompanying acculturative stress (popularly called culture shock; see C. L. Williams & Berry, 1991), can be a factor in understanding family dynamics with minority adolescents. Intergenerational conflicts may be an issue. This can occur when adolescents adopt the new or dominant culture's mores at the same time older family members are trying to maintain traditional values and behaviors (Westermeyer et al., 1991; C. L. Williams & Westermeyer, 1983, 1986).

Compulsory education is a universal experience for adolescents in developed countries around the world, with a trend toward increasing the minimum age for quitting school (16 years in the United States). Refugees and other migrants to developed countries may come from societies in which schooling was not accessible because of military conflicts or extreme poverty. The degree of rote learning, active classroom participation, expectations about parental involvement, and even the quality of the school can differ significantly across cultures or even communities or cities within the same geographic area. The growth of home-schooling is another example of diversity in compulsory education in the United States.

Many school environments bring together adolescents from different cultures, thus providing opportunities for peer group relations across cultures. These can be positive or negative interactions that can have parental approval or disapproval. Adolescents wanting to fit in with a peer group with the dominant culture's norms can cause tensions in the family. Clothing choices, dating, and time spent outside the home are examples of potential sources of conflicts between family members with traditional values and a young person's attempts to fit in with peers.

Anne Frank's diary gives us insights into the powerful community and society influences on her development from her 13th birthday until she turned 15 and was captured by the Nazis. Her diary starts with her life as a German immigrant in Amsterdam, attending a segregated Jewish school, before the Nazi occupation of the Netherlands. Her community becomes severely constricted when she and her family, along with four others, go into hiding in the Secret Annex, helped by a handful of former employees of Otto Frank. These former employees, and a radio, keep the eight residents of the Annex informed about the larger society in occupied Amsterdam and the various battles of the Allied Forces and the Germans. Anne's diary entries reflect her psychological reactions to the influences of this small community of individuals and the broader societal context of life of a young Jewish girl in hiding during World War II.

Community and societal influences can have either positive or negative impacts on adolescent and parenting behaviors that must be considered in a psychological evaluation (refer to Chapter 1 for more information). Anne Frank's life illustrates an extreme set of circumstances not experienced by the majority of psychologists practicing today in countries like the United States. However, there are minority groups in other cultures who come to the attention of psychologists who have been exposed to horrific stressors, such as ethnic genocide in Rwanda or the former Yugoslavia; female genital mutilation (i.e., partial or total removal of or other injuries to external female genitalia for nonmedical reasons)[1]; or the experiences of refugees fleeing from Cambodia, Laos, or Somalia, to mention a few examples. In addition, stressors like prejudice against members of ethnic or religious minorities, poverty, homelessness, violence, and crime are more frequent examples of community or societal influences that may be particularly salient for some minority adolescents.

---

[1]Go to the World Health Organization website (http://www.who.int/topics/female_genital_mutilation/en/) for further information.

Learning About Other Cultures

The key to conducting useful psychological evaluations across cultures is to understand how the similar influences on adolescent personality and behavior illustrated in Figure 1.1 (p. 8) have differing manifestations across cultures, languages, religions, and ethnic groups. It is important for psychologists to be aware of the factors in a person's background that can influence the results of a psychological evaluation. Assessment procedures must be tailored to provide fair and accurate appraisals when circumstances require an evaluation.

When working with any client, psychologists must seek out information about how the influences may be expressed differently in the young person's culture. Reading about the person's culture of origin, talking with knowledgeable individuals, and asking questions about these influences, rather than making assumptions based on one's own experiences, are ways to become more culturally sensitive.

There are a number of resources available for obtaining culturally relevant information regarding a given individual's background:

- A basic information source about the country of origin for a recent arrival to the United States or other country is the online *World Factbook* of the Central Intelligence Agency (https://www.cia.gov/library/publications/the-world-factbook/index.html). It includes detailed demographic information about 266 countries, including population characteristics (e.g., age, religion, ethnicities), major health issues (e.g., life expectancy, morbidity/mortality, prevalence of HIV, major infectious diseases), education (e.g., literacy, school life expectancy), government, history, geography, economy, communication, transportation, military, and transnational issues.
- Searches of the psychological literature can be conducted using keywords such as acculturation, American Indians, Native Americans, Asian Americans (as well as specific groups such as Koreans, Chinese, Japanese, Lao, Hmong, Vietnamese, Khmer, Cambodian), assimilation, cross-cultural, cross-cultural generalizability, cultural equivalence, diversity, ethnic minorities, ethnocentrism, Hispanics (as well as specific groups such as Chicanos, Mexican, Hondurans, Puerto Ricans), immigrants, intergenerational conflicts, migrants, multicultural, nomothetic/idiographic, psychometric equivalence, translators, translations, and refugees.
- Several books published by the American Psychological Association provide relevant discussion and information about the cultural factors in personality assessment (e.g., Butcher, Cabiya, Lucio, & Garrido, 2007; Hays, 2001, 2008; Phelps, 2009).

- Community or religious leaders can provide information about cultural differences and/or concerns facing the particular minority group.

- Psychologists can observe how members of the community greet each other. Gestures such as handshakes or maintaining eye contract are not universal. Touching certain parts of the body (e.g., the head) or pointing the feet at someone during an interview can be seen as rude or disrespectful in some cultural groups.

- Teachers can explain about diversity issues at school and in the classrooms. Especially useful may be English as a Second Language instructors. Observations at the school of the individual adolescent, as well as of the overall environment, can provide information about how accepting the school is of its minority students.

- Psychologists can attend cultural celebrations in the community. Some are public events (e.g., Chinese, Japanese, or Hmong New Years; Cinco de Mayo; Juneteenth); others are private and require an invitation (e.g., Bar or Bat Mitzvah celebrations; Eid Ul-Fitr, the Festival of Breaking the Fast at the end of Ramadan).

- Home visits can be quite helpful in understanding the young person's daily life. Although this might not be feasible for all clients, if a psychologist is seeing a number of patients from a particular minority community, a few visits to some of their homes will likely give a better sense of their circumstances than no visits at all. Discussions with social workers can also be useful. C. L. Williams (1987) provided a case illustration of a home visit.

- Take a language class. Believe it or not, this can be useful even if you drop out! One of the current authors, Carolyn L. Williams, is a dropout from a Hmong language class after being unable to hear, let alone reproduce, the tonal differences in Hmong. However, the experience provided a stark illustration of how different English and Hmong are, as well as the difficulties facing refugees and others in the United States from language backgrounds vastly different from English.

- Ask questions of the young person and his or her family members about their background. Avoid making assumptions. Be humble. You will learn new things about their culture and experiences.

As we will discover in the rest of this chapter, the MMPI–A can be a useful part of a psychological evaluation of a young person from a diverse background. Appendix A includes a section of references on the use of the MMPI–A across cultures and ethnic groups. The recognition of the utility of the MMPI across cultures came early in its history in the post–World War II period with efforts to translate the instrument for use by psychologists in other countries, including Cuba, Italy, Germany, and Japan (Butcher & Williams, 2009). Despite its widespread use in other countries, questions have been raised about the utility of the MMPI instruments with minority populations in the United States (e.g., Dana, 2005; Hays, 2001). In the last sections of this chapter, we cover how the MMPI–A can be used with adolescents from diverse backgrounds living in the United States. First, we describe its use internationally.

International Applications of the MMPI–A

In the decades that followed the 1950s and the MMPI developments in Cuba, Italy, Germany, and Japan, more than 150 translations of the original MMPI were made (for more information, see Butcher, 1996, 2004, 2005b; Butcher, Cheung, & Lim, 2003; Butcher, Derksen, Sloore, & Sirigatti, 2003; Butcher, Tsai, Coelho, & Nezami, 2006; Butcher & Williams, 2009; Farias, Duran, & Gomez-Maqueo, 2003; Quevedo & Butcher, 2005). By the time of the completion of the MMPI Restandardization Project for adults in 1989, the revised test, the MMPI–2, rapidly became the most widely used personality measure worldwide. One of the constructive international developments after the publication of the MMPI–2 in the United States was the consolidation of competing translations in various countries with one version. For example, in Japan there were 15 competing translations of the original MMPI. But, in a study concurrent with the Restandardization Project (i.e., Shiota, Krauss, & Clark, 1996), a single version of the MMPI–2 for Japan was developed (Butcher & Williams, 2009). Worldwide there are now more than 33 translations of the MMPI–2 in use today.

The impetus for this expansion of the MMPI–2 outside the United States was, in part, the expansion of applied psychology as a profession in other countries. As clinical psychology developed, practitioners wanted a useful assessment instrument. They found that the MMPI scales and interpretive research base, when appropriately translated and adapted, worked as well for describing patients in their countries as it did in the United States. Exhibit 6.1 provides a brief answer to a FAQ about the techniques necessary to ensure an appropriate adaptation of the MMPI instruments. As Exhibit 6.1 reveals, an adequate adaptation is not simply having an interpreter read MMPI–A items to a young person or one person attempting to write a translation. Useful adaptations, as with its parent instruments the MMPI–2 and MMPI–A, are developed through careful research procedures summarized in Exhibit 6.1. In a later section in this chapter, we describe some of these research techniques used in the development of a Hispanic version of the MMPI–A used in the United States (Butcher, Cabiya, et al., 1998).

EXHIBIT 6.1

MMPI–A FAQs: Adapting the MMPI–A Across Languages and Cultures

---

How do you determine whether a translated version of the MMPI–A is equivalent to the original MMPI–A?
There are four primary types of equivalence to be established when adapting the MMPI–A across cultures: linguistic, construct, psychological, and psychometric. Various research procedures are used to establish the equivalence of a translated version of the MMPI–A to the original.

What is linguistic equivalence?
Linguistic equivalence determines whether test items address the same qualities or characteristics in the target culture as in the source culture. The linguistic characteristics of an item include vocabulary, idioms, and grammatical structure. In order to assure accuracy, multiple independent translators who are bilingual and experienced in both cultures are used. For example, a back translation check requires a translation of the original MMPI–A into the target language. A different translator then translates the target language version back into English. The translators and an MMPI–A expert work together to resolve any differences in how individual items are translated.

What is construct equivalence?
Construct equivalence refers to similarity of the concepts being conveyed in both versions of the test. Construct equivalence or conceptual equivalence indicates that the personality variables or characteristics being assessed in the test address the same factors in both the source culture and the target culture. Bilingual test–retest procedures are helpful to establish construct equivalence. In these studies, samples of bilingual individuals take one version of the MMPI–A at one time and the other version within a week or two to determine if the original produces the same pattern of scores as the translated version.

What is psychological equivalence?
Psychological equivalence assures that the meaning of test items is familiar to real life experiences in both the target and source cultures. Psychological equivalence is established with cross-cultural validation studies (e.g., does the translated version differentiate between psychiatric and general population samples; do depressed patients in the target population score high on Scale 2 or *A-dep*?). Clinical case studies can also provide support for the psychological equivalence of a translated version.

Psychometric equivalence indicates whether the test or a given scale possesses similar psychometric properties across different cultures. For example, various psychometric studies are used to determine whether comparable reliability, item–scale correlations, item endorsement frequencies, interitem correlations, interscale correlations, and factor structure exist.

Note. See Butcher et al. (2006) and Cheung (2009) for more information.

When an appropriately adapted version of the test is administered, comparability of the MMPI and MMPI–2 Clinical Scales in assessing clinical problems is often demonstrated. For example, Butcher (1996) demonstrated that MMPI profiles for a single diagnostic group (paranoid schizophrenia) from several different countries—the United States,

Italy, Chile, Thailand, China, and India—produced highly similar profile patterns regardless of language or the country (i.e., an 8-6/6-8 code type). A study of patients diagnosed with paranoid schizophrenia in Japan (Hayama, Oguchi, & Shinkai, 1999) showed the same MMPI–2 code type, providing further support for the cross-cultural generalizability of the test. These studies are examples of how psychological and psychometric equivalence (Exhibit 6.1) can be demonstrated.

Such consistency in responding to MMPI–2 and MMPI–A items is not surprising given that disorders such as schizophrenia also tend to show similar rates across cultures (Westermeyer, 1991). Indeed, a descriptive study of over 17,000 patients from 37 countries in Asia, Europe, South America, Africa, and the Middle East reported striking similarities in symptoms and the response of patients to most measures in the study, despite the inherent regional diversity in patients and health care systems (Karagianis et al., 2009). Keep in mind, however, that rates for some psychiatric problems such as substance abuse or posttraumatic stress disorder can vary cross-culturally when the precipitating factors vary (i.e., the availability of alcohol or drugs in the culture or the prerequisite significant stressful life experiences, respectively).

Like its predecessors the MMPI and the MMPI–2, the MMPI–A has been widely studied in other cultures. Some have included

- Chile (e.g., Vinet & Alarcon, 2003; Vinet & Gomez-Maqueo, 2005),
- China (e.g., Cheung & Ho, 1997),
- Holland (e.g., Derksen, Ven Dijk, & Cornelissen, 2003),
- Italy (e.g., Sirigatti, 2000),
- Mexico (e.g., Lucio-Gomez, Ampudia-Rueda, Duran-Patino, Gallegos-Mejia, & Leon-Guzman, 1999), and
- Russia (Atlis, 2004).

Lucio and her colleagues have provided support for the adaptability of the MMPI–A as a self-report personality measure across language and countries. Lucio, Hernandez-Cervantes, Duran, and Butcher (2010) studied the application of MMPI–A norms for 13-year-olds. They found that younger adolescents, if they read well enough to comprehend the items, provide profiles that can be interpreted. Moreover, they found that adolescents in Mexico produce test scores that are highly similar to those of the MMPI–A normative sample (Butcher, Williams, et al., 1992).

A multinational case study (Butcher et al., 2000) examined the applicability of the computer-based Adolescent Interpretive System of the Minnesota Report (Butcher & Williams, 1992b, 2007; see Chapter 7 for a detailed description of computerized MMPI–A interpretations and the Minnesota Report). Adolescent patients from 15 countries (i.e., Greece, Israel, Korea, France, Hong Kong, Thailand, Netherlands, Spain, Italy, Norway, Mexico, Peru, United Kingdom, South Africa, and Russia) were evaluated with the MMPI–A, and their answer sheets were used to produce the Minnesota Report. Clinical practitioners from each country provided a detailed case description of their clients. The patients' Minnesota Reports were then sent to the practitioners, who were asked to compare the computer-generated narrative report with the information they collected about the young persons. In general, this group of clinicians indicated that the Minnesota Report interpretations, based on American norms and interpretive statements, accurately reflected their clients' MMPI–A profiles and were useful resources for their evaluations. Several of the practitioners reported using the Minnesota Reports in feedback sessions with their clients (see Chapter 9).

Illustration of an International Case From Russia

PRESENTING COMPLAINT

Iliya, a 16-year-old boy, was admitted to an inpatient treatment unit at a regional psychiatric hospital subsequent to his sexual assault of an 8-year-old boy on his way home from school (Iliya forced the boy to perform fellatio). It was a voluntary admission, and the local authorities declined to pursue criminal charges against him. Instead, the detective recommended he see a psychiatrist. This was Iliya's first psychiatric, psychological, or neurological evaluation.

BACKGROUND INFORMATION

When Iliya was 8 years old, he experienced a similar sexual assault by a teenage boy. This assault happened in the presence of several boys from his school. It was not reported at the time to his family or others. Iliya described four other assaults over the intervening years involving adolescent boys, oral sex, and beatings in which he was the victim, an observer, or a participant in the beatings. Iliya reported that "everyone was doing it and they did the same to me." His motivations for the assault on the young boy included anger, a desire to cause suffering to another similar to what he had experienced, and wanting to prove that he was no longer a victim.

When he saw the young boy he assaulted at school, Iliya reported feeling shame and fear that his peer group would learn details about the incident. When the young boy told his mother, she reported the assault to the police, and eventually it became known among Iliya's peer group.

According to Iliya, his friends became hostile and stopped talking to him. In response, he transferred to another school.

His grades in school are below average to average, although he reports loving to read. An interview with one of his teachers indicates difficulties with concentration, poor memory, delayed cognitive abilities, oversensitivity, and irritability. Although he can be rude to his teachers, behavior problems were not seen to be overly prominent.

Iliya lives near Magadan, one of the 46 *oblasts* (regions) in the Russian Federation, located in Siberia on the Sea of Okhotsk. Magadan is isolated, has a harsh subarctic climate, and is sparsely populated (estimated at 169,000 in 2007; ArcticStat, 2009). The region was part of Stalin's system of gulags—forced labor camps—used to mine gold discovered there and build infrastructure (Paxton, 2009). The city of Magadan, founded officially in 1939, served as a transport hub to the gulags until after Stalin's death in 1953. The "Mask of Sorrow" monument, unveiled in 1996, commemorates these victims. Typical of many provinces outside of central Russia, in the 1990s the region's economy suffered after the breakup of the Soviet Union, resulting in extreme poverty and population loss (Bloch & Kendall, 2004). Among the significant social changes that occurred during this time were increased openness to discussion of social problems and greater international travel and cooperation—public and international discussion of Iiya's situation would have been impossible several years prior. As a further testament to the global reach of the MMPI instruments, Mera Atlis, the developer of the Russian version of the MMPI–A, is a former resident of Magadan who completed her doctoral work at the University of Minnesota with dissertation research on the cross-cultural equivalency of a Russian translation of the MMPI–A (Atlis, 2004). Iliya's case study was included previously in Butcher et al. (2000).[2]

FAMILY HISTORY

Iliya lives alone with his mother. She worked as a clerk but was laid off recently. His father, who has a history of alcohol abuse, left the region 2 years ago and has had no contact with them. The father was physically and verbally abusive. Iliya's older brother and two younger sisters moved to his maternal grandmother's home near St. Petersburg. Iliya would like to join them. However, his grandmother told him that he could not live with her because of his poor behavior.

---

[2]Demographic information and some of the assessment details in this case and the next one in this chapter (Joseph), as well as in others throughout the book, were altered for privacy and didactic purposes. In addition, the Minnesota Report included here was scored using the second edition of the *Minnesota Report: Adolescent Interpretive System*, revised in 2007 by Butcher and Williams.

During the intake sessions, Iliya's mother made no mention of any problems she had with alcohol abuse. However, as the hospitalization progressed, staff learned of her positive history of alcohol abuse, including during her pregnancy with Iliya. A developmental delay, possibly due to fetal alcohol syndrome, was among his diagnoses after psychological and neurological evaluations.

BEHAVIORAL OBSERVATIONS, TEST ADMINISTRATION, AND SCORING

Iliya's appearance is more like that of an 11-year-old than his 16 years. He tends to speak reluctantly, hesitates, gets ashamed, and hides his eyes. His mood is somewhat low and anxious. In his conversations with staff, he maintains emotional control, but he can be irritable in interactions with other patients. He appears to have difficulty talking about himself, which is often expressed in nervous body movements. It is possible to talk about personal issues with Iliya but only for brief periods of time, or he becomes visibly tense and nervous.

Iliya was administered the Russian version of the MMPI–A within the first week of his admission. He completed it in approximately 60 minutes. Administration was spread over two supervised sessions. He worked quietly in a small testing room near the unit. The computerized Minnesota Report was used to process Iliya's responses to the MMPI–A. Figure 6.1 contains the first 11 pages of Iliya's 16-page Minnesota Report. As with the other Minnesota Reports in the remaining chapters of this book, the missing pages in Iliya's report contain items that are not reproduced here to prevent distribution of MMPI–A item content to nonqualified users. For space reasons, the printout of each adolescent's responses to every MMPI–A item is not reproduced either.

DISCUSSION: ILIYA'S MMPI–A INTERPRETATION

Iliya produced a valid MMPI–A profile showing no signs of reading difficulties and exaggerated or defensive responding. Unlike the observations from interviews about his difficulties in talking about himself, Iliya was able to reveal significant problems on the MMPI–A. Staff in the residential treatment facility found striking similarities in the narrative section of the Minnesota Report and their observations from interviews and other records about his significant conduct problems and antisocial behaviors.

Exploration of the focus of his reports of intense family problems (*A-fam*) would be helpful in deciding on a future placement. An area that had not yet come to the attention of the treatment staff was the likelihood of significant problems with alcohol or other drugs given his

FIGURE 6.1

MMPI-A
Minnesota Multiphasic
Personality Inventory— ADOLESCENT™

Inpatient Mental Health Interpretive Report

MMPI-A™

The Minnesota Report™: Adolescent Interpretive System, 2nd Edition

James N. Butcher, PhD, & Carolyn L. Williams, PhD

ID Number:	Iliya
Age:	16
Gender:	Male
Date Assessed:	12/10/2010

PEARSON

PsychCorp

FIGURE 6.1 *(Continued)*

MMPI-A™ Inpatient Mental Health Interpretive Report   ID: Iliya
12/10/2010, Page 2

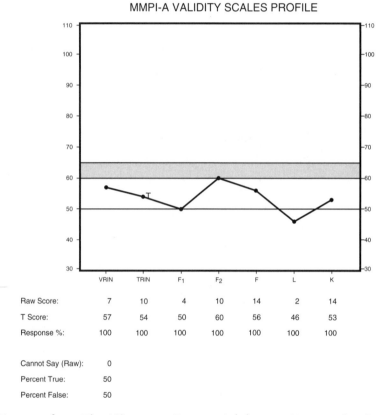

MMPI-A VALIDITY SCALES PROFILE

	VRIN	TRIN	F₁	F₂	F	L	K
Raw Score:	7	10	4	10	14	2	14
T Score:	57	54	50	60	56	46	53
Response %:	100	100	100	100	100	100	100

Cannot Say (Raw):   0
Percent True: 50
Percent False: 50

Excerpts from *The Minnesota Report: Adolescent Interpretive System*
(Rev. ed.), by Butcher and Williams, 2007.

elevation on *ACK* (Alcohol/Drug Problem Acknowledgment) and moderate elevation on *MAC–R* (MacAndrew Alcoholism Scale—Revised), described in the Diagnostic Considerations section of the narrative portion of the Minnesota Report in Figure 6.1. After review of Iliya's Minnesota Report, his primary therapist began to inquire about his alcohol and other drug use history. Iliya revealed he began smoking cigarettes

FIGURE 6.1 *(Continued)*

MMPI-A™ Inpatient Mental Health Interpretive Report 12/10/2010, Page 3

ID: Iliya

MMPI-A CLINICAL AND SUPPLEMENTARY SCALES PROFILE

	Hs	D	Hy	Pd	Mf	Pa	Pt	Sc	Ma	Si		MAC-R	ACK	PRO	IMM	A	R
Raw Score:	6	24	23	32	21	13	13	33	24	26		26	8	20	16	18	13
T Score:	47	58	54	78	49	50	44	60	54	50		61	67	58	54	55	49
Response %:	100	100	100	100	100	100	100	100	100	100		100	100	100	100	100	100

Welsh Code: 4'+8-2<u>39</u> <u>60/5</u>17: FK/L:

Mean Profile Elevation: 55.6

Excerpts from *The Minnesota Report: Adolescent Interpretive System* (Rev. ed.), by Butcher and Williams, 2007.

around age 7 as a way of coping with his interpersonal issues. His first full drink of alcohol was shortly thereafter; prior to that he would take sips from adults' beverages. He described a period between fifth and seventh grades of significant inhalant use, specifically glue, resulting in delirium with visual hallucinations. He reportedly stopped inhalant use because of concerns about what his peers would think. He endorsed the

FIGURE 6.1 (Continued)

MMPI-A™ Inpatient Mental Health Interpretive Report   **ID: Iliya**
12/10/2010, Page 4

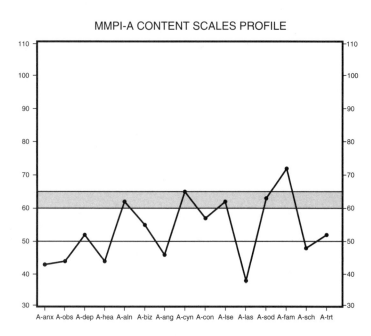

MMPI-A CONTENT SCALES PROFILE

	A-anx	A-obs	A-dep	A-hea	A-aln	A-biz	A-ang	A-cyn	A-con	A-lse	A-las	A-sod	A-fam	A-sch	A-trt
Raw Score:	5	5	9	4	10	6	7	18	13	9	2	14	22	6	11
T Score:	43	44	52	44	62	55	46	65	57	62	38	63	72	48	52
Response %:	100	100	100	100	100	100	100	100	100	100	100	100	100	100	100

Excerpts from *The Minnesota Report: Adolescent Interpretive System* (Rev. ed.), by Butcher and Williams, 2007.

MMPI–A item about excessive use of alcohol. Drinking was a factor during several of the sexual assault episodes. Currently, he denies other drug use, although this is now a factor in his clinical picture that the treatment staff plans to monitor.

Iliya's case and Minnesota Report illustrate how MMPI–A measures can be used in a psychological evaluation even in a cultural setting so different from that of the United States. Although accused of a

FIGURE 6.1 *(Continued)*

MMPI-A™ Inpatient Mental Health Interpretive Report **ID: Iliya**
12/10/2010, Page 5

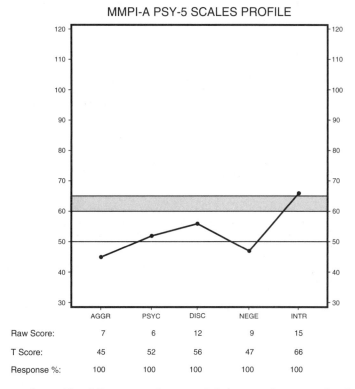

MMPI-A PSY-5 SCALES PROFILE

	AGGR	PSYC	DISC	NEGE	INTR
Raw Score:	7	6	12	9	15
T Score:	45	52	56	47	66
Response %:	100	100	100	100	100

Excerpts from *The Minnesota Report: Adolescent Interpretive System*
(Rev. ed.), by Butcher and Williams, 2007.

sexual offense against someone younger, Iliya's admission was voluntary, in marked contrast to what would probably happen in the United States, where he would be most likely facing criminal charges. His cynicism (*A-cyn*), pessimism, and social withdrawal (*INTR* [Introversion/Low Positive Emotionality]) might be a result of his long history of abuse in an environment characterized by social breakdown, evident by his reports of multiple instances of sexual victimization of the boys in his school and the lax attitude of the police regarding Iliya's abuse of an 8-year-old.

FIGURE 6.1 (Continued)

MMPI-A™ Inpatient Mental Health Interpretive Report   ID: Iliya
12/10/2010, Page 6

VALIDITY CONSIDERATIONS

This adolescent responded to the items in a cooperative manner, producing a valid MMPI-A. His profiles are likely to be a good indication of his current personality functioning.

SYMPTOMATIC BEHAVIOR

This adolescent's MMPI-A clinical profile indicates multiple serious behavior problems including school maladjustment, family discord, and authority conflicts. He can be moody, resentful, and attention-seeking. At times he may appear rebellious, impulsive, and argumentative. His poor judgment may get him into trouble. He can be self-centered and may show little remorse for his bad behavior. He may run away or lie to avoid punishment. Difficulties with the law or juvenile authorities could occur.

This MMPI-A clinical profile contains the most frequent high point, the Pd score, among clinical samples. Over 25% of boys in treatment have this well-defined profile (i.e., with the Pd scale at least 5 points higher than the next scale). Less than 4% of boys in the normative sample have this well-defined high-point profile.

Moreover, in a large archival sample of cases scored by Pearson Assessments (n = 19,048), a well-defined high-point Pd scale (T equal to or greater than 65 and more than 5 points separating it from the next highest scale) was found for 16.4% of the boys. The Pd high-point peak was the most prominent elevation in this large data set.

An examination of the adolescent's underlying personality factors with the PSY-5 scales might help explain any behavioral problems he might be presently experiencing. He shows a meager capacity to experience pleasure in life. Persons with high scores on the Introversion/Low Positive Emotionality scale tend to be pessimistic, anhedonic (unable to experience pleasure), and socially withdrawn with few or no friends.

INTERPERSONAL RELATIONS

Initially, he may seem likable and may make a good impression on others; however, his relationships tend to be very troubled. His behavior is primarily hedonistic and self-centered, and he is quite insensitive to the needs of other people, exploiting them and feeling no guilt about it.

Some interpersonal issues are suggested by his MMPI-A Content Scales profile. Family problems are quite significant in this person's life. He reports numerous problems with his parents and other family members. He describes his family in terms of discord, jealousy, fault finding, anger, serious disagreements, lack of love and understanding, and very limited communication. He looks forward to the day when he can leave home for good, and he does not feel that he can count on his family in times of trouble. His parents and he often disagree about his friends. He indicates that his parents treat him like a child and frequently punish him without cause. His family problems probably have a negative effect on his behavior in school.

Excerpts from *The Minnesota Report: Adolescent Interpretive System* (Rev. ed.), by Butcher and Williams, 2007.

FIGURE 6.1 *(Continued)*

MMPI-A™ Inpatient Mental Health Interpretive Report   **ID: Iliya**
12/10/2010, Page 7

This young person has very misanthropic attitudes. He believes that others are out to get him and will use unfair means to gain advantage. He is distrustful, looking for hidden motives when people do nice things. He feels that it is safer to trust no one. He is on guard when people seem friendlier than he expects. He often reports being misunderstood by others and sees others as being quite jealous of him. He reports several problems in social relationships. He finds it difficult to be around others, and he prefers to be alone. He may feel distant from others, believing that they do not understand or care about him. He may feel that he has no one to rely on.

BEHAVIORAL STABILITY

The relative elevation of the highest scale (Pd) in his clinical profile shows very high profile definition. His peak score is likely to remain very prominent in his profile pattern if he is retested at a later date. Adolescents with this clinical profile may have a history of acting-out behaviors and relationship problems.

DIAGNOSTIC CONSIDERATIONS

More information is needed about his behavior problems before a definitive diagnosis can be made. His Pd elevation suggests that behavior problems should be considered.

He has some personality characteristics that are associated with the development of alcohol- or other drug-use problems. An evaluation of his use of alcohol or other drugs is recommended. He may be a risk-taker and he may enjoy being the center of attention.

He has endorsed items that confirm his increasing involvement with alcohol or other drugs. He recognizes that his use is problematic, and he may be aware that others are critical of it. Using alcohol or other drugs may be a coping strategy for him.

TREATMENT CONSIDERATIONS

His conduct disturbance should figure prominently in any treatment planning. His clinical scales profile suggests that he is a poor candidate for traditional, insight-oriented psychotherapy. A behavioral strategy is suggested. Clearly stated contingencies that are consistently followed are important for shaping more appropriate behaviors.

His potential for developing alcohol or drug problems requires attention in therapy if important life changes are to be made. He has acknowledged some problems in this area, which is a valuable first step for intervention.

His family situation, which is full of conflict, should be considered in his treatment planning. Family therapy may be helpful if his parents or guardians are willing and able to work on conflict resolution. However, if family therapy is not feasible, it may be profitable during the course of his treatment to

Excerpts from *The Minnesota Report: Adolescent Interpretive System* (Rev. ed.), by Butcher and Williams, 2007.

FIGURE 6.1 (Continued)

MMPI-A™ Inpatient Mental Health Interpretive Report
12/10/2010, Page 8   **ID: Iliya**

explore his considerable anger at and disappointment in his family. Alternate sources of emotional support from adults (e.g., foster parent, teacher, other relative, friend's parent, or neighbor) could be explored and facilitated in the absence of caring parents.

His cynical attitudes and beliefs about others and their hidden motivations may create difficulties in therapy. His therapist should be aware of his general mistrust of others.

He did endorse content suggesting a desire to succeed in life. There may be some positive aspects about school that could be reinforced. This could be an asset to build on during treatment.

Excerpts from *The Minnesota Report: Adolescent Interpretive System* (Rev. ed.), by Butcher and Williams, 2007.

Use of the MMPI–A With Minority Groups in the United States

The United States is a diverse, multicultural society with many ethnic, cultural, religious, and linguistic minorities. Translations of the MMPI instruments in other countries can be useful to clinicians in the United States when they are seeing patients without the requisite English-language skills. For example, C. L. Williams (1987) presented the case of a Thai woman seen in a general medical clinic in Minneapolis. This patient had sufficient English skills to produce a valid MMPI profile. However, the resulting profile suggested a psychotic process, not at all consistent with her presenting complaint, clinical interview, or behavioral observations. When she was readministered a version of the MMPI adapted in Thailand, the profile suggested a somatoform disorder, more consistent with her problems. Apparently, she was sufficiently fluent in English to produce a valid profile, yet she did not understand the nuances of the language well enough to provide an accurate self-description with the English version.

There is an extensive research base for use of both the MMPI–2 and MMPI–A with minority U.S. populations (e.g., Gomez, Johnson, Davis, & Velasquez, 2000; Gray-Little, 2009; Greene, Robin, Caldwell, Albaugh,

FIGURE 6.1 *(Continued)*

MMPI-A™ Inpatient Mental Health Interpretive Report   **ID: Iliya**
12/10/2010, Page 9

ADDITIONAL SCALES

A subscale or content component scale should be interpreted only when its corresponding parent scale has an elevated T score of 60 or above. Subscales and content component scales printed below in bold meet that criterion for interpretation.

	Raw Score	T Score	Resp %
Harris-Lingoes Subscales			
Depression Subscales			
Subjective Depression (D$_1$)	16	67	100
Psychomotor Retardation (D$_2$)	9	71	100
Physical Malfunctioning (D$_3$)	4	55	100
Mental Dullness (D$_4$)	4	52	100
Brooding (D$_5$)	7	71	100
Hysteria Subscales			
Denial of Social Anxiety (Hy$_1$)	3	49	100
Need for Affection (Hy$_2$)	3	41	100
Lassitude-Malaise (Hy$_3$)	6	58	100
Somatic Complaints (Hy$_4$)	4	50	100
Inhibition of Aggression (Hy$_5$)	4	59	100
Psychopathic Deviate Subscales			
Familial Discord (Pd$_1$)	**8**	**75**	**100**
Authority Problems (Pd$_2$)	**5**	**60**	**100**
Social Imperturbability (Pd$_3$)	3	48	100
Social Alienation (Pd$_4$)	**9**	**69**	**100**
Self-Alienation (Pd$_5$)	**7**	**61**	**100**
Paranoia Subscales			
Persecutory Ideas (Pa$_1$)	5	53	100
Poignancy (Pa$_2$)	2	42	100
Naivete (Pa$_3$)	3	45	100
Schizophrenia Subscales			
Social Alienation (Sc$_1$)	**12**	**68**	**100**
Emotional Alienation (Sc$_2$)	2	48	100
Lack of Ego Mastery, Cognitive (Sc$_3$)	3	50	100
Lack of Ego Mastery, Conative (Sc$_4$)	3	46	100
Lack of Ego Mastery, Defective Inhibition (Sc$_5$)	**6**	**62**	**100**
Bizarre Sensory Experiences (Sc$_6$)	7	56	100
Hypomania Subscales			
Amorality (Ma$_1$)	6	73	100
Psychomotor Acceleration (Ma$_2$)	5	43	100
Imperturbability (Ma$_3$)	4	55	100
Ego Inflation (Ma$_4$)	3	42	100

Excerpts from *The Minnesota Report: Adolescent Interpretive System* (Rev. ed.), by Butcher and Williams, 2007.

FIGURE 6.1 (*Continued*)

MMPI-A™ Inpatient Mental Health Interpretive Report   ID: Iliya
12/10/2010, Page 10

	Raw Score	T Score	Resp %
Social Introversion Subscales			
Shyness / Self-Consciousness (Si_1)	5	46	100
Social Avoidance (Si_2)	6	67	100
Alienation--Self and Others (Si_3)	6	45	100
Content Component Scales			
Adolescent Depression			
Dysphoria (A-dep_1)	3	63	100
Self-Depreciation (A-dep_2)	1	45	100
Lack of Drive (A-dep_3)	3	54	100
Suicidal Ideation (A-dep_4)	0	42	100
Adolescent Health Concerns			
Gastrointestinal Complaints (A-hea_1)	0	46	100
Neurological Symptoms (A-hea_2)	2	43	100
General Health Concerns (A-hea_3)	0	38	100
Adolescent Alienation			
Misunderstood (A-aln_1)	**4**	**64**	**100**
Social Isolation (A-aln_2)	**3**	**62**	**100**
Interpersonal Skepticism (A-aln_3)	2	56	100
Adolescent Bizarre Mentation			
Psychotic Symptomatology (A-biz_1)	5	62	100
Paranoid Ideation (A-biz_2)	1	53	100
Adolescent Anger			
Explosive Behavior (A-ang_1)	2	44	100
Irritability (A-ang_2)	5	54	100
Adolescent Cynicism			
Misanthropic Beliefs (A-cyn_1)	**11**	**62**	**100**
Interpersonal Suspiciousness (A-cyn_2)	**7**	**61**	**100**
Adolescent Conduct Problems			
Acting-Out Behaviors (A-con_1)	6	60	100
Antisocial Attitudes (A-con_2)	7	68	100
Negative Peer Group Influences (A-con_3)	0	41	100
Adolescent Low Self-Esteem			
Self-Doubt (A-lse_1)	**6**	**61**	**100**
Interpersonal Submissiveness (A-lse_2)	**3**	**61**	**100**
Adolescent Low Aspirations			
Low Achievement Orientation (A-las_1)	1	36	100
Lack of Initiative (A-las_2)	1	42	100

Excerpts from *The Minnesota Report: Adolescent Interpretive System* (Rev. ed.), by Butcher and Williams, 2007.

FIGURE 6.1 (*Continued*)

MMPI-A™ Inpatient Mental Health Interpretive Report   ID: Iliya
12/10/2010, Page 11

	Raw Score	T Score	Resp %
Adolescent Social Discomfort			
Introversion (A-sod$_1$)	**11**	**74**	**100**
Shyness (A-sod$_2$)	3	44	100
Adolescent Family Problems			
Familial Discord (A-fam$_1$)	**14**	**66**	**100**
Familial Alienation (A-fam$_2$)	**5**	**63**	**100**
Adolescent School Problems			
School Conduct Problems (A-sch$_1$)	1	50	100
Negative Attitudes (A-sch$_2$)	3	52	100
Adolescent Negative Treatment Indicators			
Low Motivation (A-trt$_1$)	2	45	100
Inability to Disclose (A-trt$_2$)	6	65	100

Uniform T scores are used for Hs, D, Hy, Pd, Pa, Pt, Sc, Ma, the content scales, the content component scales, and the PSY-5 scales. The remaining scales and subscales use linear T scores.

Excerpts from *The Minnesota Report: Adolescent Interpretive System* (Rev. ed.), by Butcher and Williams, 2007.

& Goldman, 2003; Nagayama Hall, Bansal, & Lopez, 1999; Negy, Leal-Puente, Trainor, & Carlson, 1997; see also Appendix A, Cross-Cultural/Ethnic Studies). MMPI–A scales provide helpful assessments of minority clients. In the last sections of this chapter, we cover use of the MMPI–A with adolescents from diverse backgrounds who live in the United States. Some of these adolescents without sufficient language skills can benefit from translations developed elsewhere, for example, the Russian, Chinese, or Italian versions. There is also a Spanish language version (Butcher, Cabiya, et al., 1998) that would be useful for new arrivals. However, as we will see in Chapter 8 with José, not all Hispanic adolescents require a translated version.

REPRESENTATIVENESS OF THE MMPI–A NORMATIVE SAMPLE

One of the main criticisms of using the original MMPI with diverse populations in the United States was its nonrepresentative normative sample, the so-called "Minnesota Normals" (see Chapter 2). The MMPI Restandardization Committee addressed this issue by evaluating the potential impact of ethnicity on responses to the items. Test norms were developed from a diverse general population sample (Butcher, Williams, et al., 1992). Participants were recruited from a number of areas of the United States with a total sample of 805 boys and 815 girls, including African Americans, American Indians, Asians, and Hispanics. The MMPI–A normative sample consisted of the following:

- 76.5% White boys; 75.9% White girls
- 12.4% Black boys; 12.3% Black girls
- 2.9% Asian boys; 2.8% Asian girls
- 2.6% American Indian boys; 3.2 % American Indian girls
- 2.2% Hispanic boys; 2.0% Hispanic girls
- 2.5% other boys; 2.1% other girls
- 0.3% not reported boys; 1.2% not reported girls

The MMPI–A normative sample closely matches U.S. census data for the country for Blacks and Whites, whereas Asian and American Indian subjects are overrepresented in comparison with census data (U.S. Census Bureau, 2000).

Hispanic adolescents were substantially underrepresented in the MMPI–A normative sample in comparison with census data (U.S. Census Bureau, 2000). Hispanics were underrepresented in the normative sample, in part, because the test was administered in English. Therefore, shortly after the MMPI–A was published, a Spanish language version was developed for the United States to tailor the instrument specifically for assessment of Spanish-speaking adolescents without sufficient language proficiency for the English version (Butcher, Cabiya, et al., 1998).

ADAPTATION OF THE HISPANIC MMPI–A

The translation team for the development of the Hispanic version of the MMPI–A for the United States constructed a provisional test booklet using two other well-adapted Spanish translations of the MMPI item pools as source materials. Because of the significant item overlap between the MMPI–2 and MMPI–A, the Spanish translation of the MMPI–2 (e.g., Garcia-Peltoniemi & Azan, 1993) was a primary source for the provisional booklet. Items that were unique to the MMPI–A had also been translated for the adaptation of the instrument in Mexico (e.g., Lucio-Gomez et al., 1999) and were the second source of translated items for the provisional booklet.

The adaptation process is detailed in Butcher, Cabiya, et al. (1998) and summarized here. Three bilingual psychologists reviewed the provisional translation of the MMPI–A booklet. These psychologists came from differing cultural backgrounds (i.e., one was a resident of Puerto Rico, another a Cuban American from Miami, and the third a Mexican American from Los Angeles). Their task was to review each item for linguistic and psychological equivalence (see Exhibit 6.1). They noted any concerns; items were rewritten until each psychologist agreed that the meaning was clear.

The third step in the translation process was a back-translation of the provisional booklet from Spanish to English by the University of Minnesota Language Center. The linguists at this center were not involved in the development of the provisional booklet. Problematic items were retranslated and back-translated until there was agreement among the three bilingual psychologists. Finally, adolescent subjects during the normative data collection were asked to identify any items that were difficult to understand. Five such items were identified and modified for the final booklet.

Native-speaking adolescent subjects were recruited at sites in San Juan, Puerto Rico; Miami, Florida; Los Angeles, California; and Mexico City, Mexico. These sites were selected to represent the major Hispanic groups resident in the United States who would be most likely to need a Spanish, rather than an English, version of the MMPI–A. A sample of 128 subjects were administered the Hispanic MMPI–A twice to provide test–retest data. Data provided in Butcher, Cabiya, et al. (1998) establish the psychometric equivalency of the Hispanic MMPI–A with the original version.

The norms for the Hispanic MMPI–A provided in Butcher, Cabiya, et al. (1998) are quite similar to the original MMPI–A norms (Butcher, Williams, et al., 1992). MMPI–A scores for the Hispanic sample of boys and girls fell within one standard deviation of the mean of the original MMPI–A norms. Moreover, most of the Hispanic MMPI–A scale scores were well within the standard error of measurement, around a *T* score of 50. Among the Basic Scales, only two showed much difference between the two groups: Masculinity/Femininity (*Mf*) for girls and True Response Inconsistency (*TRIN*). The *TRIN* results indicate that the adolescents in the Hispanic sample responded somewhat inconsistently to a few more item pairs (in the "true" direction) than did the original normative sample. This tendency was by no means extreme, and most scale scores were highly comparable.

In general, a given raw score would fall at approximately the same *T* score in both the original and Hispanic MMPI–A norm sets. Therefore, either set of norms would likely provide a clear picture of the adolescent's psychological adjustment problems. The original MMPI–A norms can be considered appropriate to use for Hispanic adolescents taking the test in Spanish as well. Butcher, Cabiya, et al. (1998) concluded that special norms are unnecessary to provide an appropriate clinical assessment of these adolescents because Hispanic adolescents respond to the test in much the same way as those taking the test in English. This equivalency was important to demonstrate empirically.

The Hispanic MMPI–A has been included in several research studies since its publication that provide further support for its psychometric equivalence (Exhibit 6.1). Scott, Butcher, Young, and Gomez, (2002) conducted a cross-cultural comparison of Spanish-speaking adolescents in five countries: Colombia, Mexico, Peru, Spain, and the United States. They found a high degree of similarity across the five countries on the Basic, Content, and Supplementary Scales, with most scales falling within a half of a standard deviation from the original normative sample. Scott, Knoth, Beltran-Quiones, and Gomez (2003) found that a general sample of adolescents in Colombia had scores on the Hispanic MMPI–A similar to those of adolescents in the United States. In addition, they reported that adolescent earthquake victims in Colombia showed some scale elevations on three scales (*D, Pt,* and *Sc*) that are commonly associated with the experience of posttraumatic stress disorder. Interpretation strategies, along with case examples, can be found in a volume focused on the use of both the MMPI–2 and MMPI–A with Hispanic clients living in the United States (Butcher et al., 2007). In the remainder of this chapter, we turn to an MMPI–A interpretation of an American Indian student living in the Midwest.

An MMPI–A Interpretation of an American Indian Adolescent

PRESENTING COMPLAINT

Joseph, a 14-year-old student in the ninth grade, attends an alternative high school for adolescents with emotional and behavioral problems. The school serves a diverse student body drawn from across a metropolitan community. Joseph's homeroom teacher referred him to the school psychologist after an angry outburst at the start of the school day. Joseph and two other students were shouting at each other as they entered the classroom. The two others calmed down fairly quickly when the teacher intervened. Joseph, however, stormed out when his teacher asked them to sit down. He did not return to school for 3 days after this episode. Prior to the referral, other teachers had reported several different instances of Joseph's anger outbursts and fighting with multiple students at the school. Joseph was also reported to have problems completing assignments, and several teachers expressed concerns about his poor peer relations and lack of friends.

BACKGROUND INFORMATION

The term *American Indian,* like the term *Hispanic,* represents heterogeneous groups with distinct communities and societal influences. Joseph is a member of the Chippewa Nation. He was born on a reservation in a remote part of the state. He lived there with his mother and three younger siblings until he was 8 years old and his mother moved to the city to look for work. For the last 6 years his residence has alternated between living in the city with his mother or on the reservation with his maternal grandparents. Currently, his mother is in jail on a drug-related charge, and Joseph is living with a maternal aunt and uncle. His younger siblings moved back to the reservation with the grandparents. Joseph has never met his father and believes he lives out of state.

Joseph's teachers describe him as immature, easily jealous, stubborn, and demanding. He is also seen as perfectionist, suspicious, and self-conscious. He frequently daydreams during his classes and has difficulty paying attention and concentrating. He is a bright student, far above grade level in math and science, although he is below grade level in social studies.

BEHAVIORAL OBSERVATIONS, TEST ADMINISTRATION, AND SCORING

Joseph agreed to meet with the school psychologist and during the interview indicated that he was willing to take the MMPI–A. Other students at the school had taken the MMPI–A, and a test feedback session with the psychologist was a routine part of the evaluation process. He told the psychologist that he was interested in learning what the test would say about him. Joseph worked quietly on the MMPI–A in the psychologist's office, completing it in 50 minutes. He answered all the items.

Joseph's hand-scored MMPI–A profiles of the Basic Scales and Content and Supplementary Scale are in Figures 6.2 and 6.3, respectively. Not surprisingly, given Joseph's expressed interest in completing the MMPI–A, he produced a valid and interpretable protocol as can be seen in Figure 6.2. Although he had a moderate elevation on the *K* (Correction) scale, showing some test defensiveness and presenting himself in a favorable way, he was sufficiently cooperative with the assessment to produce a valid profile. His Clinical, Content, and Supplementary Scale profiles are likely to present a clear picture of his problems and symptoms. In addition to the scales included on the profiles in Figures 6.2 and 6.3, Joseph obtained the following *T* scores on the PSY-5 (Personality Psychopathology Five) Scales: 70 on *AGGR* (Aggressiveness), 69 on *DISC* (Disconstraint), 60 on *PSYC* (Psychoticism), 53 on *NEGE* (Negative Emotionality/Neuroticism), and 46 on *INTR* (Introversion/Low Positive Emotionality).

DISCUSSION: JOSEPH'S MMPI–A INTERPRETATION

Joseph's elevations on three MMPI–A scales—*Ma* (Hypomania), *A-con* (Conduct Problems), and *DISC*—indicate a pattern of impulsive acting-out without regard to the consequences or impact on others. He reported a number of serious behavior problems, including stealing, shoplifting,

FIGURE 6.2

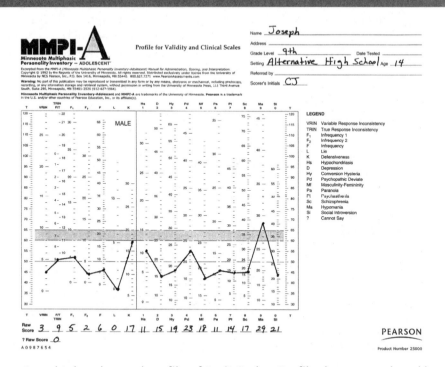

Joseph's hand-scored profile of Basic Scales. Profile sheet reproduced by permission of the University of Minnesota Press. All rights reserved. "Minnesota Multiphasic Personality Inventory®—Adolescent" and "MMPI®–A" are trademarks owned by the University of Minnesota.

lying, breaking or destroying property, swearing, and, in general, being oppositional. His responses to the MMPI–A suggest that his behavior problems likely occur regardless of setting. His *AGGR* score indicates that he is likely to be seen as a highly aggressive person who intimidates others, consistent with the teacher's observations of problematic encounters with his peers.

In addition to the acting-out behaviors indicated in his MMPI–A scores, Joseph also acknowledged unusual symptoms including having several strange thoughts and experiences, which may include hallucinations, persecutory ideas, or feelings of being controlled by others, given his elevated score on *A-biz* (Bizarre Mentation; Figure 6.3) and moderate elevation on *PSYC* (i.e., a *T* score of 60). He reported that he worries that there is something wrong with his mind. It is possible that these symptoms are the result of substance abuse, particularly given his

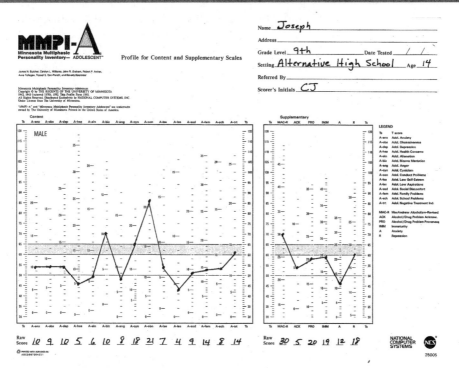

Joseph's hand-scored profile of Content and Supplementary Scales. Profile sheet reproduced by permission of the University of Minnesota Press. All rights reserved. "Minnesota Multiphasic Personality Inventory®—Adolescent" and "MMPI®–A" are trademarks owned by the University of Minnesota.

high elevation on the *MAC–R* scale. Given the background information about his mother's arrest for a drug-related charge, further assessment of Joseph's possible drug involvement is necessary. If the unusual beliefs indicated by *A-biz* and *PSYC* cannot be explained by substance use or his experiences of being uprooted over the years, then the possibility of an underlying psychotic process should be considered.

Joseph appears to be extraverted and generally comfortable in social situations as reflected in his relatively low score on the *Si* (Social Introversion) scale. However, his elevation on *A-cyn* (Cynicism) suggests that he has negative interpersonal relationships that are marked by his aggressiveness and generally misanthropic attitudes. He appears to be mistrustful of others and is on guard when he is around other people.

It is noteworthy, given the setting in which he was seen, that his score on *A-sch* (School Problems) is so low. Joseph provides an example of the distinction between a "troubling" and a "troubled" adolescent. He is not troubled by problems in school, although his extreme *A-con* score indicates numerous problems in that setting and elsewhere that are likely to trouble others.

Joseph's moderate score on *Ma* (Hypomania) and his extreme elevation on *A-con* suggest a moderate to severe conduct disorder. His score on *MAC–R* suggests that he has some personality or behavioral characteristics associated with alcohol or other drug use, including risk-taking behaviors and the desire to be the center of attention. He also reported having bizarre thoughts and behaviors as noted on *A-biz* and *PSYC*.

The behavior problems noted by the Content Scales and the PSY-5 Scales suggest that his current placement in a structured, behaviorally oriented program with close supervision is appropriate. His elevation on the *K* scale suggests that he may be reluctant to self-disclose in a treatment context. As noted by his *A-cyn* scale elevation, he may be distrustful of mental health professionals. His cynical attitudes and beliefs about others and their hidden motivations would likely create relationship difficulties in therapy.

The psychologist should gather more details, if he or she does not already know them from experiences with other students at the school, about the specific band of Chippewa (also know as Ojibwa) and the reservation from which Joseph comes to determine how cultural factors may be influencing Joseph's psychological adjustment and responding to the MMPI–A. A feedback session on the MMPI–A could be structured to include exploration of issues including the following (see Chapter 9 for more details):

- In addition to drug or alcohol intoxication, can his elevations on *A-biz* and *PSYC* be attributed to being moved back and forth between the city and the reservation? How much of a factor is his background in contributing to his feelings of being controlled by others or having persecutory ideas?
- Has he been exposed to messages in his native culture or about his native culture that have led to his elevation on *A-cyn?*
- How does Joseph's adjustment on the reservation compare with living in the city? Are resources there adequate to meet his needs compared with what is available at his school? How does Joseph feel about his current placement? Does he have a preference for the city or the reservation?

Different and Yet the Same

With Iliya and Joseph we have seen how the MMPI–A is being used both internationally and with ethnic minority adolescents within the United States. It is a robust instrument that psychologists find useful for providing a set of hypotheses about a young person's behavior and psychological issues. Both Iliya and Joseph were willing to complete the MMPI–A and responded to its items in a manner that resulted in interpretable profiles. The treatment staff in Russia and at Joseph's school in the United States learned information from the MMPI–A that had not been revealed previously.

The Minnesota Report was introduced in Iliya's case. We saw how a computerized interpretive system was used as part of an objective personality assessment in a very different culture than that of the United States. In the next chapter, we will examine computer-based assessment more closely and provide further case illustrations of the utility of the Minnesota Report in interpreting the MMPI–A.

The MMPI–A and the Digital Age 7

In the future, computers may weigh no more than 1.5 tons.

—Popular Mechanics, *1949*

The MMPI was developed at a time when computers filled entire rooms with their bulk and their ubiquitous presence in people's home or work environments was but a fantasy. The computer and the MMPI grew in tandem over the decades, one suited to the other (see reviews in Butcher, Perry, & Dean, 2009; Fowler, 1985, 1987). After all, an individual's responses to the MMPI—true or false—are binary (1, 0), the language of computers. By this century, MMPI–2 expert Roger Greene (2005) concluded, "Computer scoring and computer interpretation of all psychological assessment techniques should become the basis for the psychological report" (p. 6).

Within a short time after the publication of the MMPI, Burton and Bright (1946, p. 101) proposed the substitution of "human fallibility" with "machine accuracy" for scoring the MMPI using IBM punch cards (also called *Hollerith cards* in honor of their 19th-century inventor) with an IBM tabulator. A decade later Hathaway (1956) adapted Burton and Bright's procedures to improve the box or card form of the MMPI so that it could be either hand-scored or processed by IBM card-sorting or tabulating machines (Exhibit 7.1).

Hathaway's boxes were still in use at University of Minnesota Hospitals until the 1980s. Adolescents, like others, preferred the novelty of sorting cards rather than using the booklet version and its accompanying answer sheet. The box version, however, was considered inefficient for administra-

MMPI Trivia Questions: Boxes and Items

What do cards in boxes have to do with the MMPI?
The first version of the MMPI consisted of 504 items typed on 3 × 5 cards kept in two small boxes. Instructions were taped to the top of the boxes. The boxes contained file-card dividers labeled True, False, and Cannot Say. Hathaway's (1956) innovation substituted the 3 × 5 cards for 550 individual IBM cards (the number of items had increased by this decade), again with one MMPI item printed on each IBM card with scoring options including use of IBM card sorting and tabulating machines or hand scoring. Each IBM card contained punches allowing for the scoring of MMPI scales, Cannot Say, and % True. The cards were kept in one box, not two.

Why did the number of MMPI items increase from 550 to 566 in the booklet forms of the MMPI?
This is actually a trick question. The number of items remained at 550. However, according to Dahlstrom et al. (1972), 16 items from Scales 6, 7, 8, and 0 were repeated to facilitate scoring of the IBM answer sheet by machine.

tions with a large group, hence the almost simultaneous development during its early days of MMPI booklet forms. And these booklet forms were also developed for machine scoring with the innovative—for its time—IBM 805 Test Scoring Machine, introduced in 1937, and its accompanying answer sheets.

The adaptability of the MMPI to scoring by the predecessors of today's computers is not the only reason for the suitability of the test to the digital age. The very nature of the MMPI Standard Scales with their empirically based scale descriptors and normative scores is uniquely suited to the development of computerized interpretive programs for the MMPI, and now the MMPI–2 and MMPI–A. As we saw in previous chapters, an important advantage of using the MMPI–A is that it brings an objective perspective to a clinical personality evaluation. Research with the MMPI instruments has been successful, over the past 70 years, at establishing empirically verified correlates to the Clinical Scales that Hathaway and McKinley developed to objectively assess symptoms and problems (see Chapter 4), as well as the other MMPI–A scales in wide use today (see Chapter 5).

Case Digression: David and the Box Form

David, a 16-year-old inpatient at the University of Minnesota Hospitals, had just completed the card form of the original MMPI in a record 15 minutes. His 566 cards (by this time the 16 repeated items were part of the item pool) were placed neatly behind the True and False dividers; he had none in Cannot Say. He was still holding the box of sorted cards as the psychologist escorted him down the hall to return to his unit. His psychologist casually inquired if David was sure of his answers because most people needed at least 45 minutes to sort through them. David assured her that he had carefully read each item and was sure of his responses. "Good," replied the psychologist, "because the computer can tell if the cards were just put in the box at random."

On hearing that, David tripped and scattered the box of cards all down the corridor, effectively losing his 15 minutes of responses. The next day, David agreed to complete the MMPI again, and this time took 70 minutes to complete the task. He produced a valid profile. This case vignette illustrates how a matter-of-fact description that inconsistent responding can be detected, coupled with an opportunity to retake the test, can lead to a valid MMPI performance on retesting.

Historical Roots of Computerized MMPI–A Interpretive Reports

Paul Meehl (1954) provided the theoretical underpinnings for empirically based personality predictions and symptom descriptions in his landmark book *Clinical Versus Statistical Prediction: A Theoretical Analysis and a Review of the Evidence*. He demonstrated the strength of actuarial prediction and description over more subjective analyses and procedures. He showed that a person using data-based actuarial methods in making clinical predictions clearly performed better than clinicians who relied on more subjective or intuitive strategies in making decisions about people. His recommendations for data-based assessment influenced a number of studies that demonstrated convincingly that empirically established MMPI test correlates could be accurately applied to new cases meeting the test criteria. Two years later, Meehl (1956; see Exhibit 7.2, p. 142) expanded on his ideas, and, as Grove (2005) pointed out,

> This led to a cottage industry of researching and cataloging MMPI, and now MMPI–2, code types (Gilberstadt & Duker, 1965; Gynther, Altman, & Sletten, 1973; Lachar, 1974; Marks & Seeman, 1963; Marks et al., 1974; McGrath & Ingersoll, 1999), the most thorough and successful application of actuarial prediction in clinical psychology. (p. 1239)

Moreover, as we saw in Chapters 4 and 5, similar research and cataloguing of empirically verified correlates for various MMPI scales were carried out with adolescents as well.

EXHIBIT 7.2

MMPI Trivia Questions: Cookbooks and Recipes

What do cookbooks have to do with the MMPI?
In arguing against the tradition of using a clinician's personal experience, skill or judgment for interpreting psychological tests, Paul Meehl (1956) pleaded for the development of an empirically based set of rules that psychologists could use to access well-validated descriptors for scores on tests like the MMPI. Countless psychologists answered his challenge by conducting research to establish the data based correlates for MMPI scales. Meehl's plea: WANTED—A GOOD COOKBOOK. These "cookbooks" resulted in descriptors based on discrete scores that could be automatically and objectively applied to individuals to describe their personality and symptoms.

What did an example MMPI "recipe" look like according to Meehl?
The following is the example "recipe" provided by Meehl (1956, p. 267): 1. *Hs* and *Hy* > 70. 2. *D* < (*Hs* and *Hy*) by at least one sigma. 3. *K* or *L* > ? and *F*. 4. F < 65. 5. Scales 4, 5, 6, 7, 8, 9, 0 all < 70.

An examination of Meehl's (1956) example "recipe" in Exhibit 7.2 shows how well suited such actuarial descriptors are to computerization. Charles C. Halbower at the University of Minnesota developed Meehl's example as part of his doctoral dissertation, and from the earliest days this profile type was called a *conversion V*. Its empirically derived correlates are symptoms of somatoform disorders. It is important to note that even though Meehl's example recipe focused on an empirically derived code type (e.g., 1-3/3-1), he also recognized that clinical judgment plays a role in determining "recipes" as shown by one of its rules being "certain additional requirements based on clinical experience" (p. 267). In the example recipe in Exhibit 7.2, Items 2 through 5 were based on clinical experience (i.e., code type descriptors are more likely to apply in well-defined code types, Rules 2 and 5; and in valid profiles, Rules 3 and 4). Meehl's observations about the interface of empirical research with clinical and practical experience with the MMPI instruments remain relevant today regarding computerized MMPI–A interpretive systems.

The first computerized psychological test interpretation involved the original MMPI and was developed at the Mayo Clinic in the 1960s by Wendell Swenson and John Pearson (Pearson & Swenson, 1967; Swenson, Rome, Pearson, & Brannick, 1965). Figure 7.1 shows a patient's report that was reprinted in a revised MMPI manual (Hathaway & McKinley, 1967). The Mayo Clinic interpretive system included more than 100 descriptive statements that had been found to be associated with various scale elevations. Patients seen at the Mayo Clinic completed a card form of the MMPI while waiting for their medical tests in the different areas of the hospital. A report was generated at the end of the day's evaluation and included in the patient's file to indicate if there were psychological issues. The Mayo Clinic's interpretation system was widely

FIGURE 7.1

THOMAS JOHN   MALE   AGE 29   REPORT DATE 7-12-67   NCS CODE 0061
MM 124 0004

MINNESOTA MULTIPHASIC PERSONALITY INVENTORY
By Starke R. Hathaway, Ph. D. and J. Charnley McKinley, M.D.

T SCORE PROFILE ——— Plotted With K

T SCORE WITH K	RAW SCORE WITH K	T SCORE WITHOUT K	RAW SCORE WITHOUT K	Scale	T Score
			0	?	
	56		6	L	
	48		2	F	
	57		16	K	
52	12	49	4	Hs +5K	
	56		19	D	
	53		18	Hy	
62	24	60	18	Pd +.4K	
	65		28	Mf	
	47		7	Pa	
46	21	43	5	Pt +1K	
44	19	41	3	Sc +1K	
45	15	45	12	Ma +.2K	
	44		19	Si	

	A	R	Es	Lb	Ca	Dy	Do	Re	Pr	St	Cn	WB
RAW SCORE →	6	13	48	10	5	16	14	22	15	19	25	9
T SCORE →	42	45	56	53	41	46	48	54	56	53	50	38
	FIRST FACTOR	SECOND FACTOR	EGO STRENGTH	LOW BACK PAIN	CAUDALITY	DEPENDENCY	DOMINANCE	SOCIAL RESPONSIBILITY	PREJUDICE	SOCIAL STATUS	CONTROL	

-PATIENT VIEWS SELF AS WELL-ADJUSTED AND
SELF RELIANT.
  -TENDS TO GIVE SOCIALLY APPROVED ANSWERS RE-
  GARDING SELF-CONTROL AND MORAL VALUES.
  -INCLINES TOWARD ESTHETIC INTERESTS.
  -INDEPENDENT OR MILDLY NONCONFORMIST.
  -VIEWS LIFE WITH AVERAGE MIXTURE OF OPTIMISM
  AND PESSIMISM.
  -NUMBER OF PHYSICAL SYMPTOMS AND CONCERN
  ABOUT BODILY FUNCTIONS FAIRLY TYPICAL FOR
  MEDICAL OUTPATIENTS.
  -RESPECTS OPINIONS OF OTHERS WITHOUT UNDUE
  SENSITIVITY.
  -HAS SUFFICIENT CAPACITY FOR ORGANIZING WORK
  AND PERSONAL LIFE.
  -LOW ENERGY AND ACTIVITY LEVEL. DIFFICULT TO
  MOTIVATE, APATHETIC.
  -HAS A COMBINATION OF PRACTICAL AND
  THEORETICAL INTERESTS.
  -PROBABLY SOCIALLY OUTGOING AND GREGARIOUS.

THE PSYCHOLOGICAL CORPORATION MMPI REPORTING SERVICE

Scored by NATIONAL COMPUTER SYSTEMS   FORM MMPI-INT

Computer printout of first MMPI interpretive system. From *The Minnesota Multiphasic Personality Inventory: Manual* (Rev. ed.), by S. R. Hathaway and J. C. McKinley, 1967, p. 31. New York: The Psychological Corporation. Copyright 1943, 1951, 1967 by the University of Minnesota. Used by permission of the University of Minnesota Press. All rights reserved. "MMPI®" and "Minnesota Multiphasic Personality Inventory®" are trademarks owned by the Regents of the University of Minnesota.

used by the medical staff at the clinic. Following the success and general acceptance of the Mayo system, several other more comprehensive and sophisticated MMPI interpretation programs were developed during the 1970s (Fowler, 1985, 1987, described this early history).

Can you figure out the possible sources for the interpretive statements found in this first MMPI computerized report (Figure 7.1)? Review the information from Chapter 4 to look for scale descriptors that are consistent with the interpretive statements included in Thomas John's MMPI interpretation in Figure 7.1. Abbreviated versions of his interpretive statements are provided in the pop quiz in Exhibit 7.3 with a place for you to record which scale and score is likely responsible for each of the 11 statements in Figure 7.1. You can compare your answers with ours provided in Appendix B. Like yours, our responses are educated guesses because we do not have access to the computer program that generated these statements. Some of the statements should be relatively easy for you to identify its source from the MMPI Basic Scales profile. Others, we warn you, will not be so obvious. Indeed, we simply speculated about several! (Can you spot which one we were most uncertain about?) The actual computer program used to generate these statements would have listed the scale names, scores, and rules similar to Meehl's example recipe in Exhibit 7.2.

EXHIBIT 7.3

MMPI Pop Quiz: What are the Likely Sources of the Computer-Generated Interpretive Statements in Figure 7.1?

Statement	Source (fill in the blank)
1. . . . views self as well-adjusted and self reliant.	
2. . . . socially approved answers . . .	
3. . . . towards esthetic interests.	
4. . . . independent . . .	
5. . . . average . . . optimism and pessimism.	
6. . . . physical symptoms . . .	
7. . . . respects opinions of others . . .	
8. . . . sufficient capacity for organizing . . .	
9. Low energy . . .	
10. . . . practical and theoretical interests.	
11. . . . socially outgoing . . .	

Today, computer-based interpretation of psychological tests has become a widely accepted clinical tool (Butcher, 2009; Butcher et al., 2009; Butcher, Perry, & Hahn, 2004). Computer-based reports are much more sophisticated than the original ones from the 1960s and 1970s. They are a central part of many clinicians' diagnostic appraisals of clients' problems. Using a computer-based report as an "outside opinion" of the client's problems can be valuable to the process of clinical decision making as well as an aid for providing feedback to clients, as we will see in Chapter 9.

How Do MMPI–A Computer Reports Work?

A computer-based psychological test interpretation program is an expert system or a form of "artificial intelligence." MMPI–A computer assessment systems use a general strategy that is quite straightforward. A computer program is written to access stored files in a way that is analogous to a psychologist consulting a text (like this book) or other sources (e.g., Meehl's cookbooks in the early days) for a listing of potential correlates for particular scale elevations from a given individual's scores on the various MMPI–A measures. The database for the MMPI–A scale correlates derives from several sources, such as the established empirical test correlate literature for the primary scales identified by the system's developer. The Standard Scales, as we said in Chapter 4, are basic sources for MMPI–A interpretative statements, whether directly generated by a human or from a computerized system (which, after all, is also written by a human). Computerized systems use information from the scales covered in Chapter 5 as well (i.e., Content, Supplementary, and Personality Psychopathology Five [PSY-5] Scales). This information is called a statement library, and in MMPI–2 or MMPI–A systems these statement libraries typically include the following procedures and information sources:

1. *Checking demographic information.* A check is done to determine if all of the relevant demographic information such as age, gender, and setting is provided. This is necessary because some interpretive statements in the library are gender specific or setting specific (see Chapters 4 and 5 for examples).
2. *Scoring of relevant scales and indices.* Counts of all of the scored items for each scale and a notation of omitted items for any scale are done, MMPI–A profiles are drawn, and nonprofiled subscales and indices are listed. (In cases in which the interpretive system does not provide scoring, these measures are inputted from hand scoring or a computer-scoring service. See description of Archer, 2003, below.)

3. *Searching the stored master file for relevant descriptors.* When the client obtains an interpretable scale elevation, then the computer searches the stored database (reference files, look-up tables, and classification or decision rules) to locate the relevant personality and symptom information for the client being assessed.

4. *Assessing protocol validity.* Similar to an interpretation made by a psychologist, the statement library includes an evaluation of the pertinent validity variables to determine if the client's MMPI–A performance was cooperative and sufficiently open to provide an adequate personality appraisal. The MMPI–A validity scales are assessed and the system reports potential hypotheses concerning the client's performance on Lie (L), Correction (K), Infrequency (F), Infrequency 1 (F_1), Infrequency 2 (F_2), Variable Response Inconsistency ($VRIN$), True Response Inconsistency ($TRIN$), or Cannot Say. Adolescents with an invalid record receive a report describing the problems with their test performance.

5. *Searching stored data files for prototypal information that matches MMPI–A scales.* Given a valid MMPI–A performance, the computer program would next search the Clinical, Content, and Supplementary Scale scores to determine if any of those scores reach an interpretive level. Information included in the report must be both pertinent and consistent. That is, diverse personality and symptom correlates must be integrated into a unified report that eliminates any low base rate or conflicting information. Some systems provide information about the client based on responses to particular item or scale relationships that address specific problems. Or, some computer systems have special base-rate data for specific settings such as correctional facilities or inpatient mental health units. The research and clinical experience of the developer is crucial here for developing the decision rules.

6. *Communicating the results in a readable format.* The narrative report that is produced often mirrors sections of a report that is written by a psychologist, as we will see later in the chapter.

7. *Indicating cautions.* Professional organizations recommend guidelines concerning computerized psychological assessment, including providing cautions to reduce the possibility of their misuse (American Educational Research Association, American Psychological Association, & National Council on Measurement in Education, 1999; American Psychological Association, 1986; Butcher et al., 2009; Eyde, Robertson, & Krug, 2009). As we will see at the end of this chapter, computerized MMPI–A interpretive reports include cautionary statements printed directly on the output for a given patient.

Research on computer-based interpretive systems has focused primarily on their use with adults. Early computer-report evaluation studies tended to use satisfaction ratings to determine whether a report was effective at characterizing the client (Moreland & Onstad, 1985). Some studies have compared computer reports with other computer reports (Eyde, Kowal, & Fishburne 1991; Fishburne, Eyde, & Kowal, 1988; J. E. Williams & Weed, 2004). However, no direct comparisons of computer-derived reports with clinically based MMPI interpretations have been published. Moreland and Onstad (1985) found that the narrative reports generated for patients were considered significantly more accurate than reports that were randomly generated. In a study from Australia, Shores and Carstairs (1998) found the Minnesota Reports to be highly accurate in detecting fake-good and fake-bad response sets. In another cross-cultural comparison study, Butcher and colleagues (Butcher, Berah, et al., 1998) found that the Minnesota Reports were highly accurate when clinicians rated the reports compared with their knowledge of the case. Finally, an international case study of the Minnesota Reports for MMPI–A has shown that the computer reports, based on U.S. norms, characterized well adolescents from clinical settings in 15 countries (Butcher et al., 2000).

Options for Using the Computer With the MMPI–A

There are several options available to psychologists who want to use the computer to assist in their use of the MMPI–A:

- Computer scoring
- Computer scoring with interpretive report
- Computer administration and scoring
- Computer administration and scoring with interpretive report

Pearson Assessments has the exclusive license with the publisher of the MMPI–A, the University of Minnesota Press, to distribute MMPI–A scoring materials and booklets. Their MMPI–A website has the most up-to-date information about the various MMPI–A administration and scoring products available (http://psychcorp.pearsonassessments.com/haiweb/cultures/en-us/productdetail.htm?pid=pag522).

The size of the practice, the volume of assessments with the MMPI–A, and the availability of computers frequently determine which of several scoring options a psychologist has in his or her practice. For low-volume clinics with limited computer availability, adolescents typically are given an MMPI–A booklet and accompanying answer sheet to complete. Different answer sheets are available depending on how the answer sheet is to be scored:

1. *Mail-in service.* Answer sheets are mailed to Pearson Assessments and then the scored protocol and/or interpretive report (depending on the option purchased) is returned to the psychologist by mail.
2. *On-site scoring.* Scoring software for the psychologist's office computer can be purchased from Pearson Assessments. With this software, a clerical assistant can directly enter the adolescent's item responses into the computer. Scored protocols and/or interpretive reports (depending on the option purchased) are obtained immediately after the adolescents' responses are entered. This approach to test processing usually requires about 10 minutes of clerical time to enter the item responses. Some practitioners will have the item responses entered twice, to assure that "human error" has not altered the adolescent's responses.
3. *Optical scanner with on-site scoring.* Some clinics invest in an optical scanner for processing the MMPI–A answer sheets to eliminate clerical time (and potential for error). The optical scanner reads the answer sheet and communicates the scores directly to the computer. The scored profile and/or interpretive report (depending on the option purchased) are immediately produced.

Computer administration, instead of the old-fashioned test booklet and answer sheet, is another digital age option for the MMPI–A. Not surprisingly, many clients, especially adolescents in the "wired generation," prefer computer administration. This administrative procedure typically requires less response time than completion of the paper-and-pencil option. The computer scores and processes the MMPI–A responses and profiles, and/or interpretive reports are printed out immediately.

There are two primary MMPI–A computerized assessment systems currently available commercially: Robert Archer's (2003) MMPI–A Interpretive System (Version 3), distributed by Psychological Assessment Resources (PAR), and the Minnesota Report: Adolescent Interpretive System, 2nd Edition, developed by us (Butcher & Williams, 2007) and distributed by Pearson Assessments. Each is far more elegant than the rudimentary first interpretive system shown in Figure 7.1 (e.g., see a sample client's 20-page report by Archer at http://psych.acer.edu.au/index.php?option=com_rubberdoc&view=doc&id=78&format=raw).

Archer's (2003) system, developed with PAR staff, initially for the original MMPI, provides a computer-based analysis of widely used MMPI–A measures for adolescents between 12 and 18 years. It includes interpretive hypotheses for the MMPI–A on profile validity, probable symptoms, treatment issues and suggestions, and possible diagnostic considerations.

The MMPI–A Interpretive System is structured to provide the following:

- Individual scale interpretations and configural information for commonly occurring 2- and 3-point code types.
- An estimate of the degree to which an adolescent's profile matches the profile database and characteristics for a given profile type.
- A detailed Structural Summary of MMPI–A scores for clients based on both a configural interpretation (of the adolescents code type) and a summary of the key score variables in the protocol.
- Setting-specific report options:
  - Outpatient
  - Inpatient
  - Medical/hospital
  - Drug/alcohol treatment
  - School/academic
  - Correctional/juvenile justice

The Archer–PAR MMPI–A Interpretive System does not have scoring software because of the exclusive agreement between the University of Minnesota Press and Pearson Assessments for scoring; thus, the practitioner needs to obtain the client's *T* scores for the various scales by either hand scoring the answer sheet and entering the *T* scores into the program or obtaining a scored file from the test distributor Pearson Assessments and entering it into the software. The system provides an important feature that allows the clinician to import data from the Pearson Assessments scoring system for MMPI–A. A manual is available for understanding the measures used and the summary format for the program (Archer, 2003).

Minnesota Report: Adolescent Interpretive System, Second Edition

The Minnesota Report is a computerized interpretation system for the MMPI instruments that were originally developed for adults (Butcher, 1982). The adult clinical version of the Minnesota Report was redeveloped in 1989 after the Restandardization Project was completed to include the new information and norms for the MMPI–2. It was more recently revised in 2005 (Butcher, 2005b). In 1992 the MMPI–A norms and clinical interpretive information were used to develop the adolescent version of the Minnesota Reports (Butcher & Williams, 1992b). This system was revised in 2007 to incorporate new research-based measures and interpretive guidelines developed since its earlier release. The following characterize the Adolescent Interpretive System for the Minnesota Report:

- Similar to the other Minnesota Reports for adults, the adolescent system provides a conservative assessment guide based on established research to provide the most accurate and research-based interpretive hypotheses.
- To provide specific information to match descriptors according to setting, we tailored the reports for the following settings:
  - Correctional
  - General medical
  - Inpatient mental health
  - Outpatient mental health
  - School settings
  - Alcohol and drug treatment
- Age and gender were taken into account in the development of the system.
- Validity Scale information was initially based on cut-offs developed in the Restandardization Project and updated in 2007 based on subsequent research.
- The interpretive reports are arranged to be clinically useful, with hypotheses and recommendations concerning symptom description, diagnostic factors, and treatment suggestions.
- Empirical correlates for the Clinical Scales that were found to apply with adolescent clinical samples were included for symptom description. Recall from the descriptions in Chapters 2 and 4 about code types that we do not use or recommend code types for interpreting MMPI–A protocols, given their poor validity.
- Pertinent descriptors derived from the Content Scales, substance abuse scales (MacAndrew Alcoholism Scale—Revised [*MAC–R*], Alcohol/Drug Problem Acknowledgment [*ACK*], and Alcohol/Drug Problem Proneness [*PRO*]), and PSY-5 Scales are included.
- The interpretive system is written in a format that allows for modification as research findings on the MMPI–A emerge.

CASE ILLUSTRATIONS OF THE MINNESOTA REPORT

Not surprisingly, an adolescent's Minnesota Report output follows the interpretive strategy we will recommend and demonstrate in the next chapter. Minnesota Reports provide an expert-to-expert consultation on a given client. They give specific hypotheses based solely on how an adolescent's responses to the MMPI–A fit research-based descriptors we developed based on our expertise with the instrument. The Minnesota Report is intended to inform clinicians about reasonable conclusions that can be made from the MMPI–A to incorporate into clinicians' psychological assessment of a young person. In addition, beginners can examine Minnesota Reports as part of learning how various scores on the MMPI–A are interpreted by an expert computer system. In this section, we present cases from four of the settings included in the Minnesota Report to illustrate both this interpretive system and to provide a preview of the interpretive strategy and report writing suggestions we cover in Chapter 8.[1]

Case 1: Emily, An Adolescent Hospitalized Following a Suicide Attempt

Emily is 16 years old, White, and middle class, with a history of depression, admitted into an inpatient treatment program following a suicide attempt. She lives with her mother and grandmother, who indicate Emily has no close friends and spends much time alone in her room. At the time of the suicide attempt (her grandmother found her in the garage with the car running), she was in outpatient treatment for depression, anxiety episodes, and an eating disorder. During the intake interview, Emily reported symptoms of depression and hopelessness, and she has, in the past, had episodes of anxiety in which she was reluctant to go out of her home. She repeated the seventh grade because of excessive school absences and is currently in eighth grade. There is a positive history of psychiatric problems in her family. Her mother has been hospitalized on three occasions for depression. Her maternal grandfather, now deceased, was hospitalized on one occasion for manic-depressive disorder.

The MMPI–A was included in a battery of psychological tests administered a week after Emily was admitted into the hospital. Emily's Minnesota Report consisted of 16 pages, and its first 11 pages are included in Figure 7.2. (Reminder: the missing pages in Emily's report, like the other Minnesota Reports in this book, contain items that are not reproduced here to prevent distribution of MMPI–A item content to nonqualified users.) As can be seen in Figure 7.2, each Minnesota Report begins with a cover sheet with setting, age, and gender indicated (clinicians can choose to use either patient names or ID numbers on this sheet). Profiles of the Validity, Clinical and Supplementary, Content, and PSY-5 Scales are provided on several pages (pp. 153–156). Relevant information, in addition to plotted scale scores, can be found on these pages as well. For example, the Validity Scales profile on p. 153 includes the Cannot Say raw score and the Percent True and Percent False indicators. Both raw and

---

[1]Demographic information and some of the assessment details in these cases, as well as in others throughout the book, have been altered for privacy and didactic purposes.

FIGURE 7.2

Inpatient Mental Health Interpretive Report

MMPI-A™

The Minnesota Report™: Adolescent Interpretive System, 2nd Edition

James N. Butcher, PhD, & Carolyn L. Williams, PhD

ID Number:	Emily
Age:	16
Gender:	Female
Date Assessed:	12/10/2010

PEARSON

PsychCorp

FIGURE 7.2 (*Continued*)

MMPI-A™ Inpatient Mental Health Interpretive Report
12/10/2010, Page 2

ID: Emily

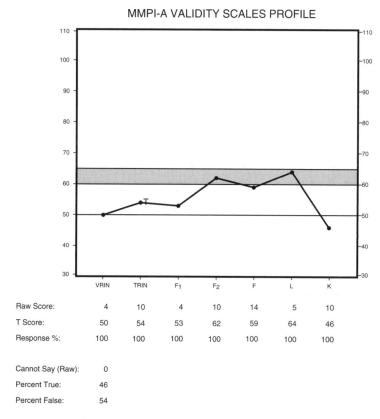

MMPI-A VALIDITY SCALES PROFILE

	VRIN	TRIN	F_1	F_2	F	L	K
Raw Score:	4	10	4	10	14	5	10
T Score:	50	54	53	62	59	64	46
Response %:	100	100	100	100	100	100	100

Cannot Say (Raw): 0
Percent True: 46
Percent False: 54

Excerpts from *The Minnesota Report: Adolescent Interpretive System*
(Rev. ed.), by Butcher and Williams, 2007.

FIGURE 7.2 (*Continued*)

MMPI-A™ Inpatient Mental Health Interpretive Report   **ID: Emily**
12/10/2010, Page 3

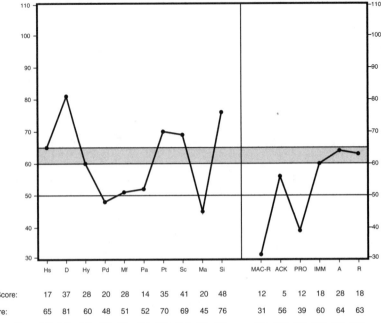

MMPI-A CLINICAL AND SUPPLEMENTARY SCALES PROFILE

	Hs	D	Hy	Pd	Mf	Pa	Pt	Sc	Ma	Si	MAC-R	ACK	PRO	IMM	A	R
Raw Score:	17	37	28	20	28	14	35	41	20	48	12	5	12	18	28	18
T Score:	65	81	60	48	51	52	70	69	45	76	31	56	39	60	64	63
Response %:	100	100	100	100	100	100	100	100	100	100	100	100	100	100	100	100

Welsh Code: 2"07'81+3-65/49: L-F/K:

Mean Profile Elevation: 61.3

Excerpts from *The Minnesota Report: Adolescent Interpretive System* (Rev. ed.), by Butcher and Williams, 2007.

FIGURE 7.2 (Continued)

MMPI-A™ Inpatient Mental Health Interpretive Report
12/10/2010, Page 4

ID: Emily

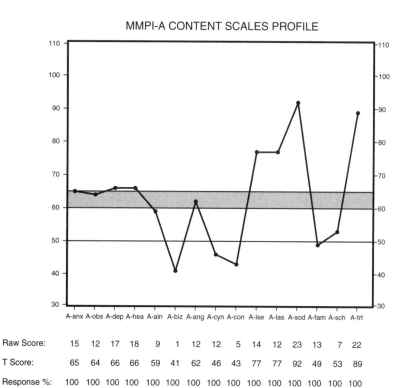

MMPI-A CONTENT SCALES PROFILE

	A-anx	A-obs	A-dep	A-hea	A-aln	A-biz	A-ang	A-cyn	A-con	A-lse	A-las	A-sod	A-fam	A-sch	A-trt
Raw Score:	15	12	17	18	9	1	12	12	5	14	12	23	13	7	22
T Score:	65	64	66	66	59	41	62	46	43	77	77	92	49	53	89
Response %:	100	100	100	100	100	100	100	100	100	100	100	100	100	100	100

Excerpts from *The Minnesota Report: Adolescent Interpretive System* (Rev. ed.), by Butcher and Williams, 2007.

T scores and the percentage of items endorsed on each scale (i.e., Response %) are provided for every scale on each of the profile pages. Emily responded to all of the MMPI–A items (i.e., her Cannot Say score is 0), thus her four profiles indicate that 100% of the items on the various scales were answered.

Following the profiles in Figure 7.2 is the narrative section of the Minnesota Report on pages 157–159. It is subdivided into Validity Considerations, Symptomatic Behavior, Interpersonal Relations, Behavioral

FIGURE 7.2 *(Continued)*

MMPI-A™ Inpatient Mental Health Interpretive Report   ID: Emily
12/10/2010, Page 5

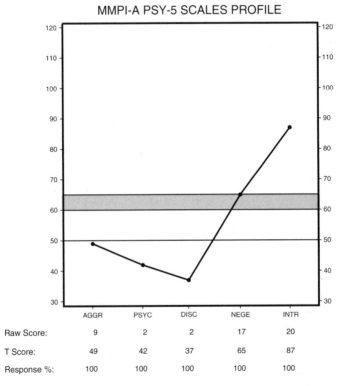

MMPI-A PSY-5 SCALES PROFILE

	AGGR	PSYC	DISC	NEGE	INTR
Raw Score:	9	2	2	17	20
T Score:	49	42	37	65	87
Response %:	100	100	100	100	100

Excerpts from *The Minnesota Report: Adolescent Interpretive System* (Rev. ed.), by Butcher and Williams, 2007.

Stability, Diagnostic Considerations, and Treatment Considerations. The next chapter provides our recommendations to clinicians for writing comparable sections for an MMPI–A report. After the narrative report, each Minnesota Report includes a listing of the various subscales and component scales described in Chapters 4 and 5. As indicated in those chapters, a subscale or component scale is only interpreted when its parent Clinical or Content Scale is elevated above a *T* score of 60 and

FIGURE 7.2 *(Continued)*

MMPI-A™ Inpatient Mental Health Interpretive Report   ID: Emily
12/10/2010, Page 6

VALIDITY CONSIDERATIONS

This is a valid MMPI-A. Her responses to the MMPI-A validity items suggest that she cooperated with the evaluation enough to provide useful interpretive information. The resulting profiles are an adequate indication of her present personality functioning.

SYMPTOMATIC BEHAVIOR

This adolescent's MMPI-A clinical profile reflects much psychological distress at this time. She has major problems with anxiety and depression. She tends to be high-strung and insecure and may also be having somatic problems. She is probably experiencing fearfulness, loss of sleep and appetite, and a slowness in personal tempo.

Her high-point MMPI-A score, D, is the second most frequent well-defined peak score among adolescent girls in treatment populations. Approximately 9% of girls in treatment programs have this peak scale elevation in their clinical profile; 7% of the normative sample have this well-defined peak score. The D score is elevated above a T of 65 for approximately 20% of clinical girls and approximately 10% of girls in the normative sample.

In a large archival sample of MMPI-A profiles scored by Pearson Assessments (n = 12,744), 9.4% of the girls had a well-defined peak score on D at or above an elevation of 65T with at least 5 points separating it from the next highest scale.

Her MMPI-A Content Scales profile reveals important areas to consider in her evaluation. She reports very limited interest in school or investment in success. She does not expect to succeed. She reports disliking reading and studying, and she may be seen as lazy. She has difficulty starting projects, tends to give up easily, and allows others to take charge. Poor academic performance, limited involvement in school activities, and multiple problems in school are likely.

She endorsed a number of very negative opinions about herself. She reported feeling unattractive, lacking self-confidence, feeling useless, having little ability and several faults, and not being able to do anything well. She may be easily dominated by others.

She reported several symptoms of anxiety, including tension, worries, and difficulties sleeping. Symptoms of depression were reported. She endorsed a variety of somatic complaints and concerns about her health.

Personality characteristics that this adolescent has reported on the PSY-5 scales might help to provide a context for the affective symptoms she is presently experiencing. She shows little capacity to experience pleasure in life. Persons with high scores on the Introversion/Low Positive Emotionality scale tend to be pessimistic, anhedonic (unable to experience pleasure), and socially withdrawn with few or no friends. She may also view the world in a negative manner and may develop a worst-case scenario to events affecting her. Her somewhat self-critical nature prevents her from viewing relationships in a positive manner.

Excerpts from *The Minnesota Report: Adolescent Interpretive System* (Rev. ed.), by Butcher and Williams, 2007.

FIGURE 7.2 *(Continued)*

MMPI-A™ Inpatient Mental Health Interpretive Report ID: Emily
12/10/2010, Page 7

INTERPERSONAL RELATIONS

She appears to be quite passive and dependent in interpersonal relationships and does not speak up for herself even when others take advantage of her. She avoids confrontation and seeks nurturance from others, often at the expense of her own independence. She may form deep emotional attachments and tends to be quite vulnerable to being hurt. She also tends to blame herself for interpersonal problems. She seems to require an excessive amount of emotional support from those around her.

She is a very introverted person who has difficulty meeting and interacting with other people. She is shy and emotionally distant, and she tends to be very uneasy, rigid, and overcontrolled in social situations. Her shyness is probably indicative of a broader pattern of social withdrawal. She is probably very timid and avoids relating to the opposite sex. She may feel weak and uncoordinated. She is probably fearful and depressed. She may think about suicide in response to the problems she has being around others.

Some problems with her relationships are evident from her extreme endorsement of items on A-sod. She reports considerable discomfort in social situations. She indicates that she has difficulties making friends and initiating conversations; she prefers to avoid group activities. She may feel depressed about her social inadequacies and she may have very limited interest in boys. She reported some irritability and impatience with others. She may have problems controlling her anger.

BEHAVIORAL STABILITY

The relative elevation of her highest clinical scales (D, Pt) suggests that her profile is not as well defined as many other profiles. That is, her highest scales are very close to her next scale score elevations. There could be some shifting of the most prominent scale elevations in the profile code if she is retested at a later date.

Adolescents with this clinical profile are often experiencing psychological distress in response to stressful events. The intense distress may diminish over time or with treatment.

DIAGNOSTIC CONSIDERATIONS

Adolescents with this clinical scales profile tend to be considered emotionally unstable and to receive diagnoses such as depression or anxiety disorder. Her Content Scales profile indicated a preoccupation with physical complaints, suggesting a somatoform component to her problems (providing that a medical evaluation is negative).

Academic underachievement, a general lack of interest in any school activities, and low expectations of success are likely to play a role in her problems.

Excerpts from *The Minnesota Report: Adolescent Interpretive System* (Rev. ed.), by Butcher and Williams, 2007.

FIGURE 7.2 *(Continued)*

MMPI-A™ Inpatient Mental Health Interpretive Report   ID: Emily
12/10/2010, Page 8

TREATMENT CONSIDERATIONS

Patients with this MMPI-A clinical profile are feeling a great deal of discomfort and are in need of symptomatic relief for their depression. Psychotherapy, particularly a supportive approach, is likely to be beneficial during the initial period of treatment. Cognitive-behavioral treatment may also be beneficial.

This individual tends to blame herself too much for her difficulties. Although she worries a great deal about her problems, she seems to have little energy left over for action to resolve them.

The passive, unassertive personality style that seems to underlie this disorder might be a focus of behavior change. Adolescents with these problems may learn to deal with other people more effectively through assertiveness training.

She should be evaluated for the presence of suicidal thoughts and any possible suicidal behaviors. If she is at risk, appropriate precautions should be taken.

She may have several attitudes and beliefs that could interfere with establishing a therapeutic relationship. These may include very negative opinions about mental health professionals, an unwillingness to self-disclose, and beliefs that her problems are unsolvable. She may be unwilling to accept responsibility for her behaviors or to plan for her future. She may doubt that others care enough to help her or that they are capable of understanding her.

Excerpts from *The Minnesota Report: Adolescent Interpretive System* (Rev. ed.), by Butcher and Williams, 2007.

---

the subscale or component scale is elevated above *T* score of 60. The subscales or component scales that can be interpreted are highlighted in bold in Emily's report. For example, Emily endorsed all of the Harris–Lingoes subscales for the Depression scale but only two of the subscales for Hysteria.

As can be seen from both Emily's MMPI–A Validity Scales profile and the Validity Considerations section of the narrative portion of the Minnesota Report, Emily was cooperative and produced a valid MMPI–A. Her MMPI–A profiles are likely to be credible summaries of her problems. Emily's MMPI–A Clinical and Content Scales indicate a number of symptoms and problems consistent with her presenting complaints. She had highly elevated scores on *D* (Depression), *Pt* (Psychasthenia), and *Sc* (Schizophrenia). She shows many symptoms of a mood disorder in which both depression and anxiety are prominent features. The Symptomatic Behavior section of the narrative in Figure 7.2 on p. 157 includes other interpretive statements from her Content and PSY-5 Scale elevations.

FIGURE 7.2 (Continued)

MMPI-A™ Inpatient Mental Health Interpretive Report
12/10/2010, Page 9

ID: Emily

ADDITIONAL SCALES

A subscale or content component scale should be interpreted only when its corresponding parent scale has an elevated T score of 60 or above. Subscales and content component scales printed below in bold meet that criterion for interpretation.

	Raw Score	T Score	Resp %
Harris-Lingoes Subscales			
Depression Subscales			
Subjective Depression (D₁)	22	76	100
Psychomotor Retardation (D₂)	9	73	100
Physical Malfunctioning (D₃)	7	71	100
Mental Dullness (D₄)	9	70	100
Brooding (D₅)	8	70	100
Hysteria Subscales			
Denial of Social Anxiety (Hy₁)	1	37	100
Need for Affection (Hy₂)	4	46	100
Lassitude-Malaise (Hy₃)	9	65	100
Somatic Complaints (Hy₄)	11	70	100
Inhibition of Aggression (Hy₅)	2	43	100
Psychopathic Deviate Subscales			
Familial Discord (Pd₁)	3	45	100
Authority Problems (Pd₂)	2	45	100
Social Imperturbability (Pd₃)	1	36	100
Social Alienation (Pd₄)	6	53	100
Self-Alienation (Pd₅)	6	55	100
Paranoia Subscales			
Persecutory Ideas (Pa₁)	3	46	100
Poignancy (Pa₂)	6	62	100
Naivete (Pa₃)	3	46	100
Schizophrenia Subscales			
Social Alienation (Sc₁)	10	61	100
Emotional Alienation (Sc₂)	7	76	100
Lack of Ego Mastery, Cognitive (Sc₃)	5	58	100
Lack of Ego Mastery, Conative (Sc₄)	11	75	100
Lack of Ego Mastery, Defective Inhibition (Sc₅)	9	72	100
Bizarre Sensory Experiences (Sc₆)	10	63	100
Hypomania Subscales			
Amorality (Ma₁)	1	39	100
Psychomotor Acceleration (Ma₂)	7	49	100
Imperturbability (Ma₃)	2	44	100
Ego Inflation (Ma₄)	5	52	100

Excerpts from *The Minnesota Report: Adolescent Interpretive System* (Rev. ed.), by Butcher and Williams, 2007.

FIGURE 7.2 *(Continued)*

MMPI-A™ Inpatient Mental Health Interpretive Report　　　　　　　　　**ID: Emily**
12/10/2010, Page 10

	Raw Score	T Score	Resp %
Social Introversion Subscales			
Shyness / Self-Consciousness (Si$_1$)	**14**	**74**	**100**
Social Avoidance (Si$_2$)	**7**	**78**	**100**
Alienation--Self and Others (Si$_3$)	11	58	100
Content Component Scales			
Adolescent Depression			
Dysphoria (A-dep$_1$)	**5**	**71**	**100**
Self-Depreciation (A-dep$_2$)	**5**	**68**	**100**
Lack of Drive (A-dep$_3$)	**5**	**65**	**100**
Suicidal Ideation (A-dep$_4$)	0	42	100
Adolescent Health Concerns			
Gastrointestinal Complaints (A-hea$_1$)	0	44	100
Neurological Symptoms (A-hea$_2$)	**11**	**69**	**100**
General Health Concerns (A-hea$_3$)	**4**	**63**	**100**
Adolescent Alienation			
Misunderstood (A-aln$_1$)	4	62	100
Social Isolation (A-aln$_2$)	4	71	100
Interpersonal Skepticism (A-aln$_3$)	0	40	100
Adolescent Bizarre Mentation			
Psychotic Symptomatology (A-biz$_1$)	1	42	100
Paranoid Ideation (A-biz$_2$)	0	43	100
Adolescent Anger			
Explosive Behavior (A-ang$_1$)	4	56	100
Irritability (A-ang$_2$)	**8**	**66**	**100**
Adolescent Cynicism			
Misanthropic Beliefs (A-cyn$_1$)	8	51	100
Interpersonal Suspiciousness (A-cyn$_2$)	4	47	100
Adolescent Conduct Problems			
Acting-Out Behaviors (A-con$_1$)	1	37	100
Antisocial Attitudes (A-con$_2$)	1	37	100
Negative Peer Group Influences (A-con$_3$)	2	65	100
Adolescent Low Self-Esteem			
Self-Doubt (A-lse$_1$)	**9**	**69**	**100**
Interpersonal Submissiveness (A-lse$_2$)	**5**	**73**	**100**
Adolescent Low Aspirations			
Low Achievement Orientation (A-las$_1$)	**6**	**63**	**100**
Lack of Initiative (A-las$_2$)	**6**	**72**	**100**

Excerpts from *The Minnesota Report: Adolescent Interpretive System* (Rev. ed.), by Butcher and Williams, 2007.

FIGURE 7.2 (*Continued*)

MMPI-A™ Inpatient Mental Health Interpretive Report   **ID: Emily**
12/10/2010, Page 11

	Raw Score	T Score	Resp %
Adolescent Social Discomfort			
Introversion (A-sod$_1$)	13	87	100
Shyness (A-sod$_2$)	10	75	100
Adolescent Family Problems			
Familial Discord (A-fam$_1$)	9	51	100
Familial Alienation (A-fam$_2$)	2	48	100
Adolescent School Problems			
School Conduct Problems (A-sch$_1$)	0	43	100
Negative Attitudes (A-sch$_2$)	1	42	100
Adolescent Negative Treatment Indicators			
Low Motivation (A-trt$_1$)	11	84	100
Inability to Disclose (A-trt$_2$)	7	71	100

Uniform T scores are used for Hs, D, Hy, Pd, Pa, Pt, Sc, Ma, the content scales, the content component scales, and the PSY-5 scales. The remaining scales and subscales use linear T scores.

Excerpts from *The Minnesota Report: Adolescent Interpretive System* (Rev. ed.), by Butcher and Williams, 2007.

Emily shows an extreme degree of social introversion on several scales, including *Si* (Social Introversion), *A-sod* (Adolescent-Social Discomfort), and *INTR* (Introversion/Low Positive Emotionality), described in the Interpersonal Relations section of the narrative in Figure 7.2 on p. 158. All of these measures point to likely personality characteristics of social withdrawal, isolation, and difficult interpersonal relationships. Her scores on the *A-trt* (Adolescent-Negative Treatment Indicators) and its component scale scores suggest difficulties in establishing a therapeutic relationship with her, which is highlighted in the last section of the narrative.

As mentioned earlier, for test security reasons, Emily's responses to the item-level indicators are not included in this book. However, clinicians find it helpful to quickly examine the listing that is available at the end of each Minnesota Report. Emily, for example, endorsed five of the six indicators of anxiety symptoms, consistent with her intake interview. Of the seven Depression/Suicidal Ideation items, she endorsed only two, a week after her suicide attempt. This is not evidence that she is at less risk for suicide, as the Treatment Considerations section of the narrative clearly indicates. In this case, it could reflect Emily's unwillingness to endorse face-valid items related to her recent attempt, or simply how she was feeling about the content of those five items at that particular moment in time. Recall that these indicators do not provide reliable measurements but can be used for follow-up questions in a clinical interview. Emily's scale scores are more valid measures and include descriptors of suicidal risk. Emily's Minnesota Report provided a wealth of clinically relevant information. Jeremy's MMPI–A results, our next case, on the other hand, did not.

Case 2: Jeremy, An Uncooperative Adolescent in a School Setting

Jeremy, a 17-year-old White 10th-grade student, was referred to the school counselor after several incidents of disrupting class, unexcused absences, and aggressive behaviors toward other students. Jeremy's disruptive behavior at school was initially reported to his mother, a single parent, with the recommendation for a psychological evaluation. His mother agreed and encouraged Jeremy to participate in the evaluation with the school psychologist. Jeremy participated reluctantly. His responses to interview questions were both brief and accompanied by sullen and angry expressions.

Jeremy completed the MMPI–A in less than 30 minutes and produced an invalid profile. Figure 7.3 contains 4 of the 12 pages of Jeremy's Minnesota Report to illustrate how this interpretive system handles invalid reports. Jeremy's Validity Scales profile and his Clinical and Supplementary Scales profile are included on pages 165 and 166 of Figure 7.3, respectively. To solidify our recommendation as the report developers that Jeremy's profiles should not be interpreted because of his extreme score on *VRIN* (*T* score = 78), his scores on these profiles are not plotted, and instead a warning statement is provided. However, like Emily's Minnesota Report in Figure 7.2, all Jeremy's scale scores are available for the clinician in the remaining eight pages of his Minnesota Report. Responses to the item-level indicators, however, are not printed out for invalid protocols.

There can be times when a psychologist would prefer to have an invalid profile plotted, for example, to use in a feedback session (see the discussion of feedback to Jeremy in Chapter 9) or to illustrate a case study in a book, article, or presentation. In those circumstances, the psychologist can enter the scores from a Minnesota Report like Jeremy's in Figure 7.3 into a spreadsheet program to create a profile like that in Figure 7.4. Figure 7.4 clearly shows an invalid validity pattern with elevations on F, F_1, and F_2 indicating extreme endorsement of rare and unusual symptoms. Combined with his *VRIN* score over 75, this validity pattern indicates that Jeremy endorsed items on the test in a random or inconsistent manner. Without attending to the Validity Scales on the left

FIGURE 7.3

Minnesota Multiphasic
Personality Inventory— ADOLESCENT™

School Interpretive Report

MMPI-A™

The Minnesota Report™: Adolescent Interpretive System, 2nd Edition
James N. Butcher, PhD, & Carolyn L. Williams, PhD

ID Number:	Jeremy
Age:	17
Gender:	Male
Date Assessed:	12/10/2010

PEARSON

⑨ *PsychCorp*

Excerpts from *The Minnesota Report: Adolescent Interpretive System* (Rev. ed.), by Butcher and Williams, 2007. Reproduced by permission of the University of Minnesota Press. All rights reserved. "MMPI®–A," "Minnesota Multiphasic Personality Inventory®—A," and "The Minnesota Report" are trademarks owned by the Regents of the University of Minnesota.

FIGURE 7.3 *(Continued)*

MMPI-A™ School Interpretive Report
12/10/2010, Page 2

ID: Jeremy

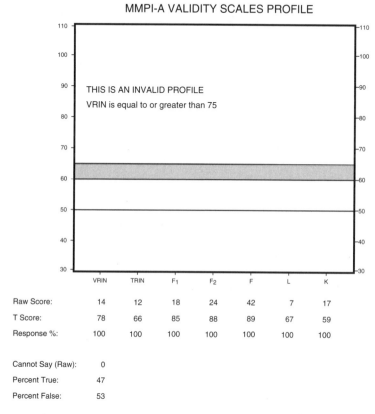

MMPI-A VALIDITY SCALES PROFILE

THIS IS AN INVALID PROFILE
VRIN is equal to or greater than 75

	VRIN	TRIN	F_1	F_2	F	L	K
Raw Score:	14	12	18	24	42	7	17
T Score:	78	66	85	88	89	67	59
Response %:	100	100	100	100	100	100	100

Cannot Say (Raw): 0
Percent True: 47
Percent False: 53

Excerpts from *The Minnesota Report: Adolescent Interpretive System* (Rev. ed.), by Butcher and Williams, 2007.

side of Figure 7.4, a psychologist would notice nothing amiss in the plotted scores on the right side of this profile.

The computer narrative for Jeremy's MMPI–A responses is provided in Figure 7.3 on p. 167, in the Validity Considerations section. The first paragraph describes Jeremy's extreme and exaggerated responding, with suggestions for possible reasons why he answered the items in this

FIGURE 7.3 *(Continued)*

MMPI-A™ School Interpretive Report
12/10/2010, Page 3

ID: Jeremy

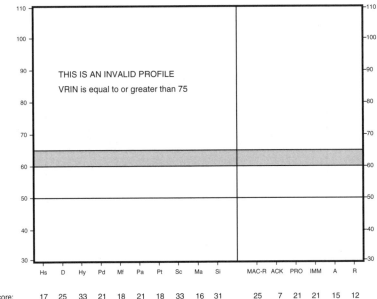

MMPI-A CLINICAL AND SUPPLEMENTARY SCALES PROFILE

THIS IS AN INVALID PROFILE
VRIN is equal to or greater than 75

	Hs	D	Hy	Pd	Mf	Pa	Pt	Sc	Ma	Si	MAC-R	ACK	PRO	IMM	A	R
Raw Score:	17	25	33	21	18	21	18	33	16	31	25	7	21	21	15	12
T Score:	71	60	71	51	42	73	49	60	41	56	59	63	60	62	51	47
Response %:	100	100	100	100	100	100	100	100	100	100	100	100	100	100	100	100

Welsh Code: 6<u>13</u>'+<u>28</u>-04/7<u>59</u>: F"'L+-K/

Mean Profile Elevation: 59.5

Excerpts from *The Minnesota Report: Adolescent Interpretive System* (Rev. ed.), by Butcher and Williams, 2007.

FIGURE 7.3 *(Continued)*

MMPI-A™ School Interpretive Report   ID: Jeremy
12/10/2010, Page 6

VALIDITY CONSIDERATIONS

His responses to the MMPI-A items were more extreme and exaggerated than those of most adolescents. He endorsed a wide variety of extreme symptoms. These symptoms may include psychotic thoughts or behaviors, alcohol- or other drug-related problems, eating difficulties, extreme family discord, or problematic interpersonal relationships. He may be exaggerating his symptoms as a plea for help. It is also possible that poor reading skills contributed to his extreme responses. These responses could also have resulted from a confused, disoriented, or intoxicated state. The resulting MMPI-A protocol may not provide a clear indication of his personality and symptoms and should only be interpreted after consideration of the likely reasons for this exaggerated response style.

His extreme elevation on VRIN indicates that his MMPI-A protocol is most likely invalid because of an inconsistent response style. He was very inconsistent in his responses to the MMPI-A item pool, apparently not taking into account the meaning of items when selecting his responses. His MMPI-A protocol should not be interpreted because of this inconsistency.

Excerpts from *The Minnesota Report: Adolescent Interpretive System* (Rev. ed.), by Butcher and Williams, 2007.

fashion. The next paragraph indicates that Jeremy was highly inconsistent in his item responding, and therefore the resulting MMPI–A profiles and scores cannot be interpreted. No further information can be obtained from Jeremy's MMPI–A; therefore there are no other narrative statements in his Minnesota Report.

The psychologist receiving this report would have his or her observations about Jeremy's condition when completing the MMPI–A and can rule in or rule out some of the hypotheses provided in the Validity Considerations narrative. For example, the school psychologist would have information about Jeremy's reading level, whether there was any reason to suspect intoxication, confusion, or an active psychotic process during the testing session. Jeremy's reluctance to participate in the clinical interview and the rapidity of his completion of the MMPI–A are other relevant pieces of information the psychologist has available for his or her psychological evaluation. At this stage of the evaluation, Jeremy appears generally uncooperative and unwilling to self-disclose. Other sources of information should be considered (e.g., information from his mother and teachers), as well as further exploration of the underlying reasons for Jeremy's anger and lack of cooperation with the evaluation. Consequently, any decisions that are made about his mental health

FIGURE 7.4

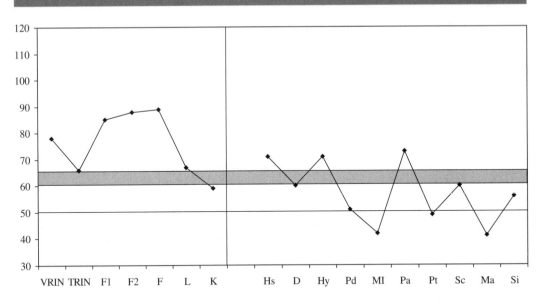

Clinician-created profile of Jeremy's Validity and Clinical Scales profile. Excerpted from the *Minnesota Multiphasic Personality Inventory®—Adolescent (MMPI®–A) Manual for Administration, Scoring, and Interpretation* by Butcher et al., 1992. Copyright © 1992 by the Regents of the University of Minnesota. Reproduced by permission of the University of Minnesota Press. All rights reserved. "MMPI®–A" and "Minnesota Multiphasic Personality Inventory®—A" are trademarks owned by the Regents of the University of Minnesota.

adjustment at this time would be based on limited information. Retesting of the adolescent is recommended if cooperation could be assured (see Chapter 9).

Case 3: Tyler, An Adolescent With Substance Abuse Problems

Tyler, a 17-year-old White 10th-grade student, was referred for substance abuse treatment following several incidents of running away from home and drinking alcohol with friends. A week prior to his referral, he and two classmates were reported to the school principal by a classmate who saw them with a bottle of whiskey. One of Tyler's friends had been suspended from school the previous year for having a marijuana cigarette on the school grounds. For the current incident, the school principal suspended the three teenagers for having alcohol at school. Tyler had also been suspended 2 months prior to his intake session for reported disruptive behaviors in the halls, fighting, and being verbally abusive to classmates. His parents were strongly encouraged by the principal to seek substance abuse treatment for Tyler.

Tyler lives at home with both parents. His parents are employed full time outside the home. His father's job requires travel most days of each week. Tyler has two adult siblings who live in other states. His 20-year-old sister, with whom he has been close, recently married and moved 200 miles away. Although Tyler expressed initial anger over his parents' plan to enter him into treatment, he was generally cooperative with the psychologist in the intake interview for the substance abuse program. He acknowledged that he has been having problems and expressed a willingness to be evaluated. He was administered the MMPI–A after the initial interview with the psychologist. The first 11 pages of his 17-page Minnesota Report are in Figure 7.5 (again, like Emily, the 3 pages of Tyler's item-level indicators are not reproduced for test security reasons, nor are his item responses).

Tyler's MMPI–A Validity Scales profile indicated that he was open and cooperative in his responses to the MMPI–A items. Although he showed some inconsistency on *VRIN*, this level of elevation was within the acceptable range (see p. 2 of his Minnesota Report in Figure 7.5 on p. 171). His performance on the Validity Scales indicates that the symptom profiles on MMPI–A are likely to be a good indication of his present functioning, as indicated in the Validity Considerations section of his Minnesota Report narrative.

The scale elevations he attained on the MMPI–A reflect a pattern of acting out and impulsive and irresponsible behaviors. His high scale elevations on the *Pd* (Psychopathic Deviate) and the PSY-5 *DISC* (Disconstraint) indicate a pattern of multiple and serious behavior problems that was apparent in the referral from school personnel and consistent with his running away from home. The Symptomatic Behavior section of his Minnesota Report highlights these problems, as well as his significant problems in school revealed by his elevation on *A-sch* (School Problems).

His elevated *MAC–R* score suggests personality characteristics associated with substance abuse problems. In addition, he acknowledged problems with substance abuse as noted by his *T* score of 63 on *ACK*. This scale elevation indicated that he was willing to acknowledge problematic use, at least through MMPI–A content. Interpretation of these scales is included in the Diagnostic Considerations section of his Minnesota Report. You can note the conservative nature of this computerized system in that we strongly encourage further evaluation rather than conclusively suggest a diagnosis of a substance use disorder.

An examination of the item-level indicators for substance use/abuse that are provided at the end of each Minnesota Report (again, they were not included in Figure 7.5 for test security reasons) reveals that he

FIGURE 7.5

Drug/Alcohol Treatment Interpretive Report

MMPI-A™

The Minnesota Report™: Adolescent Interpretive System, 2nd Edition

James N. Butcher, PhD, & Carolyn L. Williams, PhD

ID Number:	Tyler
Age:	17
Gender:	Male
Date Assessed:	12/10/2010

PEARSON   **PsychCorp**

FIGURE 7.5 (*Continued*)

MMPI-A™ Drug/Alcohol Treatment Interpretive Report
12/10/2010, Page 2

ID: Tyler

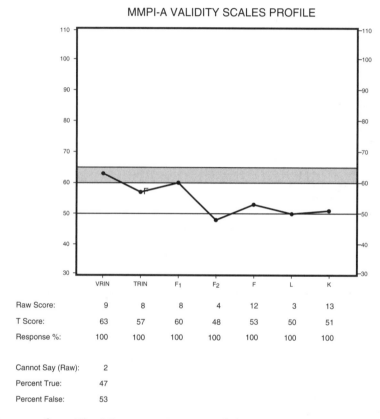

MMPI-A VALIDITY SCALES PROFILE

	VRIN	TRIN	F₁	F₂	F	L	K
Raw Score:	9	8	8	4	12	3	13
T Score:	63	57	60	48	53	50	51
Response %:	100	100	100	100	100	100	100

Cannot Say (Raw): 2
Percent True: 47
Percent False: 53

Excerpts from *The Minnesota Report: Adolescent Interpretive System* (Rev. ed.), by Butcher and Williams, 2007.

endorsed five of the nine items in this category. He willingly acknowledged problems resulting from his alcohol and drug use and admitted to marijuana use. In the last chapter of this book, we describe how an MMPI–A feedback session can be used both therapeutically and for further information gathering. Feedback sessions can be especially useful when addressing sensitive areas such as an adolescent's use of alcohol or

FIGURE 7.5 (*Continued*)

MMPI-A™ Drug/Alcohol Treatment Interpretive Report   ID: Tyler
12/10/2010, Page 3

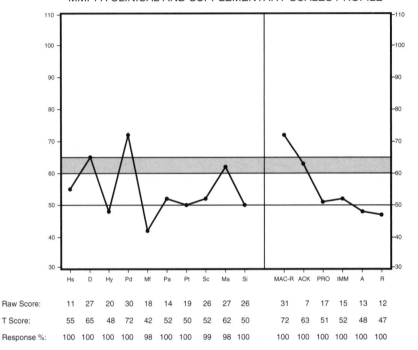

MMPI-A CLINICAL AND SUPPLEMENTARY SCALES PROFILE

	Hs	D	Hy	Pd	Mf	Pa	Pt	Sc	Ma	Si	MAC-R	ACK	PRO	IMM	A	R
Raw Score:	11	27	20	30	18	14	19	26	27	26	31	7	17	15	13	12
T Score:	55	65	48	72	42	52	50	52	62	50	72	63	51	52	48	47
Response %:	100	100	100	100	98	100	100	99	98	100	100	100	100	100	100	100

Welsh Code: 4'2+9-1<u>68</u> <u>70</u>/35: F<u>KL</u>/

Mean Profile Elevation: 57.0

Excerpts from *The Minnesota Report: Adolescent Interpretive System*
(Rev. ed.), by Butcher and Williams, 2007.

other drugs, as we will see in Chapter 9. Tyler also endorsed items related to illegal behaviors such as stealing and problems with the law, issues that had not yet come up at intake and that could be explored further when going over his responses to the MMPI–A.

Although Tyler's conduct problems are prominent in his profiles, there are also indicators of a potential for suicidal thoughts and/or

FIGURE 7.5 (*Continued*)

MMPI-A™ Drug/Alcohol Treatment Interpretive Report
12/10/2010, Page 4

ID: Tyler

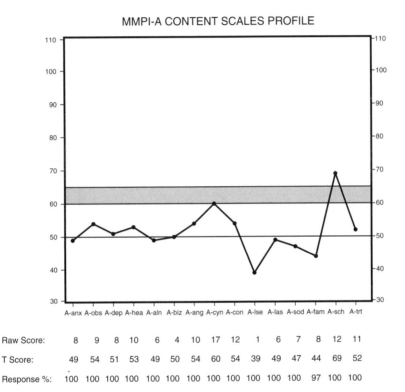

MMPI-A CONTENT SCALES PROFILE

	A-anx	A-obs	A-dep	A-hea	A-aln	A-biz	A-ang	A-cyn	A-con	A-lse	A-las	A-sod	A-fam	A-sch	A-trt
Raw Score:	8	9	8	10	6	4	10	17	12	1	6	7	8	12	11
T Score:	49	54	51	53	49	50	54	60	54	39	49	47	44	69	52
Response %:	100	100	100	100	100	100	100	100	100	100	100	100	97	100	100

Excerpts from *The Minnesota Report: Adolescent Interpretive System* (Rev. ed.), by Butcher and Williams, 2007.

behaviors, given his elevation on *D*, that also require further assessment, as indicated in the Diagnostic Considerations narrative. Recall, also in Chapter 4, that boys in clinical settings with elevations on *Pd* can respond with suicidal ideations and gestures when in trouble. An examination of Tyler's Harris–Lingoes scores for *D* indicate that D_3, Physical Malfunctioning, is the only elevated subscale, suggesting a preoccupation with somatic symptoms. Again, this is an issue not yet raised in Tyler's referral or intake session. Of the nine item-level indicators

FIGURE 7.5 *(Continued)*

MMPI-A™ Drug/Alcohol Treatment Interpretive Report
12/10/2010, Page 5

ID: Tyler

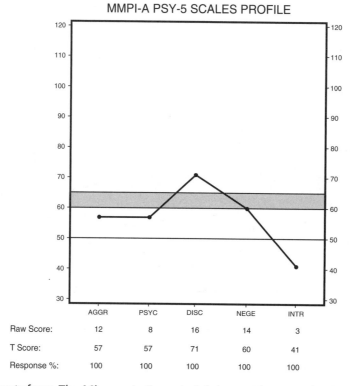

MMPI-A PSY-5 SCALES PROFILE

	AGGR	PSYC	DISC	NEGE	INTR
Raw Score:	12	8	16	14	3
T Score:	57	57	71	60	41
Response %:	100	100	100	100	100

Excerpts from *The Minnesota Report: Adolescent Interpretive System*
(Rev. ed.), by Butcher and Williams, 2007.

for Somatic Complaints, Tyler endorsed six. Many of his endorsements had to do with neurological symptoms like balance and tremors. Further assessment is suggested to determine the prominence and origin of these symptoms and if a medical consult is warranted. Note, given the absence of an elevation on *Hs* (Hypochondriasis) or *Hy* (Hysteria), these issues were not raised in the narrative section of the Minnesota Report.

FIGURE 7.5 (*Continued*)

MMPI-A™ Drug/Alcohol Treatment Interpretive Report   ID: Tyler
12/10/2010, Page 6

VALIDITY CONSIDERATIONS

This is a valid MMPI-A. His responses to the MMPI-A validity items suggest that he cooperated with the evaluation enough to provide useful interpretive information. The resulting profiles are an adequate indication of his present personality functioning.

SYMPTOMATIC BEHAVIOR

This adolescent's MMPI-A clinical profile indicates multiple serious behavior problems including school maladjustment, family discord, and authority conflicts. He can be moody, resentful, and attention-seeking. At times he may appear rebellious, impulsive, and argumentative. His poor judgment may get him into trouble. He can be self-centered and may show little remorse for his bad behavior. He may run away or lie to avoid punishment. Difficulties with the law or juvenile authorities could occur.

His two highest MMPI-A clinical scales, Pd and D, are the second most frequent high-point scale elevations among adolescents in mental health or alcohol/drug treatment settings. Approximately 12% of boys in treatment programs have these two scales prominent in their clinical profile. It should be noted that this high-point pair is infrequent in the normative sample, occurring in less than 3% of the sample. The Pd and D scale elevations are usually lower in the normative sample than in adolescent treatment samples.

In a large archival sample of MMPI-A cases scored by Pearson Assessments (n = 19,048), this high-point pair of scale elevations (Pd and D) was found for 2.9% of the boys, using well-defined peak scores of 65 or above, and more than 5 points separation from the third highest scale.

His MMPI-A Content Scales profile reveals important areas to consider in his evaluation. This young person reports numerous difficulties in school. He probably has poor academic performance and does not participate in school activities. He may have a history of truancy or suspensions from school. He probably has very negative attitudes about school, possibly reporting that the only positive aspect of school is being with his friends.

An examination of the adolescent's underlying personality factors with the PSY-5 scales might help explain any behavioral problems he might be presently experiencing. He shows a pattern of disinhibition given his elevation on the Disconstraint scale that can be manifest through high risk-taking, impulsivity, and irresponsibility. He appears to be less bound by moral restraints than other people and shows callous disregard for others.

INTERPERSONAL RELATIONS

Initially, he may seem likable and may make a good impression on others; however, his relationships tend to be very troubled. His behavior is primarily hedonistic and self-centered, and he is quite insensitive to the needs of other people, exploiting them and feeling no guilt about it.

Excerpts from *The Minnesota Report: Adolescent Interpretive System* (Rev. ed.), by Butcher and Williams, 2007.

FIGURE 7.5 *(Continued)*

MMPI-A™ Drug/Alcohol Treatment Interpretive Report
12/10/2010, Page 7

ID: Tyler

The MMPI-A Content Scales profile provides some additional information about his interpersonal relationships. He reported some misanthropic attitudes, indicating distrust of others and their motivations. He may be on guard when people seem friendlier than he thinks they should be.

BEHAVIORAL STABILITY

The relative scale elevation of the highest scale (Pd) in his clinical profile reflects high profile definition. If he is retested at a later date, the peak score on this test is likely to retain its relative salience in his profile pattern. Adolescents with this clinical profile may have a history of acting-out behaviors and relationship problems.

DIAGNOSTIC CONSIDERATIONS

More information is needed about his behavior problems before a definitive diagnosis can be made. His Pd elevation suggests that behavior problems should be considered.

Given his elevation on the School Problems scale, his diagnostic evaluation could include assessment of possible academic skills deficits and behavior problems.

His extremely high score on the MAC-R scale suggests substantial problems with alcohol or other drugs. He probably engages in risk-taking behaviors and tends towards exhibitionism. Further evaluation of his alcohol or other drug use is strongly recommended.

He has endorsed items that confirm his increasing involvement with alcohol or other drugs. He acknowledges that his use is problematic and reports being criticized for it. He may feel that alcohol or other drugs facilitate social interactions, thus serving as a coping strategy.

TREATMENT CONSIDERATIONS

His conduct disturbance should figure prominently in any treatment planning. His clinical scales profile suggests that he is a poor candidate for traditional, insight-oriented psychotherapy. A behavioral strategy is suggested. Clearly stated contingencies that are consistently followed are important for shaping more appropriate behaviors.

His very high potential for developing alcohol or drug problems requires attention in therapy if important life changes are to be made. He has acknowledged some problems in this area, which is a valuable first step for intervention.

He should be evaluated for the presence of suicidal thoughts and any possible suicidal behaviors. If he is at risk, appropriate precautions should be taken.

Excerpts from *The Minnesota Report: Adolescent Interpretive System* (Rev. ed.), by Butcher and Williams, 2007.

FIGURE 7.5 (*Continued*)

MMPI-A™ Drug/Alcohol Treatment Interpretive Report   ID: Tyler
12/10/2010, Page 8

He did endorse content suggesting a desire to succeed in life. There may be some positive aspects about school that could be reinforced. This could be an asset to build on during treatment.

Excerpts from *The Minnesota Report: Adolescent Interpretive System* (Rev. ed.), by Butcher and Williams, 2007.

However, the Minnesota Report is designed for clinicians knowledgeable about the MMPI–A and provides scores from various subscales and item indicators that must also be considered by the psychologist completing an evaluation, as illustrated in Tyler's case example. The computerized narrative section summarizes the most salient problems. A clinician's expertise is required for examining symptoms from the lower probability indicators like the subscales or item indicators.

Tyler also attained a moderate elevation on *A-cyn* (Cynicism), with most of its elevation due to items on $A\text{-}cyn_2$, Interpersonal Suspiciousness (see p. 10 of his Minnesota Report in Figure 7.5, p. 179). This indicates interpersonal problems such as interpersonal suspiciousness and problems in interpersonal relationships. He is likely to be very distrustful of others and expects the worst. This may interfere with establishing a therapeutic relationship. A savvy clinician, recalling Tyler's reported closeness to his older sister, could explore this relationship further to determine if she is a potential resource in his treatment (of course, her use of alcohol or other drugs is an area for further exploration). The lack of elevation on the *A-fam* (Family Problems) scale, despite his history of running away, indicates that Tyler does not view his problems as centered in the family. This is unlike Grace, our last case example.

Case 4: Grace, An Adolescent in a Family Dispute Assessment

Grace, a 15-year-old Black, upper-middle-class adolescent in seventh grade, was evaluated in a domestic court referral to determine if she required mental health treatment, in part as a result of the stress she is

FIGURE 7.5 *(Continued)*

MMPI-A™ Drug/Alcohol Treatment Interpretive Report   ID: Tyler
12/10/2010, Page 9

ADDITIONAL SCALES

A subscale or content component scale should be interpreted only when its corresponding parent scale
has an elevated T score of 60 or above. Subscales and content component scales printed below in bold
meet that criterion for interpretation.

Harris-Lingoes Subscales	Raw Score	T Score	Resp %
Depression Subscales			
Subjective Depression (D_1)	11	56	100
Psychomotor Retardation (D_2)	6	56	100
Physical Malfunctioning (D_3)	**7**	**75**	**100**
Mental Dullness (D_4)	5	56	100
Brooding (D_5)	3	51	100
Hysteria Subscales			
Denial of Social Anxiety (Hy_1)	3	49	100
Need for Affection (Hy_2)	1	33	100
Lassitude-Malaise (Hy_3)	5	54	100
Somatic Complaints (Hy_4)	7	60	100
Inhibition of Aggression (Hy_5)	2	44	100
Psychopathic Deviate Subscales			
Familial Discord (Pd_1)	4	53	100
Authority Problems (Pd_2)	**6**	**67**	**100**
Social Imperturbability (Pd_3)	4	54	100
Social Alienation (Pd_4)	**9**	**69**	**100**
Self-Alienation (Pd_5)	5	53	100
Paranoia Subscales			
Persecutory Ideas (Pa_1)	8	64	100
Poignancy (Pa_2)	1	36	100
Naivete (Pa_3)	3	45	100
Schizophrenia Subscales			
Social Alienation (Sc_1)	6	49	95
Emotional Alienation (Sc_2)	0	37	100
Lack of Ego Mastery, Cognitive (Sc_3)	2	46	100
Lack of Ego Mastery, Conative (Sc_4)	2	42	100
Lack of Ego Mastery, Defective Inhibition (Sc_5)	6	62	100
Bizarre Sensory Experiences (Sc_6)	11	68	100
Hypomania Subscales			
Amorality (Ma_1)	4	59	100
Psychomotor Acceleration (Ma_2)	**9**	**62**	**100**
Imperturbability (Ma_3)	3	49	100
Ego Inflation (Ma_4)	4	48	89

Excerpts from *The Minnesota Report: Adolescent Interpretive System*
(Rev. ed.), by Butcher and Williams, 2007.

FIGURE 7.5 *(Continued)*

MMPI-A™ Drug/Alcohol Treatment Interpretive Report   ID: Tyler
12/10/2010, Page 10

	Raw Score	T Score	Resp %
Social Introversion Subscales			
Shyness / Self-Consciousness (Si$_1$)	7	53	100
Social Avoidance (Si$_2$)	2	47	100
Alienation--Self and Others (Si$_3$)	7	48	100
Content Component Scales			
Adolescent Depression			
Dysphoria (A-dep$_1$)	2	55	100
Self-Depreciation (A-dep$_2$)	3	59	100
Lack of Drive (A-dep$_3$)	2	47	100
Suicidal Ideation (A-dep$_4$)	0	42	100
Adolescent Health Concerns			
Gastrointestinal Complaints (A-hea$_1$)	1	59	100
Neurological Symptoms (A-hea$_2$)	6	56	100
General Health Concerns (A-hea$_3$)	2	51	100
Adolescent Alienation			
Misunderstood (A-aln$_1$)	2	50	100
Social Isolation (A-aln$_2$)	1	46	100
Interpersonal Skepticism (A-aln$_3$)	3	64	100
Adolescent Bizarre Mentation			
Psychotic Symptomatology (A-biz$_1$)	1	43	100
Paranoid Ideation (A-biz$_2$)	1	53	100
Adolescent Anger			
Explosive Behavior (A-ang$_1$)	4	55	100
Irritability (A-ang$_2$)	5	54	100
Adolescent Cynicism			
Misanthropic Beliefs (A-cyn$_1$)	9	54	100
Interpersonal Suspiciousness (A-cyn$_2$)	**8**	**65**	**100**
Adolescent Conduct Problems			
Acting-Out Behaviors (A-con$_1$)	5	55	100
Antisocial Attitudes (A-con$_2$)	5	57	100
Negative Peer Group Influences (A-con$_3$)	1	51	100
Adolescent Low Self-Esteem			
Self-Doubt (A-lse$_1$)	1	40	100
Interpersonal Submissiveness (A-lse$_2$)	0	38	100
Adolescent Low Aspirations			
Low Achievement Orientation (A-las$_1$)	3	47	100
Lack of Initiative (A-las$_2$)	2	49	100

Excerpts from *The Minnesota Report: Adolescent Interpretive System* (Rev. ed.), by Butcher and Williams, 2007.

FIGURE 7.5 (*Continued*)

MMPI-A™ Drug/Alcohol Treatment Interpretive Report   **ID: Tyler**
12/10/2010, Page 11

	Raw Score	T Score	Resp %
Adolescent Social Discomfort			
Introversion (A-sod$_1$)	4	50	100
Shyness (A-sod$_2$)	3	44	100
Adolescent Family Problems			
Familial Discord (A-fam$_1$)	8	50	95
Familial Alienation (A-fam$_2$)	0	39	100
Adolescent School Problems			
School Conduct Problems (A-sch$_1$)	**3**	**69**	**100**
Negative Attitudes (A-sch$_2$)	**5**	**63**	**100**
Adolescent Negative Treatment Indicators			
Low Motivation (A-trt$_1$)	3	49	100
Inability to Disclose (A-trt$_2$)	5	59	100

Uniform T scores are used for Hs, D, Hy, Pd, Pa, Pt, Sc, Ma, the content scales, the content component scales, and the PSY-5 scales. The remaining scales and subscales use linear T scores.

Excerpts from *The Minnesota Report: Adolescent Interpretive System* (Rev. ed.), by Butcher and Williams, 2007.

reportedly experiencing over her parents' impending divorce. Both parents are professionals in executive positions and hold graduate degrees. Grace's father, through his attorney, requested the evaluation following his discovery that Grace's mother is living with another man in the family residence. Her father reports concerns that Grace and her two younger siblings are being neglected when in his wife's care. He is troubled about Grace's socially distant and alienated behaviors when he sees her during his weekend visitations with his children. Her father is worried that she is left home alone or in the presence of her mother's significant other without adequate supervision.

In separate interviews, both parents indicate Grace spends a great deal of time alone in her room and has no close friends. Grace is increasingly absent from school and fails to complete her assignments, a marked departure from her interest in school in earlier grades. Grace's mother contends that her father's concerns are feigned to contest the current custody arrangements as a way of punishing her for "moving on with her life." During an interview, Grace's mother noted that the constant fighting and upcoming divorce have been hard on the children and suggested that a teen divorce support group offered at their church might be beneficial for Grace.

While the psychologist was interviewing her mother, Grace agreed to complete the MMPI–A on a laptop computer. She worked quietly and had no questions when the assistant checked her progress intermittently. She finished in slightly over an hour. Figure 7.6 contains the Minnesota Report that was available as soon as Grace completed the test (11 pages of her 15-page Minnesota Report are reproduced, minus the printout of her item indicators and responses). Grace's scores on the MMPI–A Validity Scales were clearly in the valid and interpretable range for adolescents. Although she had a slight elevation on *K* (*T* score of 58), suggesting that she was somewhat defensive or self-protective, her score was not in the range that would suggest uncooperative or invalidating performance, consistent with the narrative section of her Minnesota Report.

Grace's scores on the Clinical, Content, and PSY-5 Scales suggest that she is experiencing significant adjustment problems at this time, including a great deal of alienation and social distress as noted by her scale elevations on *Pa* (Paranoia), *Si, A-sod,* and *INTR.* She feels socially isolated and has difficulties in interpersonal relationships. Her high scores on *A-aln* (Alienation) and *A-lse* (Low Self-Esteem) suggest that she is feeling alienated from others and experiencing low feelings of self-worth at this time. Low mood (as indicated by her elevation on *D* and high elevation on *INTR*) is likely part of her symptomatic picture.

The conservative nature of this computerized report is evident in the Diagnostic Considerations section of the narrative in Figure 7.6 on p. 188. Here the psychologist is advised that paranoid features may be present. In Grace's case, given that the MMPI–A was administered early in the assessment, the psychologist will incorporate further assessment of potential psychotic processes, given this statement, as well as her high elevation on *Pa* and moderate elevation on *PSYC* (Psychoticism). The Harris–Lingoes subscale *Pa₃*, Naiveté, is the only one elevated and suggests an overly trusting attitude and denial of feelings of hostility toward others rather than overt suspiciousness and projection, which is characterized by an elevation on *Pa₁*, Persecutory Ideas (Grace's *T* score on this subscale was not elevated at 57; refer to Figure 7.6, p. 189, for this information). However, this suggestion from the Harris–Lingoes subscales that correlates related to feeling threatened and misunderstood may be less relevant than naiveté is offset by her elevations on the full scales like *A-aln* and *PSYC*. Again, recall that subscales provide less reliable measurements than full scales.

Notably absent from Grace's Content Scales profile is any indication of family or school problems given her scores on *A-fam* and *A-sch* (*T* scores of 37 and 35, respectively). She is well below the norm for indicating problems in these important areas of an adolescent's life, despite the reason for the referral and information about problems in school. This is likely due to her guarded and suspicious nature. In addition, she is attempting to deal with her significant problems with denial. Despite this, one of her item-level indicators poignantly illustrates her alienation from

FIGURE 7.6

Outpatient Mental Health Interpretive Report

MMPI-A™

The Minnesota Report™: Adolescent Interpretive System, 2nd Edition

James N. Butcher, PhD, & Carolyn L. Williams, PhD

ID Number:	Grace
Age:	15
Gender:	Female
Date Assessed:	12/10/2010

PEARSON

PsychCorp

Excerpts from *The Minnesota Report: Adolescent Interpretive System* (Rev. ed.), by Butcher and Williams, 2007. Reproduced by permission of the University of Minnesota Press. All rights reserved. "MMPI®–A," "Minnesota Multiphasic Personality Inventory®—A," and "The Minnesota Report" are trademarks owned by the Regents of the University of Minnesota.

FIGURE 7.6 (*Continued*)

MMPI-A™ Outpatient Mental Health Interpretive Report ID: Grace
12/10/2010, Page 2

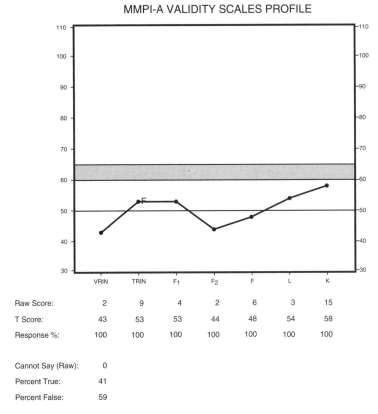

MMPI-A VALIDITY SCALES PROFILE

	VRIN	TRIN	F_1	F_2	F	L	K
Raw Score:	2	9	4	2	6	3	15
T Score:	43	53	53	44	48	54	58
Response %:	100	100	100	100	100	100	100

Cannot Say (Raw):	0
Percent True:	41
Percent False:	59

Excerpts from *The Minnesota Report: Adolescent Interpretive System*
(Rev. ed.), by Butcher and Williams, 2007.

FIGURE 7.6 (*Continued*)

MMPI-A™ Outpatient Mental Health Interpretive Report   ID: Grace
12/10/2010, Page 3

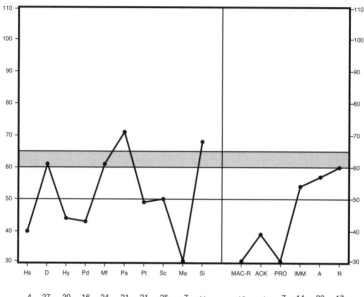

MMPI-A CLINICAL AND SUPPLEMENTARY SCALES PROFILE

	Hs	D	Hy	Pd	Mf	Pa	Pt	Sc	Ma	Si	MAC-R	ACK	PRO	IMM	A	R
Raw Score:	4	27	20	16	24	21	21	25	7	41	10	1	7	14	22	17
T Score:	40	61	44	43	61	71	49	50	30	68	30	39	30	54	57	60
Response %:	100	100	100	100	100	100	100	100	100	100	100	100	100	100	100	100

Welsh Code: 6'0+25-8/7 341:9# KL/F:

Mean Profile Elevation: 48.5

Excerpts from *The Minnesota Report: Adolescent Interpretive System*
(Rev. ed.), by Butcher and Williams, 2007.

FIGURE 7.6 (Continued)

MMPI-A™ Outpatient Mental Health Interpretive Report
12/10/2010, Page 4

ID: Grace

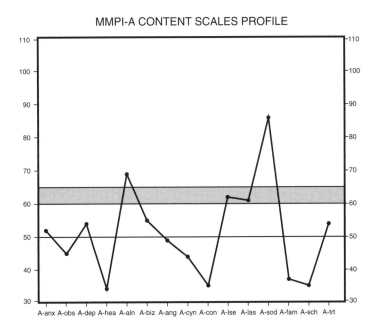

MMPI-A CONTENT SCALES PROFILE

	A-anx	A-obs	A-dep	A-hea	A-aln	A-biz	A-ang	A-cyn	A-con	A-lse	A-las	A-sod	A-fam	A-sch	A-trt
Raw Score:	11	7	12	1	12	6	9	10	2	10	9	21	4	1	12
T Score:	52	45	54	34	69	55	49	44	35	62	61	86	37	35	54
Response %:	100	100	100	100	100	100	100	100	100	100	100	100	100	100	100

Excerpts from *The Minnesota Report: Adolescent Interpretive System* (Rev. ed.), by Butcher and Williams, 2007.

FIGURE 7.6 (*Continued*)

MMPI-A™ Outpatient Mental Health Interpretive Report
12/10/2010, Page 5

ID: Grace

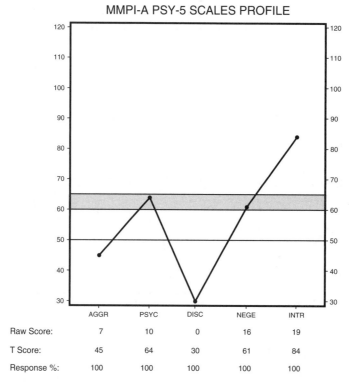

MMPI-A PSY-5 SCALES PROFILE

	AGGR	PSYC	DISC	NEGE	INTR
Raw Score:	7	10	0	16	19
T Score:	45	64	30	61	84
Response %:	100	100	100	100	100

Excerpts from *The Minnesota Report: Adolescent Interpretive System* (Rev. ed.), by Butcher and Williams, 2007.

FIGURE 7.6 (*Continued*)

MMPI-A™ Outpatient Mental Health Interpretive Report   **ID: Grace**
12/10/2010, Page 6

VALIDITY CONSIDERATIONS

This adolescent's approach to the MMPI-A was open and cooperative. The resulting MMPI-A is valid and is probably a good indication of her present level of personality functioning. This may be viewed as a positive indication of her involvement with the evaluation.

SYMPTOMATIC BEHAVIOR

Adolescents with this MMPI-A clinical profile are likely to be experiencing intense problems at this time. Overly sensitive to criticism, this individual reacts to even minor problems with resentment. She feels that other people take advantage of her at times. She is highly suspicious of others and constantly on guard to avoid being taken advantage of; this touchiness often makes her argumentative. She may be experiencing increased disagreements with adults.

Adolescents with this pattern are usually aloof and distant and may show rigid, moralistic thinking. This adolescent's lack of trust makes her feel particularly wary of others. When she feels threatened, she may react with self-righteous indignation and may complain that she has been wronged. Adolescents with this profile tend to project and externalize blame. They typically do not assume responsibility for their problems and tend to blame others or to rationalize their faults.

Her high-point MMPI-A score, Pa, is one of the least frequent well-defined peak scores among adolescent girls in treatment centers. Only 2% of girls in treatment programs have this peak scale elevation in their profile pattern. It should be noted that this high-point score also occurs with relatively low frequency (4%) as a peak score for girls in the normative sample and at a lower level of elevation than in treatment program samples.

In a large archival sample of cases scored by Pearson Assessments (n = 12,744 girls), 3.2% of the sample had a well-defined peak score on Pa that was at or above a T score of 65 and separated from the next highest scale by more than 5 points.

An understanding of the adolescent's underlying personality from her PSY-5 scales could provide a context in which to view the extreme psychological symptoms she is presently experiencing. She shows a meager capacity to experience pleasure in life. Persons with high scores on the Introversion/Low Positive Emotionality scale tend to be pessimistic in outlook, anhedonic (unable to experience pleasure) in daily life, and withdrawn from others with few or no friends.

INTERPERSONAL RELATIONS

She is overly sensitive, rigid, and hostile, and she tends to brood a great deal. She bears grudges and may actively work to get even with others when she feels they are doing her wrong. Her lack of trust and inability to compromise often disrupt interpersonal relationships and may prevent her from developing warm, close relationships. She tends to feel insecure in personal relationships, is hypersensitive to rejection, and may become jealous at times. She tends to need a great deal of reassurance.

Excerpts from *The Minnesota Report: Adolescent Interpretive System* (Rev. ed.), by Butcher and Williams, 2007.

FIGURE 7.6 (Continued)

MMPI-A™ Outpatient Mental Health Interpretive Report   **ID: Grace**
12/10/2010, Page 7

She is quite shy and inhibited in social situations and may avoid others for fear of being hurt. She is likely to have very few friends and to be thought of as distant and hard to get to know. She is quiet and submissive, and she lacks self-confidence in dealing with other people. She is timid and unlikely to be interested in dating.

Some problems with her relationships are evident from her extreme endorsement of items on A-sod. She reports considerable discomfort in social situations. She indicates that she has difficulties making friends and initiating conversations; she prefers to avoid group activities. She may feel depressed about her social inadequacies and she may have very limited interest in boys.

In addition to her extreme endorsements on the MMPI-A Content Scales, she reported other significant interpersonal issues. She feels considerable emotional distance from others. She may believe that other people do not like, understand, or care about her. She reports having no one, including parents or friends, to rely on.

BEHAVIORAL STABILITY

The relative elevation of the highest scale (Pa) in her clinical profile shows very high profile definition. Her peak score is likely to remain very prominent in her profile pattern if she is retested at a later date.

DIAGNOSTIC CONSIDERATIONS

Only tentative diagnoses can be provided for this clinical profile, because it is important to consider other factors. There is some indication that the client may have paranoid features.

TREATMENT CONSIDERATIONS

Adolescents with this clinical profile tend to be guarded, making it difficult to establish rapport with them. In psychological treatment, they deny responsibility for their problems, may have stormy treatment sessions, and may terminate therapy prematurely. A behavioral approach, with mutually established goals, may be more helpful than insight-oriented sessions. This adolescent's emotional distance and discomfort in interpersonal situations must be considered in developing a treatment plan. She may have difficulty self-disclosing, especially in groups. She may not appreciate receiving feedback from others about her behavior or problems.

Excerpts from *The Minnesota Report: Adolescent Interpretive System* (Rev. ed.), by Butcher and Williams, 2007.

FIGURE 7.6 (Continued)

MMPI-A™ Outpatient Mental Health Interpretive Report
12/10/2010, Page 8
ID: Grace

ADDITIONAL SCALES

A subscale or content component scale should be interpreted only when its corresponding parent scale has an elevated T score of 60 or above. Subscales and content component scales printed below in bold meet that criterion for interpretation.

Harris-Lingoes Subscales	Raw Score	T Score	Resp %
Depression Subscales			
Subjective Depression (D₁)	**18**	**68**	**100**
Psychomotor Retardation (D₂)	**11**	**84**	**100**
Physical Malfunctioning (D₃)	3	46	100
Mental Dullness (D₄)	6	58	100
Brooding (D₅)	**7**	**65**	**100**
Hysteria Subscales			
Denial of Social Anxiety (Hy₁)	1	37	100
Need for Affection (Hy₂)	6	55	100
Lassitude-Malaise (Hy₃)	6	55	100
Somatic Complaints (Hy₄)	2	40	100
Inhibition of Aggression (Hy₅)	3	51	100
Psychopathic Deviate Subscales			
Familial Discord (Pd₁)	2	40	100
Authority Problems (Pd₂)	0	31	100
Social Imperturbability (Pd₃)	0	30	100
Social Alienation (Pd₄)	7	57	100
Self-Alienation (Pd₅)	4	47	100
Paranoia Subscales			
Persecutory Ideas (Pa₁)	6	57	100
Poignancy (Pa₂)	5	57	100
Naivete (Pa₃)	**8**	**72**	**100**
Schizophrenia Subscales			
Social Alienation (Sc₁)	10	61	100
Emotional Alienation (Sc₂)	3	54	100
Lack of Ego Mastery, Cognitive (Sc₃)	3	50	100
Lack of Ego Mastery, Conative (Sc₄)	5	52	100
Lack of Ego Mastery, Defective Inhibition (Sc₅)	2	40	100
Bizarre Sensory Experiences (Sc₆)	3	43	100
Hypomania Subscales			
Amorality (Ma₁)	1	39	100
Psychomotor Acceleration (Ma₂)	1	30	100
Imperturbability (Ma₃)	1	37	100
Ego Inflation (Ma₄)	1	30	100

Excerpts from *The Minnesota Report: Adolescent Interpretive System* (Rev. ed.), by Butcher and Williams, 2007.

FIGURE 7.6 (*Continued*)

MMPI-A™ Outpatient Mental Health Interpretive Report   **ID: Grace**
12/10/2010, Page 9

	Raw Score	T Score	Resp %
<u>Social Introversion Subscales</u>			
Shyness / Self-Consciousness (Si$_1$)	**11**	**65**	**100**
Social Avoidance (Si$_2$)	**7**	**78**	**100**
Alienation--Self and Others (Si$_3$)	6	44	100
<u>Content Component Scales</u>			
Adolescent Depression			
Dysphoria (A-dep$_1$)	5	71	100
Self Depreciation (A dep$_2$)	2	48	100
Lack of Drive (A-dep$_3$)	3	52	100
Suicidal Ideation (A-dep$_4$)	0	42	100
Adolescent Health Concerns			
Gastrointestinal Complaints (A-hea$_1$)	0	44	100
Neurological Symptoms (A-hea$_2$)	0	35	100
General Health Concerns (A-hea$_3$)	0	37	100
Adolescent Alienation			
Misunderstood (A-aln$_1$)	2	49	100
Social Isolation (A-aln$_2$)	**4**	**71**	**100**
Interpersonal Skepticism (A-aln$_3$)	**3**	**65**	**100**
Adolescent Bizarre Mentation			
Psychotic Symptomatology (A-biz$_1$)	3	51	100
Paranoid Ideation (A-biz$_2$)	2	68	100
Adolescent Anger			
Explosive Behavior (A-ang$_1$)	4	56	100
Irritability (A-ang$_2$)	5	49	100
Adolescent Cynicism			
Misanthropic Beliefs (A-cyn$_1$)	5	41	100
Interpersonal Suspiciousness (A-cyn$_2$)	5	52	100
Adolescent Conduct Problems			
Acting-Out Behaviors (A-con$_1$)	2	43	100
Antisocial Attitudes (A-con$_2$)	0	32	100
Negative Peer Group Influences (A-con$_3$)	0	42	100
Adolescent Low Self-Esteem			
Self-Doubt (A-lse$_1$)	**7**	**62**	**100**
Interpersonal Submissiveness (A-lse$_2$)	3	59	100
Adolescent Low Aspirations			
Low Achievement Orientation (A-las$_1$)	5	58	100
Lack of Initiative (A-las$_2$)	3	54	100

Excerpts from *The Minnesota Report: Adolescent Interpretive System* (Rev. ed.), by Butcher and Williams, 2007.

FIGURE 7.6 (*Continued*)

MMPI-A™ Outpatient Mental Health Interpretive Report　　　　　　　**ID: Grace**
12/10/2010, Page 10

	Raw Score	T Score	Resp %
Adolescent Social Discomfort			
Introversion (A-sod$_1$)	**12**	**84**	**100**
Shyness (A-sod$_2$)	**9**	**71**	**100**
Adolescent Family Problems			
Familial Discord (A-fam$_1$)	2	33	100
Familial Alienation (A-fam$_2$)	1	43	100
Adolescent School Problems			
School Conduct Problems (A-sch$_1$)	0	43	100
Negative Attitudes (A-sch$_2$)	0	37	100
Adolescent Negative Treatment Indicators			
Low Motivation (A-trt$_1$)	4	53	100
Inability to Disclose (A-trt$_2$)	5	60	100

Uniform T scores are used for Hs, D, Hy, Pd, Pa, Pt, Sc, Ma, the content scales, the content component scales, and the PSY-5 scales. The remaining scales and subscales use linear T scores.

Excerpts from *The Minnesota Report: Adolescent Interpretive System* (Rev. ed.), by Butcher and Williams, 2007.

her family, with her endorsement of the item stating her family cannot be relied on in times of trouble.

As indicated in the Treatment Considerations section of the narrative in Figure 7.6 on p. 188, it will be difficult to establish rapport with Grace. However, her psychological problems are significant and unlikely to be met at the present time simply with a support group, given her denial, difficulty with self-disclosure, and discomfort in interpersonal situations. The Minnesota Report will be useful to the psychologist as an outside and objective illustration to her parents about her need for individual therapy rather than a support group at this time.

Cautions Regarding Computer-Based Report Use

Computer-based personality reports provide a useful summary of hypotheses, descriptions, and test inferences about patients in a rapid and efficient manner. However, as described earlier and illustrated with the

---

FIGURE 7.6 *(Continued)*

MMPI-A™ Outpatient Mental Health Interpretive Report   **ID: Grace**
12/10/2010, Page 13

NOTE: This MMPI-A interpretation can serve as a useful source of hypotheses about adolescent clients. This report is based on objectively derived scale indexes and scale interpretations that have been developed with diverse groups of clients from adolescent treatment settings. The personality descriptions, inferences, and recommendations contained herein need to be verified by other sources of clinical information because individual clients may not fully match the prototype. Only a qualified, trained professional should use the information in this report.

This and previous pages of this report contain trade secrets and are not to be released in response to requests under HIPAA (or any other data disclosure law that exempts trade secret information from release). Further, release in response to litigation discovery demands should be made only in accordance with your profession's ethical guidelines and under an appropriate protective order.

Excerpts from *The Minnesota Report: Adolescent Interpretive System* (Rev. ed.), by Butcher and Williams, 2007.

Minnesota Report in four cases, computer reports are not substitutes for a clinician's expertise or judgment (see Eyde et al., 2009, for more case illustrations with the MMPI–2). Rather, computerized reports provide a professional-to-professional consultation. Clinicians using computerized reports must fully understand the psychological test for which the reports were developed, including its strengths and limitations. Because of this, each Minnesota Report has a cautionary statement, as can be seen in Grace's report in Figure 7.6, this page.

The Minnesota Report is a type of psychological evaluation written for sharing information between professionals who are qualified to use it. The MMPI–A contains personal information about the adolescent's psychological functioning and, as with other psychological records, should be kept in secure files and only released under appropriate circumstances. Many psychologists prefer to keep computerized reports in their office files as part of the "raw test data" used to develop the psychological evaluation. The Minnesota Report is not written in language appropriate for sharing with clients or others without expertise in the MMPI–A. Clinicians who prefer providing written information to their clients about the findings from their testing should write a summary of the computerized report tailored to the client. Similarly, if the client requests a copy of the Minnesota Report, we suggest that a written summary be provided instead.[2]

Keep in mind that computer reports are based on modal findings and correlates that may not fully apply to a particular individual. It is the clinician's responsibility to parse out the most appropriate and well-fitted interpretations. There are instances, as we saw with Tyler and Grace, in which the computer-based reports present problems or issues not revealed at intake. The computer report may contain information that provides for a clearer and more detailed understanding of the case. However, new information that is provided in computerized systems such as the Minnesota Report should be carefully evaluated to determine if there are issues or problems that the practitioner has not obtained from other sources. Our next chapter presents a flow chart of how to use all the information coming from the MMPI–A, including computerized interpretative systems such as the Minnesota Report, to develop a comprehensive report.

---

[2]See the cautionary statement in Figure 7.6 on page 192 for information about sharing the Minnesota Report under Health Insurance Portability and Accountability Act (HIPPA) requests.

Putting It All Together

An Interpretive Strategy and Report Writing

8

When you're prepared, you're more confident. When you have a strategy, you're more comfortable.

—*Fred Couples, professional golfer*

Now that we have summarized the foundation for the MMPI–A, described the MMPI–A scales and their external correlates, and examined computerized interpretive reports, we turn to a strategy for clinicians to incorporate MMPI–A measures into an integrated clinical picture. How does the practitioner approach interpretation of the MMPI–A scales given the number of variables that can influence an adolescent's performance on psychological tests and the extensive number of scales the MMPI–A provides? What should an MMPI–A report include?

There is not necessarily a one-size-fits-all MMPI–A report because different referral sources have differing levels of expertise in psychometric testing and differing reasons for requesting an evaluation. In some cases, the referral source is another mental health professional, but in other cases it could be a teacher, parent, social worker, parole officer, attorney, or physician with limited understanding of the MMPI–A. The level of expertise of the consumer of the report should be considered when writing up the results of an MMPI–A evaluation. For example, as we saw in Chapter 7, reports generated as part of the Minnesota Reports (Butcher & Williams, 2007) are written for sophisticated users (i.e., psychologists, psychiatrists, and other qualified clinicians) who have a basic knowledge of the strengths and limitations of the MMPI–A as an assessment tool. As such, it would be inappropriate to share a young person's Minnesota Report with his or her teacher. Rather, in cases in which the referral source does not have the level of training to understand the technical information in the computerized report, the psychologist should use the Minnesota Report as "raw test data" to develop a report that addresses the questions from and expertise of the referral source. In some cases, the MMPI–A report will be embedded in a more comprehensive psychological report. It is beyond the scope of this book to provide recommendations for comprehensive psychological reports. The reader is referred to Ownby (2009) for a detailed discussion of writing comprehensive reports (see also Chapter 3, the section "Sources to Augment a Personality Assessment With the MMPI–A," on pp. 43–47).

Figure 8.1 provides a flow chart for a MMPI–A interpretation and report. It can also be used for developing a section of a comprehensive psychological evaluation that covers the MMPI–A administration and interpretation. Each MMPI–A interpretive report should include information about the reason for the evaluation (i.e., questions to be addressed), behavioral observations from the test administration and interviews, any validity concerns about the responses to the MMPI–A, and relevant MMPI–A descriptors covering clinical symptoms, interpersonal relations, diagnostic considerations, and treatment planning. If a collaborative feedback session is included, then the MMPI–A report should include information from it (Chapter 9 covers collaborative feedback sessions).

In the sections that follow, we describe a sequence of steps to bring into focus the appropriate behavioral correlates and test-based hypotheses that can have a bearing on understanding a young person. To provide a practical focus to the interpretive strategy, we begin with a case description of José that will be used in the following sections to highlight the process of using information about personality and symptoms based on the MMPI–A.[1]

Case Description of José

REFERRAL QUESTION

José was administered the MMPI–A as part of a court-ordered evaluation subsequent to his arrest after a gang-related incident in which city property was destroyed. Police found both marijuana and methamphet-

---

[1]Demographic information and some of the assessment details have been altered for privacy and didactic purposes.

FIGURE 8.1

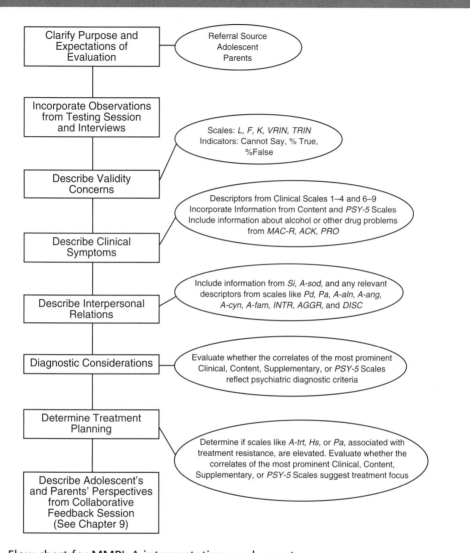

Flow chart for MMPI–A interpretations and reports.

amines in his possession. Restraint was required because José became verbally aggressive and threatened the arresting officer. José is being detained at a state juvenile detention facility awaiting a hearing. During his stay he has made several requests for medications for a number of physical symptoms, including headaches and neck pain. The court ordered a psychological evaluation to determine the existence of any mental health or substance abuse disorders that should be considered and if treatment is indicated.

BACKGROUND

José emigrated to the United States from Mexico with his parents when he was 5 years old. Spanish is the predominant language at home. José has attended school in the United States since kindergarten and is fluent in English. He lives with his parents and four younger siblings.

PRIOR HISTORY

José's history includes multiple previous arrests, the first when he was 11 years old and arrested for shoplifting in a department store. Another arrest for destroying property occurred at the same shopping center 12 months later when José and two friends were caught on a surveillance camera breaking car antennas and stealing.

INFORMATION FROM PARENTS

José's mother works as a housekeeper at a local hotel and his father is employed as a janitor. In recent months, José has failed to return home on several occasions, reportedly staying with friends. On two occasions when he was entrusted with care of his two youngest brothers, he left them unattended and went out with friends. His parents also learned that on one occasion José gave alcohol to his 9-year-old brother when the parents were both working. As a result, his parents no longer trust him to babysit and have tried to arrange their work schedules so that one of them is always home.

BEHAVIORAL OBSERVATIONS OF JOSÉ'S MMPI–A TESTING SESSION

During his interview and MMPI–A test administration sessions at the juvenile detention center 1 week after his arrest, José was sociable, cooperative, and responsive to the examiner's questions. He was fluent in English and reported no reading difficulties. He was open in his descriptions of his prior arrests, behavior problems, and history of alcohol and drug use in his initial interview. José completed the booklet form of the MMPI–A in English in one session of approximately 50 minutes at a small table in the examiner's office. The examiner was present throughout the session. José would occasionally ask the examiner for the definition of a word (e.g., *brood*) but otherwise worked quietly on his own. At the end of the testing session, José expressed curiosity about the evaluation and asked what this test is supposed to show about him and whether he could find out the results. Figure 8.2 shows 6 pages from José's 16-page Minnesota Report.

FIGURE 8.2

Correctional Interpretive Report

MMPI-A™

The Minnesota Report™: Adolescent Interpretive System, 2nd Edition

James N. Butcher, PhD, & Carolyn L. Williams, PhD

ID Number:	Jose
Age:	16
Gender:	Male
Date Assessed:	12/10/2010

PEARSON

🖲 **PsychCorp**

FIGURE 8.2 (*Continued*)

MMPI-A™ Correctional Interpretive Report   ID: Jose
12/10/2010, Page 2

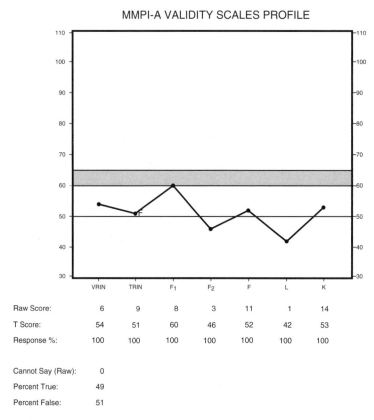

MMPI-A VALIDITY SCALES PROFILE

	VRIN	TRIN	F₁	F₂	F	L	K
Raw Score:	6	9	8	3	11	1	14
T Score:	54	51	60	46	52	42	53
Response %:	100	100	100	100	100	100	100

Cannot Say (Raw): 0
Percent True: 49
Percent False: 51

Excerpts from *The Minnesota Report: Adolescent Interpretive System* (Rev. ed.), by Butcher and Williams, 2007.

FIGURE 8.2 *(Continued)*

MMPI-A™ Correctional Interpretive Report
12/10/2010, Page 3

ID: Jose

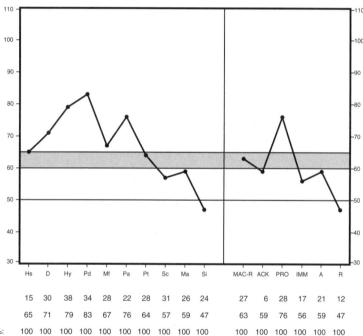

MMPI-A CLINICAL AND SUPPLEMENTARY SCALES PROFILE

	Hs	D	Hy	Pd	Mf	Pa	Pt	Sc	Ma	Si		MAC-R	ACK	PRO	IMM	A	R
Raw Score:	15	30	38	34	28	22	28	31	26	24		27	6	28	17	21	12
T Score:	65	71	79	83	67	76	64	57	59	47		63	59	76	56	59	47
Response %:	100	100	100	100	100	100	100	100	100	100		100	100	100	100	100	100

Welsh Code: 4"362'51+7-98/0: KF/L:

Mean Profile Elevation: 69.3

Excerpts from *The Minnesota Report: Adolescent Interpretive System* (Rev. ed.), by Butcher and Williams, 2007.

FIGURE 8.2 *(Continued)*

MMPI-A™ Correctional Interpretive Report
12/10/2010, Page 4

ID: Jose

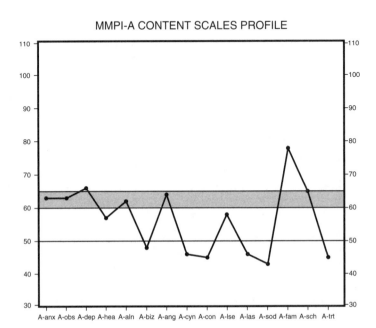

MMPI-A CONTENT SCALES PROFILE

	A-anx	A-obs	A-dep	A-hea	A-aln	A-biz	A-ang	A-cyn	A-con	A-lse	A-las	A-sod	A-fam	A-sch	A-trt
Raw Score:	13	11	15	13	10	3	12	12	8	8	5	5	24	11	7
T Score:	63	63	66	57	62	48	64	46	45	58	46	43	78	65	45
Response %:	100	100	100	100	100	100	100	100	100	100	100	100	100	100	100

Excerpts from *The Minnesota Report: Adolescent Interpretive System* (Rev. ed.), by Butcher and Williams, 2007.

FIGURE 8.2 (*Continued*)

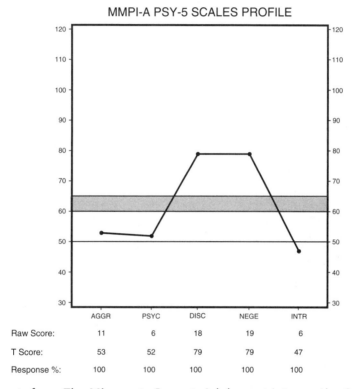

MMPI-A PSY-5 SCALES PROFILE

	AGGR	PSYC	DISC	NEGE	INTR
Raw Score:	11	6	18	19	6
T Score:	53	52	79	79	47
Response %:	100	100	100	100	100

Excerpts from *The Minnesota Report: Adolescent Interpretive System* (Rev. ed.), by Butcher and Williams, 2007.

FIGURE 8.2 (*Continued*)

MMPI-A™ Correctional Interpretive Report   ID: Jose
12/10/2010, Page 9

ADDITIONAL SCALES

A subscale or content component scale should be interpreted only when its corresponding parent scale has an elevated T score of 60 or above. Subscales and content component scales printed below in bold meet that criterion for interpretation.

Harris-Lingoes Subscales	Raw Score	T Score	Resp %
Depression Subscales			
Subjective Depression (D$_1$)	19	75	100
Psychomotor Retardation (D$_2$)	4	46	100
Physical Malfunctioning (D$_3$)	6	68	100
Mental Dullness (D$_4$)	6	60	100
Brooding (D$_5$)	8	76	100
Hysteria Subscales			
Denial of Social Anxiety (Hy$_1$)	6	66	100
Need for Affection (Hy$_2$)	9	67	100
Lassitude-Malaise (Hy$_3$)	12	81	100
Somatic Complaints (Hy$_4$)	6	57	100
Inhibition of Aggression (Hy$_5$)	2	44	100
Psychopathic Deviate Subscales			
Familial Discord (Pd$_1$)	6	64	100
Authority Problems (Pd$_2$)	5	60	100
Social Imperturbability (Pd$_3$)	4	54	100
Social Alienation (Pd$_4$)	12	83	100
Self-Alienation (Pd$_5$)	8	65	100
Paranoia Subscales			
Persecutory Ideas (Pa$_1$)	8	64	100
Poignancy (Pa$_2$)	6	67	100
Naivete (Pa$_3$)	4	50	100
Schizophrenia Subscales			
Social Alienation (Sc$_1$)	12	68	100
Emotional Alienation (Sc$_2$)	1	43	100
Lack of Ego Mastery, Cognitive (Sc$_3$)	5	59	100
Lack of Ego Mastery, Conative (Sc$_4$)	6	57	100
Lack of Ego Mastery, Defective Inhibition (Sc$_5$)	3	48	100
Bizarre Sensory Experiences (Sc$_6$)	5	50	100
Hypomania Subscales			
Amorality (Ma$_1$)	2	45	100
Psychomotor Acceleration (Ma$_2$)	8	57	100
Imperturbability (Ma$_3$)	2	43	100
Ego Inflation (Ma$_4$)	7	64	100

Excerpts from *The Minnesota Report: Adolescent Interpretive System* (Rev. ed.), by Butcher and Williams, 2007.

Purpose and Expectations for the MMPI–A Evaluation

The psychologist needs to be aware of the expectations and referral issues prompting the evaluation when beginning to write up results from the MMPI–A. Some questions that could be considered include the following:

- What is the source of the referral?
- What are the primary complaints that prompted the referral?
- What is the young person's view of the referral? What would she or he like to gain from the evaluation?
- What do the parents hope to obtain from the evaluation? (Recall from Chapter 1 that for any given young person, significant parental figures are not necessarily limited to his or her biological parents.)
- What are relevant influences in the young person's environment? (See the description in Chapter 1, pp. 8–14, for key points to consider.)
- Are there cultural factors that need to be considered? (See Chapter 6.)
- Is there a history of medical or psychiatric illness or previous evaluations in the adolescent and/or his or her immediate family?
- Has the adolescent been involved in delinquent acts in the past?
- Is there a history of substance use in the adolescent or alcohol or other drug abuse in the family?
- Is there a history of physical or sexual abuse?

Occasionally, psychologists receive referrals that are unclear or require conclusions about a client that cannot be addressed by a psychological assessment, such as "Please evaluate the strange dress of this 13-year-old." In this example, more information is needed to provide a focused and effective psychological assessment, that is, to be able to select assessment strategies and collect the information needed to provide an appropriately targeted report. A brief consultation with the referral source may be useful to clarify expectations. José's referral was a straightforward request for a psychological evaluation to determine the mental health status and needs of an incarcerated youth. There are unique considerations for psychologists working in forensic settings, as we describe in the next section.

The Special Case of Forensic Evaluations

The MMPI–A is the most widely used personality measure with adolescents such as José who are evaluated in a forensic setting. Among the primary reasons for its widespread use in these settings are its objectivity, empirical research base, and ability to provide an assessment of a broad range of adolescent problems. Undoubtedly, much of what has been covered so far in this book accounts for the use of the MMPI–A in forensic evaluations. Its objective scoring and processing by computer is a distinct advantage in contentious forensic settings.

Because the MMPI–A requires about a sixth-grade reading level, it is manageable for a large percentage of adolescents in these settings (see Chapter 3 for alternative formats for administration to those with reading problems or limited English proficiency). It requires a short amount of professional time to administer, and a technician can be trained to do the administration. It is easy to administer in either individual or group settings in about an hour. However, testing in juvenile correctional facilities requires close supervision for both individual and group testing sessions to ensure the individual is completing the test in a serious manner without "assistance" from others.

It is never appropriate to send an adolescent home with an MMPI–A booklet to complete because the psychologist cannot be certain whose MMPI–A responses are being evaluated. Such flawed, unsupervised administrations are especially troublesome in forensic settings. Information about the conditions under which the MMPI–A was administered is important to detail, particularly an indication that the adolescent was closely supervised and did not have opportunities to discuss his or her responses with others (including parents or his or her peers in a residential placement). Note that José completed the MMPI–A in an office with the examiner present and quietly doing paperwork.

Although adolescents are generally comfortable with the true–false format of the MMPI–A and are usually willing to disclose psychological problems by responding in this manner, they, like adults (especially in forensic evaluations), may attempt to present themselves in ways different than they actually feel. They may have strong motivations to avoid disclosing personal information. How credible is the information that is being obtained from the adolescent in a psychological evaluation? Is the young person being cooperative in presenting his or her problems, experiences, and attitudes? McCann (1998) described the importance for the practitioner to carefully evaluate the adolescent's response attitudes in forensic testing to ensure that the evaluation is based on credible information.

Assessments in the legal context, such as juvenile court-ordered evaluations, evaluations in family court proceedings, or personal injury litigation cases, require that psychologists attend to special ethical and legal considerations when administering the MMPI–A and presenting the results of the evaluation. MMPI–A assessments of adolescents in forensic cases are markedly different from clinical assessments conducted for or at the request of their families. Weithorn (2006) described the challenge well: "Psychologists enlisted to perform psycholegal assessment of children, adolescents or families typically find themselves thrust into worlds that operate quite differently from the range of clinical contexts most familiar to their profession" (p. 11).

The expectations and reasons for the evaluation must be clearly presented to the young person and his or her legal guardians. The psychologist often has a legal obligation to ensure the young person and his or her legal guardian completely understand the process, including who will be receiving a report, and freely consent to participation in the evaluation (Pope, Butcher, & Seelen, 2006). Written reports are tailored specifically to the requirements of the referral source. Further information on conducting psychological evaluations on adolescents in the legal context can be found in several valuable resources (Borum, 2006; Butcher & Pope, 2006; Condie, 2006; Gardner, 1997; Goldberg, 2006; Grisso, 2005; Koocher, 2006; Pope et al., 2006; Smith, 2006; Sparta & Koocher, 2006; Weithorn, 2006).

Observations From Testing and Interviews

Any unusual circumstances or behaviors on the part of the adolescent should be noted in a behavioral observations section of an MMPI–A report. Any accommodations in the test administration procedures should be described (e.g., if the adolescent is known to be learning disabled, visually impaired, or have reading difficulties and the audio version of the MMPI–A is used rather than the booklet or computer versions). Examples of the adolescent's behavioral responses to the testing that should be described include whether the adolescent appeared to be minimally involved in the testing, walked around the room during the administration, answered the items feverously and quickly, complained of boredom, or asked a lot of questions. Such behaviors can provide a backdrop for an adolescent's high score on the Variable Response Inconsistency (*VRIN*) scale or having produced excessive Cannot Say scores. Or, if the adolescent initially refused testing and only reluctantly agreed to take the test, that might be an explanation a high score on the Lie (*L*) or Correction (*K*) scale. Such behavioral information is recommended for inclusion in the behavioral observations section of the clinical report to provide a context for understanding the conclusion of the evaluation. For a discussion on incorporating behavioral observations into a clinical assessment, see Craig (2009). Relevant information for the observations section of a MMPI–A report include the following:

- Was there an assessment of the individual's reading ability?
- How much time did the adolescent take to complete the booklet?

- Was the testing broken down into several short sessions over a period of time?
- Which form of the test was administered: booklet, computer administration, audiotape, language other than English? (Chapter 6 describes the special considerations for making culturally inclusive interpretations.)
- Was the young person engaged in the task? Did he or she show signs of fatigue, lack of interest, or distraction during the session?
- Were there any behaviors during the session that may have affected the adolescent's responses to the MMPI–A items?
- Were there observations from the intake interviews with either the adolescent or parent that might be relevant?

Behavioral observations are an important component of other aspects of a psychological assessment, including the clinical interview (Kearney, Cook, Wechsler, Haight, & Stowman, 2008; Leichtman, 2009). The clinician should be alert to the following:

- Did the adolescent make eye contact?
- Were speech and communication skills age appropriate?
- Were the adolescent's motor skills coordinated?
- Were there signs of inattention, tics, or unusual behaviors?
- How cooperative was the adolescent? Was she or he forced to come for the evaluation?

See page 198 for behavioral observations of José's evaluation sessions.

Validity Considerations

In the development of a psychological report with MMPI–A information, it is initially important to evaluate the adolescent's cooperation with the testing before his or her personality patterns and clinical symptoms can be evaluated with the Standard, Content, or other MMPI–A Scales (see Chapter 4 for more information). The psychologist needs to be assured that the adolescent was sufficiently cooperative with the evaluation and has provided credible personality information. The following questions should be addressed in approaching the validity determination:

- Were there any item omissions in the protocol that suggested a reluctance to endorse particular items?
- Were there any unusual response sets, such as high true or high false responding?
- Was there any evidence of inconsistent test responding (i.e., elevations on *VRIN* or *TRIN* [True Response Inconsistency])?

■ Were there any indications of test defensiveness (e.g., elevated L or K scale scores) that indicate that the adolescent was uncooperative with the testing through lack of sufficient disclosure?

■ Were there any suggestions of symptom exaggeration (e.g., significant scale elevations on Infrequency scales F, F_1 or F_2)?

José's Validity Scales profile can be found in his Minnesota Report in Figure 8.2 on page 200. It indicates a valid and interpretable MMPI–A performance. José followed directions and endorsed all of the items on the MMPI–A (i.e., a 0 on the Cannot Say indicator). He demonstrated no problems suggestive of reading difficulties, as noted by his normal-range *VRIN* score indicating that his responding to the MMPI–A items was consistent and his relatively low F, F_1 and F_2 scores indicating that he did not approach the testing with an inconsistent or extreme response attitude. His average *TRIN* score indicates he did not use a "yea-saying" or "nay-saying" response pattern. Moreover, he was open in describing his symptoms and problems as noted by the relatively low L and K scale scores. Although research with the MMPI–2 with Hispanics has shown slight elevations on L (Butcher, 2011), José's L score was quite low at a T score of 42.

The following are possible interpretive statements to put in the validity section of José's MMPI–A report written for professionals other than psychologists who do not have psychometric expertise and extensive knowledge of the instrument and its scales. These statements do not have the level of detail provided earlier about scale names and inferences, although they do assume some knowledge about the MMPI–A:

> José was open and cooperative in responding to the MMPI–A, answering all the items on the test. None of the Validity Scales was elevated in the range suggestive of either defensive or exaggerated responding. There do not appear to be any negative or uncooperative test-taking attitudes present that suggest caution in interpretation. It is, therefore, likely that José's scores on the symptom and problem scales are valid and interpretable.

Clinical Symptom Patterns

A valuable strategy in the development of a symptom picture of the client's problems and personality is to begin with summarizing the adolescent's performance on the most well-established Clinical Scales to obtain an objective overview of the likely symptoms and personality characteristics the client manifests. The correlates for the most prominent Clinical Scales should be cited; when more than one scale is elevated in an adolescent's clinical profile, it is important to assure that all of the relevant symptoms or personality characteristics are taken into consideration. For example, if Depression (*D*) and Psychasthenia (*Pt*) are elevated in the clinical range ($T \geq 65$), then the descriptors from both measures need to be considered. The psychologist then proceeds to examine the relative elevations of the various other MMPI–A scales to supplement and refine the general framework provided by the Clinical Scales. Relevant content themes that the adolescent acknowledged through the MMPI–A Content Scales can be incorporated. Further information shown in the Personality Psychopathology Five (PSY-5) Scales may provide hypotheses about personality functioning that are not addressed by other scales. Finally, the possibility of alcohol and drug involvement needs to be considered. (More information about this interpretive approach is provided in Chapters 4 and 5.) Some questions to consider are the following:

- What are the most prominent Clinical Scale elevations in the profile?
- What salient behavioral correlates are suggested by these Clinical Scale elevations?
- Is there any indication of substance abuse problems as shown by the MacAndrew Alcoholism Scale–Revised (*MAC–R*), Alcohol/Drug Problem Acknowledgment (*ACK*), or Alcohol/Drug Problem Proneness (*PRO*)?
- Are there any content themes that require consideration in understanding the adolescent's clinical symptoms? For example, are there specific areas acknowledged, such as anxiety, depression, anger, or family, school, or conduct problems?
- Does the adolescent disclose personality adjustment problems or attitudinal problems on the MMPI–A? Are problems reflected in the PSY-5 Scales, such as Disconstraint (*DISC*) suggesting acting-out potential?

ASSESSMENT OF ACTING-OUT POTENTIAL

An important aspect of adolescent personality assessment involves an appraisal of acting-out potential. The prediction of acting-out behavior and related acts such as overt aggression and dangerousness is a complicated matter (Megargee, 2009, provided a valuable perspective on personality factors in the assessment of dangerousness). Such predictions require that practitioners have information about personality variables, past history of aggressive acts, an awareness of the person's use of drugs and alcohol, and a picture of the person's current stressors and environmental demands. Having the results of a personality measure that has been substantially related to aggressive correlates can clearly add to the equation. Although personality structure and processes are not the whole story in determining acting out, aggression, and dangerousness characteristics, they are an important component. The MMPI–A contains several measures that reflect behavioral problems involving impulsive, acting-out behaviors.

MMPI–A Clinical Scales that effectively address acting-out potential include Psychopathic Deviate (*Pd*); Hypomania (*Ma;* e.g., Borkhuis & Patalano, 1997; Craig, 2008; Schill, Wang & Thomsen, 1986); and, to a lesser extent, Schizophrenia (*Sc*) and Paranoia (*Pa*). An assessment of potential acting-out behavior should initially evaluate the range of elevation on these measures. The *Pd* and *Ma* scales can provide information about persistent personality characteristics that are associated with hedonistic behavior, impulsiveness, and self-oriented behavior. Adolescents scoring high on these scales are considered to have a potential for acting-out behaviors. When the *Pa* scale is also elevated, the type of acting-out behavior is often characterized by hostile aggressive behavior. The *Sc* scale can be associated with acting-out behavior that results from personality and cognitive deterioration.

Several of the MMPI–A Content Scales also offer important sources of information for determining possible acting-out behavior. For example, the Adolescent-Conduct Problems (*A-con*) scale is a well-established measure of conduct problems, and the Adolescent-Anger (*A-ang*) scale suggests significant anger control problems. Similarly, two of the PSY-5 Scales, Aggressiveness (*AGGR*) and Disconstraint (*DISC*), are associated with acting-out behaviors and aggression. In addition, *AGGR* suggests the use of offensive or instrumental aggression for achieving goals. The adolescent tends to intimidate others and act out in an aggressive manner.

SELECTING MOST LIKELY DESCRIPTORS FOR THE CLINICAL SCALES

Beginning MMPI–A interpreters are often puzzled over which of the many descriptors or correlates of the Clinical Scales are most pertinent for a particular case. Each of the MMPI–A Clinical Scales contains a number of empirically based descriptors of symptoms and personality. One approach for refining interpretation of the Clinical Scales is to organize the various descriptors in a hierarchy of the most likely empirical descriptors using information from content-based measures such as the Harris–Lingoes subscales or the Content Scales, as we described in Chapters 4 and 5.

For example, if the highest elevation on the adolescent's Clinical Scales profile is the Hysteria (*Hy*) scale and an examination of the Harris–Lingoes subscales shows that Denial of Social Anxiety (Hy_1) and Need for Affection (Hy_2) are the only elevated subscales, then the MMPI–A report should include a primary focus on the behavioral correlates that are suggestive of extroversion, being comfortable around others, trusting, strong need for attention and affection, and so forth. Similarly, family discord and behavior problems within the family should be highlighted with a *Pd* elevation in the 60 to 64 *T*-score range, if the Harris–Lingoes Pd_1 (Family Discord) is elevated and Pd_2 (Authority Problems) is not.

Confidence in highlighting the family problem correlates for *Pd* over the delinquent behavior correlates is increased if there is an elevation on the Adolescent-Family Problems (*A-fam*) Content Scale with no elevation on the Adolescent-Conduct Problems (*A-con*) Content Scale. However, a high elevation on *A-con*, even in the absence of an elevation on Pd_2, indicates the adolescent has endorsed a large number of items indicating behavior problems in multiple areas that should be described in the report. Elevations on the alcohol and drug problems scales can also help in the interpretation of an elevation on *Pd*. It is in circumstances like this that a feedback interview and an examination of the item-level indicators (see the case demonstration below) can be useful in the psychological evaluation.

The following are the general questions and steps to determine which of the empirical correlates from the MMPI–A Clinical Scales to highlight in the report:

- What are the most highly elevated Clinical Scales in the profile?
- Using the information in Chapter 4, list the most likely and valid behavioral correlates for each elevated Clinical Scale.
- Which of the Harris–Lingoes subscales are elevated, and how do they relate to the list of empirical correlates for the respective Clinical Scale elevations?
- Do any of the Content Scale elevations relate to the empirical correlates of the Clinical Scales? (Refer to Chapter 5 for this information.)
- Do any of the Supplementary Scales or PSY-5 Scales relate to the empirical correlates of the Clinical Scales? (Chapter 5 details this information.)

José's Clinical and Supplementary Scales profile is in his Minnesota Report in Figure 8.2 on page 201. It reveals three prominently elevated Clinical Scales: *Pd*, *Hy*, and *Pa*. The *Pd* score is often the peak clinical score among adolescents in general and in correctional facilities specifically; however, the elevation that José attained is more extreme than most young people. His *Pd* elevation suggests that he is likely to show antisocial behaviors including rebelliousness, disrupted family relations, impulsiveness, and delinquent behaviors, all of which are consistent with his current circumstances. He is likely to be deceptive, manipulative, hedonistic, and exhibitionistic. He is likely to show poor judgment and engage in unreliable, immature, hostile, and aggressive behaviors. High scores on *Pd* usually reflect long-standing character problems that are resistant to treatment. High scorers may enter treatment but usually terminate quickly, unless compelled by external pressure. José's combination of high elevations on *Pd, Hy,* and *Pa* suggests impulsive acting-out behaviors and loss of control resulting in aggression.

In addition, the high elevation José attained on *Hy* suggests that he may rely on denial and repression to deal with stress. He may show dependent, naive, outgoing, infantile, and narcissistic attitudes and have interpersonal relations that are often disrupted. His high elevation on *Pa* should also be considered. High scorers may project or externalize blame and harbor grudges against others. High scorers are generally hostile and argumentative and are not likely to benefit from traditional psychotherapy.

José's elevated scores on *Pd* and *Hs* (Hypochondriasis) suggest further assessment of possible physical or sexual abuse. His item-level indicators showed that he endorsed one item indicating worries about sex and another item indicating being the recipient of "many beatings." These issues could be explored further in an MMPI–A feedback session (see Chapter 9 for details).

An examination of José's responses on the Harris–Lingoes subscales (Figure 8.2, p. 204) provides some confirmation of the abovementioned Clinical Scales correlates. With the exception of *Pd₃* (recall from Chapter 4 that this contains items reflecting comfort and confidence in social situations; he endorsed only 4 of its 12 items), José endorsed all the subscales for *Pd,* which supports the hypotheses above about the *Pd* descriptors applying to him. His pattern of endorsement for *Hy* suggests multiple endorsements of items reflecting poor health, fatigue, and sleep problems, also consistent with his *T* score of 65 on *Hs.* The Harris–Lingoes subscales reveal a somewhat mixed picture of his social relationships, in that some suggest denial of problems in social situations (e.g., *Hy₁*), whereas others (e.g., *Pd₄, Pa₁*) suggest feelings of mistrust and suspicion toward others. Finally, the Harris–Lingoes subscales suggest feelings of depression may be part of his symptom picture.

Interpreting the MMPI–A Content, Supplementary, and PSY-5 Scales

The MMPI–A Content Scales, alcohol and drug problem scales (i.e., *MAC–R, ACK, PRO*), and the PSY-5 Scales are all validated measures that can provide important information in addition to helping to decide which Clinical Scale correlates to emphasize in the report. The Content Scales, as well as *ACK,* give the psychologist a good vantage point from which he or she can view the problems the adolescent endorsed. As noted in Chapter 5, items on the Content Scale, as well as items on *ACK* and the PSY-5 Scales, are generally obvious, thus answering in the scored direction involves a frank and open expression of problems. As a result, these scales provide valuable clues to what the adolescent considers his or her problems to be and indicate a willingness to disclose this information to others:

▪ What do the alcohol and other drug problems scales indicate?
▪ How do the Content Scales relate to the referral questions? For example, if the young person is being evaluated because of school behavior or performance problems, is the Adolescent-School Problems (*A-sch*) or Adolescent-Low Aspirations (*A-las*) scale elevated?
▪ Are there content themes in the adolescent's MMPI–A performance that provide new information regarding the adolescent's current problem situation that should be included in the report?
▪ Is there additional information from the PSY-5 Scales to be included in the report?

As revealed in Figure 8.2 in José's Minnesota Report on page 201, both of the substance abuse scales that address a proclivity to develop alcohol or drug problems were elevated in José's profile (the *PRO* scale was at a *T* score of 76 and the *MAC–R* scale at 63), suggesting likely personality factors associated with substance use disorder. It is interesting to note that although José was forthcoming about his alcohol and drug use during the interview, he only endorsed three of the possible substance use items on the MMPI–A and did not produce an elevation on *ACK*. This raises the question about whether he sees his reported significant use as problematic. Indeed, one of his item-level indicators indicates he enjoys marijuana use. Therefore, although he shows clear problems with substance abuse (moreover, his arrest charges included possession of illegal substances), he did not acknowledge problems on the *ACK* scale, indicating a denial of problems or reluctance to deal with them.

As often occurs in adolescent assessment, José's Content Scales and PSY-5 elevations provide clarification on his problems situations. First, he acknowledged problems on the Content Scales (Figure 8.2, p. 202) that reflect extensive family problems (*A-fam*) and school problems (*A-sch*), indicating that his adjustment in these two important areas, as he views his problems, is severely disturbed. He did respond differentially to problems in these important areas, as revealed by his endorsement of the Content Component Scales (e.g., $A\text{-}fam_1$ was elevated at *T* score of 76 and $A\text{-}fam_2$ was not elevated at *T* score of 58). This suggests that even in the presence of extreme discord within his family, José may not have disengaged completely and may still have some connection to family members. A similar pattern was found for the *A-sch* Content Component Scales ($A\text{-}sch_1$ was elevated at 69, but $A\text{-}sch_2$ was not elevated at 57). José reported numerous conduct problems at school but did not report having significant negative attitudes toward school. He also reported feeling both depressed (*A-dep*) and angry (*A-ang*) over his current situations.

It is noteworthy that *A-con* is not elevated, given his significant elevation on *Pd*. This illustrates how scales that are developed using different methods (e.g., empirical vs. content-based strategies) sometimes differ in their ability to identify significant problems, even in cases like José who was willing to admit to significant problems on the MMPI–A and in interviews. (See earlier comments about José's scores on the empirically derived *PRO* and *MAC–R* scales contrasted with his score on the content-based *ACK* as another example.)

José had two extreme elevations on his PSY-5 profile included in Figure 8.2, page 203: *DISC* and *NEGE* (Negative Emotionality/Neuroticism). *DISC* is a strong indicator of acting-out potential. High scores reflect risk taking, impulsivity, and low acceptance of moral values. Adolescents with high scores on *DISC* have been found to have histories of impulsive, acting-out, and irresponsible behaviors, also consistent with the descriptors for his elevated *Pd* score. His elevation on *NEGE* supports including internalizing symptoms (e.g., worries, anxious, guilt prone) as part of his MMPI–A interpretation.

Interpersonal Relations

The MMPI–A can provide clues as to the adolescent's effectiveness in or difficulties with interpersonal relationships. Several scales focus on potential problems that can emerge in social situations. The Social Introversion (*Si*), Adolescent-Social Discomfort (*A-sod*), and *INTR* scales address, in general, the extent to which the adolescent is introverted and withdrawn in social relationships. *INTR* suggests an inability to experience positive emotions or engage positively with others.

Other scales focus on different interpersonal issues. For example, the *A-ang, A-con*, and *AGGR* scales provide information about the adolescent's aggressiveness and likelihood of engaging in behavior that would be disruptive in relationships. Moreover, the Adolescent-Cynicism (*A-cyn*), Adolescent-Alienation (*A-aln*), and *Pa* scales include information about the adolescent's personality characteristics that include such factors as suspicion and mistrust in relationships and wariness about becoming involved with others. *Pd* elevations suggest a tendency toward manipulating others or superficial relationships. Some questions to consider are the following:

▪ Does the adolescent report having problems in dealing with social relationships? Are the *Si, A-sod,* or *INTR* scales elevated suggesting that the adolescent has difficulty in social relationships?

▪ Does the adolescent show personality features of interpersonal suspicion and mistrust? Are the *Pa, A-aln,* or *A-cyn* scales elevated in the clinical range?

▪ Does the adolescent show personality characteristics that are associated with aggressive acting out, for example, elevations on *Pd, DISC, AGGR, A-ang,* or *A-con?*

All of José's scores on the introversion–extraversion measures on the MMPI–A (e.g., *Si, A-sod, INTR*) are relatively low, indicating a socially extraverted lifestyle. José appears on the MMPI–A to be a person with some social skills, but he also may be likely to manipulate others in social situations (given the high *Pd* score). He admitted to an item-level indicator that others complain that he uses his temper to get his way. Given his score on *PRO,* he likely belongs to a peer group that is often in trouble, which is also consistent with one of his responses to an item-level indicator, as well as his arrest record.

His high *Pa* score and moderate elevation on *A-aln* suggest areas of interpersonal difficulties. He is likely to be suspicious and mistrustful. He may blame others for things that go wrong. Further exploration of José's distrust and suspicion will be useful: Do they center within his family or are they part of his gang-related experiences or both?

José would likely be hypersensitive to criticism and has a tendency to respond aggressively. The moderate elevation that he obtained on *A-ang* and the elevation on *DISC* scale indicate a potential for acting out in an explosive manner, which should be taken into consideration in the psychological evaluation. This potential for loss of control was evident in his arrest record. Given his possession of methamphetamines at the time of his arrest, further exploration of his drug use is warranted to determine if his impulsivity and loss of control are related to periods of intoxication.

Clinical Diagnostic Considerations

Although the MMPI–A was not designed to provide explicit diagnostic categorization following terminology from the *Diagnostic and Statistical Manual of Mental Disorders* (4th ed., text revision; American Psychiatric Association, 2000), many of the scales can provide clues to currently experienced symptoms and behavior that can be incorporated into the process of formulating a clinical diagnosis. The behavioral correlates for the Clinical Scales and the relationships of the Supplementary, Content, and PSY-5 Scales provide hypotheses about the client's symptoms, behaviors, and personality characteristics. This information from the MMPI–A can be used along with behavioral observations, interview information, and other testing to arrive at an appropriate diagnosis in situations when this is necessary or desirable. It is important to realize that an MMPI–A interpretation does not result in a definitive diagnosis. Rather, it results in a series of hypotheses for the clinician to consider through further assessment. The following are some examples of diagnostic hypotheses given various scale elevations (the reader should consult Chapters 4 and 5 for more information):

■ An extremely elevated score on the Clinical Scale *D* or on *A-dep* indicates that the adolescent is experiencing symptoms of low mood suggestive of an affective disorder.

■ A high elevation on *Hs* or *A-hea* indicates that the adolescent is reporting a large number of symptoms or beliefs suggestive of a somatoform disorder.

■ Elevations on *Pd, A-con, A-ang,* and *DISC* suggest acting-out problems, impulsivity, poor judgment, and antisocial attitudes that could be related to the development of a conduct disorder or antisocial personality disorder features.

■ Elevations on any of the substance abuse scales (*MAC–R, ACK,* or *PRO*) raise the possibility of the adolescent having drug or alcohol problems.

In considering potential clinical diagnoses for José in the current evaluation, the practitioner would want to consider a number of problems and negative attitudes he has expressed through the MMPI–A items including the following: negative attitudes toward authority (*Pd* and *Pa* elevations), impulsivity and risk taking (*Pd* and *DISC*), involvement with negative peer groups (*PRO*), and aggressive responses toward others in interpersonal relationships and anger control problems (*A-ang* and *DISC*). Conduct disorders and emerging personality disorders are possible with this extreme elevation on *Pd*.

In addition, the clinician should examine other sources of information concerning the internalizing symptoms evident from some of José's elevated and moderately elevated scores (e.g., *D, A-dep, A-anx, A-obs* [Adolescent-Obsessiveness], *NEGE*) on the MMPI–A. His risk for suicidal gestures or attempts as an impulsive reaction to mounting external pressures should be evaluated. Finally, it is likely that José meets the diagnostic criteria for one of the substance use disorders, another area for further assessment.

Treatment Planning

In addition to diagnostic hypotheses, the MMPI–A scales provide useful information about an adolescent's need for treatment, openness to change, and potential resistance to therapy (e.g., Butcher & Perry, 2008; Cumella & Lafferty-O'Connor, 2009). Some scale elevations (e.g., *D, Pt, A-anx, A-dep*) indicate a willingness to acknowledge psychological problems, as well as considerable psychological distress, suggestive of a willingness to engage in therapy. Other MMPI–A scales (e.g., *Si, A-sod, A-aln,* or *A-cyn*) suggest difficulties in forming close interpersonal relationships—personality factors that could impede treatment. Chapters 4 and 5 provide descriptors for the various scales that provide information for this section of the report. The following is a summary of some of these issues:

- Do the adolescents' profiles suggest clinical or personality problems that indicate the need for intervention or treatment?
- How aware are they of their problems?
- How credible is their self-report?
- How likely are they to disclose personal information to a therapist?
- How motivated for treatment are they likely to be?
- Are there specific treatments suggested by the MMPI–A?
- How likely is it that the adolescents will gain insight into their problems?
- How willing are they to change their behaviors?
- Have they reported psychological problems or symptoms that are amenable to treatment (e.g., elevations on *D, Pt, A-anx, A-dep,* or *NEGE*)?
- Are there elevations on scales (e.g., *Pa, Hs, A-cyn,* or *A-trt* [Adolescent-Negative Treatment Indicators]) that address personality characteristics that suggest resistance to psychological treatment?
- Are there elevations suggesting strengths or assets the adolescents have?

Although the referral for assessment in José's case was part of a forensic dispositional evaluation and not a psychological treatment referral, the question of a mental health intervention could become relevant at some point in the proceedings of his case. His prominent elevations on both *Pd* and *Pa* suggest that he would not likely be motivated for traditional psychotherapy. He would likely be highly resistant to psychological treatment and unlikely to enter into a self-change treatment program with enthusiasm. He is unlikely to recognize his own responsibility in the problems. Nor does he appear to view his alcohol or other drug use as problematic.

Even though José showed a number of problems that suggest resistance to intervention at this time, there are some indications that he might, under some circumstances, be open to change, an asset or strength to be built upon with the appropriate approach. He seems to have interpersonal relationship skills that allow, under positive circumstances, the development of a treatment relationship, and he has a relatively low scale elevation on *A-trt*, a scale that focuses on negative treatment indicators. He indicated an interest in learning about his performance on the MMPI–A, suggesting that he might be a good candidate for therapeutic assessment (see Chapter 9). The distress he feels given indications of some internalizing symptoms may make him more amenable to change than what would otherwise be the case in the absence of such symptoms (e.g., his relatively high *D* and *A-dep* scores, as well as other indications of anxiety issues, suggest psychological conflict that might provide motivation for change). His need for affection and attention could contribute to the formation of an alliance with adults in a setting with adequate supervision.

In any event, José would more likely benefit from a behavioral approach with contingencies for appropriate behaviors than from traditional psychotherapy. Anger management training may prove beneficial. His illness behaviors should be evaluated for secondary gain and a program developed to reduce any secondary gain. His reports of significant problems in school (*A-sch*) suggest that a more structured approach with incremental reinforcement of positive behaviors in the classroom could prove useful. His considerable anger and disappointment with his parents must be considered in any treatment planning.

Not Done Yet!

We used José's MMPI–A scores to describe the process for interpreting and writing a report based on the MMPI–A. We covered all the steps in the flow chart in Figure 8.1 except the last one, "Describe Adolescent's and Parents' Perspective From Collaborative Feedback Session." That is the topic of the last chapter of this book.

The Feedback Loop

Sharing MMPI–A Information With Adolescents and Parents

9

You know, you psychologists are all alike! I spent
hours taking all those tests for the last psychologist.
Even told her I wanted to know what they said. And,
nothing, not a word about what they meant!

I n many cases, clients like this teenager are left in the dark
about the results of their MMPI–A evaluations. Often, the
assessor's task ends with the completion of a written MMPI–A
interpretive report sent to the referral source. This traditional
model of psychological assessment, called the *information-
gathering assessment model*, was used (and still is used) to
facilitate communications between professionals. Traditional
assessment relies on data gathered about the young person
(e.g., test scores, interviews, consultations with the referral
source) to reach decisions that are based on the psychologist's
interpretation of the assessment data collected. Typically the
psychologist works unilaterally to determine what questions
to address in the evaluation and which methods or tests to
use (Finn & Kamphuis, 2006; Riddle, Byers, & Grimesey,
2002). Indeed, seeking input from the client or providing
feedback about test results was actually once discouraged
as potentially harmful to patients (Finn & Tonsager, 1992;
Riddle et al., 2002).

However, a number of us began describing how client participation in the assessment process can be useful for assessment in general (e.g., Fischer, 1970, 1985, 1994, 2000) and
with the MMPI specifically (e.g., Butcher, 1990; Butcher &
Williams, 2000; Finn & Tonsager, 1992; C. L. Williams, 1982,
1983, 1986). These techniques came to be called *collaborative*

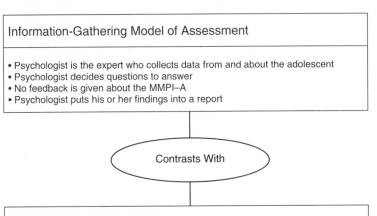

FIGURE 9.1

Information-Gathering Model of Assessment

• Psychologist is the expert who collects data from and about the adolescent
• Psychologist decides questions to answer
• No feedback is given about the MMPI–A
• Psychologist puts his or her findings into a report

Contrasts With

Collaborative Model of Assessment

• Adolescent and psychologist are a team working together
• Both formulate questions to answer
• After a standardized administration and scoring, MMPI-A feedback is given and the adolescent is asked to evaluate its accuracy
• Adolescent's opinions are incorporated into the psychologist's written evaluation

Comparison of information-gathering and collaborative models of assessment.

assessment models. Figure 9.1 contrasts these two primary models for assessment. This chapter describes how to administer, interpret, and present the MMPI–A using a collaborative assessment strategy.

We recommend collaborative assessment as a best practice that can be an additional source of information about the young person's functioning as well as providing possible therapeutic benefits to the adolescent. Collaborative assessment involves communicating and enhancing the test findings in feedback sessions. In addition, some therapists recommend written communications to the adolescent and his or her parents in the form of a letter or report (e.g., Purves, 2002; Riddle et al., 2002; Tharinger, Finn, Wilkinson, & Schaber, 2007).

Collaborative Assessment Complements Traditional Methods

Collaborative assessment need not be mutually exclusive from the traditional information-gathering methods; they can be used in a complementary fashion. Psychologists can still work with referral sources to come up with questions to address in the evaluation and incorporate the additional step of including the young person and his or her family members as another important source for topics to consider during the evaluation, as we indicated in Chapter 8. The psychologist selects the most appropriate tests and assessment techniques given the questions to be addressed. Tests like the MMPI–A are administered with standardized instructions, but additional steps involving feedback are added to the procedures, as can be seen in Figure 9.2.

Collaborative assessment is a generic label for an assortment of techniques involving feedback and the incorporation of the client's reactions to the testing experience and interpretation. Therapeutic assessment is a specific type of collaborative assessment developed by Stephen Finn and colleagues at the University of Texas and the Center for Therapeutic Assessment in Austin (e.g., Finn, 2007; Finn & Kamphuis, 2006; Finn & Tonsager, 1992; Tharinger et al., 2007, 2008). The traditional goals of psychological assessment (i.e., accurately classifying and describing patients to assist in treatment planning or educational placement) are augmented with efforts to produce therapeutic change. Therapeutic assessment is a semistructured brief intervention technique in addition to being a psychological assessment.

Research has shown therapeutic benefits for this brief intervention with clients seen in college counseling centers in the United States (Finn & Tonsager, 1992) and Australia (Newman & Greenway, 1997). Newman (2004) compared therapeutic assessment of a brief psychotherapy group with a sample of 36 secondary school students (ages 16–18 years). He found the adolescents who participated in therapeutic assessment using the MMPI–A showed a significant decline in symptomatic distress and an increase in self-esteem compared with the brief psychotherapy group. Both groups showed significant decrease in self-reports of depression over time. They also reported less levels of hopelessness and loneliness, with the therapeutic assessment group reporting significantly lower levels than the brief psychotherapy group. Newman (2004) concluded that therapeutic assessment showed superior therapeutic gains with adolescents when compared with a general cognitive–behavior approach.

Michel (2002) suggested that therapeutic assessment might be especially useful with patients hospitalized for eating disorders given typical problems of denial or minimization of the eating disorder and psychological issues, lack of insight, and treatment resistance. She presented two case examples, a 22-year-old administered the MMPI–2 and a 15-year-old administered the MMPI–A. Her case illustrations showed how the MMPI instruments were integrated into a comprehensive psychological evaluation that led to direct treatment recommendations. The younger adolescent, for example, questioned why her eating disorder developed and why she was so unhappy. During feedback sessions, her MMPI–A scores reflecting depression, family problems, school problems, and difficult interpersonal problems were linked to her eating disorder. One of the

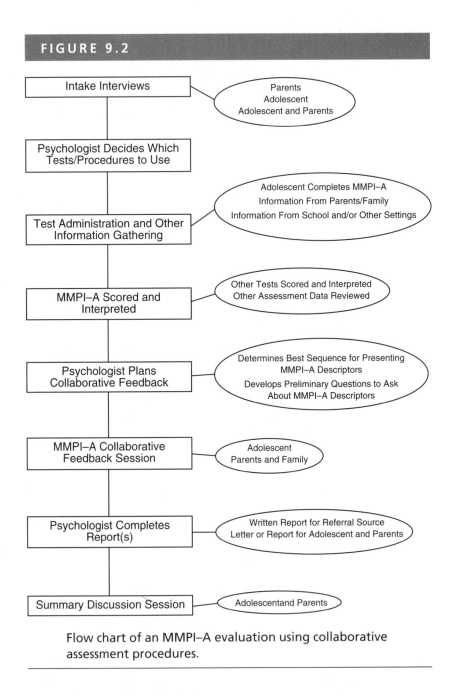

FIGURE 9.2

Intake Interviews — (Parents / Adolescent / Adolescent and Parents)

Psychologist Decides Which Tests/Procedures to Use

Test Administration and Other Information Gathering — (Adolescent Completes MMPI–A / Information From Parents/Family / Information From School and/or Other Settings)

MMPI–A Scored and Interpreted — (Other Tests Scored and Interpreted / Other Assessment Data Reviewed)

Psychologist Plans Collaborative Feedback — (Determines Best Sequence for Presenting MMPI–A Descriptors / Develops Preliminary Questions to Ask About MMPI–A Descriptors)

MMPI–A Collaborative Feedback Session — (Adolescent / Parents and Family)

Psychologist Completes Report(s) — (Written Report for Referral Source / Letter or Report for Adolescent and Parents)

Summary Discussion Session — (Adolescent and Parents)

Flow chart of an MMPI–A evaluation using collaborative assessment procedures.

discussion points during the feedback (and in subsequent group therapy sessions) was how her focus on her weight distracted her from the significant psychosocial issues found on testing.

Therapeutic assessment is a promising combination of psychological assessment and brief psychotherapy with some evidence of efficacy for both adolescents and adults. However, it is not appropriate in all settings in which the MMPI–A is included as part of a psychological evaluation. For that reason, we refer readers to Finn and his colleagues for guidelines on its use (e.g., Finn, 2007; Finn & Kamphuis, 2006; Finn & Tonsager, 1992; Tharinger et al., 2007, 2008). We do recommend consideration of collaborative assessment techniques as a best practice for many circumstances in which the MMPI–A is included as part of a psychological evaluation.

We do so with the caveat that collaborative assessment may not be appropriate in all settings, perhaps particularly in forensic evaluations such as child custody or other court-ordered evaluations. However, we saw with Grace in Chapter 7 (pp. 177–192) a circumstance in which information about her need for individual therapy, highlighted in her Minnesota Report, could prove useful in helping her mother understand the seriousness of Grace's problems. Recall in Grace's case that her father had requested the court to order a psychological evaluation, whereas her mother thought his request was retaliatory and suggested that Grace's needs might be met in a church support group. The objective nature of a computerized report might prod Grace's mother to see beyond the disagreements with her soon-to-be former spouse. And José in Chapter 8 (pp. 196–204), who was tested in a juvenile detention facility, was interested in receiving feedback about his MMPI–A performance, which could be used as an entrée into a therapeutic relationship.

Purves (2002) described the use of collaborative or therapeutic assessment in a specific, and involuntary forensic setting: the evaluation of foster children and their mothers. She suggested that collaborative techniques help facilitate the development of a working alliance with initially resistant clients. Other challenges in this setting—low remuneration and time constraints—are discussed. Step-by-step suggestions, beginning with discussions with the referral source, usually a social worker or child welfare officer, are provided. These suggestions are consistent with our discussions in Chapter 8 about referral questions and with the guidelines for collaborative assessment below.

General Guidelines for Collaborative Assessment With the MMPI–A

Figure 9.2 presents a flow chart of the steps to follow when using the collaborative assessment model with the MMPI–A. It begins at intake when the psychologist works with the young person and his or her parents or guardians to formulate questions to be addressed in the psychological evaluation. Depending on the reason for referral, it is usually best to have individual sessions with the parents and the adolescent, followed by a session with both. After conferring with the referral source and hearing what the adolescent and parents want to accomplish during the evaluation (including the development of a list of questions from each), the psychologist selects which tests and other procedures to be used for the psychological evaluation. These tests and procedures are administered in their standardized fashion, scored, and interpreted. At this point, the psychologist plans the collaborative feedback session using the following guidelines (for more details, see Butcher, 1990; Butcher & Perry, 2008, Butcher & Williams, 2000; C. L. Williams, 1982, 1983, 1986).

GUIDELINE 1: PREPARE, IN ADVANCE, THE PERSONALITY-BASED INFORMATION TO BE SHARED IN A LANGUAGE THAT IS APPROPRIATE TO THE ADOLESCENT'S ABILITY AND MATURITY

It is important to rely on the most likely personality factors shown by the test scores. Avoid using psychological jargon; when possible, use lay terms to describe the likely symptoms and behaviors reflected by the scale elevations. It is also important to select the most pertinent attributes and problem areas rather than present every one. Instead of overloading the young person with information, the main points need to be selective, by choosing the most relevant features that the adolescent can incorporate. The feedback provided should be framed in such a way to be understandable and useful to the adolescent's development level. It is best that test results not be presented in a judgmental or authoritarian manner but as a cooperative interactive process. In the event that the adolescent has difficulty accepting and incorporating feedback on some points, the psychologist should avoid getting into an argument (Finn, 1996).

GUIDELINE 2: CONSIDER THE ADOLESCENT'S DEVELOPMENTAL LEVEL

The adolescent's developmental accomplishments, cognitive ability, areas of vulnerability, and so forth should be used to determine the level of detail to include in the feedback. The most successful approach is through a collaborative process in which rapport has been well established. Butcher and Perry (2008) pointed out that the ability of the client to incorporate personality feedback needs to be taken into consideration. The client's level of intellectual functioning should be understood and any problems or deficits considered in deciding the amount and type of feedback to provide. The presentation should be varied to suit each individual's general fund of information and psychological sophistication.

GUIDELINE 3: STRUCTURE THE FEEDBACK SESSION AS AN INTERACTIVE PROCESS

It is important to seek responses or questions from the client during the feedback session. An interactive process can identify any misconceptions that need to be cleared up. Providing an active interchange over issues raised by the MMPI–A can promote a treatment-oriented atmosphere that encourages self-knowledge and problem solving on the part of the client. Be alert to the fact that a client might become fixated on an irrelevant or inconsequential point and become sidetracked from the process.

Butcher and Perry (2008) suggested that with some clients, it is important to schedule more than one test feedback session to evaluate whether the person has incorporated or rejected the test feedback. In addition, after a few days' consideration, many clients will raise questions they were hesitant to ask the first time around.

GUIDELINE 4: EXPLAIN WHY THE MMPI–A WAS SELECTED AS PART OF THE EVALUATION

It is important to describe why the MMPI–A was used and what the test has been designed to show. Provide a brief description of how the MMPI–A can provide an objective framework to view an adolescent's problems by reference to comparison groups such as the MMPI–A normative sample or various clinical groups. In feedback sessions, it is useful to explain the credibility and objectivity of the MMPI–A, for example, by describing its wide and long-standing use in assessing young people's problems.

GUIDELINE 5: DESCRIBE HOW THE TEST WORKS

Briefly explain how the MMPI–A scales were developed and point out that a great deal of research has supported its effectiveness at describing the problems that adolescents experience. Using a sample profile, show an example performance such as an adolescent who is depressed and having a high score on the Depression scale, or consider using the adolescent's own profile, as described in the case demonstration below. Begin with an explanation of the test profiles. Point out what an "average" or typical performance would be shown by each scale. Explain elevated scores (e.g., the shaded area between 60 and 65 and above a T score of 65). Indicate that the majority of adolescents fall below a T score of 65.

GUIDELINE 6: DESCRIBE HOW THE MMPI–A EVALUATES TEST-TAKING ATTITUDES

Point out that the MMPI–A contains several measures of the adolescent's attitudes toward taking the test. Describe how the adolescent approached the test and whether his or her performance was a valid indication of problems. Incorporating information about the adolescent's performance on the validity measures can be a fruitful aspect of the feedback process because it allows the practitioner to approach and or confront the teenager's willingness to engage in any psychological interventions that emerge from the assessment. For example, if the adolescent has endorsed a number of items that reflect test defensiveness, his or her level of cooperation with the evaluation can be addressed. Or, if the client has endorsed an extreme number of Infrequency (*F*) scale items, then their motivation for presenting a great number of mental health problems can be addressed.

GUIDELINE 7: HIGHLIGHT THE MOST PROMINENT SCALE ELEVATIONS THAT THE ADOLESCENT SHOWED ON THE CLINICAL SCALES

Point out the adolescent's highest clinical scores and summarize the possible attitudes or symptoms that these high points reflect. The psychologist needs to be aware that the adolescent may have little insight into his or her behavior and may have problems accepting feedback about some issues or problem areas.

GUIDELINE 8: PRESENT PROMINENT CONTENT THEMES OR PROBLEM AREAS THE ADOLESCENT HAS ACKNOWLEDGED

Providing test feedback on content themes that the client has acknowledged is a more straightforward process than interpreting the Clinical Scales because the adolescent has openly acknowledged the symptoms and attitudes that constitute the content measures. The adolescent is more likely to "see" and accept the interpretations of results from elevated scores on Content Scales than those of the Clinical Scales because of their more obvious nature since these themes were explicitly endorsed. The psychologist can augment these content-based themes with item responses from the item-level indicators as well.

GUIDELINE 9: EVALUATE THE CLIENT'S OVERALL ACCEPTANCE OF THE TEST FEEDBACK

It is a good idea to obtain a closing summary from clients to show how they understood the information presented and how they feel about the test's characterization of their problems. The clinician can evaluate whether there were aspects of the test results that were particularly surprising, distressing, or objectionable. Equally as important are the areas of agreement or aspects that "make sense" to the young person. Any "aha" moments should be described.

From the General to the Specific: A Case Illustration of Collaborative Assessment

We now illustrate these general guidelines for an MMPI–A collaborative assessment using a specific case, Kayla, a bright, 16-year-old, upper-middle-class adolescent brought in by her parents for a psychological evaluation.[1] A mental health professional referred them for a collaborative psychological assessment to assist in treatment planning. Kayla's parents reported a history of mood disturbances, acting out, and extreme risk-taking behaviors. She has a previous history of both inpatient and outpatient treatment. Her parents felt at their wit's end and believed that the previous interventions had failed. Kayla reports feeling scapegoated, very alone, and misunderstood. She believes that her parents no longer love her and feels compelled to change who she is in order to regain their love.

Not surprisingly, Kayla was distrustful that another evaluation would be helpful to her. After some prodding, she came up with only two questions she wanted addressed in the evaluation:

Am I bipolar?
Why am I so angry all the time?

Her parents, on the other hand, came up with almost 10 times as many questions as Kayla, most of which described negative behaviors including manipulation, projection, lack of empathy, problems regulating mood, and low academic achievement—for example,

Why does she lie so much?
Why aren't her grades any better?
Why is she so chaotic and self-destructive?

This imbalance in questions from Kayla and her parents reflects the frequent reality of psychological assessment of adolescents: someone else's concerns have brought them in and their expectations that anything useful will occur can be quite low. On a positive note, Kayla's parents also included several questions about what parenting techniques they could use to help her and what treatment options were available for them, for example:

It seems like we've tried everything. What else is left?
Are there things we can do differently to help her?

---

[1]Demographic information and some of the assessment details have been altered for privacy and didactic purposes.

STEP 1: PRESENT RATIONALE FOR MMPI–A ASSESSMENT TO KAYLA

A brief explanation of why the MMPI–A was among the tests selected is an important part of collaborative assessment, especially for young people like Kayla with a history of mental health interventions. The following is an example of how to introduce the MMPI–A:

> Kayla, you've come up with a couple of questions you'd like me to look into, and your parents have others, too. One of the tests that I think would be helpful is the MMPI–A. It's a long one, more than 450 true–false questions, but it is likely to give us a lot of information. You weren't sure if you'd taken this before, but it's probably been a while, so I think it would be good to do today. When you're done with it, I will have the computer score it, and in your next session, I want the two of us to look at what the computer says about your scores. You and I together will try to figure out if the computer got it right or if it didn't.

STEP 2: REVIEWING KAYLA'S MMPI–A RESULTS AND PLANNING THE FEEDBACK SESSION

Figure 9.3 presents the first 12 pages of Kayla's 17-page Minnesota Report generated for her MMPI–A responses. As in the other chapters in this book, the pages containing her item-level indicators are not included because of test security reasons, nor are the pages with her responses to each MMPI–A item. We use Kayla's Minnesota Report to illustrate how a feedback session with her could be structured. A quick examination of Kayla's Minnesota Report reveals a wealth of information to discuss in a feedback session and opportunities for further assessment of her alcohol and other drug use behaviors, as well as the possibility of a history of sexual abuse and her potential for sexual acting out. For these reasons, the psychologist tentatively should plan for more time in an individual feedback session with Kayla, followed by a shorter amount of time with her parents. Any feedback session should begin by asking the young person what he or she thought of the test, followed by a description of how the MMPI–A works. In Kayla's case, the Validity Scales profile from the Minnesota Report on page 232 can be used to explain the test in the following way:

> All those questions you answered the other day on the MMPI–A are scored into various scales and graphed on profiles like this one. The individual scales are along the bottom [point to *VRIN* (Variable Response Inconsistency), *TRIN* (True Response Inconsistency), F_1 (Infrequency 1), etc.]. This line here [point to 50 *T*-score line] tells us what the average teenager is likely to score, so you were about average on five of these scales. The more important lines are the ones in this gray shaded area [point to the 60-to-64 area]

FIGURE 9.3

Outpatient Mental Health Interpretive Report

MMPI-A™

The Minnesota Report™: Adolescent Interpretive System, 2nd Edition

James N. Butcher, PhD, & Carolyn L. Williams, PhD

ID Number:	Kayla
Age:	16
Gender:	Female
Date Assessed:	12/10/2010

PEARSON

PsychCorp

FIGURE 9.3 (*Continued*)

MMPI-A™ Outpatient Mental Health Interpretive Report   ID: Kayla
12/10/2010, Page 2

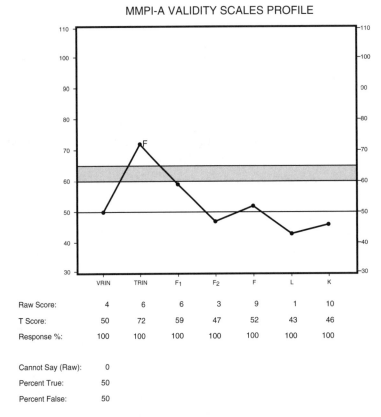

MMPI-A VALIDITY SCALES PROFILE

	VRIN	TRIN	F₁	F₂	F	L	K
Raw Score:	4	6	6	3	9	1	10
T Score:	50	72	59	47	52	43	46
Response %:	100	100	100	100	100	100	100

Cannot Say (Raw): 0
Percent True: 50
Percent False: 50

Excerpts from *The Minnesota Report: Adolescent Interpretive System*
(Rev. ed.), by Butcher and Williams, 2007.

FIGURE 9.3 (*Continued*)

MMPI-A™ Outpatient Mental Health Interpretive Report
12/10/2010, Page 3

ID: Kayla

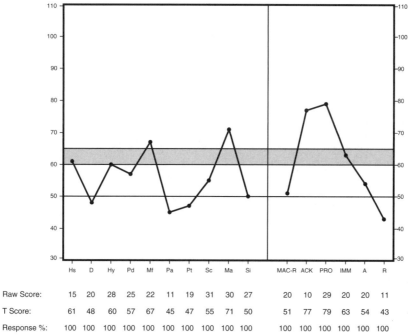

MMPI-A CLINICAL AND SUPPLEMENTARY SCALES PROFILE

	Hs	D	Hy	Pd	Mf	Pa	Pt	Sc	Ma	Si	MAC-R	ACK	PRO	IMM	A	R
Raw Score:	15	20	28	25	22	11	19	31	30	27	20	10	29	20	20	11
T Score:	61	48	60	57	67	45	47	55	71	50	51	77	79	63	54	43
Response %:	100	100	100	100	100	100	100	100	100	100	100	100	100	100	100	100

Welsh Code: 9'5+13-480/276: F/KL:

Mean Profile Elevation: 55.5

Excerpts from *The Minnesota Report: Adolescent Interpretive System* (Rev. ed.), by Butcher and Williams, 2007.

FIGURE 9.3 (*Continued*)

MMPI-A™ Outpatient Mental Health Interpretive Report
12/10/2010, Page 4

ID: Kayla

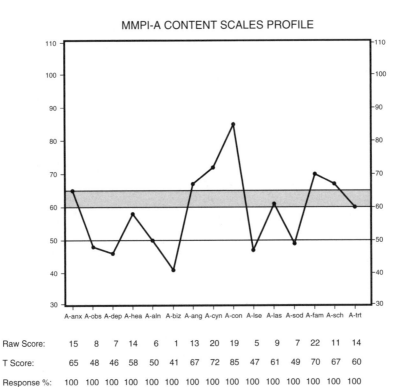

MMPI-A CONTENT SCALES PROFILE

	A-anx	A-obs	A-dep	A-hea	A-aln	A-biz	A-ang	A-cyn	A-con	A-lse	A-las	A-sod	A-fam	A-sch	A-trt
Raw Score:	15	8	7	14	6	1	13	20	19	5	9	7	22	11	14
T Score:	65	48	46	58	50	41	67	72	85	47	61	49	70	67	60
Response %:	100	100	100	100	100	100	100	100	100	100	100	100	100	100	100

Excerpts from *The Minnesota Report: Adolescent Interpretive System* (Rev. ed.), by Butcher and Williams, 2007.

FIGURE 9.3 (*Continued*)

MMPI-A™ Outpatient Mental Health Interpretive Report
12/10/2010, Page 5

ID: Kayla

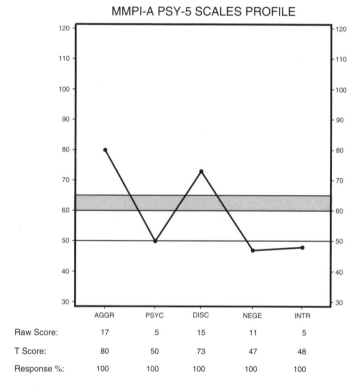

MMPI-A PSY-5 SCALES PROFILE

	AGGR	PSYC	DISC	NEGE	INTR
Raw Score:	17	5	15	11	5
T Score:	80	50	73	47	48
Response %:	100	100	100	100	100

Excerpts from *The Minnesota Report: Adolescent Interpretive System* (Rev. ed.), by Butcher and Williams, 2007.

FIGURE 9.3 (*Continued*)

MMPI-A™ Outpatient Mental Health Interpretive Report   ID: Kayla
12/10/2010, Page 6

VALIDITY CONSIDERATIONS

She had a tendency to inconsistently respond False without adequate attention to item meaning. Although her TRIN score is not elevated enough to invalidate her MMPI-A, caution is suggested in interpreting and using the resulting profiles.

SYMPTOMATIC BEHAVIOR

This individual appears to be overactive, according to her clinical scales profile. She may have unrealistic plans and agitated behavior, and she may be unable to complete tasks. She tends to be disorganized and has little patience for details.

Such individuals appear overly self-confident, and when things do not go their way, they become frustrated, irritable, and moody. In addition, this adolescent is easily bored and will act impulsively, sometimes showing poor judgment and behaving in ways that create difficulties for herself or others. She is a risk-taker.

Her high-point MMPI-A score, Ma, is the third most frequent well-defined peak score among adolescent girls in treatment settings. Approximately 5% of girls in treatment programs obtained this peak scale elevation in their profile pattern. The Ma scale is the most frequent well-defined peak score for girls in the normative sample (12%), although it usually has a lower level of elevation than in treatment program samples.

In a large archival sample of MMPI-A profiles scored by Pearson Assessments (n = 12,744), 8.4% of the girls had a well-defined elevated Ma scale as their most frequent peak score at or above a T score of 65 and separated from the next highest scale by more than 5 points.

She endorsed an unusual pattern of interests compared to other young women her age. She acknowledged interests that seem stereotypically masculine.

Her MMPI-A Content Scales profile reveals important areas to consider in her evaluation. She reports many behavioral problems including stealing, shoplifting, lying, breaking or destroying property, being disrespectful, swearing, or being oppositional. She may belong to a peer group that is frequently in trouble and encourages deviant behavior. Poor academic performance and behavioral problems in school are also possible, as are behavior problems at home. She may be sexually active, flirtatious, provocative, or promiscuous.

She may be assaultive or aggressive when she is angry, and she may be overly interested in violence. She reported numerous problems in school, both academic and behavioral. She reported several symptoms of anxiety, including tension, worries, and difficulties sleeping.

An examination of the adolescent's underlying personality factors with the PSY-5 scales might help explain any behavioral problems she might be presently experiencing. She is likely to be considered by others as a highly aggressive person given her high elevation on the Aggressiveness scale. This aggression may be manifest through use of intimidating tactics or physical aggression in order to

Excerpts from *The Minnesota Report: Adolescent Interpretive System* (Rev. ed.), by Butcher and Williams, 2007.

FIGURE 9.3 (*Continued*)

accomplish her immediate goals. Elevated Aggressiveness scores also suggest she may engage in sexual acting out. She also shows a pattern of disinhibition given her elevated score on the Disconstraint scale that can be reflected in high risk-taking, irresponsibility, and impulsive behavior. She appears to be less bound by moral restraints than other people.

INTERPERSONAL RELATIONS

She is likely to use others, which results in difficult interpersonal problems. She might be experiencing strained relationships owing to her poor judgment and acting-out behaviors. She may need a lot of interpersonal stimulation; she tends to become easily bored and irritated with others.

Her social behavior might be punctuated with periods of moodiness and open expression of negative feelings.

Some problems with her relationships are evident from her extreme endorsement of items on A-cyn. This young person has numerous misanthropic attitudes. The world is a very hostile place to her and she believes that others are out to get her. She looks for hidden motives whenever someone does anything nice for her. She believes that it is safer to trust no one because people make friends in order to use them. Because she believes that people inwardly dislike helping each other, she reports being on guard when people seem friendlier than she expects. She feels misunderstood by others and thinks they are very jealous of her.

In addition to her extreme endorsements on the MMPI-A Content Scales, she reported other significant interpersonal issues. Family problems are quite significant in this person's life. She reports numerous problems with her parents and other family members. She describes her family in terms of discord, jealousy, fault finding, anger, serious disagreements, lack of love and understanding, and very limited communication. She looks forward to the day when she can leave home for good, and she does not feel that she can count on her family in times of trouble. Her parents and she often disagree about her friends. She indicates that her parents treat her like a child and frequently punish her without cause. Her family problems probably have a negative effect on her behavior in school. She reports being irritable and impatient with others, and she may throw temper tantrums to get her way.

BEHAVIORAL STABILITY

The relative elevation of the highest scale (Ma) in her clinical profile shows very high profile definition. Her peak score is likely to remain very prominent in her profile pattern if she is retested at a later date. Adolescents with this clinical profile are often emotionally labile and may have high moods for no apparent reason and downswings that serve as marked contrasts.

Excerpts from *The Minnesota Report: Adolescent Interpretive System* (Rev. ed.), by Butcher and Williams, 2007.

FIGURE 9.3 *(Continued)*

MMPI-A™ Outpatient Mental Health Interpretive Report   **ID: Kayla**
12/10/2010, Page 8

DIAGNOSTIC CONSIDERATIONS

Adolescents with this clinical profile should be evaluated for a mood disorder. Possible authority problems and impulsivity should also be considered.

Her highly elevated Conduct Problems scale may indicate the presence of an oppositional-defiant disorder or a conduct disorder.

Given her elevation on the School Problems scale, her diagnostic evaluation could include assessment of possible academic skills deficits and behavior problems. Her endorsement of several anxiety-based symptoms should be considered in her diagnostic work-up.

Adolescents with very high scores on the PRO scale typically report being involved with a peer group that uses alcohol or other drugs. This adolescent's involvement in an alcohol- or drug-using lifestyle should be further evaluated. Problems at home or in school are likely considering her involvement with alcohol or other drugs.

She has endorsed items that confirm her increasing involvement with alcohol or other drugs. She acknowledges that her use is problematic and reports being criticized for it. She may feel that alcohol or other drugs facilitate social interactions, thus serving as a coping strategy.

TREATMENT CONSIDERATIONS

Adolescents with high scores on Ma are typically unwilling to explore feelings in therapy and tend to be insensitive to feedback. They may overuse denial, and they do not like to discuss details of personal problems. Because they are not introspective, they are not good candidates for insight-oriented psychotherapy. Behavioral approaches designed to increase self-control may prove more fruitful.

Her very high potential for developing alcohol or drug problems requires attention in therapy if important life changes are to be made. She has acknowledged some problems in this area, which is a valuable first step for intervention.

Her family situation, which is full of conflict, should be considered in her treatment planning. Family therapy may be helpful if her parents or guardians are willing and able to work on conflict resolution. However, if family therapy is not feasible, it may be profitable during the course of her treatment to explore her considerable anger at and disappointment in her family. Alternate sources of emotional support from adults (e.g., foster parent, teacher, other relative, friend's parent, or neighbor) could be explored and facilitated in the absence of caring parents.

There are some symptom areas suggested by the Content Scales profile that the therapist may wish to consider in initial treatment sessions. Her behavior problems may respond best to behavior management strategies such as contracting. Her endorsement of several anxiety-based symptoms could be explored further.

Excerpts from *The Minnesota Report: Adolescent Interpretive System* (Rev. ed.), by Butcher and Williams, 2007.

FIGURE 9.3 (*Continued*)

MMPI-A™ Outpatient Mental Health Interpretive Report   **ID: Kayla**
12/10/2010, Page 9

Conditions in her environment that may be contributing to her aggressive and hostile behaviors could be explored. Adolescents with anger-control problems may benefit from modeling approaches and rewards for appropriate behaviors. Stress-inoculation training or other cognitive-behavioral interventions could be used to teach self-control. Angry outbursts during therapy sessions can provide opportunities for her to learn about her impulse-control problems and to practice new skills.

During the course of her treatment, it may be important to discuss her sexual behavior. Her knowledge about sexuality and protecting herself from sexually transmitted diseases and unwanted pregnancies could be assessed and information provided, if needed. Perhaps in a trusting therapeutic relationship, she will be able to discuss the extent of her sexual activity and its meaning in her life. Alternatives to risky, promiscuous behavior could be discussed and promoted. If she is flirtatious and provocative, a greater awareness of this on her part may prevent unwanted sexual advances or possible victimization. Social skills training may be helpful in changing possibly inappropriate behaviors.

She endorsed some items that indicate possible difficulties in establishing a therapeutic relationship. She may be reluctant to self-disclose, she may be distrustful of helping professionals and others, and she may believe that her problems cannot be solved. She may be unwilling to assume responsibility for behavior change or to plan for her future. Her cynical attitudes and beliefs about others and their hidden motivations may create difficulties in therapy. Her therapist should be aware of her general mistrust of others.

Excerpts from *The Minnesota Report: Adolescent Interpretive System* (Rev. ed.), by Butcher and Williams, 2007.

and above 65. Pretty much all the graphs I'll show you today will be like this one. Am I making sense? Do you understand the general picture of how psychologists look at the MMPI–A?

This first graph is important because it tells us how well you cooperated with the test, and you did just fine. The only one that got above the important line is this one [point to *TRIN*]. It says that you may have sometimes filled in "false" on the answer sheet without really paying close attention. I'm wondering if you got a little bored or distracted?

In Kayla's case, the Validity Scales profile offers a low-key entry into the feedback session and can be used to explain the general concepts of MMPI–A interpretation. Kayla's elevation on Scale 9 (*Ma*, Hypomania) provides another entry point for her feedback session because it addresses her concerns about a possible mood disturbance that could be handled like this:

Okay, now that you've got the general picture of how the MMPI–A is designed, let's look at this next profile that actually

FIGURE 9.3 *(Continued)*

MMPI-A™ Outpatient Mental Health Interpretive Report   ID: Kayla
12/10/2010, Page 10

ADDITIONAL SCALES

A subscale or content component scale should be interpreted only when its corresponding parent scale has an elevated T score of 60 or above. Subscales and content component scales printed below in bold meet that criterion for interpretation.

Harris-Lingoes Subscales	Raw Score	T Score	Resp %
Depression Subscales			
Subjective Depression (D_1)	9	48	100
Psychomotor Retardation (D_2)	3	40	100
Physical Malfunctioning (D_3)	5	58	100
Mental Dullness (D_4)	7	62	100
Brooding (D_5)	3	46	100
Hysteria Subscales			
Denial of Social Anxiety (Hy_1)	4	54	100
Need for Affection (Hy_2)	1	34	100
Lassitude-Malaise (Hy_3)	7	58	100
Somatic Complaints (Hy_4)	**12**	**73**	**100**
Inhibition of Aggression (Hy_5)	2	43	100
Psychopathic Deviate Subscales			
Familial Discord (Pd_1)	5	56	100
Authority Problems (Pd_2)	5	65	100
Social Imperturbability (Pd_3)	4	55	100
Social Alienation (Pd_4)	7	57	100
Self-Alienation (Pd_5)	5	51	100
Paranoia Subscales			
Persecutory Ideas (Pa_1)	6	57	100
Poignancy (Pa_2)	1	36	100
Naivete (Pa_3)	1	36	100
Schizophrenia Subscales			
Social Alienation (Sc_1)	7	52	100
Emotional Alienation (Sc_2)	2	48	100
Lack of Ego Mastery, Cognitive (Sc_3)	4	54	100
Lack of Ego Mastery, Conative (Sc_4)	6	56	100
Lack of Ego Mastery, Defective Inhibition (Sc_5)	7	63	100
Bizarre Sensory Experiences (Sc_6)	10	63	100
Hypomania Subscales			
Amorality (Ma_1)	**5**	**70**	**100**
Psychomotor Acceleration (Ma_2)	9	59	100
Imperturbability (Ma_3)	3	50	100
Ego Inflation (Ma_4)	6	58	100

Excerpts from *The Minnesota Report: Adolescent Interpretive System* (Rev. ed.), by Butcher and Williams, 2007.

FIGURE 9.3 *(Continued)*

MMPI-A™ Outpatient Mental Health Interpretive Report   ID: Kayla
12/10/2010, Page 11

	Raw Score	T Score	Resp %
Social Introversion Subscales			
Shyness / Self-Consciousness (Si_1)	3	40	100
Social Avoidance (Si_2)	3	56	100
Alienation--Self and Others (Si_3)	11	58	100
Content Component Scales			
Adolescent Depression			
Dysphoria (A-dep_1)	1	43	100
Self-Depreciation (A-dep_2)	2	48	100
Lack of Drive (A-dep_3)	4	59	100
Suicidal Ideation (A-dep_4)	0	42	100
Adolescent Health Concerns			
Gastrointestinal Complaints (A-hea_1)	0	44	100
Neurological Symptoms (A-hea_2)	9	63	100
General Health Concerns (A-hea_3)	3	56	100
Adolescent Alienation			
Misunderstood (A-aln_1)	3	56	100
Social Isolation (A-aln_2)	3	63	100
Interpersonal Skepticism (A-aln_3)	0	40	100
Adolescent Bizarre Mentation			
Psychotic Symptomatology (A-biz_1)	0	38	100
Paranoid Ideation (A-biz_2)	1	55	100
Adolescent Anger			
Explosive Behavior (A-ang_1)	**7**	**73**	**100**
Irritability (A-ang_2)	6	55	100
Adolescent Cynicism			
Misanthropic Beliefs (A-cyn_1)	**12**	**64**	**100**
Interpersonal Suspiciousness (A-cyn_2)	**8**	**65**	**100**
Adolescent Conduct Problems			
Acting-Out Behaviors (A-con_1)	**9**	**79**	**100**
Antisocial Attitudes (A-con_2)	**8**	**78**	**100**
Negative Peer Group Influences (A-con_3)	1	53	100
Adolescent Low Self-Esteem			
Self-Doubt (A-lse_1)	5	54	100
Interpersonal Submissiveness (A-lse_2)	0	37	100
Adolescent Low Aspirations			
Low Achievement Orientation (A-las_1)	5	58	100
Lack of Initiative (A-las_2)	**4**	**60**	**100**

Excerpts from *The Minnesota Report: Adolescent Interpretive System* (Rev. ed.), by Butcher and Williams, 2007.

FIGURE 9.3 (*Continued*)

MMPI-A™ Outpatient Mental Health Interpretive Report   ID: Kayla
12/10/2010, Page 12

	Raw Score	T Score	Resp %
Adolescent Social Discomfort			
Introversion (A-sod$_1$)	4	53	100
Shyness (A-sod$_2$)	3	46	100
Adolescent Family Problems			
Familial Discord (A-fam$_1$)	**14**	**63**	**100**
Familial Alienation (A-fam$_2$)	**5**	**63**	**100**
Adolescent School Problems			
School Conduct Problems (A-sch$_1$)	**2**	**65**	**100**
Negative Attitudes (A-sch$_2$)	**5**	**65**	**100**
Adolescent Negative Treatment Indicators			
Low Motivation (A-trt$_1$)	4	53	100
Inability to Disclose (A-trt$_2$)	**7**	**71**	**100**

Uniform T scores are used for Hs, D, Hy, Pd, Pa, Pt, Sc, Ma, the content scales, the content component scales, and the PSY-5 scales. The remaining scales and subscales use linear T scores.

Excerpts from *The Minnesota Report: Adolescent Interpretive System* (Rev. ed.), by Butcher and Williams, 2007.

has two sets of scales [turn to the Clinical and Supplementary Scales profile shown on p. 233]. First, I want you to look at the left side of this page. What is the highest scale there? Scale 9. [Note: it is best to use the scale numbers or abbreviations in a feedback session rather than the scale names from the 1940s.] So, your score on this scale suggests that you are like teens who tend to be overactive, easily frustrated or bored, irritable, and sometimes show poor judgment that can create difficulties for you or others. That sounds a little like the problems you described the first time we met. What do you think? Does this sound like you?

Kayla's Clinical Scales profile also shows an elevation on Scale 5 (*Mf*, Masculinity/Femininity) and moderate elevations on Scale 1 (*Hs*, Hypochondriasis) and Scale 3 (*Hy*, Hysteria). However, there are other more significant elevations on the Supplementary and Content Scales profiles. Keeping Guideline 8 (see earlier section in this chapter) in mind, rather than overload Kayla with descriptors from those scales, it is probably best to turn to interpretations from the other profiles at this point in the feedback session. However, some adolescents quickly become engaged in this process and will ask about the other scales above 65 and in the shaded area. The psychologist should be prepared to quickly answer Kayla's questions, if asked. For example, a response about her Scale 5 elevation could be,

> This probably is more a measure of interests. This score could indicate that you may be more interested in activities favored by boys than girls. What do you think?

Similarly, if Kayla were to ask a question about the moderate elevations on Scales 1 and 3, the psychologist could respond as follows:

> These two scales are in that gray area and tend to be elevated in young people who report physical problems like headaches and stomachaches. Your mom mentioned that you had some problems with headaches. Would you agree? Can you tell me more about your headaches? What about any other health concerns?

There are two significant elevations on the Alcohol and Drug Problems scales *ACK* (Acknowledgment) and *PRO* (Proneness) on Kayla's Supplementary Scales profile. However, substance abuse problems were not mentioned during the intake session. Therefore, rather than bringing this issue up early in the feedback session, it is best to turn to a discussion of other scale descriptors that are concordant with information presented during intake:

> Okay, I do want to talk about the scales on this side of the profile, because you see that you do have two high ones, but let's look at these scales first [turn to the Content Scales profile on p. 234]. Now, if I forget to get back to those other two scales, remind me, because they are important. This set of scales provides a good summary of what you said on the MMPI–A as it compares with the average teenager. These three in the center are really noticeable. The highest one indicates a lot of serious behavior problems like problems with the law, vandalism, running away, and having friends who get into trouble. [Note that these descriptors come directly from the item-level indicators that Kayla endorsed in the scored direction and are provided on the full Minnesota Report available to clinicians.] Can you tell me a little bit about what you were thinking when you answered "true" to those questions?
>
> This one here is an Adolescent-Anger scale [point to *A-ang*]. It confirms what you told me in the first session, that you are much more angry and aggressive than other teens. These problems spill over into your school and family life, as these two scales indicate [point to *A-fam* (Adolescent-Family Problems) and *A-sch* (Adolescent-School Problems)]. What do you think? Does anything about this seem incorrect? Is this what you expected? [Note that discussion of these scales lends itself to questions about specific examples in the family and at school of problematic events.]

Similarly, Kayla could be asked for examples of recent times when she became angry or aggressive:

> We haven't talked about this one yet [point to *A-cyn* (Adolescent-Cynicism)]. It worries me from the perspective of trying to figure

out how best to help you cope with these problems. It is a scale that measures something called *cynicism,* or your ability to trust others and believe that others want to or can help you. You're not likely to believe that people like me want to help you. Looking at this profile, it seems your world is pretty bleak; trouble is everywhere and there's no one you can trust. Is that an accurate picture of your life right now?

There's one final scale to discuss here, and that's this one, over here [point to *A-anx* (Adolescent-Anxiety)]. This shows that your problems may be overwhelming you right now, causing worries and difficulties sleeping. Is this true? What sorts of things do you lie awake worrying about?

Up until this point in the feedback session, although a much more detailed picture has been revealed, the descriptors from the MMPI–A parallel information provided in the intake sessions. Although these are serious problems, they are not discordant with what Kayla and her parents described. Adolescents like Kayla, even when hearing these negative descriptors, often feel understood and somewhat relieved. After all, in Kayla's case, given the elevations on the Content Scales and her responses to the item-level indicators, the feedback involves validating what she already knows about herself, telling her that someone else (i.e., the psychologist) has a similar understanding of her problems and that there are other young people like her out there.

Now it is time in the feedback session to address two specific issues (i.e., alcohol and drug use history and sexual problems) not previously detailed although perhaps hinted at (i.e., the extreme risk-taking behaviors mentioned by her parents). The MMPI–A feedback session provides a nonconfrontational way of doing so, given Kayla's scores:

Well, the MMPI–A certainly has given us a lot of ideas about what's been troubling you. Remember that there were two other scales on your profiles that I wanted to discuss with you. They were on this page [return to the Supplementary Scales profile shown on page 233 in this chapter and point to the *ACK* and *PRO* scales]. You see that these are really high and they're something we haven't talked about yet—alcohol and other drug problems. This first one, *ACK,* indicates that you answered "true" to the MMPI–A questions about alcohol and other drug problems, and this one, *PRO,* suggests your scores are like other teens who have been in treatment for alcohol and drug problems. You indicated that you drink too much, that you've gotten into fights while drinking, and that you've experienced blackouts [note these all come from her responses to the item-level indicators provided in the full Minnesota Report]. That really hasn't come up before in our discussions. Can you tell me a little more about this?

Depending on how much time is available and how Kayla is responding to the feedback session, the final topic that could be discussed in this session is the sexual behavior correlates associated with her scale elevations; some of these are highlighted in the Treatment Considerations section of the Minnesota Report (i.e., see p. 9 of her Minnesota Report in Figure 9.3 on p. 239). Clinical judgment is necessary to determine if this session is the appropriate time for this discussion.

> Kayla, there is one final area that the MMPI–A suggests may be an issue for young women who have scores like yours, and that has to do with sexuality. One of the scales that you scored high on is associated with young women who have a history of sexual abuse. [Note: this is a correlate of an elevated *A-fam* scale score.] By no means is that true of all the young women who score like you did—only some, not all. Is that something you are comfortable talking to me about?
>
> Other young women who have high scores on some of the scales you did are sexually active, often have several partners, and may be at risk for sexually transmitted diseases or unwanted pregnancies. It may be useful to have a discussion about this as well. What do you think?

Given Kayla's MMPI–A responses indicating high levels of cynicism, distrust, and family problems, it would be best to have her present when giving initial feedback to her parents. After a lengthy feedback session as is likely with such a rich MMPI–A profile as Kayla's, a few wrap-up comments and questions are helpful.

> I really appreciated your openness and honesty when you took the MMPI–A, as well as during today's session when we discussed what the MMPI–A suggested about your problems. Overall, what did you think about the MMPI–A? How would you rate its accuracy? Our next step is to briefly report to your parents about the MMPI–A. But before we ask them to come into the room, let's just touch base about whether there's anything we discussed today that you prefer that I not mention to them.[2] Would it be okay with you if I asked you to summarize briefly what you and I discussed about the MMPI–A? [Kayla should be free to decline this request.] After we finish today, I'm going to think about what we discussed and what the other tests indicate and prepare a final set of recommendations for you and your parents. Is there anything that we haven't talked about that you want me to know about as I think about putting all this information together for you?

---

[2]The assumption here is that the psychologist has explained to the young person and his or her parents confidentiality and its limitations (e.g., danger to self or others, reporting obligations in situations of child physical or sexual abuse) as part of the intake process.

STEP 3: PLANNING THE MMPI–A FEEDBACK SESSION WITH KAYLA'S PARENTS

As mentioned earlier, given the amount of material to be covered in Kayla's MMPI–A feedback, as well as the areas for further assessment in a feedback interview, less time will be available to go over the results with her parents. And to increase rapport and trust with Kayla, it is important that she be present to hear and discuss what is told to her parents.

> We made a lot of progress today in trying to figure out what's going on in Kayla's life and how best to approach some of the problems. Most of today's session was spent talking about her MMPI–A results. She was very cooperative, open, and honest during the testing and in today's session. That was very helpful. Kayla, would you be willing to give your parents a brief summary of what you learned about yourself from the MMPI–A?

The psychologist will be prepared to provide additional information from the MMPI–A, depending on Kayla's response. How Kayla participates in this brief session with her parents will provide another sample of the interactions between Kayla and her parents.

STEP 4: PULLING IT ALL TOGETHER

Once data from all the testing, interviews, observations, rating scales, and the like are collected, the psychologist should reexamine the referral questions and provide answers. In Kayla's specific case the primary reason for the referral was treatment planning. In addition, Kayla asked a specific diagnostic question, "Am I bipolar?" Her parents' questions, on the other hand, focused primarily on conduct problems. Here is an illustration of how the psychologist can address the questions in a joint session with Kayla and her parents. The psychologist includes information presented in Chapter 1 of this volume about the nature of adolescence.

> This is our final session, the one in which we pull everything together and try to come up with a plan for the future. I'd like to start where we began. Kayla, do you remember the two questions you asked me to answer? We've already talked a fair amount about what you meant by *bipolar*. You gave me several specific examples of your concerns and what the word *bipolar* means to you.
>
> Some of the things you described, as well as things your parents told me, are really stuff that scholars and professionals have described about being an adolescent from Day 1. Would you believe that both Plato and Aristotle—from the 4th century BCE—identified moodiness and impulsivity as a key characteristic of adolescence? Even today, some psychologists still consider adolescence as a time of storm and stress.

I think one of the more exciting areas of research that helps us understand what being an adolescent is all about is from studies of brain growth and development. Not all that long ago, we used to think that the brain was fully formed about the time puberty started. Now, however, we know that there are many changes in the brain that occur beginning in early adolescence and perhaps continuing until early adulthood. Here's a picture of the areas of the brain that have important changes during adolescence [referring to the illustration shown in Figure 1.2 on p. 10].

This part of the brain, the prefrontal cortex, is involved with mood regulation, decision making, and problem solving, among other things. The limbic system is also associated with very important aspects of behavior, emotions, learning, and memory. Because these areas of the brain are not yet fully formed, adult-level control of behavior may fail at times, perhaps accounting for greater risk taking. And, there is great concern among brain researchers about what the introduction of drugs like alcohol can do to the developing brain. These areas of the brain are very much related to some of the problems that your parents described and included in their questions for me. Am I making sense? Do you have any questions about how this might relate to the problems that you or your parents described?

The information in the preceding paragraphs is presented to demonstrate a developmental context for Kayla's behavior. Given this family's sophistication, the information is presented at a relatively high level that could be modified for clients with less capacity for understanding. At any rate, it is important for the psychologist to check in frequently, as in this example, to make sure the information is coming across as intended.

So far we've talked in general about what adolescence is all about and how it relates to some of the problems that you thought might be part of being bipolar. And, some of the issues you and your parents described—moodiness, irritability, poor decision making—characterize adolescents in general. Let's go back to what we learned from the MMPI–A. When we compared your responses to the MMPI–A with other young people's responses, we learned that your problems are more severe than those of the average teenager, and we did find some evidence of a mood disturbance. Do you remember the other issues we discussed related to your MMPI–A profiles?

The psychologist can use this as an entry into a discussion of the conduct and alcohol and other drug use problems discussed in the feedback session and other evaluation methods.

Turning back to your question about whether you are bipolar, I can't give you a definitive answer today. You do have some characteristics of that label, but it is pretty rare in people your age, and some other problems came out as more prominent during the evaluation: your anger control problems, difficulties with authorities, and drinking too much and being with friends who are into other drugs. [Refer to the section in Chapter 1, "Psychopathology in Adolescence," on pages 14 to 16 for prevalence information.] We talked about how overwhelming your problems seem to be for you and how you don't have anyone you can trust.

All of us spent a fair amount of time discussing the problems within your family—the yelling and the fighting that distresses all the family members. It also bubbles up at school; your level of anger and aggressive behavior toward others appears to be greater than most young people your age and has gotten you into trouble. [A discussion of specific examples would be helpful.] But I also heard from all three of you that there's still a lot of love and commitment to try to get along better. And, Kayla, you've talked about how bad you feel when you get into trouble, indicating that you want to change. Can you tell us a little more about your bad feelings? Can you remember some of the things you've told me that you would like to change? [These questions are designed to help Kayla reveal to her parents some of her feelings underlying the conduct problems that are so visible to them.]

Given our discussions and the testing you completed and the duration of your problems, you and your family need more support than what you're getting. We talked about that the last time we met. [If possible, the psychologist should begin to prepare Kayla and her family for the treatment recommendations before this final session.] For those reasons, I'm recommending that you and your parents consider either a day treatment or residential facility that will focus on techniques to help you learn how to control your anger and develop other ways of expressing your emotions. I think more attention needs to be paid to the role of alcohol and other drugs in your life. There are better ways to relax or deal with your problems than putting drugs into your body. Let's keep that brain healthy while it's growing up, too! You and your parents could probably benefit from a breather from all the fighting. The places I'm recommending have strong family therapy components that I think will help you and your parents to confront the issues that have been driving you apart and creating such grief for all three of you. Have any of you thought about these options before? Do they seem to fit from what you've learned during the evaluation?

Feedback Sessions With Uncooperative or Unrevealing Adolescents

Kayla is an example of a sophisticated and bright young person who produced a valid MMPI–A that generated a wealth of information for discussion in a feedback session. What about the noncooperative young persons, those with invalid response styles or those who produce normal limits profiles? Can feedback sessions be useful with them? We described two such teens in Chapter 7—recall David (pp. 140–141) and Jeremy (pp. 163–168)? David announced that he had completed the MMPI box form in 15 minutes. His psychologist, even without the benefit of having a scored protocol but based on knowledge of test administration time, provided David with feedback about scoring procedures that would determine if he had simply responded randomly. The psychologist did this in a matter-of-fact, nonjudgmental fashion, with the result that David withdrew his responses (albeit in a creative way; see Chapter 7) and agreed to complete the MMPI the next day. As is often the case when individuals agree to a retesting, David produced a valid MMPI on retesting.

Jeremy's Minnesota Report (see Figure 7.3, pp. 164–167) revealed an inconsistent response style with multiple possible reasons for it. Here is a vignette about how a psychologist might provide feedback. Because the Minnesota Report's profiles were not plotted and contained the Invalid Profile warning statement (see Figure 7.3, pp. 165–166), Jeremy's psychologist decided to use the profile in Figure 7.4 on page 168 in his feedback session.

> Jeremy, do you remember that long true–false test you filled out for me last week? I got the results back and wondered if you would like me to go over them with you. What did you think about the test? Any ideas about what it might say about you?
>
> All those questions you answered the other day on the MMPI–A are scored into various scales and graphed on profiles like this one. This side of the profile usually tells us what types of problems a person might be experiencing, like depression or anxiety or behavior problems or confusion [point to the Clinical Scales in Figure 7.4]. This line here [point to 50 *T* score line] tells us what the average teenager is likely to score. The more important lines are the ones in this gray shaded area [point to the 60-to-64 area] and above 65. Am I making sense? Do you understand the general picture of how psychologists look at the MMPI–A?
>
> But, before psychologists can tell what kinds of problems you might be having, we have to look at this side of the graph, and you'll see that most of your scores are way above the gray shaded area. These scores are important because they tell us how well you cooperated with the test—and you'll see a major problem here, especially with this first one [point to *VRIN*]. It says that you might not have been paying attention to the meaning of the items when you answered them. I did notice that it only took you about 30 minutes to complete it. The fastest I've ever seen anyone do the test is 45 minutes. What do you think? Could you have gone too fast?
>
> Well, because of this first score, we can't trust the scores on this side of the graph [point to Clinical Scales], so we just

have to disregard all these scales even though you have three above the gray area. But, we can look at these three scales [point to F, F_1, and F_2]. These tell me that you answered questions indicating lots of different and serious problems. I'm not sure if that's because you were going too fast, if you had trouble understanding the items, or if you got confused. [Wait for response.] Well, another possibility is that your responses to the MMPI–A were about times when you get confused or have unusual experiences. [Evaluate possibility of thought disorder.] Or it could be times when you were under the influence of alcohol or other drugs. [Evaluate alcohol and other drug use.] How about problems with your family? Do you remember answering questions like that?

Depending on what is revealed during the feedback session and whether Jeremy becomes more engaged in the psychological evaluation, his psychologist could suggest a retest MMPI–A. Feedback sessions often result in a more engaged young person who might be willing to retake the MMPI–A. However, if Jeremy remains as reluctant and angry as he was at intake, a retake is unlikely to result in a valid MMPI–A.

Sometimes, even with cooperative adolescents, a normal limits profile is produced, which limits what can be discussed in a feedback session. However, a feedback session, even with normal limits profiles, can sometimes provide useful information. This may be particularly the case when there is a discrepancy from the clinical interviews, intake information, or school records as in the following three examples:

- Both you and your parents talked about lots of fighting and disagreements, yet look at this scale, which is Family Problems. You scored in the range of others your age that don't have these types of problems. What do you think about that?
- To a parent: You've been really worried about how your daughter is reacting to the divorce. Yet there's no indication on the MMPI–A of signs of depression or anxiety. What do you make of that? Is the test wrong? Or are you reassured?
- I'm really puzzled about all the problems you've been reporting at school, including your first suspension. Yet look at this score here—it's School Problems, and it's well below the shaded area. What do you think?

Ending the Beginner's Guide to the MMPI–A

As we hope we demonstrated with Kayla, David, Jeremy, and the other young people whose MMPI–A profiles are described in this book, the

MMPI–A has the potential for providing valuable assistance in describing a young person's personality and psychopathology. In this beginner's guide, we have focused somewhat exclusively on how to use the MMPI–A in a psychological evaluation. Our goal was to provide step-by-step guidelines for the most widely used objective measure in the clinical appraisal of adolescents. It is our hope that readers are now ready to go to the next level and effectively incorporate this instrument into their clinical practices.

Appendix A: References on the MMPI–A

General References

Archer, R. P. (1997). Future directions for the MMPI–A: Research and clinical issues. *Journal of Personality Assessment, 68,* 95–109.

Archer, R. P. (1999). Overview of the Minnesota Multiphasic Personality Inventory—Adolescent (MMPI–A). In M. E. Maruish (Ed.), *The use of psychological testing for treatment planning and outcomes assessment* (2nd ed., pp. 341–380). Mahwah, NJ; Erlbaum.

Archer, R. P. (2005). *MMPI–A: Assessing adolescent psychopathology* (3rd ed.). Mahwah, NJ: Erlbaum.

Archer, R. P., & Baker, E. M. (2005). Minnesota Multiphasic Personality Inventory—Adolescent. In T. Grisso, G. Vincent, & D. Seagrave (Eds.), *Mental health screening and assessment in juvenile justice* (pp. 240–252). New York, NY: Guilford Press.

Archer, R. P., & Krishnamurthy, R. (2002). *Essentials of MMPI–A assessment.* New York, NY: Wiley.

Ben-Porath, Y. S., & Davis, D. L. (1996). *Case studies for interpreting the MMPI–A.* Minneapolis: University of Minnesota Press.

Butcher, J. N., Graham, J. R., Williams, C. L., & Kaemmer, B. (1992). *MMPI–A: Minnesota Multiphasic Personality Inventory—Adolescent test booklet.* Minneapolis: University of Minnesota Press.

Butcher, J. N., & Williams, C. L. (2000). *Essentials of MMPI–2 and MMPI–A interpretation* (2nd ed.). Minneapolis: University of Minnesota Press.

Butcher, J. N., Williams, C. L., Graham, J. R., Tellegen, A., Ben-Porath, Y. S., Archer, R. P., & Kaemmer, B. (1992). *Manual for the administration, scoring, and interpretation of the adolescent version of the MMPI.* Minneapolis: University of Minnesota Press.

Cumella, E. J., & Lafferty-O'Connor, J. (2009). Assessing adolescents with the MMPI–A. In J. N. Butcher (Ed.), *Handbook of personality assessment* (pp. 485–500). New York, NY: Oxford University Press.

Pope, K. S., Butcher, J. N., & Seelen, J. (2006). *The MMPI, MMPI–2 & MMPI–A in court: A practical guide for expert witnesses and attorneys* (3rd ed.). Washington, DC: American Psychological Association.

Twenge, J. M., Gentile, B., DeWall, N., Ma, D., Lacefield, K., & Schurtz, D. R. (2010). Birth cohort increases in psychopathology among young Americans, 1938–2007: A cross-temporal meta-analysis of the MMPI. *Clinical Psychology Review, 30,* 145–154.

Abuse

Forbey, J. D., Ben-Porath, Y. S., & Davis, D. L. (2000). A comparison of sexually abused and non-sexually abused adolescents in a clinical treatment facility using the MMPI–A. *Child Abuse & Neglect, 24,* 557–568.

Holifield, J. E., Nelson, W. M., III, & Hart, K. J. (2002). MMPI profiles of sexually abused and nonabused outpatient adolescents. *Journal of Adolescent Research, 17,* 188–195.

Perfect, M. M. (2005). Incremental validity of the Minnesota Multiphasic Personality Inventory (MMPI–A) and Rorschach Inkblot Test in predicting the number and severity of adolescents' maltreatment histories. *Dissertation Abstracts International: Section A. Humanities and Social Sciences, 65*(8-A), 2909.

Age

See Scale Development/Psychometric Issues

Alcohol and Other Drug Use

Aharoni, D. M. (1999). The effectiveness of the MMPI–A in the assessment of adolescent substance abuse (Minnesota Multiphasic Personality Inventory). *Dissertation Abstracts International: Section B. Sciences and Engineering, 60*(6-B), 2932.

Dimino, R. A. (2003). Early memories, attachment style, the role of peers, and adolescent substance use. *Dissertation Abstracts International: Section B. Sciences and Engineering, 63*(12-B), 6091.

Gallucci, N. T. (1997). On the identification of patterns of substance abuse with the MMPI–A. *Psychological Assessment, 9,* 224–232.

Ingersoll, J. B. (2003). Predicting the underreporting of substance abuse symptoms in adolescent males in an outpatient substance abuse treatment program. *Dissertation Abstracts International: Section B. Sciences and Engineering, 63*(10-B), 4906.

Micucci, J. A. (2002). Accuracy of MMPI–A scales *ACK, MAC–R,* and *PRO* in detecting comorbid substance abuse among psychiatric inpatients. *Assessment, 9,* 111–122.

Palmer, G. A. (1999). Cluster analysis of MMPI–A profiles of adolescents with substance dependence. *Dissertation Abstracts International: Section B. Sciences and Engineering, 59*(8-B), 4479.

Perry, C. L., Lee, S., Stigler, M. H., Farbakhsh, K., Komro, K. A., Gewirtz, A. H., & Williams, C. L. (2007). The impact of Project Northland on selected MMPI–A problem behavior scales. *Journal of Primary Prevention, 28,* 449–465.

Price, B. H. (1999). Personality variables of chemically dependent adolescents as reflected in the MMPI and the Millon Adolescent Personality Inventory. *Dissertation Abstracts International: Section B. Sciences and Engineering, 60*(2-B), 0864.

Sieving, R., Maruyama, G., Williams, C. L., & Perry, C. L. (2000). Pathways to adolescent alcohol use: Potential mechanisms of parent influence. *Journal of Research on Adolescence, 10,* 489–514.

Stein, L. A. R., & Graham, J. R. (2001). Use of the MMPI–A to detect substance abuse in a juvenile correctional setting. *Journal of Personality Assessment, 77,* 508–523.

Stein, L. A. R., & Graham, J. R. (2005). Ability of substance abusers to escape detection on the Minnesota Multiphasic Personality Inventory—Adolescent (MMPI–A) in a juvenile correctional facility. *Assessment, 12,* 28–39.

Stevens, M., Passetti, L., & Johnson, J. (2004). MMPI–A profiles of substance-abusing adolescents. *International Journal of Psychology, 39,* 408–408.

Weed, N., Butcher, J. N., & Williams, C. L. (1994). Development of MMPI–A alcohol and drug problem scales. *Journal of Studies on Alcohol, 55,* 296–302.

Williams, C. L., Perry, C. L., Farbakhsh, K., & Veblen-Mortenson, S. (1999). Project Northland: Comprehensive alcohol use prevention for young adolescents, their parents, schools, peers, and communities. *Journal of Studies on Alcohol, Suppl. 13,* 112–124.

Williams, C. L., Toomey, T. L., McGovern, P., Wagenaar, A. C., & Perry, C. L. (1995). Development, reliability, and validity of self-report alcohol-use measures with young adolescents. *Journal on Child and Adolescent Substance Abuse, 4,* 17–40.

Basic Scales

See Clinical/Standard Scales; Validity Assessment

Chemical Dependency

See Alcohol and Other Drug Use

Clinical/Standard Scales

See also Cross-Cultural/Ethnic Studies

Abbas, M., Kaiser, R., Shaw, J., & Yu, S. (2007). Criterion validity of the BDI–II and MMPI–A Depression scale in tertiary care adolescent headache patients. *Cephalalgia, 27,* 634–634.

Archer, R. P., & Krishnamurthy, R. (1997). MMPI–A and Rorschach indices related to depression and conduct disorder: An evaluation of the incremental validity hypothesis. *Journal of Personality Assessment, 69,* 517–533.

Brophy, A. L. (2005). Note on Meunier and Bodkins's (2005) "Interpretation of MMPI–A Scale 5 with Female Patients." *Psychological Reports, 97,* 673–674.

Figuered, B. V. (2002). The concurrent validity of the Minnesota Multiphasic Personality Inventory—Adolescent in the assessment of depression. *Dissertation Abstracts International: Section B. Sciences and Engineering, 62*(10-B), 4782.

Finlay, S. W., & Kapes, J. T. (2000). Scale 5 of the MMPI and MMPI–A: Evidence of disparity. *Assessment, 7,* 97–101.

Lilienfeld, L. R. (1994). *The use of the MMPI–A in the identification of risk factors for the future development of eating disorders.* Unpublished doctoral dissertation, University of Minnesota, Minneapolis.

Meunier, G., & Bodkins, M. (2005). Interpretation of MMPI–A Scale 5 with female patients. *Psychological Reports, 96,* 545–546.

Rychlak, R. P. (2005). Implications of MMPI/MMPI–A findings for understanding adolescent development and psychopathology. *Journal of Personality Assessment, 85,* 257–270.

Sabatino, D. A., Webster, B. G., & Vance, H. B. (2001). Childhood mood disorders: History, characteristics, diagnosis and treatment. In H. B. Vance & A. Pumariega (Eds.), *Clinical assessment of child and adolescent behavior* (pp. 413–449). New York, NY: Wiley.

Stein, L. A. R., McClinton, B. K., & Graham, J. R. (1998). Long-term stability of MMPI–A scales. *Journal of Personality Assessment, 70,* 103–108.

Computer Interpretation

Archer, R. P. (1995). *MMPI interpretive system, Version 2.* Lutz, FL: Psychological Assessment Resources Inc.

Archer, R. P. (2003). *MMPI interpretive system, Version 3.* Lutz, FL: Psychological Assessment Resources Inc.

Butcher, J. N. (2009). How to use computer-based reports. In J. N. Butcher (Ed.), *Oxford handbook of clinical and personality assessment* (pp. 693–706). New York, NY: Oxford University Press.

Butcher, J. N., & Williams, C. L. (1992). *User's guide to the Minnesota Report: Adolescent clinical system.* Minneapolis: University of Minnesota Press.

Butcher, J. N., & Williams, C. L. (2007). *User's guide for the Minnesota Report: Adolescent Interpretive System* (Rev. ed.). Minneapolis: University of Minnesota Press.

Carlson, D. A. J. (2001). Computerized vs. written administration of the MMPI–A in clinical and non-clinical settings. *Dissertation Abstracts International: Section B. Sciences and Engineering, 62*(2-B), 1130.

Eyde, L. D., Robertson, G. J., & Krug, S. E. (2009). *Responsible test use: Case studies assessing human behavior* (2nd ed.). Washington, DC: American Psychological Association.

Forbey, J. D., Handel, R. W., & Ben-Porath, Y. S. (2000). A real-data simulation of computerized adaptive administration of the MMPI–A. *Computers in Human Behavior, 16,* 83–96.

Greene, R. L. (2005). Computer scoring and interpretation in psychological report writing. *SPA Exchange, 17,* 6.

Hays, S. K. (2003). A computer-administered version versus paper-and-pencil-administered version of the MMPI–A. *Dissertation Abstracts International: Section B. Sciences & Engineering, 63*(12-B), 6132.

Hays, S., & McCallum, R. S. (2005). A comparison of the pencil-and-paper and computer-administered Minnesota Multiphasic Personality Inventory—Adolescent. *Psychology in the Schools, 42,* 605–613.

McGrath, R. E., & Ingersoll, J. (1999). Writing a good cookbook: A review of MMPI high-point code system studies. *Journal of Personality Assessment, 73,* 149–178.

Powis, D. M. (1999). Actuarial use of the MMPI–A: Generation of clinical correlate data for frequently occurring code types in an adolescent inpatient sample. *Dissertation Abstracts International: Section B. Sciences and Engineering, 59*(11-B), 6107.

Content Scales

Arita, A. A., & Baer, R. A. (1998). Validity of selected MMPI–A Content Scales. *Psychological Assessment, 10,* 59–63.

Didonato, K. (2007). The use of Harris–Lingoes subscales to identify substance use in a population including juvenile offenders and substance users. *Dissertation Abstracts International: Section B. Sciences and Engineering, 68,* 2644.

Forbey, J. D. (2002). Incremental validity of the MMPI–A Content Scales and interpretative utility of the Content Component Scales of the MMPI–A in a residential treatment facility. *Dissertation Abstracts International: Section B. Sciences and Engineering, 63*(1-B), 522.

Forbey, J. D., & Ben-Porath, Y. S. (2003). Incremental validity of the MMPI–A Content Scales in a residential treatment facility. *Assessment, 10,* 191–202.

Kopper, B. A., Osman, A., Soman, J. R., & Hoffman, J. (1998). Clinical utility of the MMPI–A Content Scales and Harris–Lingoes subscales in the assessment of suicidal risk factors in psychiatric adolescents. *Journal of Clinical Psychology, 54,* 191–200.

McCarthy, L., & Archer, R. P. (1998). Factor structure of the MMPI–A Content Scales: Item-level and scale-level findings. *Journal of Personality Assessment, 71,* 84–97.

Milne, L. C., & Greenway, P. (1999). Do high scores on the Adolescent–School Problems and Immaturity scales of the MMPI–A have implications for cognitive performance as measured by the WISC–III? *Psychology in the Schools, 36,* 199–203.

Rinaldo, J. C. B., & Baer, R. A. (2003). Incremental validity of the MMPI–A Content Scales in the prediction of self-reported symptoms. *Journal of Personality Assessment, 80,* 309–318.

Sherwood, N. E., Ben-Porath, Y. S., & Williams, C. L. (1997). *The MMPI–A Content Component Scales: Development, psychometric characteristics, and clinical applications.* Minneapolis: University of Minnesota Press.

Williams, C. L., Butcher, J. N., Ben-Porath, Y. S., & Graham, J. R. (1992). *MMPI–A Content Scales: Assessing psychopathology in adolescents.* Minneapolis: University of Minnesota Press.

Cross-Cultural/Ethnic Studies

Atlis, M. M. (2004). Russian translation of the MMPI–A: Evaluation of cross-cultural equivalence. *Dissertation Abstracts International: Section B. Sciences and Engineering, 64*(7-B), 3512.

Butcher, J. N. (1996). *International adaptations of the MMPI–2: Research and clinical applications.* Minneapolis: University of Minnesota Press.

Butcher, J. N. (2004). Personality assessment without borders: Adaptation of the MMPI–2 across cultures. *Journal of Personality Assessment, 83,* 90–104.

Butcher, J. N., Cabiya, J., Lucio, E., & Garrido, M. (2007). *Assessing Hispanic clients using the MMPI–2 and MMPI–A.* Washington, DC: American Psychological Association.

Butcher, J. N., Cabiya, J., Lucio, E., Pena, L., Scott, R., & Ruben, D. (1998). *Hispanic version of the MMPI–A manual supplement.* Minneapolis: University of Minnesota Press.

Butcher, J. N., Ellertsen, B., Ubostad, B., Bubb, E, Lucio, E., Lim, J., . . . Elsbury, S. (2000). *International case studies on the MMPI–A: An objective approach.* Minneapolis: MMPI–2 Workshops.

Butcher, J. N., & Williams, C. L. (1996). *Fondamentiper l'interpretazione del MMPI–2 e del MMPI–A* [Essentials of MMPI–2 and MMPI–A interpretation]. Firenze, Italy: O.S. Organizzazioni Speciali.

Butcher, J. N., & Williams, C. L. (2009). Personality assessment with the MMPI–2: Historical roots, international adaptations, and current challenges. *Applied Psychology: Health and Well-Being, 1,* 105–135.

Calderon, I. (2002). Effects of acculturation on the performance of Mexican-American adolescents on selected scales of the MMPI–A (*L, K, SC,* and *MA*). *Dissertation Abstracts International: Section B. Sciences and Engineering, 63*(2-B), 1083.

Cheung, F. M., & Ho, R. M. (1997). Standardization of the Chinese MMPI–A in Hong Kong: A preliminary study. *Psychological Assessment, 9,* 499–502.

Contini de Gonzalez, E. N., Figueroa, M. I., Cohen Imach, S., & Coronel de Pace, P. (2001). El MMPI–A en la identificatión de rasgos psicopatológicos. Un estudio con adolescents de Tucumán (Argentina) [The use of the MMPI–A in the identification of psychopathological traits in adolescents of Tucuman (Argentina)]. *Revista Iberoamericana de Diagnostico y Evaluacion Psicologica, 12,* 85–96.

Deeds, O. G. V. (2006). The influence of regional area and socioeconomic status on Mexican adolescents' performance on the MMPI–A. *Dissertation Abstracts International: Section B. Sciences and Engineering, 67,* 2868.

Derksen, J., Ven Dijk, J., & Cornelissen, A. (2003). De Nederlandse adolescentenversie van de MMPI [The Dutch version of the MMPI–A]. *Psycholoog, 38,* 304–311.

Farias, J. M. P., Duran, C., & Gomez-Maqueo, E. L. (2003). Un estudio sobre la estabilidad temporal del MMPI–A con un diseño test–retest en estudiantes Mexicanos [MMPI–A temporal stability study through a·test–retest design in a Mexican student sample]. *Salud Mental, 26*(2), 59–66.

Figuered, B. V. (2002). The concurrent validity of the Minnesota Multiphasic Personality Inventory—Adolescent in the assessment of depression. *Dissertation Abstracts International: Section B. Sciences and Engineering, 62*(10-B), 4782.

Garrido, M., & Velasquez, R. (2006). Interpretation of Latino/Latina MMPI–2 profiles: Review and application of empirical findings and cultural-linguistic considerations. In J. N. Butcher (Ed.), *MMPI–2: A practitioner's guide* (pp. 477–504). Washington, DC: American Psychological Association. doi:10.1037/11287-017

Gomez, F. C. J., Johnson, R., Davis, Q., & Velasquez, R. J. (2000). MMPI–A performance of African and Mexican American adolescent first-time offenders. *Psychological Reports, 87,* 309–314.

Gumbiner, J. (2000). Limitations in ethnic research on the MMPI–A. *Psychological Reports, 87*(3, Pt. 2), 1229–1230.

Henry, L. M. (1999). Comparison of MMPI and MMPI–A response patterns of African American adolescents. *Dissertation Abstracts International: Section B. Sciences and Engineering, 60*(6-B), 2945.

Lucio, E., Duran, C., Graham, J. R., & Ben-Porath, Y. S. (2002). Identifying faking bad on the Minnesota Multiphasic Personality Inventory—Adolescent with Mexican adolescents. *Assessment, 9,* 62–69.

Lucio, E. M., Hernandez-Cervantes, Q., Duran, C., & Butcher, J. N. (2010). Effect of age and type of school on MMPI–A scores in a 13–18 year old Mexican adolescent sample. *Journal of Hispanic Psychology, 2,* 177–192.

Lucio-Gomez, E., Ampudia-Rueda, A., Duran-Patino, C., Gallegos-Mejia, L., & Leon-Guzman, I. (1999). La nueva versión del Inventario Multifásico de la Personalidad de Minnesota para adolescentes Mexicanos [The new version of the Minnesota Multiphasic Personality Inventory for Mexican adolescents]. *Revista Mexicana de Psicologia, 16,* 217–226.

Mendoza-Newman, M. C. (2000). Level of acculturation, socio-economic status, and the MMPI–A performance of a non-clinical Hispanic adolescent sample. *Dissertation Abstracts International: Section B. Sciences and Engineering, 60*(9-B), 4897.

Moore, A. T. (2006). Predictive validity of the MMPI–A for depression in Caucasian and racial minority adolescents. *Dissertation Abstracts International: Section B. Sciences and Engineering, 66*(11-B), 6285.

Negy, C., Leal-Puente, L., Trainor, D. J., & Carlson, R. (1997). Mexican American adolescents' performance on the MMPI–A. *Journal of Personality Assessment, 69,* 205–214.

Newman, M. L. (2004). *Psychological assessment as brief psychotherapy: Therapeutic effects of providing MMPI–A test feedback to adolescents.* Unpublished doctoral dissertation, La Trobe University, Bundoora, Victoria, Australia.

Perez, J. M., Farias, J. M., Gomez-Maqueo, M. E. L. (2001). Theoretical and conceptual aspects of the validity and reliability of the MMPI–A with Mexican adolescents. *Revista Mexicana de Psicologia, 18,* 54–55.

Quevedo, K. M., & Butcher, J. N. (2005). The use of MMPI and MMPI–2 in Cuba: A historical overview from 1950 to the present. *International Journal of Clinical and Health Psychology, 5,* 335–347.

Scott, R. L., Butcher, J. N., Young, T. L., & Gomez, N. (2002). The Hispanic MMPI–A across five countries. *Journal of Clinical Psychology, 58,* 407–417.

Scott, R. L., Knoth, R. L., Beltran-Quiones, M., & Gomez, N. (2003). Assessment of psychological functioning in adolescent earthquake victims in Colombia using the MMPI–A. *Journal of Traumatic Stress, 16,* 49–57.

Sirigatti, S. (2000). Verso un adattamento italiano del Minnesota Multiphasic Personality Inventory—Adolescent [Toward an Italian version of the MMPI–Adolescent]. *Bollettino di Psicologia Applicata, 230,* 67–72.

Vinet, E. V., & Alarcon B. P. (2003). Evaluación psicométrica del inventario Multifásico de Personalidad de Minnesota para Adolescentes (MMPI–A) en muestras Chilenas [Psychometric evaluation for the Minnesota Multiphasic Personality Inventory for Adolescent (MMPI–A) in Chilean samples]. *Terapia Psicologica, 21*(2), 87–103.

Vinet, E. V., & Gomez-Maqueo, M. E. L. (2005). Applicabilidad de las normas Mexicanas y Estadounidenses del MMPI–A en la evaluación de adolescentes Chilenos [Applicability of Mexican and United States norms for the MMPI–A in the assessment of Chilean adolescents]. *Revista Mexicana de Psicologia, 22,* 519–528.

Delinquency

See Forensic Assessment/Delinquency

Depression/Suicide

See also Clinical/Standard Scales; Cross-Cultural/Ethnic Studies; Content Scales

Archer, R. P., & Slesinger, D. (1999). MMPI–A patterns related to the endorsement of suicidal ideation. *Assessment, 6,* 51–59.

Friedman, A. F., Archer, R. P., & Handel, R. W. (2005). Minnesota Multiphasic Personality Inventories (MMPI/MMPI–2, MMPI–A) and suicide. In R. I. Yufit & D. Lester (Eds.), *Assessment, treatment, and prevention of suicidal behavior* (pp. 63–91). Hoboken, NJ: Wiley.

Drug Use

See Alcohol and Other Drug Use

Eating Disorders

See Feedback; Inpatient Studies; Scale Development/Psychometric Issues

Ethnic Studies

See Cross-Cultural/Ethnic Studies

Factor Analysis/Item Analysis Studies

Archer, R. P., & Gordon, R. (1994). Psychometric stability of MMPI–A item modifications. *Journal of Personality Assessment, 62,* 418–426.

Archer, R. P., Handel, R. W., & Lynch, K. D. (2001). The effectiveness of MMPI–A items in discriminating between normative and clinical samples. *Journal of Personality Assessment, 77,* 420–435.

Archer, R. P., & Krishnamurthy, R. (1997). MMPI–A scale-level factor structure: Replication in a clinical sample. *Assessment, 4,* 337–349.

Archer, R. P., & Newsom, C. R. (2000). Psychological test usage with adolescent clients: Survey update. *Assessment, 7,* 227–35.

Baldwin, B. M. (2001). Reading ability and the MMPI–A: Creation of the READ Scale. *Dissertation Abstracts International: Section B. Sciences and Engineering, 62*(5-B), 2475.

Janus, M. D., Tolbert, H., Calestro, K., & Toepfer, S. (1996). Clinical accuracy ratings of MMPI approaches for adolescents: Adding ten years and the MMPI–A. *Journal of Personality Assessment, 67,* 364–383.

Krishnamurthy, R., & Archer, R. P. (1999). A comparison of two interpretive approaches for the MMPI–A structural summary. *Journal of Personality Assessment, 73,* 245–259.

Newsom, C. R., Archer, R. P., Trumbetta, S., & Gottesman, I. I. (2003). Changes in adolescent response patterns on the MMPI/MMPI–A across four decades. *Journal of Personality Assessment, 81,* 74–84.

Williams, C. L., Ben-Porath, Y. S., & Hevern, B. W. (1994). Item level improvements for use of the MMPI with adolescents. *Journal of Personality Assessment, 63,* 284–293.

Feedback

Finn, S. E. (2007). *In our clients' shoes: Theory and techniques of therapeutic assessment.* Mahwah, NJ: Erlbaum.

Finn, S. E., & Tonsager, M. E. (1992). Therapeutic effects of providing MMPI–2 test feedback to college students awaiting therapy. *Psychological Assessment, 4,* 278–287.

Fischer, C. T. (2000). Collaborative individualized assessment. *Journal of Personality Assessment, 74,* 2–14.

Michel, D. M. (2002). Psychological assessment as a therapeutic intervention in patients hospitalized with eating disorders. *Professional Psychology: Research and Practice, 33,* 470–477.

Newman, M. L. (2004). *Psychological assessment as brief psychotherapy: Therapeutic effects of providing MMPI–A test feedback to adolescents.* Unpublished doctoral dissertation, La Trobe University, Bundoora, Victoria, Australia.

Tharinger, D. J., Finn, S. E., Austin, C. A., Gentry, L. B., Bailey, K. E., Fisher, M. E., & Parton, V. T. (2008). Family sessions as part of child psychological assessment: Goals, techniques, clinical utility, and therapeutic value. *Journal of Personality Assessment, 90,* 547–558.

Tharinger, D. J., Finn, S. E., Wilkinson, A. D., & Schaber, P. M. (2007). Therapeutic assessment with a child as a family intervention: A clinical and research case study. *Psychology in the Schools, 44,* 293–309.

Forensic Assessment/ Delinquency

Archer, R. P. (2002). Editor's introduction to a special section on the MMPI–A structural summary. *Assessment, 9,* 317–318.

Archer, R. P., Bolinskey, P. K., Morton, T. L., & Farris, K. L. (2002). A factor structure for the MMPI–A: Replication with male delinquents. *Assessment, 9,* 319–326.

Archer, R. P., Bolinskey, P. K., Morton, T. L., & Farris, K. L. (2003). MMPI–A characteristics of male adolescents in juvenile justice and clinical treatment settings. *Assessment, 10,* 400–410.

Archer, R. P., Zoby, M., & Stredny, R. V. (2006). The Minnesota Multiphasic Personality Inventory—Adolescent. In R. P. Archer (Ed.), *Forensic uses of clinical assessment instruments* (pp. 57–87). Mahwah, NJ: Erlbaum.

Bannen, M. A. (2000). Part A: Disruptive disorders in adolescent girls: A neglected group. Part B: The clinical utility of the MMPI–A in the assessment of disruptive disordered adolescent girls. *Dissertation Abstracts International: Section B. Sciences and Engineering, 61*(2-B), 1070.

Baron, A. T. (2003). Differences in psychopathology, temperament, and family/social history relative to the onset of sexual perpetration in youthful offenders. *Dissertation Abstracts International: Section B. Sciences and Engineering, 63*(10-B), 4889.

Borkhuis, G. W., & Patalano, F. (1997). MMPI personality differences between adolescents from divorced and non-divorced families. *Psychology: A Journal of Human Behavior, 34*(2), 37–41.

Butcher, J. N. (1965). Manifest aggression: MMPI correlates in normal boys. *Journal of Consulting Psychology, 29,* 446–455.

Butcher, J. N., & Pope, K. S. (2006). The MMPI–A in forensic assessment. In S. N. Sparta & G. P. Koocher (Eds.), *Forensic mental health assessment of children and adolescents* (pp. 401–411). New York, NY: Oxford University Press.

Cashel, M. L., Ovaert, L., & Holliman, N. G. (2000). Evaluating PTSD in incarcerated male juveniles with the MMPI–A: An exploratory analysis. *Journal of Clinical Psychology, 56,* 1535–1550.

Cashel, M. L., Rogers, R., Sewell, K. W., & Holliman, N. B. (1998). Preliminary validation of the MMPI–A for a male delinquent sample: An investigation of clinical correlates and discriminant validity. *Journal of Personality Assessment, 71,* 49–69.

Glaser, B. A., Calhoun, G. B., & Petrocelli, J. V. (2002). Personality characteristics of male juvenile offenders by adjudicated offenses as indicated by the MMPI–A. *Criminal Justice & Behavior, 29,* 183–201.

Green, A. N. (2000). Minnesota Multiphasic Personality Inventory—Adolescent excitatory scales and demographics as predictors of male juvenile delinquent placement. *Dissertation Abstracts International: Section B. Sciences and Engineering, 61*(3-B), 1635.

Gumbiner, J., Arriaga, T., & Stevens, A. (1999). Comparison of MMPI–A, Marks and Briggs, and MMPI–2 norms for juvenile delinquents. *Psychological Reports, 84,* 761–766.

Hammel, S. D. (2001). An investigation of the validity and clinical usefulness of the MMPI–A with female juvenile delinquents. *Dissertation Abstracts International: Section B. Sciences and Engineering, 61*(11-B), 6135.

Hunter, L. M. (2000). Use of selected MMPI–A factors in the prediction of clinical outcomes in a community-based treatment program for juvenile sexual offenders. *Dissertation Abstracts International: Section B. Sciences and Engineering, 60*(11-B), 5775.

Losada-Paisey, G. (1998). Use of the MMPI–A to assess personality of juvenile male delinquents who are sex offenders and nonsex offenders. *Psychological Reports, 83,* 115–122.

Moore, J. M., Jr., Thompson-Pope, S. K., & Whited, R. M. (1996) MMPI–A profiles of adolescent boys with a history of firesetting. *Journal of Personality Assessment, 67,* 116–126.

Morton, T. L., & Farris, K. L. (2002). MMPI–A structural summary characteristics of male juvenile delinquents. *Assessment, 9,* 327–333.

Morton, T. L., Farris, K. L., & Brenowitz, L. H. (2002). MMPI–A scores and high points of male juvenile delinquents: Scales 4, 5, and 6 as markers of juvenile delinquency. *Psychological Assessment, 14,* 311–319.

Pena, L. M. (2001). The association of MMPI–A scales with measures of adjustment among institutionalized male juvenile delinquents. *Dissertation Abstracts International: Section B. Sciences and Engineering, 62*(5-B), 2527.

Pena, L. M., Megargee, E. I., & Brody, E. (1996). MMPI–A patterns of male juvenile delinquents. *Psychological Assessment, 8,* 388–397.

Pennuto, T. O., & Archer, R. P. (2008). MMPI–A forensic case studies: Uses in documented court cases. *Journal of Personality Assessment, 90,* 215–236.

Pope, K. S., Butcher, J. N., & Seelen, J. (2006). *The MMPI/MMPI–2/ MMPI–A in court* (3rd ed.). Washington, DC: American Psychological Association.

Riethmiller, R. J. (2003). A look at personality change among conduct disordered adolescents in residential treatment. *Dissertation Abstracts International: Section B. Sciences and Engineering, 63*(12-B), 6104.

Toyer, E. A., & Weed, N. C. (1998). Concurrent validity of the MMPI–A in counseling program for juvenile offenders. *Journal of Clinical Psychology, 54,* 395–400.

Vande Streek, H. E. (2000). Concurrent validity of the Minnesota Multiphasic Personality Inventory, Jesness Inventory, and the Carlson Psychological Survey in a sample of juvenile delinquents. *Dissertation Abstracts International: Section B. Sciences and Engineering, 60*(9-B), 4951.

Weis, R., Crockett, T. E., & Vieth, S. (2004). Using MMPI–A profiles to predict success in a military-style residential treatment program for adolescents with academic and conduct problems. *Psychology in the Schools, 41,* 563–574.

Zonno, J. S. (2004). Correlates of behavioral infractions among institutionalized male juvenile offenders. *Dissertation Abstracts International: Section B. Sciences and Engineering, 64,* 5244.

Inpatient Studies

Cumella, E. J., Wall, A. D., & Kerr-Almeida, N. (1999). MMPI–A in the inpatient assessment of adolescents with eating disorders. *Journal of Personality Assessment, 73,* 31–44.

Deluca, V. A. (2003). The relationship of the MMPI–A and Rorschach, to psychosis in adolescent psychiatric inpatients. *Dissertation Abstracts International: Section B. Sciences and Engineering, 64*(2-B), 959.

Hilts, D., & Moore, J. M. (2003). Normal range MMPI–A profiles among psychiatric inpatients. *Assessment, 10,* 266–272.

Pogge, D. L., Stokes, J. M., McGrath, R. E., Bilginer, L., & DeLuca, V. A. (2002). MMPI–A structural summary variables: Prevalence and correlates in an adolescent inpatient psychiatric sample. *Assessment, 9,* 334–342.

Ryan, N. (2005). The clinical utility of the Cognitive Assessment System (CAS) in a child and adolescent psychiatric inpatient population. *Dissertation Abstracts International: Section B. Sciences and Engineering, 65*(8-B), 4333.

Stage, S. A. (1999). Predicting behavior functioning of adolescents in residential treatment with profiles from the MMPI–A, CBCL/4–18, and CBCL/TRF. *Residential Treatment for Children & Youth, 17*(2), 49–74.

Item Analysis Studies

See Factor Analysis/Item Analysis Studies

Psychometric Issues

See Scale Development/Psychometric Issues

Reading Level

See Scale Development/Psychometric Issues

Scale Development/ Psychometric Issues

Archer, R. P., Tirrell, C. A., & Elkins, D. E. (2001). Evaluation of an MMPI–A Short Form: Implications for adaptive testing. *Journal of Personality Assessment, 76,* 76–89.

Bolinskey, P. K., Arnau, R. C., Archer, R. P., & Handel, R. W. (2004). A replication of the MMPI–A PSY-5 scales and development of facet subscales. *Assessment, 11*, 40–48.

Fontaine, J. L. (2000). The effects of varying clinical elevation demarcations on classification accuracy of the MMPI–A. *Dissertation Abstracts International: Section B. Sciences and Engineering, 61*(2-B), 1080.

Fontaine, J. L., Archer, R. P., Elkins, D. E., & Johansen, J. (2001). The effects of MMPI–A *T*-score elevation on classification accuracy for normal and clinical adolescent samples. *Journal of Personality Assessment, 76*, 264–281.

Harkness, A. R., McNulty, J. L., Ben-Porath, Y. S., & Graham, J. R. (2002). *The Personality Psychopathology Five (PSY-5) scales: Gaining an overview for case conceptualization and treatment planning.* Minneapolis: University of Minnesota Press.

Janus, M.-D., de Groot, C., & Toepfer, S. M. (1998). The MMPI–A and 13-year-old inpatients: How young is too young? *Assessment, 5*, 321–332.

Mcentee, B. K. (1999). MMPI–A Personality Psychopathology Five. *Dissertation Abstracts International: Section B. Sciences and Engineering, 60*(2-B), 0837.

McNulty, J. L., Harkness, A. R., Ben-Porath, Y. S., & Williams, C. L. (1997). Assessing the Personality Psychopathology Five (PSY-5) in adolescents: New MMPI–A scales. *Psychological Assessment, 9*, 250–259.

Moyer, R. D., & Schuerger, J. M. (1999). Disorder concept scales and personality dimensions in a young adult sample. *Psychological Reports, 85*(3, Pt. 2), 1135–1138.

Rouse, S. V., Williams, C. L., Perry, C. L., Komro, K. A., Farbakhsh, K., & Grechanaia, T. (2009). *Reliability of five MMPI–A scales across age, sex, intervention status, alcohol/drug use, and culture/language.* Manuscript submitted for publication.

Toyer, E. A. (1999). Development and validation of the A-ADHD: An MMPI–A scale to assess attention-deficit hyperactivity disorder in adolescents. *Dissertation Abstracts International: Section B. Sciences and Engineering, 60*(3-B), 1319.

Williams, C. L., & Butcher, J. N. (1989a). An MMPI study of adolescents: I. Empirical validity of the standard scales. *Psychological Assessment: A Journal of Consulting and Clinical Psychology, 1*, 251–259.

Williams, C. L., & Butcher, J. N. (1989b). An MMPI study of adolescents: II. Verification and limitations of code types classifications. *Psychological Assessment: A Journal of Consulting and Clinical Psychology, 1*, 260–265.

Williams, P. E. (1999). Development of a sexual abuse scale for the MMPI–A: The Aversive Sexual Experience Scale. *Dissertation Abstracts International: Section B. Sciences and Engineering, 59*(12-B), 6516.

Zinn, S., McCumber, S., & Dahlstrom, W. G. (1999). Cross-validation and extension of the MMPI–A IMM scale. *Assessment, 6*(1), 1–6.

Standard Scales

See Clinical/Standard Scales

Suicide

See Depression/Suicide

Substance Abuse

See Alcohol and Other Drug Use

Validity Assessment

See also Clinical/Standard Scales

Alpern, J. J., Archer, R., & Coates, G. D. (1996). Development and effects of an MMPI–A *K* correction. *Journal of Personality Assessment, 67*, 155–168.

Archer, R. P., & Elkins, D. E. (1999). Identification of random responding on the MMPI–A. *Journal of Personality Assessment, 73*, 407–421.

Archer, R. P., Handel, R. W., Lynch, K. D., & Elkins, D. E. (2002). MMPI–A Validity Scale uses and limitations in detecting varying levels of random responding. *Journal of Personality Assessment, 78*, 417–431.

Baer, R. A., Ballenger, J., Berry, D. T. R., & Wetter, M. W. (1997). Detection of random responding on the MMPI–A. *Journal of Personality Assessment, 68*, 139–151.

Baer, R. A., Ballenger, J., & Kroll, L. S. (1998). Detection of under-reporting on the MMPI–A in clinical and community samples. *Journal of Personality Assessment, 71*, 98–113.

Baer, R. A., Kroll, L. S., Rinaldo, J., & Ballenger, J. (1999). Detecting and discriminating between random responding and overreporting on the MMPI–A. *Journal of Personality Assessment, 72*, 308–320.

Bagdade, P. S. (2004). Malingering on the MMPI–A: An investigation of the standard validity scales and the Infrequency–Psychopathology Scale—Adolescent version (*Fp-A*). *Dissertation Abstracts International: Section B. Sciences and Engineering, 64*(7-B), 3513.

Barrios, D. R. (2004). The MMPI–A normal K+ profile: Prevalence and codetype characteristics in an adolescent inpatient population. *Dissertation Abstracts International: Section B. Sciences and Engineering, 65,* 1068.

Conkey, V. A. (2000). Determining the sensitivity of the MMPI–A to random responding and malingering in adolescents (Minnesota Multiphasic Personality Index, Validity Scales). *Dissertation Abstracts International: Section B. Sciences and Engineering, 60*(7-B), 3608.

Handel, R. W., Arnau, R. C., Archer, R. P., & Dandy, K. L. (2006). An evaluation of the MMPI–2 and MMPI–A True Response Inconsistency (*TRIN*) scales. *Assessment, 13*, 98–106.

McCann, J. T. (1998). *Malingering and deception in adolescents.* Washington, DC: American Psychological Association.

McGrath, R. E., Pogge, D. L., Stein, L. A. R., Graham, J. R., Zaccario, M., & Piacentini, T. (2000). Development of an Infrequency–Psychopathology scale for the MMPI–A: The *Fp-A* scale. *Journal of Personality Assessment, 74*, 282–295.

McGrath, R. E., Pogge, D. L., & Stokes, J. M. (2002). Incremental validity of selected MMPI–A Content Scales in an inpatient setting. *Psychological Assessment, 14*, 401–409.

Pinsoneault, T. B. (2002). A variable response inconsistency scale and a true response inconsistency scale for the Millon Adolescent Clinical Inventory. *Psychological Assessment, 14*, 320–328.

Pinsoneault, T. B. (2005). Detecting random, partially random, and non-random Minnesota Multiphasic Personality Inventory—Adolescent protocols. *Psychological Assessment, 17*, 476–480.

Rivera, A. C. (2006). Detection of faking bad with the MMPI–A among adolescents with behavioral problems. *Dissertation Abstracts International: Section B. Sciences and Engineering, 67*(5-B), 2843.

Rogers, R., Hinds, J. D., & Sewell, K. W. (1996). Feigning psychopathology among adolescent offenders: Validation of the SIRS, MMPI–A, and SIMS. *Journal of Personality Assessment, 6,* 244–257.

Stein, L. A. R. (1999). Detecting fake-good MMPI–A profiles in a correctional facility. *Dissertation Abstracts International: Section B. Sciences and Engineering, 59*(8-B), 4486.

Stein, L. A. R., & Graham, J. R. (1999). Detecting fake-good MMPI–A profiles in a correctional facility. *Psychological Assessment, 11,* 386–395.

Stein, L. A. R., Graham, J. R., & Williams, C. L. (1995). Detecting fake-bad MMPI–A profiles. *Journal of Personality Assessment, 65,* 415–427.

Stroupe, M. A. (1999). The effects of *K*-correction on the validity of MMPI–A. *Dissertation Abstracts International: Section B. Sciences and Engineering, 59*(10-B), 5615.

Appendix B: Butcher and Williams's Responses to Pop Quiz in Exhibit 7.3

Statement	Source
1. . . . views self as well-adjusted and selfreliant	None of Mr. John's Clinical Scales was elevated over a *T* score of 70 (the cut-off score for the original MMPI), which is the likely source for this interpretive statement.
2. . . . socially approved answers . . .	This statement is most likely related to his *T* scores of 57 on the K scale and 56 on the *L* scale. Although these are relatively low scores, the Mayo Clinic patients were primarily seen in medical clinics where lower range scores were typical. The computer appears to be programmed to interpret these scores as a tendency toward socially desirable responding. Today we interpret *T* scores below 60 as responding in a cooperative fashion, resulting in a valid profile.
3. . . . aesthetic interests . . .	This interpretive statement is most certainly due to his *T* score of 65 on the *Mf* scale.
4. . . . independent . . .	His moderate elevation on *Pd* scale (*T* score = 60 which is a standard deviation above the mean) likely resulted in descriptions of nonconformity and independence. Note the conservative nature of these *Pd* descriptors, appropriate for this moderate elevation (i.e., none of the antisocial descriptors found in Chapter 3 were included by the system authors).
5. . . . average optimism and pessimism.	Not sure where this statement comes from; perhaps it is a hypothesis, given that there are no elevations on the Clinical Scales.

Statement	Source
6. . . . physical symptoms . . .	The obvious place to look for statements about somatic complaints is *Hs* and *Hy,* yet Mr. John's scores were 49 and 53, respectively, which should not generate such an interpretive statement. Among the other scales listed along the bottom of Mr. John's report is *Lb* or Low Back Pain with its *T* score of 53. Since *Lb* is not used today, it is not described in Chapter 3. Although we would not include an interpretive statement for this average score on *Lb* in an interpretive system today, it is a possible candidate for the source of this statement because his *Lb* score indicates that he did endorse some pain symptoms.
7. . . . respects opinions of others . . .	The interpretation about respecting opinions of others may be due to the low scale elevation on the *Pa* scale (*T* score of 47). Recall from Chapter 3 that elevations on *Pa* are related to oversensitivity and a tendency to look down on others with contempt. The corollary (i.e., respecting others without undue sensitivity) is a descriptor of a low *Pa* score.
8. . . . sufficient capacity for organizing . . .	The interpretation about being able to organize his work and personal life may come from Mr. John's low elevation on *Pt* with his *T* score of 43. Recall that *Pt* elevations are associated with ruminations, self-doubt, concentration problems, and the like, which would impede a capacity to organize one's life.
9. Low energy . . .	Two scale scores could have influenced the printout of the statement about low energy, motivation problems, and apathy. Mr. John had a low score on *Ma* (*T* score of 45) combined with a *T* score of 56 on *D*. This is the possible source of these interpretations.
10. . . . practical and theoretical interests.	*Mf* is the only scale on the MMPI that focuses on interests, and his score of 65 likely resulted in this descriptor.
11. . . . socially outgoing . . .	Undoubtedly, this statement comes from his *T* score of 44 on *Si,* indicative of extroversion.

Note. As noted in No. 2 above, the Mayo interpretive system was developed for patients seen in medical clinics. In medical settings, lower elevations are common on the Clinical Scales (with the possible exception of *Hs* and *Hy*). Mr. John's report included several statements for low range scores on *Pa, Pt, Ma,* and *D.* In general, this practice of interpreting low elevations is not often used in contemporary computer reports—with the exception of *Si* and some content-based measures.

Glossary of MMPI–A Terms

A-ALN: Adolescent Alienation Content Scale on the MMPI–A. (Chapter 5)

A-ANG: Adolescent Anger Content Scale on the MMPI–A. (Chapter 5)

A-ANX: Adolescent Anxiety Content Scale on the MMPI–A. (Chapter 5)

A-BIZ: Adolescent Bizarre Mentation Content Scale on the MMPI–A. (Chapter 5)

A-CON: Adolescent Conduct Problem Content Scale on the MMPI–A. (Chapter 5)

A-CYN: Adolescent Cynicism Content Scale on the MMPI–A. (Chapter 5)

A-DEP: Adolescent Depression Content Scale on the MMPI–A. (Chapter 5)

A-FAM: Adolescent Family Problems Content Scale on the MMPI–A. (Chapter 5)

A-HEA: Adolescent Health Concerns Content Scale on the MMPI–A. (Chapter 5)

Some definitions were adapted or modified from *A Beginner's Guide to the MMPI–2* (3rd ed.), by J. N. Butcher, 2011, Washington, DC: American Psychological Association. Copyright 2011 by the American Psychological Association.

A-LAS: Adolescent Low Aspirations Content Scale on the MMPI–A. (Chapter 5)

A-LSE: Adolescent Low Self-Esteem Content Scale on the MMPI–A. (Chapter 5)

A-OBS: Adolescent Obsessiveness Content Scale on the MMPI–A. (Chapter 5)

A-SCH: Adolescent School Problems Content Scale on the MMPI–A. (Chapter 5)

A-SOD: Adolescent Social Discomfort Content Scale on the MMPI–A. (Chapter 5).

A-TRT: Adolescent Negative Treatment Indicators Content Scale on the MMPI–A. (Chapter 5)

A OR ANXIETY SCALE: The first factor that emerges from a factor analysis of the MMPI Standard Scales. One of the Supplementary Scales developed from research on the original MMPI. (Chapter 5)

ACK OR ALCOHOL AND DRUG PROBLEM ACKNOWLEDGMENT SCALE: One of the Supplementary Scales. (Chapter 5)

ACTUARIAL PREDICTION: The empirical determination of the relationships between test scores and external behavior by statistical rules. Contrasted with clinical prediction. (Chapter 7)

AGGR: Aggressiveness, one of the PSY-5 Scales. (Chapter 5)

ANHEDONIA: A mental health symptom, associated with both depression and schizophrenia, in which the person becomes less involved or interested in things that typically give pleasure. (Chapter 4)

BASIC SCALES: Typically used to refer to both the Validity and Standard or Clinical Scales. It is the starting point for a MMPI assessment. (Chapter 4)

CANNOT SAY SCORE: An MMPI–A validity score (often shown as "?"). It is the number of unanswered items the client had on the test. (Chapter 4)

CLINICAL PREDICTION: The use of clinical guidelines or accumulated wisdom of a given practitioner in making judgments and predictions. This approach is contrasted with actuarial prediction. (Chapter 7)

CLINICAL SCALES: Scales 1–4 and 6–9 developed by Hathaway and McKinley to measure common diagnostic groupings of their patients seen at University of Minnesota Hospitals in the 1940s. Term is often used interchangeably with "Standard Scales" or "Basic Scales," although there are subtle differences in meaning. (Chapter 4)

CONTENT SCALES: Fifteen scales developed to assure homogeneous groupings of items onto scales. (Chapter 5)

CONVERSION V: A term used to describe the relationships between *Hs, Hy,* and *D* that are found to be associated with the presentation of physical symptoms (e.g., numbness, fainting spells) for which no physical basis is found. Scales *Hs* and *Hy* are highly elevated and *D* is not. (Chapters 4, 7)

CORRELATE OR DESCRIPTOR: A characteristic found to be associated with an elevation on an MMPI–A Scale. Correlates are frequently identified using correlation coefficients. (Chapters 4, 5, 7)

CRITICAL ITEMS (ITEM-LEVEL INDICATORS): Sets of items that have been determined to suggest the presence of specific problems. These items are used to provide cues to psychopathology. They are not used as predictor scales.

D: Depression Clinical Scale (i.e., Scale 2) on the MMPI–A. (Chapter 4)

DISC: Disconstraint, one of the PSY-5 personality dimensions. (Chapter 5)

EMPIRICAL SCALE CONSTRUCTION: The development of scales by selecting items that contrast a group known to possess particular qualities (e.g., depressed patients) with another group of individuals without such problems (e.g., the normative sample). (Chapters 2, 7)

F: MMPI–A Validity Scale created to measure exaggeration of symptoms. (Chapter 4)

F_1: MMPI–A Validity Scale created to measure exaggeration of symptoms on the items that appear at the front of the MMPI–A. (Chapter 4)

F_2: MMPI–A Validity Scale created to measure exaggeration of symptoms on the items that appear at the end (or back) of the MMPI. (Chapter 4)

Hs: Hypochondriasis Clinical Scale (i.e., Scale 1) on the MMPI–A. (Chapter 4)

Hy: Hysteria Clinical Scale (i.e., Scale 3) on the MMPI–A). (Chapter 4)

IDIOGRAPHIC APPROACH: Idiographic observations or measures, in contrast with nomothetic observations, focused on individual characteristics, for example, case studies. (Chapter 6)

IMM: Immaturity scale; one of the Supplementary Scales. (Chapter 5)

INTR: Introversion/Low Positive Emotionality; one of the PSY-5 Scales. (Chapter 5)

K OR CORRECTION SCALE: MMPI–A Validity Scale measuring defensiveness. (Chapter 4)

L OR LIE SCALE: MMPI–A Validity Scale measuring claims of excessive virtue. (Chapter 4)

LINEAR *T* SCORES: A statistical term in which the mean of the distribution equals 50 and the standard deviation equals 10; the type of scaling used by the original MMPI and for some of the MMPI–A scales. (Chapters 2 and 3)

MAC–R: MacAndrew Alcoholism Scale—Revised; one of the Supplementary Scales. (Chapter 5)

Ma: Hypomania Clinical Scale (i.e., Scale 9) of the MMPI–A. (Chapter 4)

Mf: Masculinity–Femininity Standard Scale (i.e., Scale 5) on the MMPI–A. (Chapter 4)

NEGE: Negative Emotionality; one of the PSY-5 personality dimensions. (Chapter 5)

NOMOTHETIC APPROACH: Nomothetic observations or measures are those obtained on a relatively large sample and provide a more general comparison perspective than the idiographic approach that focuses on individual characteristics. (Chapter 6)

NORMATIVE SAMPLE: A sample drawn from the general population used to develop the standard scores (or norms) for tests like the MMPI–A. (Chapters 2 and 3)

P_A: Paranoia Clinical Scale (i.e., Scale 6) on the MMPI–A. (Chapter 4)

P_D: Psychopathic Deviate Clinical Scale (i.e., Scale 4) on the MMPI–A. (Chapter 4)

PERCENTILE RANK: Shows what proportion of the group falls below a particular point. (Chapter 2)

PRO: Alcohol and Drug Problem Proneness scale; one of the Supplementary Scales. (Chapter 5)

PROFILE: A chart that graphically shows several scale score results of a test taker. (Chapters 2–5)

PROTOCOL VALIDITY: A measure of the extent to which a particular performance on a psychological test is credible. (Chapter 4)

PSY-5 SCALES: Five personality measures developed by rational/statistical procedures to assess the major dimensions of personality referred to as the "Big Five": *AGGR, PSYC, DISC, NEGE,* and *INTR.* (Chapter 5)

PSYC: Psychoticism; one of the PSY-5 personality dimensions. (Chapter 5)

P_T: Psychasthenia Clinical Scale (i.e., Scale 7) on the MMPI–A. (Chapter 4)

R: Repression scale. The second factor that emerges from a factor analysis of the MMPI Standard Scales. One of the Supplementary Scales developed from research on the original MMPI. (Chapter 5)

RATIONAL SCALE DEVELOPMENT: Scale construction strategy based on the combination of similar content items, for example, the MMPI–2 and MMPI–A Content Scales. (Chapter 5)

RAW SCORE: A measure of performance (e.g., the total number of scored answers) for a particular scale. These raw scores are typically converted to scale scores using a test distribution, referred to as a norm. (Chapters 2 and 3)

STANDARD DEVIATION: A statistical measure of the spread or dispersion of scores (or other measures) around the mean; the square root of the variance. (Chapters 2 and 3)

S_C: Schizophrenia Clinical Scale (i.e., Scale 8) on the MMPI–A. (Chapter 4)

SCALE: A group of items in a personality inventory that is assumed to measure a particular personality construct. (Chapters 2 and 3)

SCALES 1–9, 0: See *Hs, D, Hy, Pd, Mf, Pa, Pt, Sc, Ma, Si.* (Chapter 4)

S_I: Social Introversion Standard Scale (Scale 0) on the MMPI–A. (Chapter 4)

STANDARD SCALES: Clinical Scales 1–4 and 6–9 plus Scales 5 and 0. (Chapter 4)

STANDARD SCORE: A score on a standardized psychological test calculated in terms of standard deviations from the statistical mean of scores. (Chapters 2 and 3)

STATEMENT LIBRARY: A compendium of interpretive statements for various test scores that serves as the basis for developing computerized test interpretations. Narrative statements are stored along with the test scores and indices with which they are associated. (Chapter 7)

SUPPLEMENTARY SCALES: Six scales make up this set: *MAC–R, PRO, ACK, IMM, A,* and *R.* (Chapter 5)

T SCORE: Standard score. MMPI–A scores falling along a distribution in which $M = 50$ and the $SD = 10$. (Chapters 2–3)

TRIN: True Response Inconsistency scale, a Validity Scale of the MMPI–A. (Chapter 4)

UNIFORM *T* SCORE: A statistical term (*T* score); the type of scaling used by the MMPI–2 and MMPI–A, resulting in comparable percentile values for a given *T* score across various Clinical or Content Scales. (Chapters 2 and 3)

VALIDITY: Degree to which a test measures what it is designed to assess. (Chapter 4)

VALIDITY SCALES: Provide methods of identifying random or inconsistent responding, underreporting, and overreporting. (Chapter 4)

VRIN: Variable Response Inconsistency scale, a Validity Scale of the MMPI–A. (Chapter 4)

References

Achenbach, T. M., & Edelbrock, C. S. (1983). *Manual for the Child Behavior Checklist and revised Child Behavior Profile.* Burlington: University of Vermont.

American Educational Research Association, American Psychological Association, & National Council on Measurement in Education. (1999). *Standards for educational and psychological testing.* Washington, DC: American Psychological Association.

American Psychiatric Association. (1952). *Diagnostic and statistical manual—Mental disorders.* Washington, DC: Author.

American Psychiatric Association. (2000). *Diagnostic and statistical manual of mental disorders* (4th ed., text revision). Washington, DC: Author.

American Psychological Association. (1986). *American Psychological Association guidelines for computer-based tests and interpretations.* Washington, DC: Author.

Andrucci, G. L., Archer, R. P., Pancoast, D. L., & Gordon, R. A. (1989). The relationship of the MMPI and Sensation Seeking Scales to adolescent drug use. *Journal of Personality Assessment, 53,* 253–266. doi:10.1207/s15327752jpa5302_4

Archer, R. P. (1987). *Using the MMPI with adolescents.* Hillsdale, NJ: Erlbaum.

Archer, R. P. (1992a). *MMPI–A: Assessing adolescent psychopathology.* Mahwah, NJ: Erlbaum.

Archer, R. P. (1992b). *MMPI Interpretive System.* Lutz, FL: Psychological Assessment Resources.

Archer, R. P. (2003). *MMPI Interpretive System, Version 3.* Lutz, FL: Psychological Assessment Resources.

Archer, R. P. (2005). *MMPI–A: Assessing adolescent psychopathology* (3rd ed.). Mahwah, NJ: Erlbaum.

Archer, R. P., & Gordon, R. A. (1988). MMPI and Rorschach indices of schizophrenic and depressive diagnoses among adolescent inpatients. *Journal of Personality Assessment, 52,* 276–287. doi:10.1207/s15327752jpa5202_9

Archer, R. P., & Gordon, R. A. (1994). Psychometric stability of MMPI–A item modifications. *Journal of Personality Assessment, 62,* 416–426. doi:10.1207/s15327752jpa6203_3

Archer, R. P., Gordon, R. A., Anderson, G. L., & Giannetti, R. A. (1989). MMPI special scale clinical correlates for adolescent inpatients. *Journal of Personality Assessment, 53,* 654–664. doi:10.1207/s15327752jpa5304_2

Archer, R. P., Gordon, R. A., Giannetti, R. A., & Singles, J. M. (1988). MMPI scale clinical correlates for adolescent inpatients. *Journal of Personality Assessment, 52,* 707–721.

Archer, R. P., Handel, R. W., Lynch, K. D., & Elkins, D. E. (2002). MMPI–A validity scale uses and limitations in detecting varying levels of random responding. *Journal of Personality Assessment, 78,* 417–431. doi:10.1207/S15327752JPA7803_03

Archer, R. P., & Krishnamurthy, R. (1997a). MMPI–A and Rorschach indices related to depression and conduct disorder: An evaluation of the incremental validity hypothesis. *Journal of Personality Assessment, 69,* 517–533. doi:10.1207/s15327752jpa6903_7

Archer, R. P., & Krishnamurthy, R. (1997b). MMPI–A scale-level factor structure: Replication in a clinical sample. *Assessment, 4,* 337–349.

Archer, R. P., & Newsom, C. R. (2000). Psychological test usage with adolescent clients: Survey update. *Assessment, 7,* 227–235. doi:10.1177/107319110000700303

ArcticStat. (2009). *Table 1.6: Population in the regions of the Russian Federation on January 1.* Retrieved from http://www.arcticstat.org/Table Viewer.aspx?S=2&ID=12573.

Arita, A. A., & Baer, R. A. (1998). Validity of selected MMPI–A Content Scales. *Psychological Assessment, 10,* 59–63. doi:10.1037/1040-3590. 10.1.59

Arnett, J. J. (1999). Adolescent storm and stress. *American Psychologist, 54,* 317–326. doi:10.1037/0003-066X.54.5.317

Arnett, J. J. (2000). Emerging adulthood: A theory of development from the late teens through the twenties. *American Psychologist, 55,* 469–480. doi:10.1037/0003-066X.55.5.469

Arnett, J. J. (2006). G. Stanley Hall's *Adolescence:* Brilliance and nonsense. *History of Psychology, 9,* 186–197. doi:10.1037/1093-4510.9.3.186

Aronow, E., Altman Weiss, K., & Reznikoff, M. (2001). *A practical guide to the Thematic Apperception Test: The TAT in clinical practice.* New York, NY: Brunner-Routledge.

Atlis, M. M. (2004). Russian translation of the MMPI–A: Evaluation of cross-cultural equivalence. *Dissertation Abstracts International: Section B. Sciences and Engineering, 64*(7-B), 3512.

Baer, R. A., Ballenger, J., & Kroll, L. S. (1998). Detection of underreporting on the MMPI–A in clinical and community samples. *Journal of Personality Assessment, 71,* 98–113. doi:10.1207/s15327752jpa7101_7

Baer, R. A., Kroll, L. S., Rinaldo, J., & Ballenger, J. (1999). Detecting and discriminating between random responding and overreporting on the MMPI–A. *Journal of Personality Assessment, 72,* 308–320. doi:10.1207/S15327752JP720213

Bakke, O. M. (2005). *When children became people: The birth of childhood in early Christianity* (B. McNeil, Trans.). Minneapolis, MN: Augsburg Fortress Press.

Ben-Porath, Y. S., Hostetler, K., Butcher, J. N., & Graham, J. R. (1989). New subscales for the MMPI–2 Social Introversion (*Si*) scale. *Psychological Assessment: A Journal of Consulting and Clinical Psychology, 1,* 169–174. doi:10.1037/1040-3590.1.3.169

Berzonsky, M. D. (2000). Theories of adolescence. In G. Adams (Ed.), *Adolescent development: The essential readings* (pp. 22–27). Malden, MA: Blackwell.

Bloch, A., & Kendall, L. (2004). *The museum at the end of the world: Encounters in the Russian far east.* Philadelphia: University of Pennsylvania Press.

Borkhuis, G. W., & Patalano, F. (1997). MMPI personality differences between adolescents from divorced and non-divorced families. *Psychology: A Journal of Human Behavior, 34*(2) 37–41.

Borum, R. (2006). Assessing risk for violence among juvenile offenders. In S. N. Sparta & G. P. Koocher (Eds.), *Forensic mental health assessment for children and adolescents* (pp. 190–202). New York, NY: Oxford University Press.

Burrow, J. A. (1986). *The ages of man: A study in medieval writing and thought.* New York, NY: Oxford University Press.

Burton, A., & Bright, C. J. (1946). Adaptation of the Minnesota Multiphasic Personality Inventory for group administration and rapid scoring. *Journal of Consulting Psychology, 10,* 99–103. doi:10.1037/h0057968

Butcher, J. N. (1982). *User's guide for the Minnesota Clinical Report.* Minneapolis, MN: National Computer Systems.

Butcher, J. N. (1990). *The MMPI–2 in psychological treatment.* New York, NY: Oxford University Press.

Butcher, J. N. (1996). *International adaptations of the MMPI–2: Research and clinical applications.* Minneapolis: University of Minnesota Press.

Butcher, J. N. (2004). Personality assessment without borders: Adaptation of the MMPI–2 across cultures. *Journal of Personality Assessment, 83,* 90–104. doi:10.1207/s15327752jpa8302_02

Butcher, J. N. (2005a). Exploring universal personality characteristics: An objective approach. *International Journal of Clinical and Health Psychology, 5,* 553–566.

Butcher, J. N. (2005b). *The Minnesota Report: Adult Clinical System—Revised Interpretive Report* (4th ed.). Minneapolis: University of Minnesota Press.

Butcher, J. N. (2009). How to use computer-based reports. In J. N. Butcher (Ed.), *Oxford handbook of clinical and personality assessment* (pp. 693–706). New York, NY: Oxford University Press.

Butcher, J. N. (2010). Personality assessment from the nineteenth to the early twenty-first century: Past achievements and contemporary challenges. *Annual Review of Clinical Psychology, 6,* 1–20. doi:10.1146/annurev.clinpsy.121208.131420

Butcher, J. N. (2011). *A beginner's guide to the MMPI–2* (3rd ed.). Washington, DC: American Psychological Association.

Butcher, J. N., Berah, E., Ellertsen, B., Miach, P., Lim, J., Nezami, E., . . . Almagor, M. (1998). Objective personality assessment: Computer-based MMPI–2 interpretation in international clinical settings. In C. Belar (Ed.), *Comprehensive clinical psychology: Sociocultural and individual differences* (pp. 277–312). New York, NY: Elsevier.

Butcher, J. N., Cabiya, J., Lucio, E., & Garrido, M. (2007). *Assessing Hispanic clients using the MMPI–2 and MMPI–A.* Washington, DC: American Psychological Association. doi:10.1037/11585-000

Butcher, J. N., Cabiya, J., Lucio, E., Pena, L., Scott, R., & Ruben, D. (1998). *Hispanic version of the MMPI–A manual supplement.* Minneapolis: University of Minnesota Press.

Butcher, J. N., Cheung, F. M., & Lim, J. (2003). Use of the MMPI–2 with Asian populations. *Psychological Assessment, 15,* 248–256. doi:10.1037/1040-3590.15.3.248

Butcher, J. N., Dahlstrom, W. G., Graham, J. R., Tellegen, A. M., & Kaemmer, B. (1989). *Minnesota Multiphasic Personality Inventory—2 (MMPI–2): Manual for administration and scoring.* Minneapolis: University of Minnesota Press.

Butcher, J. N., Derksen, J., Sloore, H., & Sirigatti, S. (2003). Objective personality assessment of people in diverse cultures: European adaptations of the MMPI–2. *Behaviour Research and Therapy, 41,* 819–840.

Butcher, J. N., Ellertsen, B., Ubostad, B., Bubb, E., Lucio, E., Lim, J., . . . Elsbury, S. (2000). *International case studies on the MMPI–A: An objective approach.* Minneapolis, MN: MMPI–2 workshops. Retrieved from http://www.umn.edu/mmpi

Butcher, J. N., Graham, J. R., Ben-Porath, Y. S., Tellegen, Y. S., Dahlstrom, W. G., & Kaemmer, B. (2001). *Minnesota Multiphasic Personality*

Inventory—2: Manual for administration and scoring (Rev. ed.). Minneapolis: University of Minnesota Press.

Butcher, J. N., Graham, J. R., Williams, C. L., & Ben-Porath, Y. S. (1989). *Development and use of the MMPI–2 Content Scales.* Minneapolis: University of Minnesota Press.

Butcher, J. N., Graham, J. R., Williams, C. L., & Kaemmer, B. (1992). *Minnesota Multiphasic Personality Inventory—Adolescent (MMPI–A) softcover test booklet.* Minneapolis: University of Minnesota Press.

Butcher, J. N., & Perry, J. N. (2008). *Personality assessment in treatment planning: Use of the MMPI–2 and BTPI.* New York, NY: Oxford University Press.

Butcher, J. N., Perry, J. N., & Dean, B. (2009). Computer-based personality assessment. In J. N. Butcher (Ed.), *Oxford handbook of clinical and personality assessment* (pp. 163–186). New York, NY: Oxford University Press.

Butcher, J. N., Perry, J. N., & Hahn, J. (2004). Computers in clinical assessment: Historical developments, present status, and future challenges. *Journal of Clinical Psychology, 60,* 331–345. doi:10.1002/jclp.10267

Butcher, J. N., & Pope, K. S. (2006). The MMPI–A in forensic assessment. In S. N. Sparta & G. P. Koocher (Eds.), *Forensic mental health assessment for children and adolescents* (pp. 401–411). New York, NY: Oxford University Press.

Butcher, J. N., Tsai, J., Coelho, S., & Nezami, E. (2006). Cross cultural applications of the MMPI–2. In J. N. Butcher (Ed.), *MMPI–2: The practitioner's handbook* (pp. 505–537). Washington, DC: American Psychological Association. doi:10.1037/11287-018

Butcher, J. N., & Williams, C. L. (1992a). *Essentials of MMPI–2 and MMPI–A interpretation.* Minneapolis: University of Minnesota Press.

Butcher, J. N., & Williams, C. L. (1992b). *The Minnesota Report: Adolescent Interpretive System.* Minneapolis: University of Minnesota Press.

Butcher, J. N., & Williams, C. L. (2000). *Essentials of MMPI–2 and MMPI–A interpretation* (2nd ed.). Minneapolis: University of Minnesota Press.

Butcher, J. N., & Williams, C. L. (2007). *The Minnesota Report: Adolescent Interpretive System* (Rev. ed.). Minneapolis: University of Minnesota Press.

Butcher, J. N., & Williams, C. L. (2009). Personality assessment with the MMPI–2: Historical roots, international adaptations, and current challenges. *Applied Psychology: Health and Well-Being, 1,* 105–135. doi:10.1111/j.1758-0854.2008.01007.x

Butcher, J. N., Williams, C. L., Graham, J. R., Tellegen, A., Ben-Porath, Y. S., Archer, R. P., & Kaemmer, B. (1992). *Manual for administration, scoring, and interpretation of the Minnesota Multiphasic Personality Inventory for Adolescents: MMPI–A.* Minneapolis: University of Minnesota Press.

Capwell, D. F. (1945a). Personality patterns of adolescent girls: I. Girls who show improvement in IQ. *Journal of Applied Psychology, 29,* 212–228. doi:10.1037/h0062853

Capwell, D. F. (1945b). Personality patterns of adolescent girls: II. Delinquents and non-delinquents. *Journal of Applied Psychology, 29,* 289–297. doi:10.1037/h0054701

Capwell, D. F. (1953). Personality patterns of adolescent girls: Delinquents and nondelinquents. In S. R. Hathaway & E. D. Monachesi (Eds.), *Analyzing and predicting juvenile delinquency with the MMPI* (pp. 29–37). Minneapolis: University of Minnesota Press.

Cashel, M. L., Rogers, R., Sewell, K. W., & Holliman, N. B. (1998). Preliminary validation of the MMPI–A for a male delinquent sample: An investigation of clinical correlates and discriminant validity. *Journal of Personality Assessment, 71,* 49–69. doi:10.1207/s15327752jpa7101_4

Cheung, F. M. (2009). The cultural perspective in personality assessment. In J. N. Butcher (Ed.), *Oxford handbook of personality assessment* (pp. 45–56). New York, NY: Oxford University Press.

Cheung, F. M., & Ho, R. M. (1997). Standardization of the Chinese MMPI–A in Hong Kong: A preliminary study. *Psychological Assessment, 9,* 499–502. doi:10.1037/1040-3590.9.4.499

Cicero, D. C., Epler, A. J., & Sher, K. J. (2009). Are there developmentally limited forms of bipolar disorder? *Journal of Abnormal Psychology, 118,* 431–447. doi:10.1037/a0015919

Colligan, R. C., & Offord, K. P. (1989). The aging MMPI: Contemporary norms for contemporary teenagers. *Mayo Clinic Proceedings, 64,* 3–27.

Condie, L. O. (2006). Evaluating the effects of domestic violence in children. In S. N. Sparta & G. P. Koocher (Eds.), *Forensic mental health assessment for children and adolescents* (pp. 149–174). New York, NY: Oxford University Press.

Costello, E. J., Mustillo, S., Erkanli, A., Keeler, G., & Angold, A. (2003). Prevalence and development of psychiatric disorders in childhood and adolescence. *Archives of General Psychiatry, 60,* 837–844. doi:10.1001/archpsyc.60.8.837

Craig, R. J. (2005). Assessing contemporary substance abusers with the MMPI Mac Andrews Alcoholism Scale: A review. *Substance Use & Misuse, 40,* 427–450. doi:10.1081/JA-200052401

Craig, R. J. (2008). MMPI-based forensic-psychological assessment of lethal violence. In H. V. Hall (Ed.), *Forensic psychology and neuropsychology for criminal and civil cases* (pp. 393–416). Boca Raton, FL: CRC Press.

Craig, R. J. (2009). The clinical interview. In J. N. Butcher (Ed.), *Oxford handbook of personality assessment* (pp. 201–225). New York, NY: Oxford University Press.

Cramer, P. (2004). *Storytelling, narrative, and the Thematic Apperception Test.* New York, NY: Guilford Press.

Cumella, E. J., & Lafferty-O'Connor, J. (2009). Assessing adolescents with the MMPI–A. In J. N. Butcher (Ed.), *Handbook of personality assessment* (pp. 485–498). New York, NY: Oxford University Press.

Cumella, E. J., Wall, A. D., & Kerr-Almeida, N. (1999). MMPI–A in the inpatient assessment of adolescents with eating disorders. *Journal of Personality Assessment, 73,* 31–44. doi:10.1207/S15327752JPA 730103

Dahl, R. E. (2004). Adolescent brain development: A period of vulnerabilities and opportunities. *Annals of the New York Academy of Sciences, 1021,* 1–22. doi:10.1196/annals.1308.001

Dahlstrom, W. G., Welsh, G. S., & Dahlstrom, L. E. (1972). *An MMPI handbook* (Vol. 1). Minneapolis: University of Minnesota Press.

Dana, R. (2005). *Multicultural assessment: Principles, applications, and examples.* Mahwah, NJ: Erlbaum.

Derksen, J., Ven Dijk, J., & Cornelissen, A. (2003). De Nederlandse adolescentenversie van de MMPI [The Dutch version of the MMPI–A]. *Psycholoog, 38,* 304–311.

Drake, L. E. (1946). A social I-E scale for the MMPI. *Journal of Applied Psychology, 30,* 51–54. doi:10.1037/h0059898

Ehrenworth, N. V., & Archer, R. P. (1985). A comparison of clinical accuracy ratings of interpretive approaches for adolescent MMPI responses. *Journal of Personality Assessment, 49,* 413–421. doi:10.1207/s15327752jpa4904_9

Eisenberg, N., Vaughan, J., & Hofer, C. (2009). Temperament, self-regulation, and peer social competence. In K. H. Rubin, W. M. Bukowski, & B. Laursen (Eds.), *Handbook of peer interactions, relationships, and groups* (pp. 473–489). New York, NY: Guilford Press.

Eyde, L. D., Kowal, D., & Fishburne, F. J. (1991). The validity of computer-based test interpretations of the MMPI. In T. B. Gutkin & S. L. Wise (Eds.), *The computer and the decision making process* (pp. 75–123). Hillsdale, NJ: Erlbaum.

Eyde, L. D., Robertson, G. J., & Krug, S. E. (2009). *Responsible test use: Case studies assessing human behavior* (2nd ed.). Washington, DC: American Psychological Association.

Farias, J. M. P., Duran, C., & Gomez-Maqueo, E. L. (2003). Un estudio sobre la estabilidad temporal del MMPI–A con un diseño test–retest en estudiantes Mexicanos [MMPI–A temporal stability study through a test–retest design in a Mexican student sample]. *Salud Mental, 26*(2), 59–66.

Finn, S. E. (1996). *Using the MMPI–2 as a therapeutic intervention.* Minneapolis: University of Minnesota Press.

Finn, S. E. (2007). *In our clients' shoes: Theory and techniques of therapeutic assessment.* Mahwah, NJ: Erlbaum.

Finn, S. E., & Kamphuis, J. H. (2006). Therapeutic assessment with the MMPI–2. In J. N. Butcher (Ed.), *MMPI–2: The practitioner's handbook* (pp. 165–191). Washington, DC: American Psychological Association. doi:10.1037/11287-008

Finn, S. E., & Tonsager, M. E. (1992). Therapeutic effects of providing MMPI–2 test feedback to college students awaiting therapy. *Psychological Assessment, 4*, 278–287. doi:10.1037/1040-3590.4.3.278

Fischer, C. T. (1970). The testee as co-evaluator. *Journal of Counseling Psychology, 17*, 70–76. doi:10.1037/h0028630

Fischer, C. T. (1985). *Individualizing psychological assessment.* Monterey, CA: Brooks/Cole.

Fischer, C. T. (1994). *Individualizing psychological assessment.* Hillsdale, NJ: Erlbaum.

Fischer, C. T. (2000). Collaborative individualized assessment. *Journal of Personality Assessment, 74*, 2–14. doi:10.1207/S15327752JPA740102

Fishburne, J., Eyde, L., & Kowal, D. (1988, August). *Computer-based test interpretations of the MMPI with neurologically impaired patients.* Paper presented at the 96th Annual Convention of the American Psychological Association, Atlanta, GA.

Flory, K., Lynam, D., Milich, R., Leukefeld, C., & Clayton, R. (2004). Early adolescent through young adult alcohol and marijuana use trajectories: Early predictors, young adult outcomes, and predictive utility. *Development and Psychopathology, 16*, 193–213. doi:10.1017/S0954579404044475

Flouri, E., & Kallis, C. (2007). Adverse life events and psychopathology and prosocial behavior in late adolescence: Testing the timing, specificity, accumulation, gradient, and moderation of contextual risk. *Journal of the American Academy of Child and Adolescent Psychiatry, 46*, 1651–1659. doi:10.1097/chi.0b013e318156a81a

Fontaine, J. L., Archer, R. P., Elkins, D. E., & Johansen, J. (2001). The effects of MMPI–A *T*-score elevation on classification accuracy for normal and clinical adolescent samples. *Journal of Personality Assessment, 76*, 264–281. doi:10.1207/S15327752JPA7602_09

Forbey, J. D. (2002). Incremental validity of the MMPI–A Content Scales and interpretative utility of the Content Component Scales of the MMPI–A in a residential treatment facility. *Dissertation Abstracts International: Section B. Sciences and Engineering, 63*(1-B), 522.

Forbey, J. D., & Ben-Porath, Y. S. (1998). *A critical item set for MMPI–A.* Minneapolis: University of Minnesota Press.

Forbey, J. D., & Ben-Porath, Y. S. (2003). Incremental validity of the MMPI–A Content Scales in a residential treatment facility. *Assessment, 10*, 191–202. doi:10.1177/1073191103010002010

Fowler, R. D. (1985). Landmarks in computer-assisted psychological test interpretation. *Journal of Consulting and Clinical Psychology, 53*, 748–759. doi:10.1037/0022-006X.53.6.748

Fowler, R. D. (1987). Developing a computer-based test interpretation system. In J. N. Butcher (Ed.), *Computerized psychological assessment* (pp. 50–63). New York, NY: Basic Books.

Frank, A. (1993). *The diary of a young girl.* New York, NY: Bantam Books. (Original work published 1947)

Fulkerson, J. A., Pasch, K. E., Perry, C. L., & Komro, K. (2008). Relationships between alcohol-related informal social control, parental monitoring, and adolescent problem behaviors among racially diverse urban youth. *Journal of Community Health, 33,* 425–433. doi:10.1007/s10900-008-9117-5

Gallucci, N. T. (1997). On the identification of patterns of substance abuse with the MMPI–A. *Psychological Assessment, 9,* 224–232. doi:10.1037/1040-3590.9.3.224

Ganellen, R. J. (2001). Weighing evidence for the Rorschach's validity: A response to Wood et al. (1999). *Journal of Personality Assessment, 77,* 1–15. doi:10.1207/S15327752JPA7701_01

Garcia-Peltoniemi, R., & Azan, A. (1993). *MMPI–2 Inventario de a Personalidad—2 Minnesota* [Minnesota Multiphasic Personality Inventory–2]. Minneapolis: University of Minnesota Press.

Gardner, M. R. (1997). *Understanding juvenile law.* New York, NY: Matthew-Bender.

Glaser, B. A., Calhoun, G. B., & Petrocelli, J. V. (2002). Personality characteristics of male juvenile offenders by adjudicated offenses as indicated by the MMPI–A. *Criminal Justice and Behavior, 29,* 183–201. doi:10.1177/0093854802029002004

Goldberg, M. A. (2006). Evaluating children in personal injury claims. In S. N. Sparta & G. P. Koocher (Eds.), *Forensic mental health assessment for children and adolescents* (pp. 245–259). New York, NY: Oxford University Press.

Gomez, F. C. J., Johnson, R., Davis, Q., & Velasquez, R. J. (2000). MMPI–A performance of African and Mexican American adolescent first-time offenders. *Psychological Reports, 87,* 309–314. doi:10.2466/PR0.87.5.309-314

Gottesman, I. I., Hanson, D. R., Kroeker, T. A., & Briggs, P. F. (1987). New MMPI normative data and power transformed *T* score tables for the Hathaway–Monachesi Minnesota cohort of 14,019 fifteen-year-olds and 3,674 eighteen-year-olds. In R. P. Archer (Ed.), *Using the MMPI with adolescents* (pp. 241–297). Hillsdale, NJ: Erlbaum.

Graham, J. R. (1977). *MMPI: Assessing personality and psychopathology.* New York, NY: Oxford University Press.

Grant, B. F., & Dawson, D. A. (1997). Age at onset of alcohol use and its association with *DSM–IV* alcohol abuse and dependence results from the National Longitudinal Alcohol Epidemiologic Survey. *Journal of Substance Abuse, 9,* 103–110. doi:10.1016/S0899-3289(97)90009-2

Gray-Little, B. (2009). The assessment of psychopathology in racial and ethnic minorities. In J. N. Butcher (Ed.), *Oxford handbook of personality and clinical assessment* (pp. 396–414). New York, NY: Oxford University Press.

Grayson, H. M. (1951). *Psychological admission testing program and manual.* Los Angeles, CA: Veterans Administration Center, Neuropsychiatric Hospital.

Greene, R. L. (1980). *The MMPI: An interpretive manual.* New York, NY: Grune & Stratton.

Greene, R. L. (2005). Computer scoring and interpretation in psychological report writing. *SPA Exchange, 17,* 6.

Greene, R. L., Robin, R. W., Caldwell, A. B., Albaugh, B., & Goldman, D. (2003). Use of the MMPI–2 in American Indians: II. Empirical correlates. *Psychological Assessment, 15,* 360–369.

Grisso, T. (2005). The empirical limits of forensic mental health assessment. *Law and Human Behavior, 29,* 1–5. doi:10.1007/s10979-005-1396-0

Grove, W. M. (2005). Clinical versus statistical prediction: The contribution of Paul E. Meehl. *Journal of Clinical Psychology, 61,* 1233–1243. doi:10.1002/jclp.20179

Hall, G. S. (1904). *Adolescence* (Vols. 1 & 2). Englewood Cliffs, NJ: Prentice Hall.

Hanawalt, B. A. (1993). *Growing up in medieval London: The experience of childhood in history.* New York, NY: Oxford University Press.

Handel, R. W., Arnau, R. C., Archer, R. P., & Dandy, K. L. (2006). An evaluation of the MMPI–2 and MMPI–A True Response Inconsistency (*TRIN*) scales. *Assessment, 13,* 98–106. doi:10.1177/1073191105284453

Harkness, A. R. (1992). Fundamental topics in the personality disorders: Candidate trait dimensions from lower regions of the hierarchy. *Psychological Assessment, 4,* 251–259. doi:10.1037/1040-3590.4.2.251

Harkness, A. R. (2009). Theory and measurement of personality traits. In J. N. Butcher (Ed.), *Oxford handbook of personality and clinical assessment* (pp. 150–162). New York, NY: Oxford University Press.

Harkness, A. R., & McNulty, J. L. (1994). The Personality Psychopathology Five (PSY-5): Issues from the pages of a diagnostic manual instead of a dictionary. In S. Strack & M. Lorr (Eds.), *Differentiating normal and abnormal personality* (pp. 291–315). New York, NY: Springer Publishing Company.

Harkness, A. R., McNulty, J. L., & Ben-Porath, Y. S. (1995). The Personality Psychopathology Five (PSY-5) constructs and MMPI–2 scales. *Psychological Assessment, 7,* 104–114. doi:10.1037/1040-3590.7.1.104

Harris, R. E., & Lingoes, J. C. (1955). *Subscales for the MMPI: An aid to profile interpretation* [Mimeograph]. Los Angeles: University of California, Department of Psychiatry.

Harris, R. E., & Lingoes, J. C. (1968). *Subscales for the Minnesota Multiphasic Personality Inventory.* Unpublished manuscript, Langley Porter Clinic, San Francisco, CA.

Harter, S. (2006). Developmental and individual difference perspectives on self-esteem. In D. K. Mroczek & T. D. Little (Eds.), *Handbook of personality development* (pp. 311–334). Mahwah, NJ: Erlbaum.

Hathaway, S. R. (1956). Scales 5 (Masculinity–Femininity), 6 (Paranoia), and 8 (Schizophrenia). In W. G. Dahlstrom & G. S. Welch (Eds.), *Basic readings in the MMPI* (pp. 104–111). Minneapolis: University of Minnesota Press.

Hathaway, S. R., Hastings, D. W., Capwell, D. F., & Bell, D. M. (1953). The relationship between MMPI profiles and later careers of juvenile delinquent girls. In S. R. Hathaway & E. D. Monachesi (Eds.), *Analyzing and predicting juvenile delinquency with the MMPI* (pp. 70–80). Minneapolis: University of Minnesota Press.

Hathaway, S. R., & McKinley, J. C. (1940). A multiphasic personality schedule (Minnesota): 1. Construction of the schedule. *Journal of Psychology, 10,* 249–254.

Hathaway, S. R., & McKinley, J. C. (1942). *The Minnesota Multiphasic Personality Schedule manual.* Minneapolis: University of Minnesota Press.

Hathaway, S. R., & McKinley, J. C. (1943). *The Minnesota Multiphasic Personality Schedule.* Minneapolis: University of Minnesota Press.

Hathaway, S. R., & McKinley, J. C. (1967). *The Minnesota Multiphasic Personality Inventory: Manual* (Rev. ed.). New York, NY: Psychological Corporation.

Hathaway, S. R., & Monachesi, E. D. (1953). *Analyzing and predicting juvenile delinquency with the MMPI.* Minneapolis: University of Minnesota Press.

Hathaway, S. R., & Monachesi, E. D. (1957). The personalities of predelinquent boys. *Journal of Criminal Law, Criminology, and Police Science, 48,* 149–153. doi:10.2307/1139488

Hathaway, S. R., & Monachesi, E. D. (1961). *An atlas of juvenile MMPI profiles.* Minneapolis: University of Minnesota Press.

Hathaway, S. R., & Monachesi, E. D. (1963). *Adolescent personality and behavior: MMPI patterns of normal, delinquent, drop-out and other outcomes.* Minneapolis,: University of Minnesota Press.

Hayama, T., Oguchi, T., & Shinkai, Y. (1999). Trial of the new psychological test MMPI–2 on the chronic schizophrenic patients: Investigation of the basic and content scales [Japanese]. *Kitasata Medicine, 29,* 281–297.

Hays, P. (2001). *Addressing cultural complexities in practice: A framework for clinicians and counselors.* Washington, DC: American Psychological Association. doi:10.1037/10411-000

Hays, P. (2008). *Addressing cultural complexities in practice: Assessment, diagnosis, and therapy* (2nd ed.). Washington, DC: American Psychological Association. doi:10.1037/11650-000

Hilts, D., & Moore, J. M. (2003). Normal range MMPI–A profiles among psychiatric inpatients. *Assessment, 10,* 266–272. doi:10.1177/1073191103255494

Holifield, J. E., Nelson, W. M., III, & Hart, K. J. (2002). MMPI profiles of sexually abused and nonabused outpatient adolescents. *Journal of Adolescent Research, 17,* 188–195. doi:10.1177/0743558402172005

Janus, M. D., de Groot, C., & Toepfer, S. M. (1998). The MMPI–A and 13-year-old inpatients: How young is too young? *Assessment, 5,* 321–332. doi:10.1177/107319119800500402

Jencks, C., & Mayer, S. (1990). The social consequences of growing up in a poor neighborhood. In J. Brooks-Gunn, G. J. Duncan, & J. L. Aber (Eds.), *Neighborhood poverty: Vol. 2. Policy implications in studying neighborhoods* (pp. 48–64). New York, NY: Russell Sage Foundation.

Johnston, L. D., O'Malley, P., Bachman, J. G., & Schulenberg, J. (2008). *Monitoring the Future national results on adolescent drug use: Overview of key findings, 2007.* Bethesda, MD: National Institute on Drug Abuse.

Josephson, A. M., & the AACAP Work Group on Quality Issues. (2007). The practice parameter for the assessment of the family. *Journal of the American Academy of Child and Adolescent Psychiatry, 46,* 922–937. doi:10.1097/chi.0b013e318054e713

Karagianis, J., Novick, D., Pecenak, J., Haro, J. M., Dossenbach, M., Treuer, T., . . . Lowry, A. J. (2009). The Worldwide-Schizophrenia Outpatient Health Outcomes study (W-SOHO). *International Journal of Clinical Practice, 63,* 1578–1588. doi:10.1111/j.1742-1241.2009.02191.x

Kearney, C. A., Cook, L. C., Wechsler, A., Haight, C. M., & Stowman, S. (2008). Behavioral assessment. In M. Hersen & A.M. Gross (Eds.), *Handbook of clinical psychology: Vol. 2. Children and adolescents* (pp. 551–574). Hoboken, NJ: Wiley.

Kling, K. C., Hyde, J. S., Showers, C. J., & Buswell, B. N. (1999). Gender differences in self-esteem: A meta-analysis. *Psychological Bulletin, 125,* 470–500. doi:10.1037/0033-2909.125.4.470

Koocher, G. P. (2006). Ethical issues in forensic assessment of children and adolescents. In S. N. Sparta & G. P. Koocher (Eds.), *Forensic mental health assessment for children and adolescents* (pp. 46–63). New York, NY: Oxford University Press.

Kopper, B. A., Osman, A., Soman, J. R., & Hoffman, J. (1998). Clinical utility of the MMPI–A content scales and Harris–Lingoes subscales in the assessment of suicidal risk factors in psychiatric adolescents. *Journal of Clinical Psychology, 54,* 191–200. doi:10.1002/(SICI)1097-4679(199802)54:2<191::AID-JCLP8>3.0.CO;2-V

Koss, M. P., & Butcher, J. N. (1973). A comparison of psychiatric patients' self-report with other sources of clinical information. *Journal of Research in Personality, 7,* 225–236. doi:10.1016/0092-6566(73)90038-X

Lachar, D. (1974). *The MMPI: Clinical assessment and automated interpretation.* Los Angeles, CA: Western Psychological Services.

Lachar, D., & Wrobel, T. A. (1979). Validating clinicians' hunches: Construction of a new MMPI critical item set. *Journal of Consulting and Clinical Psychology, 47,* 277–284. doi:10.1037/0022-006X.47.2.277

Lachar, D., & Wrobel, T. A. (1990, August). Predicting adolescent MMPI correlates: Comparative efficiency of self-report and other informant assessment. In R. C. Colligan (Chair), *The MMPI and adolescents: Historical perspectives, current research, and future developments.* Symposium conducted at the 98th Annual Convention of the American Psychological Association, Boston, MA.

Leichtman, M. (2009). Behavioral observations. In J. N. Butcher (Ed.), *Oxford handbook of clinical and personality assessment* (pp. 187–200). New York, NY: Oxford University Press.

Leon, G. R., Gillum, B., Gillum, R., & Gouze, M. (1979). Personality stability and change over a 30-year period: Middle age to old age. *Journal of Consulting and Clinical Psychology, 47,* 517–524. doi:10.1037/0022-006X.47.3.517

Leventhal, T., & Brooks-Gunn, J. (2000). The neighborhoods they live in: The effects of neighborhood residence on child and adolescent outcomes. *Psychological Bulletin, 126,* 309–337. doi:10.1037/0033-2909.126.2.309

Lilienfeld, S. O., Wood, J. M., & Garb, H. N. (2001). What's wrong in this picture? *Scientific American, 284,* 80–87. doi:10.1038/scientificamerican0501-80

Lippa, R. A. (2005). *Gender, nature, and nurture* (2nd ed.). Mahwah, NJ: Erlbaum.

Loevinger, J. (1976). *Ego development: Conception and theories.* San Francisco, CA: Jossey-Bass.

Lopez, B., Schwartz, S. J., Prado, G., Campo, A. E., & Pantin, H. (2008). Adolescent neurological development and its implications for adolescent substance abuse prevention. *Journal of Primary Prevention, 29,* 5–35. doi:10.1007/s10935-007-0119-3

Lucio, E., Duran, C., Graham, J. R., & Ben-Porath, Y. S. (2002). Identifying faking bad on the Minnesota Multiphasic Personality Inventory—Adolescent with Mexican adolescents. *Assessment, 9,* 62–69.

Lucio, E. M., Hernandez-Cervantes, Q., Duran, C., & Butcher, J. N. (2010). Effect of age and type of school on MMPI–A scores in a 13–18 year old Mexican adolescent sample. *International Journal of Hispanic Psychology, 2,* 177–192.

Lucio-Gomez, E., Ampudia-Rueda, A., Duran-Patino, C., Gallegos-Mejia, L., & Leon-Guzman, I. (1999). La nueva versión del Inventario Multifásico de la Personalidad de Minnesota para adolescentes Mexicanos [The new version of the Minnesota Multiphasic Personality Inventory for Mexican adolescents]. *Revista Mexicana de Psicología, 16,* 217–226.

Luna, B., & Sweeney, J. A. (2004). The emergence of collaborative brain function. *Annals of the New York Academy of Sciences, 1021,* 296–309. doi:10.1196/annals.1308.035

MacAndrew, C. (1965). The differentiation of male alcoholic outpatients from nonalcoholic psychiatric outpatients by means of the MMPI. *Quarterly Journal of Studies on Alcohol, 26,* 238–246.

Marks, P. A., Seeman, W., & Haller, D. L. (1974). *The actuarial use of the MMPI with adolescents and adults.* Baltimore, MD: William & Wilkins.

Mash, S. J., & Barkley, R. A. (2007). *Assessment of childhood disorders* (4th ed.). New York, NY: Guilford Press.

Masten, A. S. (2007). Competence, resilience, and development in adolescence. In D. Romer & E. F. Walker (Eds.), *Adolescent psychopathology and the developing brain* (pp. 31–53). New York, NY: Oxford University Press. doi:10.1093/acprof:oso/9780195306255.003.0002

Masten, A. S., Cutuli, J. J., Herbers, J. E., & Gabrielle-Reed, M. J. (2009). Resilience in development. In C. R. Snyder & S. J. Lopez (Eds.), *The handbook of positive psychology* (2nd ed., pp. 117–131). New York, NY: Oxford University Press.

McCann, J. T. (1998). *Malingering and deception in adolescents.* Washington, DC: American Psychological Association. doi:10.1037/10249-000

McGrath, R. E., Pogge, D. L., & Stokes, J. M. (2002). Incremental validity of selected MMPI–A content scales in an inpatient setting. *Psychological Assessment, 14,* 401–409. doi:10.1037/1040-3590.14.4.401

McKinley, J. C., & Hathaway, S. R. (1942). A multiphasic schedule (Minnesota): IV. Psychasthenia. *Journal of Applied Psychology, 26,* 614–624. doi:10.1037/h0063530

McKinley, J. C., & Hathaway, S. R. (1944). The MMPI: V. Hysteria, hypomania and psychopathic deviate. *Journal of Applied Psychology, 28,* 153–174. doi:10.1037/h0059245

McNulty, J. L., Harkness, A. R., Ben-Porath, Y. S., & Williams, C. L. (1997). Assessing the Personality Psychopathology Five (PSY-5) in adolescents: New MMPI–A scales. *Psychological Assessment, 9,* 250–259. doi:10.1037/1040-3590.9.3.250

MedlinePlus. (2010, August 19). *Sydenham chorea.* Retrieved from http://www.nlm.nih.gov/medlineplus/ency/article/001358.htm

Meehl, P. E. (1954). *Clinical versus statistical prediction: A theoretical analysis and a review of the evidence.* Minneapolis: University of Minnesota Press. doi:10.1037/11281-000

Meehl, P. E. (1956). Wanted: A good cookbook. *American Psychologist, 11,* 263–272. doi:10.1037/h0044164

Megargee, E. I. (2009). Understanding and assessing aggression and violence. In J. N. Butcher (Ed.), *Oxford University handbook of personality and clinical assessment* (pp. 542–566). New York, NY: Oxford University Press.

Michel, D. M. (2002). Psychological assessment as a therapeutic intervention in patients hospitalized with eating disorders. *Professional Psychology: Research and Practice, 33,* 470–477. doi:10.1037/0735-7028.33.5.470

Micucci, J. A. (2002). Accuracy of MMPI–A scales ACK, MAC-R, and PRO in detecting comorbid substance abuse among psychiatric inpatients. *Assessment, 9,* 111–122. doi:10.1177/10791102009002001

Minnesota Department of Corrections. (2009). *History of the Minnesota Department of Corrections.* Retrieved from http://www.doc.state.mn.us

Monachesi, E. D. (1948). Some personality characteristics of delinquents and nondelinquents. *Journal of Criminal Law and Criminology, 38,* 487–500. doi:10.2307/1138925

Monachesi, E. D. (1950a). Personality characteristics and socioeconomic status of delinquents and nondelinquents. *Journal of Criminal Law and Criminology, 40,* 570–583. doi:10.2307/1137847

Monachesi, E. D. (1950b). Personality characteristics of institutionalized and noninstitutionalized male delinquents. *Journal of Criminal Law and Criminology, 41,* 167–179. doi:10.2307/1138422

Monachesi, E. D. (1953). The personality patterns of juvenile delinquents as indicated by the MMPI. In S. R. Hathaway & E. D. Monachesi (Eds.), *Analyzing and predicting juvenile delinquency with the MMPI* (pp. 38–53). Minneapolis: University of Minnesota Press.

Moore, J. M., Jr., Thompson-Pope, S. K., & Whited, R. M. (1996). MMPI–A profiles of adolescent boys with a history of firesetting. *Journal of Personality Assessment, 67*(1), 116–126. doi:10.1207/s15327752jpa6701_9

Moreland, K. L., & Onstad, J. (1985, March). *Validity of the Minnesota Clinical Report: I. Mental health outpatients.* Paper presented at the 20th Annual Symposium on Recent Developments in the Use of the MMPI, Honolulu, HI.

Murray, H. A. (1943). *Manual for the Thematic Appreciation Test.* Cambridge, MA: Harvard University Press.

Nagayama Hall, G. C., Bansal, A., & López, I. R. (1999). Ethnicity and psychopathology: A meta-analytic review of 31 years of comparative MMPI/MMPI 2 research. *Psychological Assessment, 11,* 186–197.

Negy, C., Leal-Puente, L., Trainor, D. J., & Carlson, R. (1997). Mexican American adolescents' performance on the MMPI–A. *Journal of Personality Assessment, 69,* 205–214. doi:10.1207/s15327752jpa6901_12

Newman, M. L. (2004). *Psychological assessment as brief psychotherapy: Therapeutic effects of providing MMPI–A test feedback to adolescents.* Unpublished doctoral dissertation, La Trobe University, Bundoora, Victoria, Australia.

Newman, M. L., & Greenway, P. (1997). Therapeutic effects of providing MMPI–2 test feedback to clients at a university counseling service: A collaborative approach. *Psychological Assessment, 9,* 122–131. doi:10.1037/1040-3590.9.2.122

Orvaschel, H. (2006). Structured and semistructured interviews. In M. Hersen (Ed.), *Clinician's handbook of child behavioral assessment* (pp. 159–179). San Diego, CA: Elsevier Academic Press. doi:10.1016/B978-012343014-4/50008-3

Ownby, R. L. (2009). Writing clinical reports. In J. N. Butcher (Ed.), *Oxford handbook of personality assessment* (pp. 684–692). New York, NY: Oxford University Press.

Park, R. D., & Buriel, R. (2006). Socialization in the family: Ethnic and ecological perspectives. In N. Eisenberg (Ed.), *Handbook of child psychology* (pp. 429–504). Hoboken, NJ: Wiley.

Paterson, D. G., Schneidler, G. G., & Williamson, E. G. (1938*). Student guidance techniques: A handbook for counselors in high schools and colleges.* New York, NY: McGraw-Hill Book Company.

Paxton, R. (2009, August 15). Let them eat cake at Gulag city birthday party. *Reuters U.S. edition.* Retrieved from http://www.reuters.com/article/idUSL7515993

Pearson, J. S., & Swenson, W. M. (1967). *A user's guide to the Mayo Clinic automated MMPI program.* New York, NY: Psychological Corporation.

Peña, L. M., Megargee, E. I., & Brody, E. (1996). MMPI–A patterns of male juvenile delinquents. *Psychological Assessment, 8,* 388–397. doi:10.1037/1040-3590.8.4.388

Perry, C. L., Lee, S., Stigler, M. H., Farbakhsh, K., Komro, K. A., Gewirtz, A. H., & Williams, C. L. (2007). The impact of Project Northland on selected MMPI–A problem behavior scales. *Journal of Primary Prevention, 28,* 449–465. doi:10.1007/s10935-007-0105-9

Perry, C. L., Williams, C. L., & Veblen-Mortenson, S. (2009). Project Northland program guide for effective alcohol-use prevention in schools and communities. Center City, MN: Hazelden Foundation.

Phelps, R. P. (Ed.). (2009). *Correcting fallacies about educational and psychological testing.* Washington, DC: American Psychological Association. doi:10.1037/11861-000

Pinsoneault, T. B. (2005). Detecting random, partially random, and nonrandom Minnesota Multiphasic Personality Inventory: Adolescent protocols. *Psychological Assessment, 17,* 476–480. doi:10.1037/1040-3590.17.4.476

Pope, K. S., Butcher, J. N., & Seelen, J. (2006). *The MMPI/MMPI–2/MMPI–A in court* (3rd ed.). Washington, DC: American Psychological Association.

Purves, C. (2002). Collaborative assessment with involuntary populations: Foster children and their mothers. *Humanistic Psychologist, 30,* 164–174. doi:10.1080/08873267.2002.9977031

Quevedo, K. M., & Butcher, J. N. (2005). The use of MMPI and MMPI–2 in Cuba: A historical overview from 1950 to the present. *International Journal of Clinical and Health Psychology, 5,* 335–347.

Rawson, B. (2003). *Children and childhood in Roman Italy*. New York, NY: Oxford University Press.

Reynolds, C. R., & Kamphuis, R. W. (2003). *Handbook of psychological and educational assessment of children: Intelligence attitude and achievement* (2nd ed.). New York, NY: Guilford Press.

Riddle, B. C., Byers, C. C., & Grimesey, J. L. (2002). Literature review of research and practice in collaborative assessment. *Humanistic Psychologist, 30,* 33–48. doi:10.1080/08873267.2002.9977021

Rinaldo, J. C. B., & Baer, R. A. (2003). Incremental validity of the MMPI–A Content Scales in the prediction of self-reported symptoms. *Journal of Personality Assessment, 80,* 309–318. doi:10.1207/S15327752JPA8003_08

Roberts, R. E., Roberts, C. R., & Xing, Y. (2007). Rates of DSM–IV psychiatric disorders among adolescents in a large metropolitan area. *Journal of Psychiatric Research, 41,* 959–967. doi:10.1016/j.jpsychires.2006.09.006

Rousseau, J. J. (1979). *Emile, or On education* (A. Bloom, Trans.). New York, NY: Basic Books. (Original work published 1762)

Rubin, K. H., Bukowski, W. M., & Laursen, B. (Eds.). (2009). *Handbook of peer interactions, relationships, and groups*. New York, NY: Guilford Press.

Rutter, M. (2007). Psychopathological development across adolescence. *Journal of Youth and Adolescence, 36,* 101–110. doi:10.1007/s10964-006-9125-7

Sampson, R. J., Morenoff, J. D., & Gannon-Rowley, T. (2002). Assessing "neighborhood effects": Social processes and new directions in research. *Annual Review of Sociology, 28,* 443–478. doi:10.1146/annurev.soc.28.110601.141114

Santrock, J. W. (2007). *Adolescence* (12th ed.). Boston, MA: McGraw-Hill Higher Education.

Satterfield, J. H., Faller, K. J., Crinella, F. M., Schell, A. M., Swanson, J. M., & Homer, L. D. (2007). A 30-year prospective follow-up study of hyperactive boys with conduct problems: Adult criminality. *Journal of the American Academy of Child and Adolescent Psychiatry, 46,* 601–610. doi:10.1097/chi.0b013e318033ff59

Savage, J. (2008). *Teenage: The prehistory of youth culture: 1875–1945*. New York, NY: Penguin.

Schill, T., Wang, S., & Thomsen, D. (1986). MMPI F, 4, and 9 as a measure of aggression in a college sample. *Psychological Reports, 59,* 949–950.

Scott, R. L., Butcher, J. N., Young, T. L., & Gomez, N. (2002). The Hispanic MMPI–A across five countries. *Journal of Clinical Psychology, 58,* 407–417. doi:10.1002/jclp.1152

Scott, R. L., Knoth, R. L., Beltran-Quiones, M., & Gomez, N. (2003). Assessment of psychological functioning in adolescent earthquake victims in Colombia using the MMPI–A. *Journal of Traumatic Stress, 16,* 49–57. doi:10.1023/A:1022011427985

Shahar, S. (1992). *Childhood in the middle ages.* London, England: Routledge.

Sherwood, N. E., Ben-Porath, Y. S., & Williams, C. L. (1997). *The MMPI–A Content Component Scales: Development, psychometric characteristics, and clinical applications.* Minneapolis: University of Minnesota Press.

Shiota, N. K., Krauss, S. S., & Clark, L. A. (1996). Adaptation and validation of the Japanese MMPI–2. In J. N. Butcher (Ed.), *International adaptations of the MMPI–2: Research and clinical applications* (pp. 67–87). Minneapolis: University of Minnesota Press.

Shores, A., & Carstairs, J. R. (1998). Accuracy of the MMPI–2 computerized Minnesota report in identifying fake-good and fake-bad response sets. *Clinical Neuropsychologist, 12,* 101–106. doi:10.1076/clin.12.1.101.1733

Sirigatti, S. (2000). Verso un adattamento italiano del Minnesota Multiphasic Personality Inventory—Adolescent [Toward an Italian version of the MMPI–Adolescent]. *Bollettino di Psicologia Applicata, 230,* 67–72.

Smith, S. R. (2006). Working with courts, judges, and lawyers: What forensic mental health professionals should know about being expert witnesses. In S. N. Sparta & G. P. Koocher (Eds.), *Forensic mental health assessment for children and adolescents* (pp. 88–96). New York, NY: Oxford University Press.

Sowell, E. R., Thompson, P. M., & Toga, A. W. (2007). Mapping adolescent brain maturation using structural magnetic resonance imaging. In D. Romer & E. F. Walker (Eds.), *Adolescent psychopathology and the developing brain* (pp. 55–85). New York, NY: Oxford University Press. doi:10.1093/acprof:oso/9780195306255.003.0003

Sparta, S. N., & Koocher, G. P. (Eds.). (2006). *Forensic mental health assessment for children and adolescents.* New York, NY: Oxford University Press.

Spear, L. P. (2000). The adolescent brain and age-related behavioral manifestations. *Neuroscience and Biobehavioral Reviews, 24,* 417–463. doi:10.1016/S0149-7634(00)00014-2

Spiro, A., III, Butcher, J. N., Levenson, M. R., Aldwin, C. M., & Bosse, R. (2000). Change and stability in personality: A 5-year study of the MMPI–2 in older men. In J. N. Butcher (Ed.), *Basic sources for the MMPI–2* (pp. 443–463). Minneapolis: University of Minnesota Press.

Spivack, G., Haimes, P. E., & Spotts, J. (1967). *Deveraux Adolescent Behavior (DAB) Rating Scale manual.* Devon, PA: Deveraux Foundation.

Stage, S. A. (2000). Predicting behavior functioning of adolescents in residential treatment with profiles from the MMPI–A, CBCL/4-18, and CBCL/TRF. *Residential Treatment for Children & Youth, 17*(2), 49–74. doi:10.1300/J007v17n02_05

Stein, L. A. R., & Graham, J. R. (1999). Detecting fake-good MMPI–A profiles in a correctional facility. *Psychological Assessment, 11,* 386–395. doi:10.1037/1040-3590.11.3.386

Stein, L. A. R., & Graham, J. R. (2001). Use of the MMPI–A to detect substance abuse in a juvenile correctional setting. *Journal of Personality Assessment, 77,* 508–523. doi:10.1207/S15327752JPA7703_10

Stein, L. A. R., & Graham, J. R. (2005). Ability of substance abusers to escape detection on the Minnesota Multiphasic Personality Inventory—Adolescent (MMPI–A) in a juvenile correctional facility. *Assessment, 12,* 28–39. doi:10.1177/1073191104270838

Stein, L. A. R., Graham, J. R., & Williams, C. L. (1995). Detecting fake-bad MMPI–A profiles. *Journal of Personality Assessment, 65,* 415–427. doi:10.1207/s15327752jpa6503_3

Steinberg, L., Dahl, R., Keating, D., Kupfer, D. J., Masten, A. S., & Pine, D. S. (2006). The study of developmental psychopathology in adolescence: Integrating affective neuroscience with the study of context. In D. Cicchetti & D. J. Cohen (Eds.), *Developmental neuroscience: Developmental psychopathology* (2nd ed., Vol. 2, pp. 710–741). New York, NY: Wiley.

Steiner, H., & Feldman, S. S. (1996). General principles and special problems. In H. Steiner (Ed.), *Treating adolescents* (pp. 1–41). San Francisco, CA: Jossey-Bass.

Swenson, W. M., Rome, H. P., Pearson, J. S., & Brannick, T. L. (1965). A totally automated psychological test: Experience in a medical center. *Journal of the American Medical Association, 191,* 925–927.

Tapert, S. E., Caldwell, L., & Burke, C. (2004–2005). Alcohol and the adolescent brain: Human studies. *Alcohol Research & Health, 28,* 205–212.

Terman, L. M., & Miles, C. C. (1936). *Sex and personality: Studies in masculinity and femininity.* New York, NY: McGraw-Hill.

Tharinger, D. J., Finn, S. E., Austin, C. A., Gentry, L. B., Bailey, K. E., Parton, V. T., & Fisher, M. E. (2008). Family sessions as part of child psychological assessment: Goals, techniques, clinical utility, and therapeutic value. *Journal of Personality Assessment, 90,* 547–558. doi:10.1080/00223890802388400

Tharinger, D. J., Finn, S. E., Wilkinson, A. D., & Schaber, P. M. (2007). Therapeutic assessment with a child as a family intervention: A clinical and research case study. *Psychology in the Schools, 44,* 293–309. doi:10.1002/pits.20224

Tobler, A. L., Komro, K. A., & Maldonado-Molina, M. M. (2009). Relationship between neighborhood context, family management practices and alcohol use among urban, multi-ethnic, young adolescents. *Prevention Science, 10,* 313–324. doi:10.1007/s11121-009-0133-1.

Toyer, E. A., & Weed, N. C. (1998). Concurrent validity of the MMPI–A in a counseling program for juvenile offenders. *Journal of Clinical*

Psychology, 54, 395–399. doi:10.1002/(SICI)1097-4679(199806)54: 4<395::AID-JCLP1>3.0.CO;2-N

Triandis, H. C. (2007). Culture and psychology: A history of the study of their relationship. In S. Kitayama & D. Cohen (Eds.), *Handbook of cultural psychology* (pp. 59–76). New York, NY: Guilford Press.

Twenge, J. M., Gentile, B., DeWall, N., Ma, D., Lacefield, K., & Schurtz, D. R. (2010). Birth cohort increases in psychopathology among young Americans, 1938-2007: A cross-temporal meta-analysis of the MMPI. *Clinical Psychology Review, 30,* 145–154. doi:10.1016/j.cpr. 2009.10.005

U.S. Census Bureau. (2000). *DP-1. Profile of general demographic characteristics: 2000.* Retrieved from http://factfinder.census.gov/servlet/ QTTable?_bm=y&-qr_name=DEC_2000_SF1_U_DP1&-geo_id= 01000US&-ds_name=DEC_2000_SF1_U&-_lang=en&-format=&- currentselections=DEC_2000_SF1_U_DP1&-CONTEXT=qt

Vinet, E. V., & Alarcon, B. P. (2003). Evaluación psicométrica del inventario Multifásico de Personalidad de Minnesota para Adolescentes (MMPI–A) en muestras Chilenas [Psychometric evaluation for the Minnesota Multiphasic Personality Inventory for Adolescent (MMPI–A) in Chilean samples]. *Terapia Psicológica, 21,* 87–103.

Vinet, E. V., & Gomez-Maqueo, M. E. L. (2005). Applicabilidad de las normas Mexicanas y Estadounidenses del MMPI–A en la evaluación de adolescentes Chilenos [Applicability of Mexican and United States norms for the MMPI–A in the assessment of Chilean adolescents]. *Revista Mexicana de Psicología, 22,* 519–528.

Weed, N. C., Butcher, J. N., & Williams, C. L. (1994). Development of MMPI–A alcohol and drug problem scales. *Journal of Studies on Alcohol, 55,* 296–302.

Weiner, I. B. (2003). *Principles of Rorschach interpretation* (2nd ed.). Mahwah, NJ: Erlbaum.

Weiner, I. B., & Meyer, G. J. (2009). Personality assessment with the Rorschach inkblot method. In J. N. Butcher (Ed.), *Oxford handbook of personality assessment* (pp. 277–298). New York, NY: Oxford University Press.

Weithorn, L. A. (2006). The legal contexts of forensic assessment of children and adolescents. In S. N. Sparta & G. P. Koocher (Eds.), *Forensic mental health assessment for children and adolescents* (pp. 11–29). New York, NY: Oxford University Press.

Welsh, G. S. (1956). Factor dimensions A and R. In G. S. Welsh & W. G. Dahlstrom (Eds.), *Basic readings on the MMPI in psychology and medicine* (pp. 264–281). Minneapolis: University of Minnesota Press.

Westermeyer, J. (1991). Special considerations. In J. Westermeyer, C. L. Williams, & A. N. Nguyen (Eds.), *Mental health services for refugees* (DHHS Publication No. ADM 91-1824). Washington, DC: U.S. Government Printing Office.

Westermeyer, J., Williams, C. L., & Nguyen, N. (Eds.). (1991). *Mental health services for refugees* (DHHS Publication No. ADM 91-1824). Washington, DC: U.S. Government Printing Office.

Wiggins, J. S. (1966). *Substantive dimensions of self-report in the MMPI item pool* (Research Monograph, Vol. 6, No. 1). Eugene, OR: Oregon Research Institute.

Williams, C. L. (1982). Can the MMPI be useful to behavior therapists? A case study example. *Behavior Therapist, 5*(3), 83–84.

Williams, C. L. (1983). Further investigation of the Si scale of the MMPI: Reliabilities, correlates, and subscale utility. *Journal of Clinical Psychology, 39*, 951–957. doi:10.1002/1097-4679(198311)39:6<951::AID-JCLP2270390621>3.0.CO;2-V

Williams, C. L. (1986). MMPI profiles from adolescents: Interpretive strategies and treatment considerations. *Journal of Child and Adolescent Psychotherapy, 3*, 179–193.

Williams, C. L. (1987). Issues surrounding psychological testing of minority patients. *Hospital and Community Psychiatry, 38*, 184–189.

Williams, C. L., Ben-Porath, Y. S., & Hevern, B. W. (1994). Item level improvements for use of the MMPI with adolescents. *Journal of Personality Assessment, 63*, 284–293. doi:10.1207/s15327752jpa6302_8

Williams, C. L., & Berry, J. W. (1991). Primary prevention of acculturative stress in refugees: The application of psychological theory and practice. *American Psychologist, 46*, 632–641. doi:10.1037/0003-066X.46.6.632

Williams, C. L., & Butcher, J. N. (1989a). An MMPI study of adolescents: I. Empirical validity of the standard scales. *Psychological Assessment: A Journal of Consulting and Clinical Psychology, 1*, 251–259. doi:10.1037/1040-3590.1.4.251

Williams, C. L., & Butcher, J. N. (1989b). An MMPI study of adolescents: II. Verification and limitations of code type classifications. *Psychological Assessment: A Journal of Consulting and Clinical Psychology, 1*, 260–265. doi:10.1037/1040-3590.1.4.260

Williams, C. L., Butcher, J. N., Ben-Porath, Y. S., & Graham, J. R. (1992). *MMPI–A content scales: Assessing psychopathology in adolescents.* Minneapolis: University of Minnesota Press.

Williams, C. L., & Uchiyama, C. (1989). Assessment of life events during adolescence: The use of self-report inventories. *Adolescence, 24*, 95–118.

Williams, C. L., & Westermeyer, J. (1983). Psychiatric problems among adolescent Southeast Asian refugees: A descriptive study. *Journal of Nervous and Mental Disease, 171*, 79–85.

Williams, C. L., & Westermeyer, J. (Eds.). (1986). *Refugee mental health in resettlement countries.* New York, NY: Hemisphere.

Williams, J. E., & Weed, N. C. (2004). Review of computer-based test interpretation software for the MMPI–2. *Journal of Personality Assessment, 83*, 78–83. doi:10.1207/s15327752jpa8301_08

Wolfson, K. P., & Erbaugh, S. E. (1984). Adolescent responses to the MacAndrew Alcoholism Scale. *Journal of Consulting and Clinical Psychology, 52,* 625–630. doi:10.1037/0022-006X.52.4.625

Wood, J. M., Nezworski, M. T., Garb, H. N., & Lilienfeld, S. O. (2001). The misperception of psychopathology: Problems with the norms of the comprehensive system. *Clinical Psychology: Science and Practice, 8,* 360–373.

Woodworth, R. S. (1919). Examination of emotional fitness for war. *Psychological Bulletin, 15,* 59–60.

Woodworth, R. S. (1920). *Personal data sheet.* Chicago, IL: Stoelting.

Woodworth, R. S., & Mathews, E. (1924). *Personal data sheet (children and adolescent).* Chicago, IL: Stoelting.

Zeigler, D. W., Wang, C. C., Yoast, R. A., Dickinson, B. D., McCaffree, M. A., Robinowitz, C. B., & Sterling, M. L. (2005). The neurocognitive effects of alcohol on adolescents and college students. *Preventive Medicine, 40,* 23–32. doi:10.1016/j.ypmed.2004.04.044

Index

About the Authors

Carolyn L. Williams, PhD, is an emeritus professor in the Division of Epidemiology and Community Health in the School of Public Health at the University of Minnesota. Her doctoral work was completed at the University of Georgia in clinical psychology with a comajor in child and family development. In 1993 she was named a fellow of the American Psychological Association Division 5 (Evaluation, Measurement, and Statistics) and a charter member and diplomate of the American Board of Assessment Psychology.

Dr. Williams has more than 30 years of experience in research, practice, and teaching about the MMPI, MMPI–2, and MMPI–A. She is a coauthor of the MMPI–A and many of its scales, including the Content Scales, Content Component Scales, the alcohol–drug problem scales (ACK and PRO), and PSY-5 Scales. With James N. Butcher, she developed the widely used computerized system *The Minnesota Report: Adolescent Interpretive System* and wrote the textbook *Essentials of MMPI–2 and MMPI–A Interpretation.*

In addition to her work on the MMPI instruments, Dr. Williams is a cocreator of *Project Northland,* published by the Hazelden Foundation. Project Northland is one of the few prevention programs in use in American schools with scientific evidence that its programs actually reduce alcohol, tobacco, and other drug use by adolescents. The National Institute on Alcohol Abuse and Alcoholism funded Project Northland research from 1990 to 2007 and is currently funding follow-up research on a cohort from Chicago.

James N. Butcher, PhD, obtained his bachelor's degree in psychology at Guilford College in Greensboro, North Carolina, and his master of arts degree in experimental psychology and PhD in clinical psychology from the University of North Carolina at Chapel Hill. He was awarded Doctor Honoris Causa by the Free University of Brussels, Belgium, and received an honorary doctorate from the University of Florence in Italy for his cross-cultural research, much of which was on the MMPI instruments. Currently, he is a professor emeritus in psychology at the University of Minnesota and is a former editor of the American Psychological Association journal *Psychological Assessment*. He consults and testifies as an expert witness in trials involving the MMPI–2 and MMPI–A.

Dr. Butcher was the lead author of both the MMPI–A and MMPI–2 and developed the Minnesota Reports, a computerized interpretive system, for the MMPI and then for the MMPI–2 and MMPI–A (with Carolyn L. Williams). Recent books include *A Beginner's Guide to the MMPI–2, Third Edition* (2011); *Oxford Handbook of Personality* (2009); *Assessing Hispanic Clients Using the MMPI–2 and MMPI–A* (2007, with José Cabiya, Emilia Lucio, and Maria Garrido); *The MMPI, MMPI–2 and MMPI–A in Court: A Practical Guide for Expert Witnesses and Attorneys, Third Edition* (2006, with Ken Pope and Joyce Seelan); and *Abnormal Psychology in Modern Life, 14th Edition* (2010, with Susan Mineka and Jill Hooley).